Toward Stonewall

NICHOLAS C. EDSALL

# Toward Stonewall

## HOMOSEXUALITY AND SOCIETY
## IN THE MODERN WESTERN WORLD

University of Virginia Press | Charlottesville & London

University of Virginia Press
© 2003 by the Rector and Visitors of the University of Virginia
All rights reserved
Printed in the United States of America on acid-free paper
*First published 2003*

9  8  7  6  5  4  3  2  1

Library of Congress Cataloging-in-Publication Data
Edsall, Nicholas C.
 Toward Stonewall : homosexuality and society in the mod-
ern western world / Nicholas C. Edsall.
   p.    cm.
Includes bibliographical references and index.
 ISBN 0-8139-2211-9 (alk. paper)
 1. Homosexuality—Europe, Western—History.
2. Homosexuality—United States—History.   3. Marginality,
Social—Europe, Western—History.   4. Marginality,
Social—United States—History.   5. Subculture—Europe,
Western—History.   6. Subculture—United States—
History.   I. Title: Homosexuality and society in the modern
western world.   II. Title.
HQ76.3 .E37 2003
306.76'6'094—dc21

                                                    2002155966

*To My Students*
*and*
*In Memory of*
*Gerald Trett*

# Contents

# Preface

As the sheer volume of writings on gay and lesbian history has grown in recent years, so too has the need for works of synthesis, pulling together this widely scattered and often not readily available material. What follows is just such a work, aimed at a general audience both within and, it is hoped, beyond the gay and lesbian community.

It is only recently that homosexuals and homosexual subcultures have joined the ranks of previously neglected or underreported minorities and subordinate groups as subjects for dispassionate study by historians and other social scientists. Few subjects are more divisive or raise issues as disquieting as the nature of sexuality and the meaning of gender identity. What is more, homosexuality is controversial not only in and of itself but for the light it throws on society at large, often from unexpected and disturbing angles. By showing how subordinate groups accommodate themselves to their subordination, often at terrible psychic cost to themselves, it reveals just what society's demands and expectations are; by showing whether, in what way, and how successfully they challenge their subordination, it reveals just how open society is to change; by showing the way society treats weak or unpopular groups, it reveals a true measure of the distance between society's professed and actual values; and by showing society's willingness to employ scapegoats and which groups it chooses for that role, it reveals the nature and level of social anxiety. That tense relationship, at least as much as the internal development of homosexual subcultures, is the subject of what follows. Indeed, neither is comprehensible without the other.

Homosexuality also raises in an acute form the vexed question where the boundary should be drawn between the public and the private. Although nothing is more personal, more intimate, than an individual's choice of a sexual partner, whether for the night or for life, that choice is often far from private. All sorts of social institutions regard it as too important a matter to be left to the individuals involved and therefore have their say: families to ensure that such choices are socially acceptable or advantageous, churches to define their morality, governments to ensure their legality, doctors to assert whether they are physically and mentally healthy. The definition of what is acceptable, moral, legal, and normal has often been quite narrow, and all other choices have been and frequently still are labeled as deviant. But of all the deviant sexual practices not involving incest, violence, or children, the one that has been most condemned by most societies in the West is homosexuality, whether or not it was practiced in private. England and Germany did not decriminalize homosexual relations between consenting adults in private until the late 1960s, and then only within strict limits, and as late as 1986 the United States Supreme Court upheld the constitutionality of state antisodomy laws in part on the grounds that a majority of the population still viewed homosexuality as "immoral and unacceptable."

Over time, of course, the labels have changed, both those imposed from outside, such as *sodomy, buggery, pederasty,* and *homosexuality* (not to mention pejorative slang terms), and those coined from within the subculture in the hope of establishing neutral or positive terminology, *gay* (following failed attempts to gain widespread acceptance for other language) and *lesbian.* The rationale for condemnation and persecution has evolved as well. Depending on the time, the place, and the circumstances, the terms *sinful, unnatural, criminal, antisocial, sick,* or combinations of any or all of these have been applied to homosexuality. The shifts in perception and self-perception implied by these changes in labeling provide perhaps the best clues to the character and development of a beleaguered minority that has all too often been, as the title of one volume of essays on the subject suggests, "hidden from history." In only a generation historians have established a generally accepted chronology, proposed and furiously debated opposing theoretical models, and identified the major players, rescuing many of them from near oblivion.

The modern history of homosexuality and homosexual subcultures as we now generally use and understand these terms appears to date back only some three hundred years, to a significant shift in attitudes toward sexuality in northwestern Europe in the late seventeenth century, although the extent and sources of that shift remain very much matters of debate. However, it is generally agreed that the subsequent development of male homosexual and, later, lesbian subcultures similar to those of the late twentieth century was centered in only about half a dozen countries, the major nations of northwestern Europe—Britain, France, Germany, and the Netherlands—and the

United States, the social and cultural descendent of the others. It was from this transatlantic axis—indeed, from the major cities at either end—that modern attitudes of and about the homosexual minority spread downward and outward to lesser urban centers and rural society, as well as to neighboring countries in Europe and North America, to Westernized countries elsewhere, and finally to non-Western societies worldwide, and it is with developments in this small group of core countries during a period of slightly less than three centuries that this work is overwhelmingly concerned.

The proliferation of local and regional studies in gay history during the last decade is a useful reminder of the limitations of approaching this or any field from the center outwards. In the words of John Howard, the leading historian of homosexuality in the American South, this approach "effects a number of exclusions," of places and classes and peoples. Yet, as Howard readily acknowledges, in the creation of homosexual communities, homosexual subcultures, both as "phenomenon" and as "concept," it was urban middle-class males who led the way. Though by no means the whole story, and certainly not the only story, that remains the central one. In addition to local histories, another often underreported aspect of that story is the history of lesbianism. Largely because of the subordinate status of women, lesbian subcultures grew up later and in the shadow of male homosexual communities, with the result that they have frequently been discussed, if at all, as an afterthought to the treatment of male homosexuality. In order to avoid repeating that pattern, I have deliberately delayed the discussion of lesbianism until the emergence of vibrant, autonomous lesbian subcultures early in the twentieth century allowed them to be treated on a par with their male counterparts. I should also note that as an American whose primary field of research and teaching for some thirty years was modern British history, I have drawn disproportionately on two of these core countries, Britain and the United States, to illustrate what I see as the most important developments, but not, I think, to the point of distorting the historical record.

All the major players, as well as many lesser ones, make an appearance, though once again not necessarily in proportion to their importance. Frequently I have paid special attention to individuals, groups, and organizations that seemed particularly interesting or revealing. As I moved deeper and deeper into the project, I was somewhat surprised at how much it became a study in individual and group biography, especially of writers. In retrospect, I should have expected that. In the early history of any social or cultural movement the role of individuals, however idiosyncratic, especially individuals able to articulate and define the self-perceptions of others like themselves, is central. Organizations follow later, often much later. There had to be a Walt Whitman before there was a Mattachine Society, a Karl Ulrichs before there was a Scientific Humanitarian Committee, an Edward Carpenter before there was a Homosexual Law Reform Society, an Arnold Aletrino before there was a Cultural and Recreational Center, an Andre Gide before there was an Arcadie, a Radclyffe Hall before there was a Daughters of Bilitis. More conscious, and earlier, of the nature of their sexuality and of their kinship with others of their kind than were the majority of homosexual men and women, such individuals were atypical, and their achievements must be set in the context of "the unknown, the unfamous, and often isolated," as one of a number of studies of ordinary members of gay and lesbian subcultures usefully reminds us. That said, it was those in the vanguard, like the major cities to which they gravitated, that gave voice and shape to a fragmented and inchoate minority.

And finally, a matter that was foreseeable, the question of terminology. I do not like the term *homosexuality,* and not because it is a bastard word, partly Greek, partly Latin in origin. The problem is that the term limits by emphasizing only one end of the spectrum of close and comradely, loving and often eroticized, but by no means necessarily sexual relations between people of the same sex. Earlier alternatives, such as *Uranian* and *homophile,* were proposed and used for a time but ultimately fell out of favor. *Gay* has the virtue of inclusiveness but is so much of our own time that its use in describing any era before World War I, at the very earliest, would be anachronistic. Lesbians are luckier; the term has a long history and is broadly inclusive of a wide range of relationships between women. But for men the term *homosexuality* will, regrettably, have to serve.

# Acknowledgments

As this is a work of synthesis, my primary debt is to those who have gone before: to those writers and scholars of the 1980s and 1990s who transformed the study of gay and lesbian history into a mature field, but most of all to their predecessors in the 1970s who created that field out of almost nothing.

Part 1

# Making a Subculture

# Chapter 1    Origins

Can there be any such thing as a history of homosexuality stretching back much beyond the late nineteenth century to the early modern, let alone the medieval or ancient worlds? Or are the terms we employ in discussing homosexuality—*gay, lesbian, homosexuality* itself—and the meanings we attach to them so much a product of modern Western thought that meaningful comparisons, let alone a sense of continuity, are chancy at best, all but impossible at worst? That, in essence, is the central issue in the theoretical debate surrounding gay history, the debate between the so-called essentialists and the so-called social constructionists. That is not, of course, a problem unique to this field of study. The terminology available to us limits as well as illuminates our understanding. To suggest just one parallel example, social inequality is universal, but the language of social class we employ is little more than two hundred years old and we apply it to earlier and increasingly different social relationships at an ever greater risk of misrepresenting and misunderstanding the past. Even younger than the modern language of class is the term *homosexuality,* coined by the German-Hungarian advocate of the decriminalization of homosexuality, Karoly Maria Kertbeny, in 1868.

Before that, homosexual acts between men were termed *sodomy.* But sodomy is not synonymous with homosexuality, far from it. Not all same-sex acts were necessarily considered sodomy. Oral sex was not always included; the legal definition was frequently limited to anal penetration, often to the point of emission. Nor was sodomy necessarily limited to same-sex acts. Non-vaginal penetration of women as well as bestiality often fell within the definition of sodomy, the only common denominator of all these varying definitions and descriptions being that they referred to nonprocreative sexual acts. The sodomite, in short, was defined by what he did. The homosexual, on the other hand, is defined by his sexual orientation, by what he is and not by what he does. Thus, in sharp contrast to the sodomite, the homosexual may engage in heterosexual acts or even be celibate and still be homosexual. As the father of social constructionism, Michel Foucault, put it, "The sodomite had been a temporary aberration; the homosexual was now a species."

Described in such terms, as most proponents of social constructionism do indeed describe it, this shift in terminology involved a shift in Western perceptions of the nature of sexuality so profound as to create an all but unbridgeable discontinuity with the thinking of earlier centuries. From this clearly defined position the social constructionists launched repeated and at first almost wholly successful attacks on their doubters and detractors, the so-called essentialists, who acknowledged the discontinuity with earlier centuries but regarded it as far from unbridgeable and as an admonition to use extreme care rather than as a deterrent to attempting to bridge the gap. Unfortunately, as in most such generalized theoretical debates in history and the social sciences, the lines between the two camps became more and more sharply drawn, both sides tended to caricature the views of the other, and the terms of the debate became increasingly removed from the social realities they purported to explain. The frustrating nature of the debate as it developed during the 1970s and early 1980s led many noncombatants as well as some who joined the conflict late to search out, if not common ground or compromise, at least a way of breaking out of the confines of the debate as it was initially defined, either by appealing to disciplines outside of history such as anthropology or biology or, staying within history, by drawing on the additional evidence that has since become available.

From such evidence it is clear that same-sex attraction is very nearly universal in human societies, past and present, while the manner in which it has been understood and expressed, let alone accommodated, regulated, or repressed, is very much a matter of specific time and place. There is also a considerable body of evidence, much of it necessarily literary or anecdotal, to suggest that the more we deal with individuals and their immediate sexual longings and fantasies or with individuals in the company of similar individuals, the closer we come to whatever is essential, transhistorical, and transcultural in the nature of sexual orientation. Conversely, the more we deal with individuals in large or diverse groups, the more we encounter socially determined attitudes and patterns of behavior. It might even be said that each of us harbors within him- or herself an essentialist and a social constructionist— and not only in matters sexual. We all experience hunger, but what and how we eat, and how we feel about what and how we eat, is largely socially determined. We all feel heat and cold, but how we dress and how we warm and cool ourselves, and how we feel about how we dress and warm and cool ourselves, is largely socially determined. Sexual attraction is of the same elemental order of things as hunger and the desire for physical comfort, and as with these most fundamental human needs, so with sexual attraction, the essentialist–social constructionist paradigm is perhaps most fruitfully seen as more a continuum than a dichotomy.

Where any of us happens to be on that continuum is subject to constant change depending on the complex interaction between the nature and intensity of our own desires and the weight of social expectations. Any sexually active person, straight or gay, from northern Europe or English-speaking North America, who visits geographically close but culturally different North Africa or Latin America knows this from firsthand experience. The culturally insensitive may act foolishly, embarrassingly, even dangerously, but the culturally aware can quite quickly adapt to the foreign rules of the game and even, precisely because such visitors can perhaps see the rules more clearly than those who have grown up with them, subtly adjust the rules to accommodate their desires. And if, as L. P. Hartley suggested, the past is like a foreign country because they do things differently there, then within the limitations—which can also be an advantage—inherent in being foreign it is possible to write a history of homosexuality.

Writing such a history is not fundamentally different from writing the history of any institution or social relationship over an extended period of time, and one of the puzzling things about the social constructionists is their singling out of the experience of homosexuality as peculiarly culture-bound. Now I have here argued that the elemental nature of sexual attraction makes it, if anything, less culture-bound than most social relationships, but even if that view is not accepted, the fact remains that we commonly study the history of such relationships and of the institutions that frame them, which have changed radically over time. As John Boswell, the leading historian of medieval homosexuality, said in an interview:

> It interests me that no one has claimed that there can't be family history. In fact many of the people who are most constructionist about sexuality are ardent advocates of family history, and yet the family has changed much more over time than ordinary forms of eroticism between two people. . . . Yet nobody says there can't be "family" history. Everyone recognizes that the family wouldn't be exactly the same in a previous age. What social phenomenon is exactly the same

in a previous age? Marriage is different, banking is different, the Church is different.

Thus, while the widespread adoption of the term *homosexuality* in the years after its coinage points to a significant development in Western thinking about sexuality, it is misleading to treat it as too sharp a line of demarcation (just as it distorts history not to acknowledge or account for the discontinuity, which is the great failing of virtually all histories of homosexuality aimed at a general audience).

Jeffrey Weeks, the most prominent historian of homosexuality in modern Britain and an avowed social constructionist, asserts that "the late nineteenth century sees a deepening hostility towards homosexuality, alongside the emergence of new definitions of homosexuality and the homosexual," and argues that such changes were so fundamental that they "can only be properly understood as part of the restructuring of the family and sexual relations consequent upon the triumph of urbanization and industrial capitalism." Furthermore, he believes that the modern homosexual subculture and the movement for homosexual rights must be seen as primarily "a basic but creative response to the culture which defined and oppressed them." The assumptions underlying this argument can be faulted on a number of grounds, but most of all because Weeks pays virtually no attention to historical continuities. He does, to be sure, note "signs of the emergence" of homosexual roles as far back as the late seventeenth century, but he treats them dismissively. Yet there is now, as there was even at the time Weeks wrote, substantial evidence suggesting the emergence of vibrant, recognizably protomodern homosexual subcultures in northwestern Europe two centuries earlier than he suggests. Furthermore, while the late nineteenth century witnessed increased hostility toward sexual deviation, this was as nothing compared with the savage repression of homosexuality early in the century (let alone in earlier centuries). This wider historical perspective opens up the possibility of interpreting the developments of the late nineteenth century in a way very different from, indeed almost opposite to, Weeks's. The repressive atmosphere of the fin de siècle can be read, not as a catalyst for the emergence of the modern homosexual subculture, but as a reaction to the earlier loosening of the constraints of mid-Victorian society, of which the emergence of a homosexual subculture was a notable, even notorious part.

Clearly it is important to understand how and when something approximating the modern homosexual subculture evolved if the significance of the defining and further developing of that subculture in the late nineteenth century is to be properly understood. In this respect the tendency of Weeks and others to see the development of that subculture as largely a reaction to hostile labeling of deviant behavior is troubling. Not only does it rob the individual and the group of autonomy but it oversimplifies a complex process. The sense of being different, of not quite fitting in, of having thoughts and feelings and interests most of one's peers do not have, and the accidental stumbling upon or actively seeking out others like oneself underlies a wide spectrum of subcultures—not only sexual but also ethnic, religious, intellectual, and artistic. Different subcultures often find common ground, sometimes through overlapping membership, often simply because they gravitate to the same places. The relationship between subcultures and society at large is often tense but not necessarily hostile. Merely dissenting or dropping out is a very long way from openly challenging social norms; subcultures may have a great deal of latitude to define themselves as different from society at large but by no means antagonistic to it. As long as that distinction is maintained society at large may even point to the diversity of its subcultures with some pride. Only when a subculture is (or is thought to be) growing rapidly, when it becomes highly visible, even assertive or challenging, or when a society feels insecure within itself does tension necessarily spill over into hostility and the freedom of self-definition give way to labeling as a mechanism of social control or scapegoating.

The earliest richly documented examples of this complex process so far as homosexual subcultures are concerned occurred at the close of the seventeenth century in London, Paris, Amsterdam, and neighboring Dutch cities. Despite the considerable differences between these cities, the similarities in the nature and development of their sodomitical subcultures are striking (which would have made it easy for a knowledgeable Parisian, say, to find his way into the demimonde of London or Amsterdam). Certain streets and districts became well known as places where men could make contact, either for a brief sexual encounter or as a preliminary to more lengthy and intimate relations in private. In Amsterdam the area around the town hall and the exchange was a major cruising ground; in the Hague the Voorhout and Vijverberg were the center of activity. The royal gardens—the Luxembourg, the Tuileries—were particularly favored in Paris, as were the boulevards built on the site of the former city walls. In London, Covent Garden and Lincoln's Inn Fields to the west and Smithfield and the area around the Royal Exchange to the east were popular haunts, though by no means to the exclusion of other places. And in all these cities, then and ever since, public urinals, parks, and secluded walkways beside canals or river banks have served as meeting grounds.

Recognition signals, often quite elaborate, were necessary to establish who was who: apparently accidental physical contact, shoe to shoe or elbow to elbow; patterns of dress, including the use of particular colors or the wearing or waving of a handkerchief in a certain way; the too intense perusal of the wares in market stall after market stall; or simply the casual glance held just a beat too long. In the most notorious cruising areas, or following a few preliminary moves, men might act more brazenly, exposing themselves or even risking overt sexual contact. There were common verbal approaches too, including the ageless requests for the time or for directions. Slang could also be used for identification purposes or, within the subculture, as an expression of solidarity. Words and phrases that might have no particular significance to outsiders might mean something different to those in the know. Male prostitutes were available in the larger cities, as were casual hustlers, perhaps soldiers or sailors, or apprentices, servants, students in need of a bit of cash, a meal, a drink, or a place to spend the night. If they were lucky and their clients were sufficiently independent or had the right contacts, they might be invited back to a private house, perhaps to a discreet party. Such private circles appear to have been especially common in the Netherlands, where informal contacts linked such circles in a number of cities. For those with lesser means or less freedom—men who lived in lodgings, men who were married—there were inns and taverns, even private clubs, that catered to their needs, providing rooms for couples or for parties. The so-called molly houses of London ranged from makeshift rooms behind lowly public houses to establishments large enough to accommodate fancy-dress balls and a dozen or more couples in private bedrooms.

If much of this seems unremarkable, that is what is so remarkable. Here we have many of the elements of a readily recognizable modern gay subculture; most of the signals are familiar, and some of the cruising areas are still in use for that purpose three centuries later. There are substantial differences, however, both from what had been and from what was to come, and not only in such ephemeral matters as slang. Though the evidence from earlier periods is thinner, the most common, or at least most commonly noted, pattern of homosexual relations before the late seventeenth century was either a passing phase of sexual contacts between adolescents or involved partners unequal in age—adults with youths—and often in social status as well—

masters with servants, teachers with pupils, employers with apprentices, and the like. The hierarchical or patronage nature of these relationships usually extended to the sex acts themselves, with the older partner or the partner having the higher social status assuming a dominant, masculine role, while the subordinate partner normally acted as the receptor. As long as these roles were adhered to, the morals of the adult partner might be questioned, but not his masculinity. Indeed, a temporary lapse into sodomy or even the active pursuit of boys did not necessarily preclude heterosexual relations or marriage, and vice versa. As one historian vividly put it, the upper-class libertine or rake with "his whore on one arm and his boy on the other" was a subject of gossip and often of social (and legal) concern but not of derision.

Such men were not so much bisexual in the modern sense as sexual opportunists, ready to satisfy themselves as chance and inclination dictated. Nor is there more than occasional or fragmentary evidence to suggest that even those among them who were more or less exclusively involved with boys over an extended period were or saw themselves as members of distinct sexual subcultures. By and large they appear to have been simply individuals whose sexual tastes or lack of other outlets led them to experiment with sodomy. Such unselfconscious sexual ambidexterity became increasingly difficult to sustain following the emergence of the molly house subculture and its Paris and Amsterdam equivalents. The general mixing of ages and ranks in the molly houses was matched by a growing flexibility in sexual roles: adults with adults and adult males accepting the passive, or "feminine," role. The issue of what one did, in short, was now supplemented, indeed often superseded, by the issue of who one did it with, and once that happened any adult male's taste for other males of any age, boys included, became suspect. Inevitably, those who preferred the sexual company of other males came to be associated in the public mind, and increasingly in their own minds, with others of their kind, as members of a distinct category of persons, not merely as men who engaged in acts of sodomy but as sodomites, as men who, because of their choice of sexual acts and partners, were deemed other than, or less than, fully men.

For the denizens of the emerging sodomitical subcultures this almost inevitably led to identifying themselves as well as being labeled by outsiders as in some sense partly feminine in their nature. With the decline of the old hierarchical paradigm of male-to-male sexual relationships, there was no pattern of explanation for the subculture other than in terms of some variant or distortion of normal gender roles, and one of the characteristics of these sodomitical subcultures as they developed during the early eighteenth century was the way they incorporated, played on, or parodied contemporary gender categories and expectations, to the point in some instances of staging mock marriages and even mock birthings. Indeed, if there is one aspect of these early modern subcultures that more than any other seems to separate them from the gay subcultures of the late-twentieth-century West, it is this elaborate and exaggerated emphasis on feminine role-playing.

That said, however, it would be misleading in our turn to exaggerate the differences between the molly house culture and what preceded or followed it. There was almost certainly more homosexual contact between adult males before the emergence of the sodomitical subcultures of the late seventeenth century than we will ever know of, simply because the consequences of acknowledging or being discovered in such a relationship could be socially catastrophic for the individuals involved. Moreover, there is substantial evidence from a number of cities in southern Europe a century or more earlier of streets, taverns, and other well-known meeting places for sodomites and their youthful partners, as well as of informal networks of adult neighbors, friends, and coworkers with shared sexual tastes, not, to be sure, for one another, but for boys (who equally often ran in groups of friends or gangs). In Renaissance Florence, and very likely elsewhere as well, "sodomy was intimately connected to the intense bonding and camaraderie so characteristic of male sociability in this culture." That did not mean, however, that there was a "truly autonomous and distinctive 'sodomitical subculture.' . . . There was only a single male sexual culture with a prominent homoerotic character." The growth of just such an increasingly highly structured, distinct, and self-conscious subculture appears to have been the novel feature of the sodomitical underworld in the major cities of northwestern Europe at the turn of the eighteenth century.

Similarly, while the emergence of these subcultures reinforced and extended the taboo to any and all homosexual relations, that taboo has never operated as completely as some would imagine. The earlier distinctions between sexual partners based on what they did survived the rise of the molly house culture and survives to this day. In his superbly researched study of gay New York at the beginning of the twentieth century George Chauncey reveals that it was common for men to seek out the services of avowedly homosexual "fairies" but that as long as the clients kept to the dominant role, their masculinity was not questioned. This carefully maintained distinction could not survive very far into the new century, Chauncey argues, as the idea of the homosexual as a type of person spread and took hold, but even casual conversations with present-day hustlers clearly show that this is not the case. Many who are new to the game cling to the fiction that they are only doing it for the money and are not "queer" by refusing to do anything other than let the client pleasure them, while any experienced hustler will have encountered clients who, on the excuse that they were not getting enough from their wives or girlfriends, sought out a male hustler for relief yet, no matter how often they did so, adamantly denied that they were gay. Such artificial distinctions may not be as carefully structured and maintained—or maintainable—today as they were a century ago or, indeed, as common, but they are there.

A similar observation applies to the exaggerated effeminacy of the sodomitical subcultures of three centuries ago. For one thing, it may not have been so, or at least not so all-pervasive. The police surveillance records from Paris, for example, contain a number of references to sodomites who, repelled by the more effeminate cliques and clubs, sought their satisfaction elsewhere; court records from a number of Dutch cities indicate a wide range of sexual tastes and preferences within the subculture; and the most thorough study of the London subculture convincingly argues that cross-dressing was usually reserved for masquerades and other special occasions. Moreover, all surviving accounts of these subcultures come from hostile sources, such as sensational pamphlets and newspapers or court testimony from informers and police agents. Emphasizing the unmanly nature of the sodomites was an effective way of horrifying (or titillating) the general public, not to mention judges and juries. But even if, as possibly was the case, gender role–playing occupied a prominent place in these early modern subcultures, the submissive queens Chauncey rediscovered in turn-of-the-century New York were no less self-consciously femme in speech, manner, and dress than their counterparts in London, Paris, and Amsterdam two hundred years earlier, and camping it up, right down to the use of feminine nicknames, remains a common feature of the modern gay subculture, just as the drag queen remains one of the representative characters within that subculture.

To be sure, effeminate behavior is rarely as elaborate and certainly not as central to the modern subculture as seems to have been the case three centuries ago. The contrast is especially striking between the variegated male hustlers of the late twentieth century and the almost uniformly effeminate male prostitutes of the early eighteenth century or of Chauncey's turn-of-the-century New York (at least according to criminal records, which must, of course, be corrected for the tendency of the authorities to single out flamboyant behavior). Moreover, much campy behavior within the modern gay world is self-consciously referential, a knowing reaching back into gay history rather than the continuation of a vital tradition. For some, however, it is a vital tradition. Many young men just entering the gay scene feel almost compelled to experiment with different gender roles in the process of defining themselves. It is almost as if, as individuals or in small groups of "sisters," they are replicating the experience of the sodomitical subcultures at large as they "came out" three hundred years ago.

Archaic, impossibly distant, as these early modern subcultures often seem, in short, they have connections with our own time, tenuous and indirect as they may be. Much of the problem lies in the limited nature of the sources. We know next to nothing about the inner emotional lives of these men, about their friendships and loving relationships, and we can rarely do more than guess whether as individuals they saw themselves as a distinct type or category of person, let alone the extent to which they shared a sense of group identity. What at first appear to the modern observer as fundamental changes in consciousness between then and now may in fact be largely changes in style (though changes in style can and do add up to changes in consciousness). Indeed, some moments and participants in these early subcultures have an astonishingly contemporary ring about them. Very occasionally someone accused of sodomy defended his actions as an expression of his nature, of who and what he was; and in one remarkable case, in London in 1726, a defendant asserted that "there is no crime in making what use I please of my own body."

Such declarations are rare, which is hardly surprising since they come down to us from trial records. Anyone brave—or foolhardy—enough to challenge the authorities in such terms risked time in the pillory or worse. Most defendants said what they thought the court wanted to hear: that they had fallen temporarily into sin, that they had been too drunk to know what they were doing (still a useful excuse), that they had been tricked or coerced, that they could not be sodomites since they were married and had children (interesting evidence that the modern view that a person must be one or the other had already taken hold in the early eighteenth century). Given the lack of evidence from within these subcultures, what is remarkable is not how few less compliant, more defiant voices are heard but that we hear any. And the most important question we can ask of the seriously unbalanced material available to us is how and why subcultures containing the germs of a modern consciousness of sexuality and personal sexual identity emerged when and where they did.

Perhaps the most fundamental precondition, if not exactly a cause, of the emergence of these subcultures was urban growth. London, Paris, and Amsterdam were the largest cities in Europe at the end of the seventeenth century. They were, moreover, major political and/or commercial capitals with far-flung trading and imperial interests. As such these three cities provided something available nowhere else, a potent combination of anonymity and cosmopolitanism. The ambitious, the restless, the merely curious, and persons on the make were drawn to these cities from the provinces, indeed from all over Europe, and, because of their peculiarly international flavor as well as their sheer size, they fostered to an almost unprecedented degree complex and sophisticated divisions of labor, not only economic but social, cultural, and, for that matter, sexual.

It would be convenient for the sake of easy historical analysis if this increasing urban openness had been paralleled by growing social tolerance, if not of sexual deviance specifically, then in more general terms. That was the case in the Netherlands and to a degree in England but not in France. the Netherlands was perhaps the most open society in Europe. The early-seventeenth-century conflict between strict and reform Calvinism had long since given way to broad religious toleration, even of both Catholics and Jews. Moreover, the Dutch were deeply suspicious of central authority, clinging tenaciously to their republican form of government and refusing to give to their rulers the kind of absolute power developing elsewhere on the Continent, even in the face of wars with England and then with France in the second half of the century. In England the even deeper divisions of the first half of the century over religion and political power, which had led to civil war and a brief experiment with republicanism, were resolved after 1660 by a restoration of the monarchy and of an established church, but of a monarchy and a church and a central authority that were limited in scope. A powerful Parliament, a degree of religious toleration, and jealously guarded local autonomy had become accepted hallmarks of English society.

Not so in France, however, where the religious and political conflicts of the seventeenth century were resolved not by toleration and the diffusion and limitation of political power but by the reversal of earlier religious toleration and the reassertion of royal authority. Under Louis XIV France had perhaps the most effective absolutist regime in Europe, generally intolerant of any suggestion of political or religious deviance. Louis had the means and certainly the inclination to stamp out sexual deviance as well—he was intensely homophobic—but he also had a younger brother, Philippe, duc d'Orléans, whose "taste . . . was not for women and he never had them," as Saint Simon matter-of-factly noted in his memoirs. Philippe had a succession of handsome young favorites, some drawn from the ranks of the aristocracy, others from further down the social ladder. Relationships with the latter tended to be fleeting but often resulted in a promotion in the Orléans household or in the military. Even when in thrall to one of his aristocratic favorites, he apparently never lost his taste for rougher trade. As his second wife reported when he was fifty-eight years old, he "is more than ever taken with boys, he takes lackeys out of the antechamber. Everything he has he squanders in this way . . . and allows himself to be ruled by these lewd boys."

With some of his aristocratic favorites Philippe had lasting relationships, one of these extending over the greater part of his adult life, and they received commensurate rewards in titles or lucrative government posts. The written commentaries on Philippe's private life contain more innuendo than fact, but the implications are, and surely were intended to be, clear. His taste for men and boys was the subject of constant rumor and gossip at court—and not only at court. One of the most engaging aspects of the sodomitical subculture in Paris was its fondness for mimicking and parodying the manners and terms of address of the closed hierarchical structures of its social betters, especially those institutions rumored to be rife with sodomy. Monasteries and convents came in for a lot of this by play, but the favorite model and target, perhaps because it served to legitimize the subculture itself, was the court, some eleven miles away at Versailles.

In the Netherlands and England gossip reached even higher. When William of Orange, stadtholder for life in the Netherlands since 1673, was elevated to a share in the English throne fifteen years later, he brought with him two of his Dutch favorites, William Bentinck and the young Arnold Joost van Keppel. Both were handsomely rewarded with high government posts, military commands, titles, and estates, and Bentinck remained what he had already been for some years, William's chief personal and political confidant. Rumors about the nature of William's relations with his favorites preceded him to England and only increased as time passed, culminating with open and bitter rivalry between Bentinck and Keppel for the king's favor. According to Jonathan Swift, the king's "vices were of two sorts—male and female—in the former he was neither cautious nor secret."

Whatever the truth of the matter, William's preference for male company, social if not sexual, was common knowledge, the stuff of broadsides and satirical poems, grist for the mill of critics of the new regime, and the proximity of the court to some of the most notorious cruising grounds of the capital simply served to fuel the gossip. London was unique among the three great urban centers of northwestern Europe in this respect; the Dutch capital in the Hague is roughly three times as far from Amsterdam as Versailles is from Paris. The public perception that there were thriving sodomitical subcultures in the city and at court and that each might be encouraging (if not directly linked to) the other was therefore especially strong in England. By contrast, the subculture was as widely dispersed in the Netherlands as it was concentrated in England. South Holland was perhaps the most densely populated and substantially urbanized area in Europe; its compactness and the ease of communication there had long fostered a complex and sophisticated regional economy. The sodomitical subculture simply echoed this, as individuals moved readily between overlapping circles centered on the university town of Leiden, the textile-manufacturing center of Haarlem, the political and diplomatic capital in The Hague, the military stronghold of Utrecht, and above all the great commercial centers of Amsterdam and Rotterdam.

The extent of urbanization in late-seventeenth-century Europe is measurable, and public awareness and even limited tolerance of social and sexual deviance in these burgeoning cities and at the courts of France, England, and the Netherlands can be demonstrated, if only anecdotally. But there were— or may have been—other developments harder to trace or define that contributed to the emergence of a distinct and self-conscious sexual subculture. A number of historians have suggested the possibility that a new family type was developing in northwestern Europe, and especially in England, in the late seventeenth century, a family type distinguished by what Lawrence Stone has called *affective individualism,* among the chief characteristics of which were closely knit, home-centered nuclear (as opposed to extended) families, marriages founded on at least the expectation of love rather than the expectation of social or economic advantage, increasing regard for the individuality and privacy of all members of the family, and a tendency to define and refine distinct and appropriate roles for each family member according to gender and generation—husbands and wives, parents and children. This thesis has been subjected to much harsh criticism. There is, for example, abundant evidence from earlier centuries of families held together by no less strong ties of marital and filial affection, and Stone himself is careful to suggest that the changes he identifies were limited to the upper middling ranks of society, rural and urban, and that it took a generation or more for them to spread to other classes. On the other hand, some of the developments he singles out as most important are undeniable, even measurable, such as changes in the design of houses from those in which rooms connect with each other to those in which rooms connect separately with a hallway.

If indeed such a family type was emerging at this time, it would, however inadvertently, have fostered and highlighted the growth of deviant subcultures. To the extent that the nuclear family based on love-centered ideas of a marriage partnership was becoming the accepted unit of respectable society, those who, for whatever reason, including sexual orientation, were unwilling or unable to form such families (or who did so but found them either more than they could cope with or less than met their needs) would necessarily be driven to define themselves, and would be defined by others, as in some measure distinct and different, outsiders. The increasingly clear demarcation of gender roles would make those who felt uncomfortable or inadequate in such roles more self-conscious, which may help to explain the emphasis on gender role–playing within the early sodomitical subcultures. And finally, growing emphasis on the autonomy of the individual was likely to make such self-awareness and self-definition far easier, and acting on such feelings more likely, while the increasing recognition of the right to privacy allowed greater scope for such actions.

If much of this analysis seems highly speculative in nature, the cumulative effects are not. The major cities of northwestern Europe at the end of the seventeenth century were perhaps uniquely endowed with conditions favorable to the growth of a wide range of culturally and socially diverse interests, subgroups, and neighborhoods. The emergence of sodomitical subcultures was but one manifestation of this process.

# Chapter 2    Patterns of Repression

The sodomitical subcultures that emerged in northwestern Europe at the close of the seventeenth century were bound sooner or later to attract public attention, hostile public attention, since the conditions that had fostered or simply allowed for their growth also ensured that they would be seen as symptoms and possibly as sources of social disorder and moral decay. The growth of London, Paris, and Amsterdam led to serious problems of criminality and public order and thus to demands from local authorities and respectable citizens for better law enforcement. The cosmopolitanism of these cities bred xenophobia; it is no accident that sodomy was often labeled a foreign vice (Italians being the favorite target). Political and religious toleration in the Netherlands and England fostered a traditionalist, conservative reaction. The opulence of court life created social resentments and class tensions; in moralistic tracts and press coverage sodomy was often portrayed as a peculiarly aristocratic vice. Growing emphasis on the nuclear family led to concern about any behavior that might threaten the integrity of the family and its mores, while greater autonomy and privacy for the individual raised the question how best to regulate the behavior of the unattached male, especially at a time when the influence of the extended family was in decline. By the early eighteenth century conditions in northwestern Europe were ripe not only for the emergence of sodomitical subcultures but for a savage reaction against them as well.

Not, of course, that sodomy had ever been viewed favorably in Christian Europe. Biblical injunctions against sodomy in both the Old Testament (Leviticus 20:13) and the New (Romans 1:26–27) unequivocally condemned it as a crime "against nature" for which the practitioner "shall surely be put to death." Moreover, the story of the destruction of Sodom and Gemorrah inextricably (though rather unfairly, since the sins of these cities of the plain were left somewhat vague) linked sodomy with natural disaster and divine retribution, while medieval conflicts within Christianity and between Christianity and Islam associated it both with heresy and with the infidel. Like the Arab enemies of Christendom, the Albigensian heretics were popularly supposed to indulge in sodomy, and their purported origins in Bulgaria gave the West its most common synonym for the practice: Latin *bulgaris*, French *bougre*, Dutch *bouger*, English *bugger*. Perhaps because it lent itself so readily to being labeled an alien vice, by the end of the thirteenth century sodomy, which had been condemned as no worse than other sexual sins (in Leviticus it was only one item in a category of abominations including bestiality, adultery, and incest), began to be singled out as especially repugnant and dangerous.

In a number of Italian cities in the fifteenth century and in Spain a century and more later, major campaigns were launched to check what the authorities, civil and religious, claimed was an increasing incidence of sodomy. In successive years early in the sixteenth century Holy Roman Emperor Charles V and King Henry VIII of England promulgated statutes prescribing the death penalty for, in the language of the English legislation, "the detestable and abominable vice of buggery committed with mankind or beast," while the imperial decree cast its net wider to include anyone "who commits lewdness with a beast, or a man with a man or a woman with a woman." Death was normally either by hanging, as in England, or, as in most of continental Europe, by burning alive. But there were variations, either as alternatives or as embellishments in especially sensational cases: stoning to death, garroting, castration or disfigurement before or even in place of execution, dismemberment after execution, and in some instances the total obliteration of the body, possibly along with all records of the crime itself.

It was not for nothing that sodomy was called the unmentionable vice. So much so, in fact, that it was often referred to even in official documents nonspecifically as the crime against nature or simply as the most awful sin. For the historian this is more than merely frustrating. Even where records escaped accidental or deliberate destruction, the exact nature of the offense is often far from clear, as is the answer to the most important question: not what the penalties were but how often they were carried out. The powerful and the privileged, children, and the clergy were often treated leniently unless their activities were especially flagrant or frequent. Standards of proof varied greatly. Sometimes both penetration and emission had to be proved, sometimes not. Sometimes a confession (often obtained by torture) was required, sometimes not. Accusations and eyewitness testimony might be accepted at face value or seriously questioned. Just how rigorously the authorities pursued cases of sodomy seems to have depended on the state of public opinion and the degree of official anxiety as much as on the nature of the offense. And the same was true of the punishments meted out. For anything less than sodomy itself—for public lewdness or attempted sodomy—punishments ranged from public humiliation to various terms of imprisonment or banishment to physical mutilation.

As for the death penalty, in the cities that have been most closely studied, such as fifteenth-century Venice or sixteenth-century Seville, it appears to have been applied with great care and sparingly most of the time but frequently and savagely in exceptional years. In Portugal, for example, there were some four hundred trials for sodomy before the inquisition from the mid-sixteenth to the early nineteenth century, very nearly one quarter of them in two troubled decades in the mid-seventeenth century, but only about 7 percent of those prosecuted were convicted and handed over to the secular authorities to be burned (and those tried represented fewer than 10 percent of those accused). In Seville a larger number, seventy-one, were burned to death for sodomy in a far shorter period, between 1567 and 1616, but most of these executions were concentrated in two clusters, from the late 1570s to the mid-1580s and about 1600. This might suggest that the frequency of sodomy was itself periodic or, more likely, that sodomites used greater caution following a crackdown or, the most intriguing possibility, that prosecutions for sodomy were an index of social and political stresses, that public and official concern with the crime against nature was less a function of its frequency than an outlet for concern about other, more intractable issues and a rallying cry for moral reformers and demagogues.

This was certainly the case in Florence at the end of the fifteenth century. Rightly or wrongly the city had long been notorious for sodomy, so much so that in 1432 the government created a special magistracy evocatively named the Officers of the Night to deal with the problem. The sexual practices they policed, almost always involving dominant older and submissive younger partners, resembled the pattern found virtually everywhere in premodern Europe. The pattern of policing was not typical, however. There were far more prosecutions in Florence than in other comparable European cities, but the punishments meted out were milder: mostly fines, less frequently public humiliation or exile, occasionally prison, and only rarely death, with the harsher penalties normally reserved for repeat offenders or those adults who accepted the passive role. As elsewhere, however, the number and severity of prosecutions fluctuated from year to year, decade to decade, depending, it would seem, on the exigencies of local politics. There was a major crackdown in the early 1460s, when Lorenzo di Medici was attempting to consolidate power. More savage penalties—the pillory, corporal punishment, and death—were introduced, and prosecutions increased dramatically again in the 1490s, during the three-year moral dictatorship of Savonarola, who denounced sodomy along with a host of other sins to which he attributed the city's recent disasters.

Similarly in Spain, the systematic persecution of sodomy followed closely upon the Council of Trent, which marked the beginning of the militant Counter-Reformation. The pattern was not as straightforward as this would suggest, however. In Seville, for example, the authorities often prosecuted sodomy and other sexual offenses in different years, perhaps in order to reinforce the impact of burnings for sodomy. In any case, few things are easier than using hindsight to find an appropriate cause for a particular event. The interesting question is why sodomy became an object of public and official concern and persecution in certain times and places but not in other, similar circumstances.

All of these considerations apply also to the waves of persecution of sodomy that followed upon the emergence of sodomitical subcultures in northwestern Europe about 1700. Before the early eighteenth century prosecutions for sodomy were, if anything, less frequent in France, the Netherlands, and England than in the large cities of Italy and Spain. A major scandal such as the infamous Castlehaven case of 1631, in which the earl of Castlehaven was found guilty of committing sodomy with his servants, might force the issue on public and official attention, but in many cases, as indeed in this one, those prosecuted, convicted, and actually put to death were often guilty of other crimes as well, from blasphemy to theft. The close surveillance and systematic prosecution of sodomy in early-eighteenth-century Paris, London, and Amsterdam was a new phenomenon.

Of these three major cities it was in Paris that the response of the authorities was the most circumspect but also the most methodical. The marquis d'Argenson, the lieutenant general of police for more than twenty years from 1697, initiated a policy of monitoring a number of deviant and potentially criminal activities, including the emerging sodomitical subculture. A couple of officers were assigned full time to keeping track of homosexual activity, watching the parks and other hangouts themselves or codifying information supplied by often anonymous informants, by confessions extracted from those arrested, or by undercover agents, most of whom were recruited from sodomites turned by the police under threat of arrest, conviction, or harsher sentences. Elaborate files were built up, recording not only the names and favorite haunts of known sodomites but also their patterns of behavior and even their conversations with undercover agents.

The primary purpose of this monitoring was not to lay the groundwork for more frequent or extensive prosecutions. On the contrary, hoping to avoid public scandal, particularly if it might involve the powerful and well-born or otherwise respectable citizens, indeed hoping to limit public awareness that there was a sodomitical subculture, D'Argenson and his subordinates appear to have viewed their work as essentially a means of social control. The police, though not some others in the government hierarchy, let alone the clergy, knew better than to accept the common belief that sodomy was a largely aristocratic vice, and they were therefore especially careful to monitor the extent of social mixing, which those in authority regarded as perhaps the most disturbing characteristic of the subculture. That the young might be seduced and corrupted by contact with sodomites was a public as well as a police concern, but like social mixing, it was a problem that D'Argenson believed could best be handled through a policy of deterrence with a minimum of publicity. Thus, first-time offenders might be let off with a warning, their families and neighborhoods being relied upon to exert a restraining influence, while repeaters or the more flagrant might spend some time in the hospital of Bicetre or in the Bastille. Foreigners were normally deported, and provincials sent back home, perhaps to be kept under surveillance by local authorities. Harsher penalties were available for the truly incorrigible, including deportation to the West Indian colonies, but the ultimate penalty for sodomy was rarely resorted to, and still more rarely publicized, in eighteenth-century France.

The most notable exception to the cool, almost detached manner in which the police carried out their surveillance policy was the Deschauffours case of 1726. Deschauffours was a pimp and procurer who enticed and in some instances forced boys into his "school and bordello of sodomy" for the deletation of wealthy and powerful clients. Deschauffours's behavior was so depraved, and the extent and importance of his clientele so great, that D'Argenson's successor as lieutenant general of police decided "that an example must be made, it not being possible to punish all those who were implicated, because that would cause too much trouble. And besides, it wasn't desirable to further illustrate this crime and to spread it, because most of the people do not know what it is." Deschauffours was arrested and jailed in the Bastille in February, and he was sentenced to death and burned alive three months later. Others were given far lighter sentences—banishment or short prison terms—in the hope of containing the scandal, limiting the possibility of its corrupting the impressionable and the young or feeding antiaristocratic sentiment, while at the same time sending a clear message about the limits of government tolerance to the upper ranks of French society. Unfortunately for the authorities, they could not escape censure no matter what course they took; critics of the government, from street hustlers to Voltaire, saw the contrast between the punishment meted out to Deschauffours and that given to his clients as an outrageous example of discrimination in favor of the powerful and the privileged.

The situation was potentially so explosive that the normally cautious police authorities would likely have avoided taking such drastic action if the Deschauffours case had been less horrifying and less far-reaching or if the political situation in France had been less uncertain. But the Deschauffours case was not an isolated matter; it was the culmination of a number of sodomitical scandals involving highly placed churchmen and courtiers, most notably a moonlight orgy on the grounds of the palace of Versailles that resulted in the banishment of a number of young nobles from court. The economic and political condition of France in the 1720s also seemed to call for decisive action in defense of public order, even in the absence of what appeared to be a dangerous decline in public morals following the death of Louis XIV in 1715. The economy had been weakened by more than a generation of war, followed by the collapse of a postwar speculative bubble, and the boy king, Louis XV, had yet to settle on a stable group of ministers and advisers. The handling of the Deschauffours case was a unique response to what was seen as a peculiarly dangerous scandal at an especially difficult time. Thereafter, the police reverted to the low-key approach pioneered by D'Argenson a generation before.

The response in England to the emerging sodomitical subculture could hardly have been more different. London had no professional police force comparable to that in Paris or, for that matter, any authority with jurisdiction over the whole city. Furthermore, the ecclesiastical courts traditionally responsible for enforcing public morals—the so-called bawdy courts—had become all but moribund by the end of the seventeenth century. The gap thus left by both church and state was filled, as so often in modern English history, by private voluntary initiatives. In the years immediately following the accession of William III, Societies for the Reformation of Manners sprang up as one facet of a broad-based reform movement aimed at securing the constitutional and religious institutions of England, threatened during the reign of James II, as well as checking what moral reformers saw as a loosening of public and private standards dating back a generation, to the reign of Charles II. The first of the Societies for the Reformation of Manners was founded in 1690 in London's East End by a group of artisans and tradesmen, respectable representatives of the lower middling ranks of society who were equally disturbed by the depravity of the poor and the moral laxity of the upper classes. Their first concern was with suppressing bawdy houses as breeding grounds for crime, licentiousness, public disorder, and disease. The movement quickly spread to wealthier sections of London and to the provinces. Perhaps sensing the risks as well as the opportunities presented by such an ad hoc popular movement, both the established church and the court took it up and gave it official sanction. From their largely Anglican origins the societies spread to other Protestant sects, and from the suppression of bawdy houses they went on to tackle other signs and symbols of immorality: blasphemy and Sabbath breaking, public lewdness, obscenity, prostitution, drunkenness—and sodomy.

As a popular movement the societies acted publicly and courted publicity, and as their title suggests, they were not content with the mere surveillance or regulation of vice but aimed at nothing less than the reformation of English society. In the absence of a professional police force the societies' methods were an opportunistic mix of the public and the private. Their agents acted as clearinghouses for complaints brought by sympathizers or themselves sought out violations. Warrants detailing offenses would then be taken to a magistrate for signature and to a local constable for serving on offenders. Perhaps inevitably the societies overreached themselves. Their use of informers and self-appointed agents and their highly publicized attempts to suppress vice rather than quietly control it (as the Paris police did) encouraged blackmail, extortion and bribery, the manufacturing of evidence, and the criminalization of otherwise relatively harmless activities. Never popular with the lower orders (their agents were often physically assaulted in the poorer parts of London), the societies were doomed once they alienated the wealthy and powerful. High churchmen disliked their evangelical zeal, and the government came to distrust their fanaticism and frequent disregard for the niceties of the law. By the time the movement disintegrated in the 1730s, however, it had achieved much of what it had hoped for. The societies claimed direct responsibility for obtaining almost one hundred thousand convictions in the nearly fifty years of their existence, and there is no question that London society had gradually become outwardly more civil and respectable (if only because vice had been driven deeper underground). And besides, the cause of moral regeneration had by that time been taken over by a movement of even greater competence and longevity: Methodism.

Before entering its final period of decline in the 1730s the movement for the reformation of manners enjoyed three major bursts of activity. The first coincided with the optimistic beginnings in the 1690s, and by the end of that decade sodomy had become one of its principal targets, alongside more traditional concerns such as bawdy houses, streetwalkers, public lewdness, and the like. The first well-publicized sodomy case and one of the societies' early coups involved the entrapment, trial, and conviction of a naval captain, Edward Rigby, for attempted sodomy in 1698. Rigby never served his sentence of time in the pillory, a fine of a thousand pounds, and a year in jail— he escaped to France—but his trial served the purposes of the societies admirably. It opened the way to a series of arrests and convictions early in the new century and, of even greater long-run significance, made sodomy a major public issue perhaps for the first time. The societies trumpeted their success in their annual reports and in a pamphlet entitled *The Sodomites' Shame and Doom* hinted darkly at the extent of the evil and promised to expose it.

In their second wave of activism, beginning in 1707, the societies made good on that threat. Over the next couple of years dozens of men were entrapped by the societies' agents, and a number of molly houses were raided and closed. But even this was only a foretaste of the wholesale crackdown on the sodomitical subculture in the third and final wave, in 1726. The way to this unprecedentedly thorough campaign was opened, as might be expected, by informers and agent provocateurs, one of each in fact, both of whom agreed to cooperate with the authorities in return for immunity from prosecution. The first, identified at the time only by one initial, *P*, agreed, following a quarrel with his lover, to introduce agents of the societies into a number of molly houses he frequented, which resulted in a series of arrests in February. The second, Thomas Newton, apparently a hustler as well as a molly house client, came to the attention of the authorities when he offered to post bail for one of those arrested in the February sweep, the proprietress of an especially infamous molly house, the wonderfully improbably named Mother Clap. Newton tentatively agreed to assist the police but kept putting the constables off until his own arrest some weeks later. From that moment on he cooperated fully, giving names and particulars of men he had slept with, entrapping others in known cruising areas and giving evidence against them in court. The circle was widened still further when some of those arrested were turned, as Newton and the other original informant had themselves been turned, by the police. All in all, at least twenty molly houses were shut down, dozens were arrested, at least three, including Mother Clap herself, were sentenced to the humiliation and danger of time in the pillory for attempted sodomy or, in Mother Clap's case, for running a disorderly house, and three were found guilty of sodomy itself and hung.

Surely not entirely coincidentally, the campaign against sodomy in London peaked at exactly the same time as the extensively reported Deschauffours case in Paris. Thereafter, in London as in Paris, the police and the courts stopped pressing the issue so publicly. The authorities in both cities always felt uncomfortable dealing with sodomy, not only on moral grounds or because they feared that by publicizing it they might encourage it and possibly further consolidate the subculture but also because it was a dangerous and volatile issue. Sodomy could be used by the authorities, but it could also be used against them. The popular prejudice that sodomy was an aristocratic vice, persistent rumors about goings-on at court, the increasingly blunt and inflammatory nature of the innuendos contained in pamphlets, popular ballads, and press coverage, and public disquiet at the class bias evident in the punishments meted out made governments on both sides of the Channel nervous. Certainly by the summer of 1726 the issue, like the Societies for the Reformation of Manners themselves, needed to be reined in. And so it was. Indeed there was only one relatively minor aftershock following the three major bursts of activity in London stretching back to the late seventeenth century. But that final eruption, in 1730, also, interestingly, coincided with similar events abroad, events that, like the Deschauffours case, received great publicity in England and soon developed into the most savage campaign to suppress a sodomitical subculture in modern times—at least until the twentieth century.

It took place, surprisingly, in the Netherlands, which, then as now, was regarded as one of the most tolerant societies in Europe. No Dutch city had a police force able or intended to carry out the sort of close surveillance of illicit activities that D'Argenson had developed in Paris, and the absence of such official means of social control may help explain the overreaction in the Netherlands once the public became aware and alarmed. As in London, therefore, arrests and prosecutions for many offenses depended on complaints brought by private citizens or information extracted from defendants. Though there was no Dutch equivalent to the Societies for the Reformation of Manners, there were signs of growing public and official concern with sexual crimes in general, sodomy included, after 1700. Before the turn of the century sodomy was rarely prosecuted unless it was associated with other crimes such as rape or extortion, but during the first quarter of the eighteenth century prosecutions for sodomy independent of other offenses increased, as did prosecutions for adultery, bigamy, and prostitution. Even given such indications of changing attitudes toward moral offenses, however, no one could have predicted the chain of events set in motion almost by chance in the winter of 1730, which quickly spread to involve towns and cities throughout the most densely populated provinces of the Netherlands and ultimately even the remotest villages.

The process began with a complaint that unnatural acts were being committed in the former cathedral in Utrecht. The two soldiers who were subsequently arrested (and ultimately executed) implicated a well-traveled former soldier, Zacharias Wilsma, who in turn implicated members of sodomitical networks from Utrecht to Amsterdam. As the information (and Wilsma himself, as chief informer) was passed along to the authorities in city after city, the reaction ranged from stunned disbelief to ferocious repression. No one had any inkling that something so extensive existed. Sodomy suddenly took on the character of a criminal conspiracy. The caution and circumspection with which the authorities had traditionally treated cases of sodomy, lest undue publicity excite public unrest or curiosity about the unmentionable sin, was replaced by the determination to "exterminate this vice to the bottom," as the provincial court of Holland declared, if necessary by making public examples of the worst offenders. Mass arrests followed inevitably, as did flights from the country to avoid arrest. Vaguely worded statutes against sodomy were strengthened and made more specific. In all, more than three hundred trials were held before the antisodomitical frenzy spent itself late in the decade.

At least in Amsterdam the percentage of those tried who were actually convicted and executed for sodomy was relatively small, since anal penetration and emission had to be proved or confessed. While some confessions were made voluntarily, perhaps in the hope of lighter sentences, many were obtained by torture, and some of these were later recanted. Lesser offenders received jail terms, corporal punishment, or both. Those who fled were often tried in absentia and sentenced to banishment, sometimes for life. The accused represented a wide spectrum of Dutch society, from soldiers, common workmen, and servants, to shopkeepers, merchants, and minor officials, to members of the aristocracy. Divergences in punishments based on social status were perhaps less glaring in the relatively egalitarian Netherlands than in France or England, but the lower orders were more likely to be imprisoned or put to death, while those from the upper ranks of society, who in any case had greater means and opportunity to flee the country, were more likely to be banished.

The first, most virulent phase of the prosecution of sodomites in major cities passed quickly—the last execution for sodomy in the decade in Amsterdam took place in September 1730—but the most horrific example was yet to come, in, of all places, the village of Faan in remote Groningen province. What began in April 1731 with perhaps a merely mischievous accusation by one adolescent boy against another mushroomed in the hands of a single magistrate, egged on by the local minister, into a relentless pursuit of men and boys throughout this rural backwater. The cycle of accusation, arrest, possible torture, confession, and the implication of others was repeated again and again. In the end, in September twenty-four of the accused were found guilty, strangled, and burned at the stake. The calamity at Faan has often been compared to the witch-hunts of earlier centuries and in particular to the witch trials in Salem, Massachusetts, in 1692. It is an apt comparison, given the atmosphere of temporary hysteria that swept a small community, the role of a judge determined to pursue the matter to its illogical conclusion, and the popular revulsion against that judge once the hysteria had passed. That revulsion was more than justified. There was no sodomitical subculture in Faan nor any connection with the subcultures unearthed in Utrecht, Amsterdam, or the Hague. The twenty-four dead of Faan were victims of a change in perception brought about by the revelation of these subcultures. Echoes of the campaign against sodomy had already reached this corner of the Netherlands. In the previous year the ubiquitous Wilsma had implicated some men in the region, and the province of Groningen, like the province of Holland, had reaffirmed and strengthened its laws against sodomy. The casual sexual encounters between a few men and boys in a small town were suddenly and irrevocably seen in a new and sinister light.

It is this change in perceptions that is the most striking aspect of what happened in the Netherlands beginning in 1730. The uncovering of a sodomitical subculture, indeed of a network of such subcultures, came as a shock. What had until then been treated as a lapse into sin or criminality by an individual was now looked upon as a social ill, a symptom of decadence and decline. In the flurry of pamphlets, broadsides, and moral tracts that followed the ever-widening investigation in 1730, sodomy was linked—as both cause and con-sequence—to all of the Netherlands' recent problems, real or imagined: the decline of moral fervor and religious observance in the Protestant churches; the concomitant penetration of Dutch society by foreign, especially Catholic, influences; the loss of the country's preeminence in world trade; and the rise of a new, ostentatious moneyed class that lacked both the moral rigor and the commercial vigor of its predecessors from the golden age of Dutch prosperity.

The Netherlands was ripe for scapegoating—economically, diplomatically, and militarily it was experiencing a painful loss of power and influence rela-tive to France and England—but it would be a mistake to look to specifi-cally Dutch causes for the persecution of sodomites in the early-eighteenth-century Netherlands, since similar crackdowns took place in France and England simultaneously. Unfortunately for the sodomitical subcultures of northwestern Europe, they emerged in circumstances in which they would be peculiarly vulnerable to attack. A generation of war stretching back to the 1680s was followed by a long and difficult transition to stable peacetime conditions, quite as much in victorious England and the Netherlands as in defeated France. In such circumstances it was tempting—it always is—for governments and the public to lash out at easy targets, and the sodomites were easy targets indeed. The subcultures were new, strange, and potentially threatening; they thrived outside, even in opposition to, the ordinary institu-tions of social control such as family and neighborhood; they were often asso-ciated with other criminal activity, if only by force of circumstance; they were almost always seen as alien intrusions. Above all, their sudden emergence had to be explained, and what better explanation than that they were the result of, or perhaps in part responsible for, society's other ills. The authorities, to be sure, were always ambivalent about how best to deal with sodomy, often preferring to ignore it for fear that it might somehow be contagious or that public anger, once aroused, might be vented at unwelcome targets. But once the issue was out of the box, they were more or less compelled to take the lead in pursuing it and often did so enthusiastically, at least for a time, if only to divert public attention from other issues. The experience of the Netherlands was not unique in this; it is simply an especially clear-cut example.

The Dutch example is instructive in another way; it perfectly illustrates the problem of lesbian invisibility. Of some eight hundred trials for sodomy before the nineteenth century in the Netherlands, fewer than twenty were of women, and none of these came during the great wave of prosecutions in the early eighteenth century. A significant number, thirteen, were tried in the 1790s, but for earlier cases it is necessary to go back to the seventeenth century, when there was a scattering of prosecutions of women. In none of these cases, however, was sodomy the primary concern of the courts. All these women had tried to pass as men, deserting their husbands in a couple of cases, marrying or attempting to marry other women in others. It was their violation of their accepted roles as women in society, not their having lain with other women, that led to their convictions and their relatively light sentences of banishment. The object of public and official alarm was male sodomy and the sodomitical subculture; lesbianism, when it was even recognized, was still regarded, and long continued to be, as an individual aberration, much as male sodomy had been before 1700 but could never quite be again.

By the late 1730s the first systematic persecution of sodomites in modern times had come to an end everywhere in northwestern Europe, and there was to be nothing like it again until the end of the century. But the emergence of these subcultures and their repression had significant lasting effects on attitudes toward and probably within the subcultures. Twice more during the next fifty years, in the 1760s and again a decade later, there were brief crackdowns in Amsterdam. The pattern was the same in both instances: men arrested for other crimes were revealed as sodomites and implicated others in networks similar to those uncovered in 1730. A few men were executed (by garroting) in the 1760s, but most were imprisoned or banished, many of the latter by default since they had fled prosecution. Clearly the subculture had survived or revived following its decimation in the 1730s, and while official attitudes toward it could hardly be called permissive in view of the numbers arrested and severely punished in 1764–65, these further revelations of the existence of a subculture did not come as a shock. Nor, it would seem, considering the much milder crackdown of the 1770s, was the total elimination of the subculture any longer considered possible.

In Paris, where control more than repression had long been official policy, a grudging recognition that the subculture was probably there to stay is even more evident in the direction police intervention took from the late 1740s on. A new lieutenant general of police reorganized the department, creating a separate inspectorate to enforce the laws against sodomy and placing at its head an officer, one Framboisier, who had served for more than a decade as an assistant in the division until then responsible for suppressing a variety of vices, including sodomy. Methods changed along with organization. No longer venturing into the field, Framboisier concentrated on amassing a huge file on the subculture by collating reports from his subordinates and information supplied by informants, most of them arrested but not charged or given a light sentence in return for cooperation. The files contained little more than names and places. Gone were the detailed arrest reports including descriptions of acts and records of conversations between undercover agents and the men who accosted them; gone also was the moralistic tone of many records from earlier in the century. There is no little irony in this. In the case of sodomy, as in the case of other crimes that were viewed as sins, the civil authorities had originally acted as the secular arm of the church. By the early eighteenth century the police had taken complete control but still employed religious sanctions and moral pressure for their own purposes, as a means of extracting confessions. By midcentury even that was gone. Sodomy was treated as a crime, as a problem of social control, not as a sin. Bureaucratic specialization had triumphed; the means had become the end.

There were exceptions to this general tolerance. In 1750 two young men were executed for sodomy, but significantly, they were workers, an apprentice cabinetmaker and a pork butcher, and they were caught in the act in public. (The other sodomites burned in Paris during the eighteenth century—five in all—had also committed other crimes.) Discretion or high social status all but guaranteed leniency under the new dispensation. Another, perhaps even more significant indicator of a permanent shift in attitudes was a change in terminology. In police reports from the late 1730s on the term *pederast* gradually replaced the traditional designation, *sodomite.* Not only was *pederast* a less emotive term but it lacked the religious connotation of *sodomite.* In addition, unlike *sodomy,* which described certain acts, *pederasty* referred only to acts of a homosexual character. We are very close here to the modern concept of the homosexual as a category. As the notion of the pederast as a type took hold, replacing the old view of the sodomite as an individual fallen into sin, it followed that as a category of persons pederasts should be identifiable to the knowledgeable observer by certain traits of personality or patterns of behavior. It was during the eighteenth century that the stereotype of the effeminate homosexual took hold. The fop, the dandy, became suspect. Once any man who engaged in sex with another male of any age came to be seen as in some sense effeminate, as less than manly, effeminate behavior was increasingly labeled as a sign of homosexuality or homosexual tendencies. The definition of manliness was narrowed and more sharply drawn; men became more self-conscious about their behavior, and traditional expressions of affection between men were abandoned or modified.

Before the middle of the century intense friendships between males with open displays of physical affection and correspondence incorporating the language and sentiments of love letters were common and unremarkable. An especially interesting example, because it involved a little-known chapter in the life of the English radical leader of the American revolutionary era, John Wilkes, centered on a group of English students at the University of Leiden in the 1740s. Wilkes received effusive declarations of their passionate attachment to him whenever he was parted from either his tutor or his closest companion in the group, and when they were all together they routinely exchanged hugs and kisses in public. At least two members of this little club went on to live more or less exclusively homosexual lives, but the same could hardly be said of Wilkes, one of the more notoriously heterosexual libertines of late-eighteenth-century England. As a group they belonged to a long-established, fairly widely accepted tradition of homoerotic friendships between young men and between students and their tutors. During the latter half of the century that tradition gradually ceased to be acceptable, especially in England. Public displays of affection between men, indeed passionate male friendships, could arouse suspicion. The once common custom of men's sharing a bed—guests with hosts, students with each other or with their tutors, travelers at inns—declined, and parents began to demand separate beds for their boys at boarding schools, which in turn advertised separate sleeping accommodations as an attraction. These trends both reinforced and were reinforced by the growing concern with privacy, though privacy, it was gradually realized, had its own dangers. It is no accident that the eighteenth century also witnessed growing concern with that most private of sexual practices, masturbation, which it was feared might lead boys into isolation and antisocial behavior, as well as to other secret sexual vices, including, of course, homosexuality.

Many of these changes in attitudes and behavior were confined to the upper middling ranks of society, to merchants, members of the professions, and to the landed gentry, or to those a bit lower on the social ladder, such as artisans and shopkeepers, who desired to better themselves. Among those of even lower status, the working poor, sharply defined gender roles, privacy, and the indulgence of children were unaffordable luxuries, while at the upper end of the social spectrum both love and sexual satisfaction were as likely to be found outside of marriage as in it, since marriage was still very much a matter of family and social alliances. In the upper ranks of society the old libertine tradition survived, and notions of what was normal and abnormal, feminine and masculine, were often vaguely defined. As one historian put it, "Throughout the century, with its taste masques and substitutions, for foppish men and dominant women, the mood of sexual ambivalence dominated cultured society." But it did so with increasing self-consciousness, since that tradition was under attack from below by those who adopted and propounded a set of norms that drew sharper lines between the acceptable and the unacceptable, the normal and the abnormal, the proper roles of men and of women. And it was in contrast with, in opposition to, these emerging norms that those who felt unable or unwilling to conform were defined or defined themselves as deviant or simply different.

# Chapter 3    Sodomy and the Enlightenment

The crystallization of the image—and self-image—of members of the sodomitical subcultures of northwestern Europe as in some way a distinct and identifiable category of persons was certainly the most important development affecting these subcultures in the decades following their emergence and repression early in the eighteenth century. Scarcely less significant was the development of similar subcultures in parts of northern Europe beyond the small Paris-London-Amsterdam triangle. Of these by far the most important was in Berlin, the city that was to be at the forefront of the movement to achieve greater knowledge and understanding of sexual deviance in the coming century. During the latter half of the eighteenth century the population of Berlin doubled to over one hundred thousand, and during the reign of Frederick the Great (1740–86) the city was transformed from a Prussian backwater into the capital of a major European power.

With population and power came an ever greater degree of cultural and social diversity, including the development of a thriving sodomitical subculture with all the characteristics familiar in the West: known cruising areas, taverns, clubs, and male brothels, a specialized slang, and elaborate visual codes of recognition. We are less dependent on police and court records for our knowledge of this subculture than for those in the West. There is in fact a firsthand account of the Berlin sexual underground in 1782 by an Austrian visitor accompanied by a knowledgeable native. Unfortunately, this account is richer in metaphor, classical allusions, and moralistic asides than in facts, so comparisons with what the official files from London, Paris, and Amsterdam reveal is difficult. As for government policy and law enforcement, the pattern appears to have been similar to that in the great urban centers to the west. In the early eighteenth century a number of convicted sodomites were put to the sword and then burned, sometimes at the insistence of Frederick the Great's father, Frederick William I, though the very young and the titled were usually treated more leniently.

Under Frederick the Great enforcement of the law, though not the law itself, was relaxed, perhaps in part due to the sexual predilections of Frederick himself. For here again we have a monarch rumored to be homosexual. The evidence, though of course circumstantial, is persuasive. He never lived with his wife but preferred all male company. He erected a temple on the palace grounds at Potsdam dedicated to friendship and decorated with portraits of close male companions from antiquity: Heracles and Philoctetis, Orestes and Pylades, and others. He purchased or commissioned both painted and sculpted representations of Ganymede, the beautiful boy whom Zeus took a fancy to and, transforming himself into an eagle, transported to Mount Olympus. Personal sexual tastes aside, however, Frederick had good reasons of policy and political philosophy to apply the law with moderation. Voltaire, during his three years as Frederick's philosopher in residence, recorded an occasion when the monarch overruled a death sentence in a case of sodomy—in this instance with a donkey—noting under his verdict that "in his states he granted freedom of conscience and of cock."

Mention of Frederick the Great and of Voltaire leads inevitably to consideration of the influence of Enlightenment thought and of the theory and practice of enlightened despotism on the proper role of the state and society in matters of private morality and deviant behavior, sexual and otherwise. That influence was, of course, profound and the phrase "freedom of conscience and of cock" sums it up surprisingly well. The leading thinkers of the eighteenth century, as well as rulers such as Frederick the Great and Joseph II of Austria, when being enlightened as well as despotic generally held that individuals should be free to believe, think, and even act as they wished, consistent with the rights of others, the maintenance of public order, and the ultimate authority of the state. Not that the philosophes countenanced libertinism; on the contrary, they were often rather prudish, at least in their public pronouncements. They strongly denounced almost all forms of sexual license or deviance, including adultery, fornication, the resort to prostitution, and sodomy, but not primarily on traditional moral grounds.

Skeptics or freethinkers for the most part, the philosophes were critical of organized religion and often savagely anticlerical. Their objections to sexual deviance emphasized practical concerns such as the maintenance of public order and the health of civil society. Sexual vices as secret vices they condemned as potentially socially disruptive, especially of the institutions of marriage and the family. Moreover, in the pre-Malthusian world of the mid-eighteenth century it was generally believed that Europe was underpopulated. At a time of intense mercantilist economic competition and frequent wars between the major states of Europe, any practice that threatened to stifle the growth of population could be seen as a threat to national prosperity and security. Thus sodomy was condemned, along with but little more severely than celibacy, especially as institutionalized in the clergy, or adultery.

Sodomy was, however, singled out by the French philosophes as especially revolting. Whenever they referred to it they were careful to do so with disgust. Voltaire, for example, called it "a vice which would destroy mankind, . . . a sordid outrage against nature," while Montesquieu denounced it as an "infamy," "a crime which religion, morality and civil government equally condemn." These writers may well have made such remarks primarily to protect themselves from the imputation of being overly indulgent toward sodomites or even of being sodomites themselves. While in Prussia, Voltaire experimented with sodomy once, but when it was suggested that he repeat the experience, he replied, "Once a philosophe, twice a sodomite." Such openness to the frank discussion of sodomy was unprecedented, and apart from their formulaic denunciations of it as personally repugnant, the philosophes tended to treat the subject most often in the context of law reform or of the analysis of the peculiar customs of other societies, ancient and modern. By and large the tone was measured as much as condemnatory, and their conclusions were as novel as their tone: that institutions should conform to human nature and that those who differed from the norm should not be repressed simply on that account.

The leading French philosophes only occasionally applied the arguments from nature or from cultural and historical relativism specifically to sodomy; greater tolerance for sexual deviance was, for the most part, implicit rather than explicit in their writings, as, for example, in Diderot's dictum that "nothing that exists can be against nature or outside nature." Illustrating his point, he did not cite sodomy, though he could well have done so. "I don't even exclude chastity and voluntary continence," he wrote, "which if it were possible to sin against nature would be the greatest of crimes against her." Those who did address sodomy directly generally did so briefly, Voltaire in an essay called "So-Called Socratic Love" in his *Philosophical Dictionary* and Montesquieu in a heated denunciation titled "Of Crimes Against Nature" in *The Spirit of the Laws*.

Both were bothered and perplexed by the existence of a vice that they, unlike Diderot, did not hesitate to condemn as against nature. "How did it come about," asked Voltaire, "that a vice which would destroy mankind if it were general, that a sordid outrage against nature, is still so natural? It seems the highest degree of deliberate corruption, and yet it is the ordinary lot of those who have not yet had time to be corrupted." He speculated that its prevalence among the young could be attributed in part to the almost feminine beauty of many early adolescent boys, but both he and Montesquieu laid the blame primarily on the peculiarities of particular societies or social institutions. Voltaire believed the vice was more common in hot climates, while Montesquieu singled out such things as nude athletic competitions in ancient Greece, Asiatic marriage customs, and single-sex boarding schools. If such practices were reformed or abolished, he suggested, the vice would largely disappear: "Let there be no customs preparatory to the crime; let it like every other violation of morals be severely proscribed by the civil magistrate; and nature will defend or resume her rights." Both he and Voltaire still regarded sodomy, at least practiced by adults, as a crime, as an antisocial vice worthy of punishment. But their belief that it was the result in large measure of a distortion of normal sexual appetites, a distortion, moreover, that had its origins primarily in faulty social institutions, led them to recoil in greater horror at the traditional punishments than at the crime itself. "It is very odd," Montesquieu observed, "that these three crimes, witchcraft, heresy, and that against nature, of which the first might easily be proved not to exist; the second to be susceptible to an infinite number of distinctions, interpretations, and limitations; the third to be often obscure and uncertain—it is very odd, I say, that these three crimes should amongst us be punished with fire." To Voltaire the Deschauffours case was an especially outrageous instance of judicial excess. "A victim was needed," he argued, so "they roasted Deschauffours in . . . place" of a more powerful transgressor. "That is too much," Voltaire concluded, "we should proportion punishments to crime."

The Italian jurist and legal reformer Cesare Beccaria wrote in similar terms. Indeed he strongly influenced Voltaire, who in turn did much to bring Beccaria's work to a wider European audience. Like most of his French contemporaries, he only mentioned sodomy in passing, in a brief section titled "Crimes Difficult to Prove" in his major work *On Crimes and Punishments.* Also like Voltaire and Montesquieu, he attributed sodomy primarily to cultural influences, such as single-sex education at an impressionable age, and therefore advocated moderate punishments designed to deter the practice.

The next logical step, toward advocating the decriminalization of sodomy, was taken by one of the leading French philosophes, the marquis de Condorcet. In a footnote to an essay by Voltaire he argued that "Sodomy, so long as there is no violence, cannot be covered by criminal law. It does not violate the rights of any other man. It only exercises an indirect influence on the good order of society, like drunkenness and gambling." Like all his contemporaries, he expressed his repugnance for what he termed "a low vice, disgusting," but nonetheless suggested that the appropriate punishment for it was not prison, let alone the stake, but "contempt."

No less radical, though writing in an entirely different, more personal vein, was Rousseau. In his memoirs he recounted that while staying in a Catholic hospice in Italy, he became the object of persistent sexual advances from another resident. He was alarmed and disgusted, particularly when his admirer, after touching him and encouraging him to reciprocate, climaxed. "My stomach turned over," Rousseau recalled, "and I rushed onto the balcony more upset, more troubled and more frightened as well, than I had been in my life. I was almost sick." Too agitated to keep to himself what had happened, Rousseau was almost as startled by the reaction of others as he had been by the incident itself. One of the principals of the hospice rebuked him for spreading the story and belittled the importance of it. "There was nothing to get so annoyed about in having been found attractive," he told Rousseau. "There was no reason to be alarmed about nothing." Intellectually, if not emotionally, Rousseau was compelled to reassess his reaction, not so much by the arguments of the principal as by his tone. "The whole matter seemed so simple to him," Rousseau recalled, "that he had not even sought privacy for our conversation. . . . This natural behavior so impressed me that I finally believed such things were no doubt general practice in the world. . . . So I listened without anger though not without disgust." What is most striking about Rousseau's recounting of this incident, apart from his constant references to his almost physical revulsion, is the total absence of any reference to absolute standards of judgment. What happened was portrayed not as criminal, let alone as sinful, but as a matter of taste (Rousseau's own versus his admirer's) or of interpretation (Rousseau's own versus the principal's). This degree of subjectivity concerning a matter as inflammatory as sodomy would have been inconceivable at least to anyone outside the subculture a century, even a generation, earlier.

Apart from Rousseau, the most advanced writers of eighteenth-century France were tantalizingly brief and, like Rousseau, clearly uncomfortable in their comments on all forms of sexual deviance. Not so their closest English counterpart, Jeremy Bentham, the founder of utilitarianism. Obsessed with covering every aspect of any subject he tackled—and he tackled hundreds—Bentham produced the longest essay on sodomy written in the eighteenth century and the longest to be written in English for more than a century thereafter. He wrote on sodomy as early as the 1770s, when he was in his twenties; as late as at the end of the Napoleonic Wars; and in an essay he may have intended for publication in the 1780s. Acutely conscious of the damage any association with the subject might do to his career, he took care to preface his 1785 essay with the usual comments disparaging the practice as "abominable" and "disgusting." But that was pure calculation. "To other subjects," he wrote, "it is expected that you sit down cool, but on this subject if you let it be seen that you have not sat down in a rage you have betrayed yourself at once." Even so, he finally decided that he dared not publish; indeed none of his writings on sodomy were published until two centuries later, in 1978. This was no easy decision for Bentham, who, uncharacteristically, wrote and saved a passionately felt memo on his conflicted feelings. "I am ashamed to own that I have often hesitated whether for the sake of the interests of humanity I should expose my personal interest so much to hazard as it must be exposed to by the free discussion of a subject of this nature." In the end, though he dared not publish, he felt compelled to write and to preserve these writings, despite the risk, if only to his historical reputation. "At any rate," he concluded, "when I am dead mankind will be the better for it."

The 1785 essay was characteristic Bentham. One by one he raised every conceivable objection to pederasty, and one by one he demolished them. To the allegation that it debilitated the individual and, by extension, society at large by, as Montesquieu put it, "giving one sex the weaknesses of the other," Bentham countered by citing the prevalence of the practice in both Greece and Rome at the height of their power. Bentham scornfully dismissed Voltaire's concern that pederasty, should it become general, might endanger the growth of population, since it was nowhere general and, unlike the celibacy of the clergy in Voltaire's France, often not exclusive. Bentham was equally dismissive of the proposition that it might rob women of their rightful sexual fulfillment, since Western society allowed women far fewer sexual outlets than men in any case. And as for the possibility that it might undermine marriage, he believed that marriage was threatened less by pederasty than by the husband's adultery with another woman.

On the perhaps most common and most telling indictment against peder-asty, at least so far as rationalist thinkers were concerned—that it was against nature—Bentham was surprisingly brief. Essentially he was content to dem-onstrate the fallibility of the argument from purpose or function: that sexual relations with the opposite sex were natural because they were necessary for the propagation of the species, while sexual relations with one's own sex were unnatural because unnecessary. If that were so, Bentham noted, "it might well be said that the taste a man has for music is unnatural." As a measure of how far rationalist arguments had come to dominate the debate on this and similar issues, at least among the audience he might hope to influence, Bentham did not even bother to treat the objections from religion seriously or at length. Moralists, he suggested, too often condemned as sinful all pleas-ures other than those that were necessary to survival, such as eating and pro-creative sex. But surely, he argued, touching on the core of his utilitarian creed, "if pleasure is not a good, what is life for, and what is the purpose of preserving it."

Having demonstrated to his satisfaction the harmlessness of pederasty to society and to the individual, Bentham went on to demonstrate the very real harm that punishing or proscribing it might well do both to society and to the individual. Punishment, he believed, was as likely to increase the frequency of the offense as it was to lessen it and would surely harden its practitioners against society at large: "The persecution they meet with . . . has the effect . . . of rendering those persons who are the objects of it more at-tached than they would otherwise be to the practice it proscribes. It renders them the more attached to one another, sympathy of itself having a powerful tendency . . . to attach a man to his own companions in misfortune. This sym-pathy has at the same time a powerful tendency to beget a proportionable an-tipathy even towards all such persons as appear to be . . . authors of such mis-fortune."

Bentham was equally concerned with the danger to civil society of crimi-nalizing behavior simply because it was generally regarded as repugnant; in a monarchy that was a license for personal tyranny, in a democracy for the tyranny of the majority. In this as in so much else in eighteenth-century En-gland's archaic and arbitrary justice system, Bentham believed, there had to be more rational and objective standards. In addition, by their very nature the antisodomy statutes encouraged official misconduct and other forms of crim-inal behavior. The law as it stood opened the way to extortion, to blackmail, and, because the offense was hard to prove, to mischievous accusations and prosecutions.

What is most striking about all these arguments is their modernity. The legislation of morality in general and the continued existence of antisodomy laws are still debated in precisely these terms. That would have been all but impossible much earlier in the eighteenth century, when the law in such matters reflected and was intended to reflect what were generally accepted as absolute moral standards. There was no such consensus beyond midcentury; the most advanced legal reformers and social critics throughout western Europe increasingly viewed the law as a social construct, a reflection of the attitudes and interests of those who governed particular societies at particular times, and therefore open to debate, change, and amelioration. Bentham's arguments for the decriminalization of pederasty were simply the logical conclusion of this trend. He chose not to publish his views not only because he was young and feared for his reputation and influence and because his views were so far in advance of almost anyone else's anywhere in Europe, but also because English legal thought was much more conservative than French. At the same time that Voltaire, Beccaria, and other legal reformers on the Continent were pressing for lesser punishments, that is, in the 1760s, the most influential English jurist of the eighteenth century, William Blackstone, in his *Commentaries on the Laws of England,* justified the death penalty for sodomy in traditional terms, and with traditional venom, as an "offense of a still deeper malignity, the infamous crime against nature . . . a subject the very mention of which is a disgrace to human nature . . . a crime not fit to be named. This the voice of nature and of reason, and the express law of God, determined to be capital. Of which we have a signal instance . . . by the destruction of two cities by fire from heaven."

To be sure, there were voices raised in England against the most savage punishments, even for crimes such as sodomy and attempted sodomy. In 1780 a man convicted of attempted sodomy died in the pillory, partly from choking on the pillory itself, partly as a result of being pelted with refuse and finally with at least one stone by the sort of abusive mob that often attended the public exhibition of sodomites. This prompted Edmund Burke to raise the issue in the House of Commons, describing the man's death in graphic terms and condemning both "the awkward and ugly instrument used in this mode of punishment" and the barbarizing effects of its use on society. Though he received some support from other members of Parliament, Burke was excoriated in the press for showing any sympathy at all to sodomites—a price for moral courage that surely entered into Bentham's calculations when he agonized over what to do with his essay on pederasty shortly thereafter. Burke's pleas for the abolition of the pillory got nowhere; the punishment remained in use as well as on the statute books and was not seriously questioned again for a generation.

In much of the rest of western Europe, however, if not yet in England, the trend of Bentham's thought toward the mitigation and perhaps even the elimination of punishments for offenses against morality, for crimes without victims, was the dominant trend, a trend that was to bear fruit in a number of states before the end of the century, most notably in revolutionary France. Not that the leaders of the French Revolution were above using imputations of sodomy to further their cause. There were a number of juicy sex scandals shortly before the revolution, and the popular view that sodomy was a peculiarly courtly, aristocratic, and clerical vice was a handy weapon in the arsenal of those who wished to discredit the ancien régime. On the other hand, a number of the central ideological underpinnings of the revolution—the decoupling of law from religion, the right to privacy, and the freedom of individual choice and contract—all pointed in the opposite direction. In the end, when it came to actually rewriting the law the latter trend won out: in the 1791 penal code and later in the Code Napoléon homosexual acts between consenting adults in private were decriminalized for the first time in modern European history. Although it might be more accurate to say that sodomy was not so much decriminalized as passed over in embarrassed silence by French legal reformers in 1791, the man who oversaw the drafting of the Code Napoléon, Jean-Jacques Cambacérès, a member of the revolutionary National Assembly and later archchancellor of the empire, was himself homosexual and well known as such, not least of all by Napoleon.

The omission of sodomy, along with other "imaginary crimes," from the penal code did not, however, end the scapegoating of sodomites in France; they were too easy and too tempting a target. The marquis de Villette, a family friend of Voltaire's, was perhaps the prime example. He had long been a favorite of the libelous scandal sheets of Paris. Quarrelsome yet cowardly when faced with the prospect of a duel, financially irresponsible, associated for a time with an actress known to be lesbian, and above all notorious for his pederastic exploits, he was often portrayed as the worst sort of dissolute aristocrat. Yet, when he emerged as a supporter of the French Revolution in its early stages the scurrilous attacks on his private life did not change, only the attackers. As a moderate revolutionary he was assaulted from both the right and the far left with wildly exaggerated accusations of innumerable acts of both active and passive sodomy. Though he was no longer at risk legally for his sexuality, his politics seemed very likely to place him in jeopardy, and Villette was perhaps lucky to die peacefully when he did, in the summer of 1793, on the eve of the Reign of Terror.

No discussion of eighteenth-century attitudes toward sexuality would be complete that did not take into account the life and writings of the Marquis de Sade. But simply to mention his name is to come face to face with potential contradictions in eighteenth-century thought, with what might well be called the dark side of the Enlightenment. On the one hand, he represented the ultimate example of the eighteenth-century concern with greater freedom of individual expression; on the other, he deliberately sought out and gloried in extremes of sexual expression. During his lifetime he was seen, as he has been seen for the most part ever since, as epitomizing the point at which liberty slides into license. In many respects he was in, or at least an extension of, the mainstream of Enlightenment thought. In perhaps his most lucid and programmatic political statement, "Yet Another Effort, Frenchmen, If You Would Become Republicans," interpolated (characteristically, it might be suggested) into his *Philosophy in the Bedroom,* written in 1795, he used arguments similar to Diderot's or to Bentham's ten year earlier to go well beyond Voltaire, Montesquieu, and Beccaria in arguing from nature: "It makes absolutely no difference whether one enjoys a girl or a boy. . . . no inclinations or tastes can exist in us save the ones we have from Nature." Sade did, however, go far, very far, beyond either Bentham or Diderot in tone by not merely questioning orthodoxy and authority but also rudely challenging and defying them, by celebrating the pleasures of deviant sexuality rather than merely arguing that it was harmless, and, most subversively, by suggesting a direct link between sexual freedom and political and religious freedom.

"New government will require new manners," he argued, a new morality—and vice versa. Traditional morality was founded on prejudice; society at large designated as sinful minority tastes it did not share. "We wonder," he questioned, speaking specifically of sodomy, "that savagery could ever reach the point where you condemn to death an unhappy person all of whose crime amounts to not sharing your tastes." Criminality in his view was equally socially determined, an arbitrary designation for the most part, or the result of repression and of gross social and economic inequality. His solution was a republican government with a rigid separation of church and state, severe restrictions on the powers of both church and state, complete freedom of belief and nonbelief, and commitment to both social equality and personal liberty. In such a society, he was certain, there would be little antisocial behavior, since "there are very few criminal actions in a society whose foundations are liberty and equality." Of particular interest to Sade, almost no sexual acts would any longer be regarded as criminal: "We are fully convinced that if anything were criminal, it would be to resist the penchants she [Nature] inspires in us, rather than to come to grips with them." He did not quite equate sexual freedom with political freedom, but he did argue that there could be no sexual freedom without political freedom and, moreover, that personal sexual freedom was both a result and a measure of the degree of personal political freedom.

This was by far the most radical statement of its kind for nearly two hundred years, until the 1960s, and it is no accident that it was in the 1960s that Sade was resurrected as something more—or other—than a monster and that attempts were made to absolve him of the worst accusations of sadism and rampant sexism. And yet in many respects he was monstrous. Not only did he shock bourgeois sensibilities through obscene and pornographic writings and challenge authority by adopting a political philosophy bordering on anarchism but he treated and regarded women as objects, and in his writings, and to some extent in his personal life, he experimented with patterns of sexual behavior that rightly bear his name. It is hardly surprising, therefore, that he was imprisoned under the ancien régime and, after being released at the time of the revolution, reincarcerated in various prisons and asylums by both the revolutionary and Napoleonic regimes. What most disturbed his critics, then and since, was that he took Enlightenment thought to its logical conclusion, and then well beyond that to its illogical conclusion, by carrying personal freedom and self-indulgence to excess. Respectable opinion, even moderate radical opinion, recoiled from him in horror, much as it recoiled from the excesses of the French Revolution itself.

The Marquis de Sade represented the perfect object lesson in one of the most troubling dilemmas of Enlightenment thought, the dangers of decoupling criminality from sin. Without a religious sanction, the way appeared open to a host of abuses and excesses. That prospect cried out for a redefinition of criminality on a secular basis, specifically in terms of the maintenance of public order. And that is where most of the philosophes ended up in condemning sexual deviance. Voltaire, Montesquieu, and Beccaria all supported humane and limited punishments for sodomy—they were, after all, seeking to deter antisocial behavior, not bring down the wrath of God—but all agreed that sexual deviance could pose a threat to the stability of society. That the postrevolutionary regimes in France went beyond this to the extent of decriminalization was neither as surprising nor as radical as might at first appear. Decriminalization was carefully limited to consensual sodomy between adults in private. The public order was protected.

Much the same thing happened as discussion of nature and the natural became divorced from issues of morality. There was little or nothing to counterbalance the proposition of Diderot, echoed by Bentham and Sade, that whatever exists in nature cannot be unnatural. To those who feared the implications of that proposition the situation demanded, as did the decoupling of criminality from sin, a redefinition in secular terms, in this instance a redefinition by medical science (or pseudoscience) of the natural as healthy and the unnatural as sick. The growing authority of medical science during the eighteenth century was remarkable, not least of all in the field of human sexuality. By the end of the century the profession had established itself as the virtually unchallenged arbiter of what was and was not healthy, natural, and therefore acceptable sexual behavior. The first practice over which the medical authorities successfully staked their claim to expertise, and certainly the most amusing (at least to us, though certainly not to generations of adolescent boys), was masturbation.

As a private vice in an age of increasing privacy, masturbation was, as we have seen, a source of growing concern to moralists. Medical authorities took up the issue early in the eighteenth century, and by the middle decades of the century they had taken it over. The most influential work on the subject, *Onanism,* by the Swiss doctor Simon André Tissot, was first published in 1758 and rapidly went through a number of editions in French and then in translation. Tissot was no crank; far from it. He was an early advocate of smallpox vaccination and of the importance of personal hygiene, and his status at the forefront of medical science ensured that his views on other matters, including masturbation, would be taken seriously. Voltaire publicized his work, and many who were otherwise predisposed to challenge authority accepted it uncritically. Bentham, for example, in his essay on pederasty, had dealt almost dismissively with moral arguments, and while he had treated the views of Voltaire and Montesquieu on sodomy more seriously and at greater length, he felt competent to criticize them as an equal. Yet he ended his daring and iconoclastic essay with an attack on the evils of masturbation, which he denounced as enervating and addictive, as leading to impotence and to indifference to other healthy sexual outlets. His authority for these assertions, an authority he did not feel competent to question, was that "physicians are all agreed about it."

Clearly Tissot had struck a nerve. The obsession with masturbation—and it was nothing short of that—like the concerns with celibacy and sodomy, spoke to general European anxieties about the relative economic and military strength of states in an era of intense competition and conflict. But masturbation was perhaps the most insidious threat in the sexual arena. Celibacy and sodomy might deprive states of needed population, but masturbation could also weaken the existing population, as well as lead to other vices and perversions. While sexual overindulgence of any kind was thought likely to enervate the individual, masturbation was regarded as especially dangerous because it could be practiced in isolation, in secret, and with great frequency. Not only could this debilitate the habitual masturbator, stunting his growth and depriving him of energy—it is no accident that ejaculation, which is now called *coming*, was then termed *spending*—but it might lead him to withdraw from society, to become morbid and self-absorbed, ultimately even insane. Sade, as might be expected, denounced all this as hysterical nonsense. Not only did he defend masturbation and its pleasures but he denied the underlying assumptions of the medical literature that the spilling of seed sapped vitality. Waste and regeneration, he argued, were part of the cycle of nature. But in this, as in so much else, Sade was hopelessly out of touch with what was rapidly becoming not only medical orthodoxy but conventional wisdom.

Parents and teachers were warned to keep an eye out for signs of overindulgence in self-abuse: listlessness, a sickly pallor, withdrawal, antisocial behavior (all, of course, common characteristics of various stages of adolescence). As alarm at the effects of masturbation spread from the medical profession to the general public, it often took bizarre forms. A wax museum opened in Paris in 1775 featured a lurid exhibit on the consequences of masturbation, and groups of schoolboys were trooped past the displays in the hope of preventing or, at the very least, arresting the practice. Among the many ills to which the weakened constitution of the habitual masturbator was thought likely to fall prey, one of the most common was a tendency to sodomy. Practitioners of one secret vice were deemed especially susceptible to indulgence in the other, the weak and listless masturbator was thought likely to seek out others like himself, and so on. Indeed, the physical characteristics and behavioral patterns identified as typical of the actual or incipient sodomite differed very little from those of the chronic masturbator. By the end of the eighteenth century sodomy had joined, and was usually joined with, masturbation as a critical concern of the growing body of medical opinion on sexual pathology.

Characteristic of the literature linking these and other sexual vices was Johann Valentin Müller's *Outline of Forensic Medicine,* published in 1796. Like most of the early literature in the field, it was based on the assumption that there were clear outward signs of specific sexual abuses that properly trained medical professionals could identify and use to assist—and thereby gain a central role in assisting—the police and the courts in identifying sexual offenders. Müller and his colleagues denied that they were in the business of making moral judgments; rather they saw themselves as engaged in the objective study and classification of human behavior. But of course they were judgmental, marshaling the full authority of medical science behind the designation of some behavior as sick, much as earlier generations had marshaled the full authority of religion behind the designation of some behavior as sinful. As the editor of the leading British medical journal, *The Lancet,* put it in 1819: "We are responsible for the employment of our peculiar authority in promoting the purification and well being of human society." The notion of what was and was not in accord with nature had, in fact, changed very little; only the sanction enforcing it had. Doctors were the new priesthood.

## Chapter 4

**Europe Divided**

Contemporary with the Enlightenment but rarely intersecting with it, the Protestant nations of northern and western Europe, Germany and England in particular, experienced religious revivals so widespread that they have often been referred to as the second reformation. There were significant differences between the movements in Germany and England, perhaps the most important being that German Pietism was quietist and inward looking, while English Methodism and later Evangelicalism within the Church of England were activist and outward looking. But the similarities were greater. Both decried the dry formalism of the established Protestant churches, which seemed to have lost their zeal, and both extolled enthusiasm and the direct personal experience of religious feeling. Both distrusted rationalism and were suspicious of the main tendencies of Enlightenment thought, and with good reason considering the indifference, even hostility, toward religion among the leading philosophes. In any case, Pietism and Methodism stressed the emotional, faith as a better guide than reason, and passionate commitment as more important than doctrine.

Both Pietism and Methodism were directed primarily at elements in society not adequately served by the established churches: lesser merchants, tradesmen, shopkeepers, artisans, and the like, the middling and lower middle ranks of society. As movements of, by, and for these classes, both Pietism and Methodism reflected and reinforced their concerns, attitudes, and prejudices. The upper and lower orders of society were often depicted as immoral, or at least amoral; the aristocracy as profligate and decadent; and the poor as lazy and undisciplined, at the lowest level even depraved. By contrast, the values of the striving middling sort—hard work, thrift, sobriety, and sexual restraint—were extolled. All too easily, outward behavior came to be seen as both a result and a measure of inward piety, or lack of it. Morality and respectability became fused. The groundwork for the eighteenth-century religious revival had been laid by the growing emphasis on family and morality at the close of the previous century. Pietism, Methodism, and Evangelicalism gave focus and drive to the revolution in manners, above all bringing it to the masses and the masses to it. By the last quarter of the eighteenth century the way was thus open to a new and unprecedentedly powerful and widespread movement for moral reform. If this has about it an air of inevitability, and it is a curious fact that similar moral reform movements have sprouted in the late decades of each of the last four or five centuries, what was not inevitable was the way in which the religious revival and the revolution in manners it wrought became linked with nationalism, specifically anti-French and therefore antirevolutionary nationalism. It was a link that reinforced the moral conservatism of the Protestant revival, tied it to political conservatism, and pushed different countries in Europe down different paths so far as the legal enforcement of morality, including codes of sexual conduct, was concerned.

In Germany the link between the Protestant revival and nationalism was forged early, before the French Revolution and French military intervention in Germany, and was at first primarily cultural, not political, in nature, since Germany was not one state but a collection of many states. The governing elites of many of these kingdoms, principalities, bishoprics, and so forth, looked to France or to Rome as much as to their own or neighboring territories for cultural models—French was the language of the Prussian court under Frederick the Great, for example—and the simple fact that Pietist ministers preached in the vernacular provided a sense of national cultural unity absent in the political realm. In England, however, and to a lesser extent in Germany, it was in response to the French Revolution and the French revolutionary and Napoleonic wars that the fusion between nationalism and the Protestant revival took place. So dramatic was the French Revolution that every class and faction in Europe read it as an object lesson for its own society, on the left as a clarion call for revolution or reform, on the right as a danger signal, and among religious leaders as a clear warning of the inevitable result of the moral decay of a decadent governing class. The call for a revolution, not political but in manners and morals, began to be made with ever greater urgency. The course of the French Revolution reinforced this message. The radicalization of the Revolution, culminating in the Terror, the execution of Louis XIV and Marie Antoinette in early 1793, and the escalating attacks on religion terrified many who had initially looked hopefully to the French example but now recoiled in horror. The outbreak of war between France and much of the rest of Europe in 1792 added an element of a clear and present physical danger and led to the coalescence of unlikely allies in defense of the established order.

In Prussia, overrun and humiliated by Napoleon's armies in 1805–6, the need for national revival and regeneration appeared especially urgent and especially sweeping. Patriotic liberals, disillusioned radicals, and enlightened conservatives joined forces to push through or rouse support for wholesale reform of government administration, economic policy, education, and the military. For many supporters of the Prussian reform movement, however, such measures would be to no avail in the absence of a moral regeneration of the nation. Preachers, poets, and pamphleteers alike looked to the young, to a generation imbued with a new German consciousness, self-disciplined and selflessly dedicated to building a stronger, purer country. The ideal type of this new German youth would combine the virtues of a medieval knight and the ancient Greek or Roman warrior athlete: physical strength, Christian virtue, cleanliness, comradeship, and dedication to a higher cause.

Luckily for the exponents of such an ideal, potent visual symbols were readily at hand in German medieval sculpture but above all in the art of ancient Greece and Rome. The classical revival, the cult of the antique, was by this time well established in Germany, largely as a result of the work of the most influential classicist of the eighteenth century, Johann Winckelmann. His writings on Greek art during the third quarter of the century not only awakened an interest in classical art in Germany as an alternative to French cultural models and the frivolousness of the rococo but also set the tone for its use in the national revival. "The quiet and repose of the body," he wrote, characteristically, of one Greek sculpture, "reveals the lofty and harmonious spirit of he who braves the greatest dangers for the sake of justice, who provides for his country's defense and brings peace to its subjects."

Obviously there was no room in this concept of manliness for anything that threatened or sullied it, as too overt a suggestion of homoeroticism clearly would have done. Yet in its emphasis on virility and the beauty of the well-developed male physique the classical ideal embodied a powerful element of homoeroticism. It was an insoluble dilemma. To the extent that neoclassical representations of the male nude were stripped of sensuality, and their virility reduced to mere monumentality, they lost much of their potency as symbols, their power to inspire (as anyone familiar with neoclassical sculpture of the Nazi era can attest). The figure of the medieval knight—fully clothed, Christian, thoroughly German—presented no such contradictions, but there was no denying the lure and power of the classical ideal. It represented reason and order, necessary ingredients of a successful national revival, particularly in a country as fragmented as Germany. The most that those who felt uncomfortable with its physical representation could do was cover the genitalia with a fig leaf or a fragment of clothing. That, however, did not resolve but only obscured the tension inherent in importing the classical nude as a model for modern German manliness.

Winckelmann, the father of German neoclassicism and philhellinism, himself appears to have embodied that tension. Speculating on the mysterious circumstances of his death, one of his biographers has suggested that Winckelmann was the victim of his inability to reconcile his appetites with his ideals. He died in Trieste in 1768, in a hotel where he had registered under an assumed name, murdered by an unemployed cook nearly twenty years his junior, with whom he had spent much of the preceding week, often in private. The possibility that this was a sexual liaison with rough trade gone terribly wrong on the part of a man who had "completely separated his intellectual ideal from his physical desires" cannot be dismissed, though the evidence for this interpretation is entirely circumstantial. Whatever the particulars of Winckelmann's death, there is no question that in his scholarship as in his life he struggled to achieve some sort of accommodation between his physical and intellectual passions.

In Rome, where he spent almost half his adult life at work in the Vatican archives and museums, he was drawn to, obsessed with, the beauty of the young male, no less in the flesh than sculpted in stone, and sought to find in both the embodiment of the highest manly virtues. He had a succession of close mentoring relationships with young Germans—tutees, the sons of collectors, travelers on the grand tour—but intense as these relationships often were, they seem to have remained nonsexual. Not so his dalliances with a number of attractive Italian youths; we know that for certain since on one occasion he was surprised in a compromising position by Casanova. Yet sadly, Winckelmann was unable to reconcile his sexual tastes and actions with his esthetic principles. He explained himself to Casanova with a catalogue of evasions and excuses: that he was only experimenting, seeking to understand the sexual proclivities of the ancients, that this was not his taste, that women were preferable.

There was a similar ambivalence in and about two of the institutions founded in the early nineteenth century to further the German national revival, the gymnast and fraternity movements. Both celebrated the beauty and virility of the well-developed young male physique, and both sought to build on the tradition, in Germany almost a cult, of passionate friendships involving the open display of physical affection as the basis of a wider sense of comradeship. That tradition had already become suspect in England, but not so in Germany even as late as the age of Goethe, at the end of the eighteenth century. Patronage and mentoring relationships between older and younger men, as well as passionate friendships between youths, often extending well into adulthood, both consciously modeled on classical precedents and both commonly expressed in language close to that of erotic love, were widely accepted and often celebrated in literature so long as such relationships and their literary representation did not stray from the sensual into the overtly sexual. Such distinctions were not always easy to maintain in practice, and authors who blurred them—even Goethe himself occasionally—were severely criticized for doing so.

Ambiguities that troubled even Winckelmann and his contemporaries were increasingly regarded as intolerable by the proponents of the German national revival in the first decade of the new century. The leaders of the gymnast and fraternity movements could hardly ignore, let alone deny, the intense male bonding that was at the core of these movements, but they could and did seek to ensure that the ideal of manly comradeship would remain untainted by even a suggestion of explicit homoeroticism and thus be compatible with the ideals of respectability, family, and service to the nation. As one modern critic put it, "The age of Winckelmann and Frederick, the age of homosocial networking, had come to an end."

Small wonder, then, that while in much of Europe conquered by and long under the sway of France, including portions of western and southern (and largely Catholic) Germany, the Code Napoleon or similar measures decriminalizing homosexual acts between consenting adults in private were imposed and then kept or voluntarily adopted, this was not true in Prussia, the leading Protestant German state and the center of the national revival and of resistance to France and French ideas. Bavaria went furthest in separating law from morality in sexual matters. In 1804 King Maximilian appointed the German jurist Anselm Feuerbach, an ardent admirer of the Code Napoleon, to rationalize and reform the Bavarian criminal code. Promulgated in 1813, the new code decriminalized virtually all consensual sexual acts. To Feuerbach the underlying principle was clear and nearly absolute: "As long as a person . . . only contravenes the commandments of morality without harming the rights of another person, then those deeds are not included in the present law code. Masturbation, sodomy, bestiality, extramarital consensual intercourse are serious contraventions against moral commandments, but as sins, they do not belong to the domain of external law codes."

No other German state adopted Feuerbach's principles in their entirety, but the Bavarian reforms, like the Code Napoleon, provided an alternative model for the legal treatment of sexual offenses that influenced policy elsewhere in Germany. But not in Prussia, where, although the death penalty for sodomy had earlier been repealed in keeping with the Enlightenment trend toward lessening the severity of punishments, sodomy itself remained a crime. Thus emerged the sharp division in the state enforcement of morals between predominantly Latin Catholic Europe (and South America) and largely Germanic Protestant Europe (and North America) under the dual impact of the Napoleonic Wars and the evangelical revival, a division that was to persist well into the twentieth century.

Britain arrived at a similar result, though by a very different route, if only because, unlike Germany, she was long established as a nation-state and was not invaded and was only briefly directly threatened by Napoleonic France. The impetus for a national revival in Britain came not from external disaster but from a growing concern with an apparent decline in both public and private morals. The generation-long war against revolutionary and Napoleonic France simply added a sense of urgency, as well as giving a public-policy dimension to what had begun as a movement for moral regeneration. As in France and Germany, there were a number of well-publicized sexual scandals in Britain in the 1780s. Among the sodomitical sensations by far the most notorious, because it involved both one of the wealthiest men in England and the under-age heir to a title, was the Beckford-Courtenay scandal.

William Beckford was the grandson of a governor of Jamaica and the son of a radical lord mayor of London. Precocious as well as flamboyant, he helped set the tone and style of English romanticism with one of the earliest exotic novels of the late eighteenth century, *Vathek*, written when he was only twenty-two, and later in life by designing and building the most ambitious Gothic Revival mansion in England, if not Europe, Fonthill. So lavish was Fonthill that it ultimately ruined Beckford financially; what ruined him socially was his homosexuality. In his late teens he fell passionately in love with the preadolescent only son of Lord Courtenay of Powderham Castle in Devon. Five years later the two were discovered in bed together by the boy's tutor. Beckford denied that anything incriminating had taken place, and perhaps correctly—in this instance. He may have been arranging an assignation with Courtenay's aunt and used the boy as a go-between. Furthermore, his wife accompanied him on this visit to Powderham. On the other hand, there is no question that Beckford had a taste for young men as well as for women; he belonged very much to the old libertine tradition. And as for Courtenay, he grew up to be the center of another series of sodomitical scandals.

What did or did not happen in young Courtenay's bedroom in 1784 is almost beside the point, however. Rumors spread and were widely accepted as fact. High society up to and including the royal household was outraged. Beckford, who had been on the verge of being ennobled, suddenly found himself disgraced. Like many in his situation before and since, he fled to the Continent, where he remained for ten years. But even away from England he could not escape the scandal. Leaders of English expatriate communities in more than one European city ensured that he would remain ostracized by threatening to ostracize anyone who associated with him. On his return to England he lived in similar isolation for most of the remainder of his long life, subject to the same relentless social pressures.

The private life of William Beckford and the scandal that destroyed his public career were symptomatic of the deep divisions on moral issues in late-eighteenth-century England, and the scandal itself had important immediate consequences, the effects of which were still discernible as much as a generation later. Beckford's disgrace and exile may well have inspired Bentham to write his essay on pederasty the following year; certainly he was later to look to Beckford as a potential supporter of his views. The lurid nature of the scandal spurred the moral reformers to greater activity and was especially repugnant to George III, thus helping to lay the foundations for an alliance between the Evangelicals and the crown that bore fruit three years later in a royal proclamation against vice. The total destruction almost overnight of the career and reputation of one of the leading lights of the first generation of English romanticism was a frightening object lesson for the second generation, and in particular to the no less precocious and equally sexually ambidextrous Lord Byron.

Byron was not yet born at the time of Beckford's downfall; his stormy life was played out in a very different climate, after the issues in the cultural conflicts of the last two decades of the eighteenth century had been decided. The battle lines of that conflict were already sharply defined well before the impact of the French Revolution on England gave it a predominantly political cast. Bentham may have decided that he dared not publish his essay on pederasty, but others were not so cautious in taking on scarcely less controversial topics, from free love and open marriage to the traditional status of women. In response, all that religious and social conservatives needed to transform their growing disquiet into an effective movement was skilled and inspired leadership. That was provided primarily by William Wilberforce, whose conversion from nominal to evangelical Christianity in 1785 gave their cause an organizational center (in the Clapham district of London, where most of them lived), access to the levers of power (through his membership and connections in Parliament), and above all, perhaps, a rationale for direct intervention in the lives and habits of their fellow countrymen. To his more cautious colleagues who argued that the enforcement of morals through legislation and public pressure only created hypocrites, not true converts, the activist Wilberforce replied: "I know that by regulating the external conduct we do not at first change the hearts of men, but even they are ultimately to be wrought upon by these means, and we should at least so far remove the obtrusiveness of temptation that it may not provoke the appetite, which might otherwise be dormant and inactive."

On that basis (the argument of moral busybodies throughout history) Wilberforce launched his national campaign for moral reformation, first by using his contacts in the hierarchy in the Church of England and at court to persuade George III to issue a "Proclamation for the Encouragement of Piety and Virtue and for the Preventing and Punishing of Vice, Profaness and Immorality" in the spring of 1787 and then by founding a Proclamation Society to help (and pressure) the authorities to carry it out. His model and inspiration were the old Societies for the Reformation of Manners, but Wilberforce's ambitions for the new movement went far beyond what had been achieved a century earlier. It was now possible to build on two generations of Methodist and Evangelical proselytizing, on his own and his allies' political skills and contacts at the highest level, and, from the early 1790s on, on the need for national purpose and discipline in the war against France, which even before the Revolution but still more afterward was looked upon as a center and source of immorality. Indeed, the length of the struggle against revolutionary and Napoleonic France ensured that the pressure would not slacken, since the government, like the Evangelicals, believed that there was an intimate relationship between French morals and French politics, clearly fearing that the first would lead to the second.

The movement for the moral reformation of England went through a number of changes in organization and emphasis over the years. The Society for the Suppression of Vice replaced the Proclamation Society in 1802, and different functions were taken up by different groups along the way. No one, whatever their political views or religious persuasion, would deny the worth of many of the Evangelicals' aims and achievements. They played a key role in the movements to abolish the slave trade and slavery, to protect child labor, to abolish blood sports, to reduce the number of capital crimes, and to foster temperance. But they were equally determined to regulate what could be published and read, seen at the theater, and done on Sundays. Inevitably their concern with sexuality was extended from its representation in books and plays to its practice, and as had been the case a century earlier, sodomy proved an especially inviting target because undefended. During the last quarter of the eighteenth century, before the vice societies reached their peak of activity and influence, the number of executions for sodomy actually declined, largely because the standard of proof was tightened in 1781 to include emission as well as penetration. Early in the new century, however, the number of prosecutions and the severity of punishments increased markedly. At a time when executions for crimes other than murder were decreasing in number due to law reform, the number of hangings for sodomy rose and then remained constant for some years, as did the number of convictions for attempted sodomy.

Also on the increase was public awareness of sodomy, along with the suspicion that it was becoming more common and the fear that it would sap the moral and physical fiber of the nation. The year 1810 perhaps marked the peak of public concern, but there were indications of what was to come more than a decade before that. In the Royal Navy a long period during which there were no courts-martial for the offense was followed by a steady stream of prosecutions and executions from 1797 on. The timing of this change in policy was no accident: 1797 witnessed the greatest naval mutiny in British history and was a year of maximum danger in the war against France. The navy was expanding rapidly, and the influx of new recruits demanded particularly strict discipline. To be sure, in a hierarchical, confined, all-male environment such as the navy sexual contacts, especially between different ranks, was regarded as a threat to good order and discipline under any circumstances. Just how serious a threat is indicated by how rarely sailors convicted of sodomy were pardoned, far less frequently in fact than those convicted of equally serious offenses such as mutiny or striking an officer. Similarly, those convicted of offenses against morals short of actual buggery received consistently harsher punishments—more lashes—than their shipmates guilty even of mutiny, desertion, or striking an officer. Courts-martial for morals offenses were, however, overwhelmingly a wartime phenomenon, and there were no executions for sodomy in the peacetime navy. As after 1797, so in the early and mid-eighteenth century it was during the long French wars that sodomy emerged as a major concern of the Admiralty.

In the civilian world the issue surfaced dramatically shortly after the turn of the century with a number of executions for sodomy, three of them in a town in northern England where a small sodomitical circle was uncovered. But the most celebrated case, because it took place in London and was extensively reported in the London press, involved mass arrests at the White Swan Tavern in Vere Street in 1810. There had been nothing like this since the raids of 1726. Presumably acting on a tip, constables in plain clothes observed and were themselves the objects of sexual approaches by regular patrons of the tavern, who were arrested and tried for "assault with intent to commit sodomy." Those convicted were given the standard sentence of time in the pillory, a cruel enough punishment for any offense but tantamount to a sentence of severe physical injury, even death, for sodomites. Both before and after the trials the accused had to be escorted by constables, and even those acquitted were attacked by the crowd despite police protection. As for the guilty, they fared far worse, not only in the pillory but on the ride across London from Newgate prison to Haymarket, where they were to be exposed. The prisoners were pelted with mud, stinking entrails of days-old fish, rotten vegetables, and offal and dung from butcher shops—this despite the fact that the caravan proceeded under armed guard, some sixty constables in front led by a City of London marshal, some forty constables in the rear commanded by the local sheriff.

We know more about the Vere Street case than we do about almost any comparable incident, earlier or later, because in addition to the sensational press coverage, it inspired an even more lurid pamphlet literature. The author of the best-known of these screeds, *The Phoenix of Sodom,* cashed in on the notoriety of the goings-on at the White Swan not only through authorship but, in league with the owner of the tavern, by extorting money from its habitués under threat of exposure. The Vere Street incident was not the only sodomitical sensation of 1810–11—a year that, like the late 1790s, marked one of the low points, economic as well as military, in Britain's war with Napoleonic France—but it was certainly the most sweeping. Sodomites were, if nothing else, a useful diversion and could even serve as scapegoats. Early in 1811 a soldier and a drummer boy, who appears to have been a hustler on the side, met in a park, went to Vere Street at the boy's suggestion, were proved to have committed sodomy, and were hanged. In addition, there were the usual, along with the not so usual, scandals. Also in 1811 the middle-aged Courtenay, who had by this time become as notorious in his not so private life as Beckford, followed the example of his admirer of a generation before and fled the country. Suggestions of scandal even reached the royal family. A valet of the duke of Cumberland, a younger brother of the future king George IV, was found murdered. Rumors circulated in radical circles that the duke himself had committed the crime to prevent the valet from revealing the duke's affair with another male servant.

All this was related in juicy detail to Lord Byron by an old college friend. Byron was on his way back from Greece, where he had indulged his tastes for the locals of both sexes, and his correspondent duly noted the contrast between where Byron had been and what he was coming home to: "That which you get for five pounds we must risk our necks for; and are content to risk them." Of Byron's bisexuality there can now be no doubt. He may have been sexually active with some of his schoolmates at Harrow and was part of a circle at Cambridge that appears to have been fairly openly homosexual (though the correspondence between its members was necessarily in carefully coded language). Also while at university he was involved in a number of passionate friendships with fellow students, one of whom, John Edlestone, was clearly among the great loves of Byron's life. To what extent it was a sexual relationship we probably shall never know. Such passionate friendships pose a perennial problem for biographers and historians since they frequently inspired letters and poetry written in the language of erotic love yet stopped well short of sexual consummation. In our post-Freudian world we speak knowingly of the "real" meaning of such expressions of loving friendship but may in fact totally misread their nature. Highly eroticized but sexually chaste friendships between men were still common, if increasingly suspect, in Byron's time and survived into the early twentieth century, as the Cambridge chapters of E. M. Forster's *Maurice* or the collegiate novels of E. F. Benson (Cambridge again) attest. The same difficulty arises in interpreting passionate friendships between women in the late nineteenth and early twentieth centuries, which are all too easily read as lesbian relationships. As for Byron's love for Edlestone, he was always careful how and to whom he revealed the depth of his feelings, both at the time and later. When young Edlestone died, Byron wrote some of his most passionate poetry in memoriam but changed the pronouns from masculine to feminine.

Whatever the nature of his relationships with his fellow students at Cambridge, we know for certain that he was actively bisexual during his early trips abroad, so much so that the college friend who wrote to tell him of the latest sodomitical scandals, arrests, and executions in England did so in part to warn Byron to be careful and discreet on returning home. And he was—at least homosexually, though not heterosexually. He soon became involved in three disastrous relationships with women: with the obsessive and possessive Lady Caroline Lamb, with his own half-sister, and in a marriage to a woman determined to reform him. He made the terrible mistake of telling Lady Caroline about the most intimate details of his personal life: when he broke with her she retaliated by spreading gossip about his relations with his half-sister and about his homosexuality. This contributed to a nasty and sensational separation from his wife and to the destruction of his public career and reputation. Reviled in the press, taunted in public, and snubbed by society, Byron left England for good in 1816. The similarity to Beckford's downfall a generation earlier was uncanny, as Byron was well aware (on his first trip abroad he had made a point of visiting the house in Portugal where Beckford had spent much of his exile). Nor did the parallel end there: Byron, like Beckford, was ostracized by various English communities abroad.

The extent and depth of the climate of homophobia revealed by the treatment of Lord Byron, following on the persecutions of 1810–11, was so great, so unlike anything that had happened in England for more than three-quarters of a century, that Bentham felt compelled to return to the issue in his writings after nearly thirty years. In part he simply updated and reinforced the arguments in his earlier essay, repeating and adding to the evidence from ancient Greece and Rome of the bravery of male lovers and citing additional anthropological evidence to demonstrate that homosexuality did not lead to the neglect of women in other cultures. In one respect he was able to turn a change in expert and public opinion to his advantage. As late as the 1780s it had been generally believed that Europe was underpopulated. The writings of T. R. Malthus, reinforced by the periodic unemployment, food shortages, and high prices of the French war years, had reversed that perception, so that Bentham was now able to suggest that if, as alleged, pederasty led to a loss of population, so much the better. Indeed, no longer content with merely demonstrating the harmlessness of pederasty, he made notes for an essay entitled "Beneficial

Effects of Certain of These Modes." Not only would pederasty not contribute to the growth of excess population, he argued, but if and when men had sex before or outside of marriage, pederasty was to be preferred, since it posed no risk of pregnancy and therefore no risk of illegitimacy, abortion, or infanticide and would not lead to the degradation of women into prostitution.

Bentham's postwar essays went beyond his earlier efforts in other, no less fundamental ways. Back in 1785 he had employed rational arguments to counter fallacies and misapprehensions based on ignorance in the hope of persuading people that the criminalization of same-sex acts was both unnecessary and wrong. Now, in the wake of the rising tide of evangelical conservatism and a new wave of persecutions, he recognized that the underlying problem was the irrational fear and hatred of pederasty and that his main task was to expose homophobia and set about destroying its roots. Just how deep these roots went Bentham had only recently come to realize. Even if it were not the case that many people feared what they did not understand and sought to suppress tastes they did not share, the persecution of permanent minorities such as pederasts served a variety of the persecutors' needs. Not only were pederasts useful as diversions or scapegoats in times of trouble and unrest but in attacking them the bigot, the hate monger, the envious, or the merely insecure could feel virtuous and superior with no risk to themselves, since their victims dared not strike back. Acutely conscious that the enemies he now had to contend with were all but impervious to reason, Bentham chose his words with great care, avoiding language that reflected or was likely to further inflame prejudice. Three decades earlier he had characterized pederasty as "abominable" and "unnatural" in order to protect himself, even while arguing for decriminalization. In 1814 he did not allow himself that cover; he was fully aware of the dangers of labeling, of the power of words to make a bad situation worse: "It is by the power of names, of signs originally arbitrary and insignificant, that the course of the imagination has in great measure been guided." New thinking required new words, and Bentham struggled to invent a neutral vocabulary for pederasty, experimenting with terms such as "irregular," "the improlific appetite," and "the Attic mode."

An even better measure of just how much the changed cultural climate since the 1780s altered Bentham's approach to the issue of pederasty was his handling of religion. In his 1785 essay he had dismissed religious arguments about the sinfulness of pederasty in a couple of paragraphs. That was no longer possible. Recognizing that the most potent source and support of homophobia derived from religious belief, in his later essays Bentham directed

more attention to this than to any other problem. In the hope of reward or because of the fear of punishment, he argued, virtually all religions preached
the propitiation of their gods through sacrifice either of material goods or of
pleasures, including, of course, sexual pleasures. However, since procreative
sex could not be denied, nonprocreative sexual practices and in particular
those of sexual minorities bore the brunt of moral condemnation. That Christianity was especially savage in its treatment of sexual deviance Bentham attributed in part to its Jewish inheritance but not to Jesus himself. The culprit,
according to Bentham, was the apostle Paul, who, uncomfortable with all
physical pleasures, had perverted the teachings of Jesus and set Christianity
down the road to asceticism and self-denial. Bentham became obsessed with
this idea and planned an ambitious program of publications designed to demonstrate that the pursuit of pleasure, including sexual pleasure, was compatible with Christian morality as preached by Jesus himself. The defense of pederasty remained Bentham's primary concern, but he recognized that it had to
be embedded, even disguised, in a wider context, if indeed it could be discussed at all. We know of his intentions because he addressed a memorandum
on his project to his old friend William Beckford, now living in isolation in his
Gothic mansion, from whom Bentham may have hoped for financial support.
But like the project itself, the memorandum was never finished. The hostile
climate that had prompted Bentham to take up the issue of pederasty once
again also led him to abandon his later essays and keep them secret. This reform was sacrificed to other reforms, for they were obtainable and it was not,
and the futile pursuit of it might well endanger his other goals. "Never did
work appear," he sadly concluded, "from which at the hands of public opinion
a man found so much to fear, so little to hope."

# Chapter 5     Conclusion to Part 1

Even without the French Revolution and the genera-
tion of war that followed, the various nations of northern and western Europe
would have followed different paths so far as their attitudes toward the proper
role of the public in private morals was concerned: the French toward a
laissez-faire policy, at least as far as state intervention was involved, England
and Prussia toward a more intrusive policy of enforcing moral norms not only
through social and religious pressure (as, of course, the French did too) but
also through law. The general tendency of Enlightenment thought, centered
in France, on the one hand, and the religious revival in the Protestant nations
of Germany and England, to which there was nothing comparable in France,
ensured that they would go in opposite directions. Revolution, counterrevo-
lution, and war exaggerated and hardened the differences, adding a political
dimension to the widening divergence over morals—and vice versa.

That said, it would be misleading to draw the distinctions too sharply. The
nineteenth-century French bourgeoisie was as concerned with respectability
as its English or German counterparts, while the middle classes of England
and Germany were as intent on protecting their privacy as the French. In
practical terms this meant that the individual was generally left free to indulge
his vices so long as he did so discreetly, but violations of public decency were
as severely censured in France as in England or Germany. The example one
set, in short, was generally regarded as at least as important as what one did.
For members of the various sodomitical subcultures of northwestern Europe,
therefore, similarities in public attitudes toward them were often of greater
importance than the differences in their legal status. Private consensual sodomy might be legal, or, more accurately, might not be illegal in France, while
still criminal in Prussia and England, but the French retained laws punishing "any person who shall have committed a public offense against decency"

or who "habitually [facilitated] debauchery or corruption of young people." These vaguely worded articles (330 and 334) of the French Penal Code of 1810 often were used to entrap sodomites in public places, to close cafés and other notorious meeting places, and the like, especially from the mid-nineteenth century on. Not that the legal distinctions were not important. Clearly they were, if only in creating a climate of opinion and a chilling threat of persecution in those countries where sodomy itself remained a crime. To be sure, sodomy was difficult to prove (though England made it easier in 1828 by no longer requiring proof of penetration and emission), but once it was proven, of course, the consequences could be devastating to the individual arrested and a terrifying object lesson for others of his kind.

Even in England and Prussia, however, there was a gradual move away from the most savage punishments for sodomy. The general European tendency toward law reform that had led France to decriminalization produced in Prussia and England a much slower, less far-reaching, but nonetheless steady mitigation in the severity of the laws themselves and in their application. Prussia, which had abolished the death penalty for sodomy in 1794, replacing it with a term of imprisonment followed by banishment, reduced the penalty still further to a term of imprisonment only as part of a general law reform in 1837. England did not replace the death penalty for sodomy with a term of imprisonment, and that a life term, until the general law reform of 1861, but the application of the death penalty fell into abeyance some time before that. The last hanging for sodomy seems to have taken place in 1835; after that the death sentence, though invoked, was routinely commuted. Earlier attempts to abolish it were, however, as routinely defeated. Abolition of the death penalty for sodomy (and rape) passed the House of Commons in 1841 but was killed in the House of Lords on the grounds that repeal, as one member put it, "would do great violence to the moral feelings of a very large class of the community." Earlier than that the tendency was simply to avoid the issue altogether. In 1836 a commission on the criminal law recommended reducing the number of capital crimes to eight. All but one, sodomy, were crimes of violence, but the commission refused to address that contradiction or, for that matter, the issue itself, stating only that "a nameless offense of great enormity we, at present, exclude from consideration."

There were some concrete, measurable changes in England before the second half of the nineteenth century, however. Thirty-five years after Edmund Burke proposed the abolition of the pillory in 1780, the issue was taken up again, this time ultimately successfully, by a private member of Parliament,

Michael Angelo Taylor. Denouncing the practice as a relic of barbarism and as a punishment whose severity and consequences were determined more by the attending mob than by the authorities, Taylor carefully avoided any more direct reference to sodomy. Not so his chief ally in the House of Lords, the earl of Lauderdale, who cited the death in the pillory in 1780 that had prompted Burke to raise the issue. Delayed in the Lords, the measure was reintroduced by Taylor early in 1816. This time he addressed the issue of sodomy directly, if disingenuously, arguing on the one hand that the public exhibition of sodomites only gave publicity to the offense and on the other that no "punishment, however severe," appeared to deter "persons addicted to this atrocious offense."

Taylor's less than forthright approach to mitigating the punishments meted out for sodomy or attempted sodomy was characteristic of the way in which the issue was almost always handled in England, where such changes, if they happened at all, usually took place in the context of general law reform, and then only with a time lag in comparison with other offenses and with other countries. But while England could therefore be taken as representing one extreme in these matters, and France another, they were far from polar opposites, given the gap between law and practice in England and the enormous latitude afforded the French police by the laws protecting the young and criminalizing public sexual expression. Rather, France and England might better and more revealingly be represented as occupying points on a spectrum, with Prussia somewhere in between but clearly closer to England. By the end of the 1830s each of these countries had arrived at a rough-and-ready response to sexual deviance, a response that reflected its prejudices and recent historical experience but was to prove surprisingly stable and durable.

Just how much a matter of chance and circumstance these outcomes were is perfectly illustrated by what happened in the Netherlands in this period. Situated culturally as well as geographically between Germany and England, but subject to strong and direct French influence as well, the Netherlands was influenced by all of the developments that shaped its larger and more powerful near neighbors during the eighteenth century. A Protestant religious revival early in the century, like similar revivals in Prussia and England, tended to reinforce traditional attitudes toward sexuality. On the other hand, the Netherlands proved as receptive as any country in Europe to Enlightenment thought, including the rationalist critique of traditional morality even in areas as sensitive as sexual deviance. In a tract published in 1777 the Dutch legal reformer Abraham Perrenot echoed Beccaria and the French philosophes in denouncing sodomy as both unnatural and repugnant, yet not as a crime warranting the death penalty. Indeed, like Montesquieu, he laid much of the blame for sodomy on faulty social institutions and believed that it would largely disappear if alternatives were more readily available. Only incorrigibles should be punished, he concluded, and then only with prison terms or other lesser penalties, depending on the nature of the offense.

This was, to be sure, very much a minority view. Significantly, it was published anonymously and, perhaps even more significantly, in the wake of one of the periodic persecutions of sodomites to which the Netherlands, more than any other country in northwestern Europe, was subject in the eighteenth century. Most of these crackdowns were minor echoes of the major persecutions of 1730–31, but the last of these, in the mid-1790s, was unprecedentedly harsh. Not only sexual acts but mere solicitation, not formerly prosecuted, was savagely dealt with. Torture was used to gain confessions, long prison sentences were meted out even in the absence of confessions, and most surprising of all, lesbians as well as male sodomites were prosecuted for the first time in over a century.

This frenzied surge of repression took place against the background of a political and military crisis. In the mid-1790s the French revolutionary armies overran the Netherlands, whose internal divisions along religious and class lines had already been exposed by the influence of the Revolution itself and the approach of the French armies. Over the following generation the country experienced a bewildering series of political and constitutional changes or proposed changes, with various groups vying for position and power as the status of the country vis-à-vis the French and later the allies shifted. Reflecting deep divisions concerning how and how much the state should enforce morals, official policy toward punishment for sodomy wavered back and forth between a long prison term followed by banishment on the one hand and decriminalization on the other, the former when the old Dutch governing elites were on the ascendant, the latter when French control was most direct.

Ironically, though the French were ultimately defeated and driven out, the Dutch nonetheless ended up with the French penal code. This happened because the victorious allies wanted a union of Belgium and the Netherlands as a barrier against French resurgence, and one price of this for the Dutch was to accept the French penal code, which was in force in Belgium. Thus the Netherlands, though culturally more akin to Prussia and England, had a French-based legal code, and had it more by imposition than because of indigenous support. Not surprisingly, therefore, there were a number of attempts during the nineteenth century to recriminalize sodomy, none of them, however, successful. Parliament was dominated by liberals who held that private acts should not be illegal simply because they were distasteful or morally reprehensible. But laws regarding sex with minors were tightened, as were those protecting subordinates from the depredations of those in authority over them, and these increasingly stringent laws, together with those directed against public lewdness, were frequently used, as they were in France, to harass and entrap individuals and raid suspect bars and clubs.

There could hardly be a better example of the error of stressing the differences rather than the similarities between the countries of northwestern Europe than the ambivalent attitudes and policies of the Dutch toward sodomy throughout the nineteenth century. All of these countries officially considered sodomy as base and repugnant, and all of them retained laws that allowed the authorities considerable latitude to confine or repress at least the public behavior of their sodomitical subcultures. At the same time, all of them ultimately abolished the death penalty for sodomy, as well as the array of cruel punishments that had commonly been employed a century earlier: torture to gain confessions, the pillory, banishment. Moreover, as penalties were decreased or eliminated, greater reliance was placed on respectable public opinion and social pressure to regulate morals. This was the case even in England, where harsh laws remained later than in most other countries. As early as 1816, when the pillory was finally abolished, one member of Parliament who opposed the change at least took comfort from the thought that social pressure might be an even better deterrent: "If such crimes were effectively checked in upper life, it would have a great effect. The wretch who stood in little fear of imprisonment, pillory or death, might perhaps be affected by the terrors of perpetual disgrace and scorn."

And that, by and large, is what did happen by the mid-nineteenth century. The stigma of sinfulness may have lost much of its traditional force, and the increasing separation of crime from sin, as well as the spread of humanitarian ideas, had led authorities throughout much of Europe to reduce or even eliminate punishment for individual immoral behavior, but the sanction of social disapproval moved in to fill the void. By labeling deviant sexual behavior— and by no means only homosexuality—as unacceptable and disreputable, and by imposing its values on other classes, middle-class opinion in western Europe built a barrier between respectable society and the individual deviant or deviant subcultures that was as effective as legal sanctions, if not more so. This did not eliminate deviance, nor was it expected to, since there would always be the weak, the susceptible, the depraved. But the very existence of an unmistakable line between the acceptable and the unacceptable was intended to deter most of those tempted to cross it and may very well have done so. Above all, perhaps, it was intended to protect society at large from infection by deviant subcultures, and it may very well have done that too; it certainly was thought to have done so.

In the late eighteenth century there had been a real fear that social and sexual deviance, including homosexuality, was on the increase. This almost certainly was not so, though its visibility and the public discussion of it undoubtedly did increase. By the mid-Victorian era even that was no longer true. The sexual underworld, including homosexual subcultures, certainly existed, even thrived, but it, and most especially the homosexual subcultures, existed in isolation and near invisibility. They had been pushed to the fringe of society, where they posed little danger, and therefore did not need to be discussed. And for the most part they were not discussed, as much because they posed little danger as because it was not respectable to discuss them. That is a point worth keeping in mind whenever we are tempted to deride the Victorians as naive and hypocritical in sexual matters. They were not, or at least not to the degree later generations have liked to caricature them to be. What appears to us as denial or simply ignorance was as often as not an approach designed to channel and control sexuality.

# Part 2

# Defining a Subculture

## Chapter 6

**Pioneers: The United States**

          Well before the middle of the nineteenth century each
of the major nations of northwestern Europe had established its own peculiar
variations on the general theme of how best to regulate deviant sexuality in
a modern, increasingly secular society and render it relatively harmless. By
drawing a clear line between the acceptable and the unacceptable, and by
enforcing that border as much through disapproval as by laws of varying
severity, they had succeeded in pushing what had once seemed threatening
sufficiently far out on the fringe that it could largely be ignored. But at that
point, inevitably, the law of unintended consequences came into play. The
more clearly the line was drawn, the more emphatically the homosexual or
any other subculture was labeled as different and distinct, the more likely it
was that such a subculture would develop a group consciousness, a sense of
its own separateness and identity. To the extent that members of such a subculture internalized the stigmas applied to them by society, regarding themselves as in some measure criminal or sick or sinful, they represented no great
threat. But group consciousness could lead as well to a sense of solidarity
within the subculture, of grievance against the society that stigmatized it,
and finally to the desire to redefine and assert itself on its own terms. Moreover, once a clear line had been drawn between acceptable and deviant behavior, then ever-increasing vigilance was required to ensure that the line was
not crossed. Indeed, the clearer the boundary, the greater the danger, since a
single transgression was more and more likely to be viewed, not as a temporary lapse, but as indicative of a deviant nature.

     It was as a result of these two unintended consequences of the labeling of
sexual deviance that the Victorian compromise and Victorian silence on the
subject of homosexuality broke down. Members of homosexual subcultures
did indeed begin to question their labeling by society and to attempt the long

and difficult task of redefining themselves on their own terms. Partly in response to that effort, and partly due to the emergence of other social problems in late-nineteenth-century Europe, problems with which homosexuality could be linked as symptom or even as cause, social critics and medical scientists broke their silence and turned their attention to homosexuality with an intensity not seen for nearly a hundred years.

Surprisingly, the first process, that of redefining the subculture from within, was pioneered most influentially by a poet, and an American poet at that— Walt Whitman. Though it is more confusing than helpful to dub him, as some have, the first modern homosexual, there is no question that he is the first iconic figure in the pantheon of the modern movement for gay self-definition and gay rights. John Addington Symonds, the English critic and cultural historian, who wrote the first scholarly account of Greek pederasty, as well as one of the earliest defenses of what he called "sexual inversion" in modern times, was deeply influenced by Whitman. Writing to him in 1872, Symonds declared the nature and extent of his indebtedness to the poet:

> I have traced passionate friendship through Greece, Rome, the medieval and the modern world. . . . It was while engaged upon this work . . . that I first read Leaves of Grass. The man who spoke to me from that Book impressed me in every way most profoundly and unalterably; but especially did I then learn confidently to believe that the Comradeship which I conceived as on a par with the Sexual feeling for depth and strength and purity and capability of all good, was real—not a delusion of distorted passions, a dream of the Past, a scholar's fancy—but a strong and vital bond of man to man.

Ten years later Oscar Wilde, while on his highly publicized (and self-promoting) visit to the United States, called on Whitman at his home in Camden, New Jersey. "There is no one in the great wide world of America whom I love and honor so much," Wilde said of Whitman. A quarter-century later, when the French novelist André Gide wrote a defense of pederasty in the form of a dialogue, his fictional protagonist had on his desk a single picture— of Walt Whitman. And one hundred years after Symonds told Whitman how greatly the poet had changed his life, the beat poet Allen Ginsberg happily and proudly related in an interview that his lover, Neal Cassady, had slept with Gavin Arthur (the grandson of President Arthur), who had slept with the English poet and advocate of social and sexual freedom Edward Carpenter, who had slept with Walt Whitman. This sexual line of succession, this—it is impossible to resist the phrase—laying on of hands, was for Ginsberg a "line of transmission" of a cultural as well as a sexual heritage.

At first glance mid-nineteenth-century America might seem an unlikely setting for the emergence of so central and defining a figure in the development of a distinctive modern homosexual subculture, and in the lives and thought of men as diverse as Symonds, Wilde, Gide, and Ginsberg. Certainly there was nothing in America's colonial or early federal history to suggest such a possibility. Public and official attitudes toward sodomy derived inevitably more or less directly from England, with only minor variations. There was the familiar ambiguity in terminology. The religious designation *sodomy* and the popular secular term *buggery* were used sometimes interchangeably, sometimes to mean different acts. Often it is unclear what was meant by either one. In some cases the offense was clearly defined in biblical language as "a man who lies with a man as those who lie with a woman," but frequently the definition of *sodomy* was broadened to include nonvaginal intercourse with a woman, bestiality, or even masturbation, in short, any nonprocreative sexual act. Indeed, the distinction between procreative and nonprocreative sex, which was often explicitly equated with the natural and the unnatural, was scarcely less a concern than the sex of a person's partner. All such acts were a threat to marriage and the family, to population growth (a major preoccupation in the colonial period), and therefore to the community. Justification for harsh punishments rested on the Bible, and the penalty in all of the American colonies was death, while the penalty for attempted sodomy was prison, whipping, banishment, or fines.

The death penalty was rarely carried out after the early eighteenth century in America, though it long remained on the books. Thomas Jefferson suggested replacing it with castration for those convicted of sodomy (and rape or polygamy) in a proposed revision of the Virginia criminal code in the late 1790s (which also took care to define its terms: "Buggery is twofold. 1. with mankind, 2. with beasts. Buggery is the Genus, of which Sodomy and Bestiality are the species"). Pennsylvania was the first state actually to repeal the death penalty for sodomy, in 1786, and others followed suit within the next generation, well ahead of England, though the Carolinas held out until after the Civil War. Another sign of the spread of Enlightenment ideas was the gradual change in legal terminology from the religious designation *sodomy* to phrases such as a *crime against nature.* To be sure, even the authors of statutes incorporating lesser penalties usually felt compelled to include language castigating homosexuality as an *unmentionable* or *abominable* vice, but at least these were terms of disgust and revulsion, not of sinfulness or damnation. Beyond that, however, even toward a more dispassionate language, reformers would not (dared not?) go. The former colonies might move faster than the mother country, but they did not move further. No one suggested decriminalization.

Nor was there anything in the early-nineteenth-century United States comparable to the urban subcultures of northwestern Europe. This is hardly surprising. In 1800 no American city had even close to one hundred thousand people; the critical mass needed to foster a sexual subculture simply did not exist. Our knowledge of the lives and attitudes of men drawn to other men in the United States is, therefore, necessarily fragmentary and discontinuous. There were infrequent trials for sodomy or attempted sodomy, as well as the occasional scandal, but these tell us more about public attitudes toward the crime against nature than about its perpetrators. More revealing are the accounts, fictional and real, of intense, loving male friendships. They are one of the great recurring themes of American literature throughout the nineteenth century and well into the twentieth, a common element in the depiction of the all-male worlds of school and college, of sailing ships, of the military, of the frontier, or of encounters with the supposedly more elemental peoples of exotic lands, from the Indians of the American West to the Arabs of North Africa to the natives of the South Sea Islands.

Far from being only highly idealized fantasies of "a friendship I deemed more precious than the love of women," as the hero of one such novel declared, deliberately echoing the lament of David over the dead Jonathan, these tales reflected an important social reality. The relationship that inspired this particular novel—*Cecil Dreeme*, by Theodore Winthrop—is especially well documented in the memoirs of the model for one main character, Thomas Wentworth Higginson, and in the biography of him written by his wife Mary. Radical abolitionist, colonel of a regiment of freed slaves during the Civil War, active supporter of women's suffrage, and, in quieter times, a central figure in Boston literary circles and the promoter and protector of Emily Dickinson's career, Higginson, while still a student at Harvard in the mid-1840s, "met one day a young man [William Hurlbut] so handsome in his dark beauty that he seemed like a picturesque Oriental; slender, keen eyed, raven haired, he arrested the eye and heart like some fascinating girl." Higginson was far from alone in falling under Hurlbut's spell—men and women alike were drawn to him, and he was the model for no less powerfully magnetic characters in two other novels—but Higginson appears to have been especially susceptible. "I never loved but one male friend with passion," he recollected, "and for him my love had no bounds—all that my natural fastidiousness and cautious reserve kept from others I poured on him; to say that I would have died for him was nothing. I lived for him." Even though Hurlbut often failed to reply, Higginson continued to write to him almost monthly for years. "Their letters were more like those between man and woman than between two men," Higginson's widow noted. Ultimately they fell out, over presidential politics in the critical wartime election of 1864 and as a result of Hurlbut's turbulent private life, what Higginson termed his "moral deterioration," but perhaps also because Higginson felt the need to free himself from the obsessive nature of what Mary Higginson called his "romantic attachment" to Hurlbut. "Concede to any person an influence over us beyond what the time relation justifies," Higginson confided to his diary, perhaps in relation to Hurlbut, "and the reaction makes us almost hate them." Yet even late in life Higginson admitted, "I strongly suspect that if, after twenty years of non-intercourse, he had written to me to come and nurse him in illness, I should have left all and gone."

The only aspect of this remarkable relationship that is likely to be more surprising to a modern audience than the intensity of Higginson's love for Hurlbut is the frankness with which he and his wife recounted it. For that reason it is virtually certain that however passionate this and similar friendships we know of may have been, they remained nonsexual. Had they been otherwise, they would surely have been kept strictly, even darkly secret. "It is possible," as one critic suggests, convincingly, "that a strict interdiction against full genital sexuality . . . at the same time allowed for a much fuller expression of male friendship, since that in no way threatened to spill over into genitality." Of explicitly sexual relationships between men in early-nineteenth-century America we therefore know very little. One tantalizing exception, revealed by a couple of letters that survive in a South Carolina family archive, involved two young men who were later to play prominent roles in antebellum southern politics. In 1826, at the age of twenty, they had other things on their minds, however. The writer of the letters asked his friend "whether you yet have the extravagant delight of poking and punching a writhing Bedfellow with your long fleshen pole—the exquisite touches of which I have often had the honor of feeling?" and so on in a lighthearted, teasing manner totally free of any suggestion of guilt or shame. This is reminiscent of, though even more flippant in tone than, a letter the twenty-three-year-old Byron received from an old college friend during his return journey to England fifteen years earlier. To attempt to draw any broader conclusions from such fragmentary evidence about the sexual lives of young middle- and upper-class men in regency England or the antebellum South would be foolish. All that can be said with some assurance is that however anomalous such correspondences may have been, they are hardly likely to have been unique.

We are on surer ground when we move lower down the social scale. As would be the case in Oscar Wilde's London (as revealed at his trials), so in Walt Whitman's New York a generation and more earlier, working-class young men and boys appear often to have had a quite matter-of-fact attitude toward casual sexual encounters with other men, particularly older men of a higher social class who could offer them money, a meal, a drink, a place to stay— or a little affectionate regard along with (and legitimated by) such material considerations. Reading between the lines of Whitman's poetry or of the jottings in his notebooks, it is clear that even before midcentury, New York had what it had not had even a few years earlier, a variegated sexual subculture. The rapidity with which that developed is hardly surprising considering the city's explosive growth; its population doubled between 1800 and 1820 and had more than doubled again by 1840, to over three hundred thousand. By the time the young Whitman settled in the city in 1841 it was as dynamic and cosmopolitan as the great cities of Europe and, in Whitman, poetically better served. Not the least of his subjects was the street life and street boys of New York; he was the first poet of sexual cruising. Scattered throughout his celebrations of the city are references, unmistakable to the observant reader, to "frequent and swift flash of eyes offering me robust, athletic love," to carefully coded exchanges with total strangers: "O I saw one passing alone, saying hardly a word, yet full of love I detected him by certain signs / O eyes ever wishfully turning! O silent eyes!"

He captured perfectly the mixture of excitement and caution, of arousal and the need to disguise it, which is at once the thrill, the frustration, and the danger inherent in the pursuit of illicit pleasures in public places:

> I too . . .
> . . . . . .
> Was call'd by my nighest name by clear loud voices of young men as they saw
>     me approaching or passing,
> Felt their arms on my neck as I stood, or the negligent leaning of their flesh
>     against me as I sat,

Saw many I loved in the street or ferry-boat or public assembly, yet never told
    them a word,
Lived the same life with the rest, the same old laughing gnawing, sleeping,
Play'd the part that still looks back on the actor or actress,
The same old role, the role that is what we make it, as great as we like,
Or as small as we like, or both great and small.

At other times he wrote with a frankness that is almost unmistakable: "I share the midnight orgies of young men / I pick out some low person for my dearest friend. He shall be lawless, rude, illiterate."

Whitman frequented certain well-known parks, public baths, the docks, places along the East River where boys swam naked, ferryboats, streetcars, and a couple of mixed bars or dance halls. From the first he preferred the company of young working-class men, a taste that lasted throughout his long life. He kept a record of the men and boys he met, talked and walked with, sometimes slept with, usually noting their age, a couple of physical characteristics, something of their nature perhaps, where they were from or what they did for a living, if indeed they were employed or even settled. From among these chance encounters developed the loves of his life, a succession of intimate companions, friends, comrades. The first of these, Fred Vaughan, then still in his teens, lived with the Whitman family in the late 1850s and was perhaps the inspiration for the Calamus poems, the first and, as a group, the most tender and touching of Whitman's celebrations of manly intimacy and love. Vaughan went off on his own before the end of the decade and married in 1862, but he kept in touch with Whitman, writing him now and then, and in 1890, more than three decades after they had ceased to live together, he paid a final visit to the poet shortly before his death. "There is never a day passes but what I think of you," Vaughan wrote sixteen years earlier, after Whitman had been felled by a stroke. "So much have you left to be remembered by a Broadway stage—a Fulton ferry boat—a bale of cotton on the dock. The 'Brooklyn Daily Times'—a ship loading or unloading at the wharf—a poor man fallen from the roof of a new building, a woman and child suffocated by smoke in a burning tenement house. All—all to me speak of thee Dear Walt.—Seeing them my friend the part thou occupiest in my spiritual nature. . . . My love my Walt—is with you always."

Vaughan was not alone in never ceasing to see New York through Whitman's eyes. For a generation of young men of similar temperament or inclinations New York was Whitman's New York, and to those also wishing "to celebrate the need of the love of athletic comrades," who "dreamed . . . of a city where all the men were like brothers," New York was a magnet. In 1866 the young Horatio Alger was surprised in a compromising position with a young member of the Unitarian congregation in the village of Brewster on Cape Cod, to which he had recently been appointed minister. To avoid a public scandal, he withdrew from the ministry and fled, but even though he had been born, bred, and educated in Massachusetts, he fled not to Boston but to New York. There he became as enthralled by the street life and street boys of the city as the youthful Walt Whitman had been twenty years earlier. (As an aspiring poet himself Alger must have read the early editions of the *Leaves of Grass,* including the Calamus poems). He befriended the street arabs and entertained groups of them in his lodgings; he actively supported the Children's Aid Society and the Newsboys' Lodging House; he used the best of them, as well as some who were not so good, as models for the heroes in his didactic tales of boys rising above their poor beginnings through hard work and straight living. Whether he also had sex with them is another matter. Alger had had at least two passionate friendships—possibly more than friendships—before his brush with disaster in 1866, one shortly after he graduated from college, another with a young soldier during the Civil War, but his most recent and best biographers suggest that he may have remained celibate after the events that nearly ruined his life. If so, his friendship and support for boys and his books for and about boys, which earned him a modest living and later status as a byword for the Victorian belief in self-help, may have sufficed to satisfy his fascination with adolescents.

Whitman found it neither necessary nor possible to make such a distinction between inclination and action (though there is ample evidence that he too was sometimes troubled by his feelings for young men). Not for Whitman, therefore, the hothouse, effeminate atmosphere of the molly house culture of European cities (which probably could be found in New York); he sought the "love of athletic comrades," of thoroughly manly men, companions as much as, or more than, sexual partners, young men with whom he could roughhouse almost in the manner of an older brother. At its core Whitman's ideal of sexuality was fresh and uncomplicated, almost innocent, joyful in its celebration of the senses, potentially heroic. "The brotherhood of lovers" he envisioned was free of guilt, shame, doubt, furtiveness; it required no antecedents, no historical precedents or models; it knew neither class nor social status; it was essentially American, only possible in a democracy and the highest expression of democracy. It was new, potential not actual, and therefore required a new vocabulary in order to be born.

And Whitman sought to provide that new vocabulary. Just as Jeremy Bentham, recognizing the power of words, had sought to replace negative with neutral terms in the hope of removing the stigma of sinfulness and unnaturalness from sexual relations between men, Whitman seized on a vocabulary that held out the promise, not of neutrality, but of affirmation. The source of that vocabulary seems curious more than a century later: phrenology. It is dismissed derisively now as the pseudoscience of reading the bumps on a person's head, but in mid-nineteenth-century Europe and America many saw it as a great advance in the science of the mind. The central propositions of phrenology are that individual mental and character traits are localized within the human brain, that the strength of any particular characteristic depends on the size and development of the appropriate portion of the brain, and, finally, that the size of any given portion of the brain will show up in the configuration of the cranium. Hence the practice, for a time a popular fad, of reading the bumps on people's heads. Whitman had his read in 1847 by Lorenzo Fowler, the brother of the leading light of American phrenology. The Fowler family ran an emporium of trendy cures (and also provided the first outlet for Whitman's poetry), including hydropathic cures and animal magnetism. Whitman was interested in the latter as well, but phrenology came to him as a revelation. Two of the traits that the reading of his head demonstrated to be most prominently developed in him—amativeness (or sexual love) and adhesiveness (or comradeship)—also became central to his art and thought. By distinguishing between amativeness and adhesiveness phrenology solved a number of problems for Whitman. By adopting the concept of adhesiveness as his own he was able to resolve his conflicted feelings about the intensity and nature of his attraction to other men; he was provided with a respectable cover for the public and poetic expression of those feelings; and above all, he now had not a neutral but a positive vocabulary with which to express them. The term *adhesiveness*, in short, did for Whitman very much what the term *gay* would do for the liberation movement of the 1970s: it freed him. He could celebrate the physical without fully or directly confronting the sexual, either publicly or privately; he could now write the Calamus poems.

Whitman's concept of adhesiveness found its near perfect practical expression in Washington during the Civil War. To be sure, he cruised the streets there, much as he had the streets of New York, only now in search of the soldiers who thronged the capital. But his main concern, his obsession, was with tending the sick, the wounded, and the dying. In makeshift hospitals in government buildings or in field hospitals near the front he distributed parcels and wrote letters for the boys of both armies, fed them, took care of their personal needs, or simply stayed with them, thousands of them. He cared for them all, the plain and the rough, most especially the rough, as well as the handsome and the mannerly, since "affection . . . is sometimes the only thing that will reach their condition." There were special cases, young men who stood out even among the hordes indiscriminately brought together in time of war. "Every now and then," he noted,

> in hospital or camp, there are beings I meet—specimens of unworldliness, disinterestedness and animal purity and heroism . . . on whose birth the calmness of heaven seems to have descended, and whose gradual growing up . . . the power of a strange spiritual sweetness, fibre and inward health, have also attended. Something veil'd and abstracted is often part of the manners of these beings. . . . They are often young men, obeying the events and occasions about them, marching, soldiering, fighting, foraging, cooking, working on farms or at some trade before the war—unaware of their own nature, (as to that, who is aware of his own nature?) their companions only understanding that they are different from the rest, more silent, "something odd about them," and apt to go off and meditate and muse in solitude.

Such men were the potential recruits to Whitman's army of comrades.

While the idea of adhesiveness allowed Whitman a freedom of expression, both physical and poetic, that he might otherwise not have dared display, it failed to satisfy those disturbed by his celebration of the senses and of sexuality in general, let alone by his all but unmistakable homoeroticism. Ralph Waldo Emerson hailed the first edition of *Leaves of Grass* "as the most extraordinary piece of wit and wisdom that America has yet produced," but even though, or perhaps because, he himself had become obsessed with a fellow student while at Harvard, he urged the poet to write with greater caution. Whitman had difficulty both getting and keeping publishers. When he sought financial support for his work on behalf of wounded soldiers, he had little success, largely because, as one friend wrote to him, "it is believed you are not ashamed of your reproductive organs." A few years after the war Whitman lost his job in the Department of the Interior in part because of his writings.

Others were dissatisfied with Whitman's adhesiveness in a different, almost opposite sense. Symonds continued to write to Whitman for almost twenty years following his first idolatrous letter in 1871, but gradually he became more and more insistent on knowing precisely what adhesiveness did and did not include. Symonds was writing his own work in defense of inversion at the time and felt that Whitman was or could be invaluable to his argument. Finally, in 1890, he asked the central question directly: "In your conception of comradeship, do you contemplate the possible intrusion of those semi-sexual emotions and actions which no doubt do occur between men?" Whitman, who had dodged the question before but could do so no longer, answered testily, calling Symonds's suggestions "gratuitous and quite at the time entirely undream'd & unreck'd possibility of morbid inferences—wh' are disavow'd by me & seem damnable." Symonds had to accept this as Whitman's authoritative last word, but he never entirely believed it, and for good reason. In a letter to Edward Carpenter, Symonds said of Whitman's denial, "I feel sure he could not have written it, when he first published Calamus. I think he was afraid of being used to lend his influence to 'Sods.' Did not quite trust me perhaps."

Symonds was almost certainly right. Whitman had always been cautious, even in his diaries and certainly in his poetry, taking care to leave room for varying interpretations even of his most explicit works. Symonds was hardly the man to whom he could let down his guard. The Englishman was married and had children, was upper-middle-class, wealthy, and educated. Whitman had no such protections, and he clearly resented Symonds's pressing and prying from a much safer position. Besides, Whitman understandably wished his works to be left to speak for themselves and not to be overly explained or used for other purposes. Symonds's increasingly direct questions also forced Whitman to confront once again his own ambivalent feelings about his sexuality. He had adopted adhesiveness as much as a way of resolving inner conflicts as of providing himself with protective cover in public or of finding a new and positive language through which to express his feelings. But the intensity of his attraction to young men and the at times obsessive manner in which he sought to satisfy it often disturbed him. During a crisis in his relationship with the best-known of his working-class comrades, the streetcar conductor Peter Doyle, he admonished himself to, "Depress the adhesive nature. It is in excess—making life a torment . . . diseased feverish disproportionate adhesiveness. . . . Remember where I am most weak, & most lacking. . . . To give up absolutely & for good, from this present hour, this feverish, fluctuating, useless undignified pursuit of [Peter Doyle]—too long (much too long) persevered in—so humiliating—It must come at last & had better come now."

At such times the distinction the idea of adhesiveness had allowed Whitman to make between different kinds of love threatened to break down and put into doubt the meaning of much of his poetry, even to himself. Two years before his vehement denial to Symonds, he confessed to a friend, "I often say to myself about Calamus, perhaps it means more or less than what I thought myself—means different; perhaps I don't know what it all means—perhaps never did know."

External pressures quite apart from Symonds's probings may have added to Whitman's discomfiture in his last years. Earlier in his life, when he was first coming to terms with his feelings for other men, the idea of adhesiveness had not only provided protective cover and a way of resolving doubts about his sexuality but also genuinely expressed the character of his sexuality. It was not only convenient but emotionally true. For the young Whitman sexual contact with other men was a natural extension of comradely love, a variant of the sort of passionate friendships still generally accepted at the time when he began his career as a poet. Open displays of physical affection between young males of the sort that are still common in Mediterranean countries appear to have been unremarkable in mid-nineteenth-century New York City. So too with the practice of men sharing accommodations, including a bed, as Fred Vaughan and Walt Whitman did in the Whitman family household; economic necessity may have dictated it, but society did not yet look on it with suspicion. Indeed, male relatives, friends, or guests sleeping in the same bed, long regarded as an invitation to vice in much of northern Europe, at least among the middle and upper classes, remained quite common in parts of the United States well into the final decades of the nineteenth century.

The author of the earliest known autobiography of an avowed American homosexual, Claude Hartland, had his first, much-longed-for sexual experience in his mid-teens, with a visitor with whom his parents asked him to share his bed—and this even though Hartland was unusually effeminate in manner and appearance. For years thereafter the necessity or opportunity of sharing his bed provided him with a succession of sexual encounters, some fleeting and superficial, others of greater depth and duration: with fellow students, with a friend of his older brother's, with a colleague after he became a teacher, with an itinerant preacher, among others. Neither family nor friends nor colleagues appear to have found his eagerness to spend the night with others remarkable; nor did those who shared a bed with him simply for the sake of a place to sleep or out of comradely affection. Frequently such physical but nonsexual intimacy was enough to satisfy him, but all too often it did not suffice and Hartland would lie sleeplessly beside his bedmate, consumed by his secret desires and able to relieve himself only by "self abuse" (which, interestingly, he regarded as "a far greater sin" than homosexuality and vowed, repeatedly but always unsuccessfully, to forgo). There were, he recalled, "scores of such nights with different men."

Hartland wrote this remarkable account of his sexual history just after the turn of the century, when he was just thirty. His declared purpose was to disabuse his readers of their naiveté, their sheer ignorance of sexual matters, which had allowed him to slip into such a life so easily. "If my parents could have seen the dark future in store for me," he lamented, "I might have been saved, but they did not understand." That they did not, he believed, could be blamed in large part on the appalling ignorance of the medical profession, to the end of whose innocence about homosexuality he dedicated his little book. That Hartland had long since lost his own innocence is clear from the later chapters of his autobiography. In his mid-twenties, almost by accident, he discovered street cruising in a big city, sex for the sake of sex, though he still longed for the transformation of such relationships into something nobler, that is, asexual. As he put it, "My love for my own sex is of two distinct kinds—spiritual and animal." That one might not only lead to the other but also include it he did not even consider; the two kinds of love were in conflict, and for the higher to triumph, the lower had to be suppressed. To that end he sought the help of ministers, even of a hypnotist, as well as physicians and a psychiatrist. None could fully understand his condition, let alone cure him of it, and he ended his autobiography resigned to his "unnatural" state, his "perverted nature," his status as "a prisoner for life in the gloomy dungeon of an abnormal passion."

To the extent that Hartland's book reflected growing social awareness of the supposed dangers of physical intimacy between men, and to the extent that his unquestioning acceptance of his condition as "unnatural," "perverted," and "abnormal" represented the spread of the medical view of homosexuality as pathological, Whitman's alternative vision of sexual relations between men as an expression of comradely love became more and more untenable. Whitman had always been subject to criticism along these lines, but in the late decades of the century the underpinnings of his views were weakened at the same time that the medical view was gaining currency. The popular vogue and professional regard for phrenology was in decline, while emphasis on the carnal as opposed to the comradely in intimate relations between men was implicit in the new and increasingly widely used term *homo-*

*sexuality.* Even as late as midcentury there had been a presumption of innocence about such relationships; well before the end of the century they had become suspect, at least among the middle and upper classes. There was little or no room left for adhesiveness.

Thomas Wentworth Higginson provides an interesting measure of the change. Whereas in his youth he had thrown himself into an especially passionate friendship with the beautiful and fascinating William Hurlbut, in late middle age, perhaps in part in reaction to the intensity of his relationship with Hurlbut but surely also reflecting growing social awareness and self-consciousness about the underlying meaning of such relationships, he savagely attacked both the aging Whitman and the young Oscar Wilde, then just beginning his year-long lecture tour of the United States. In 1882, in an editorial in the *Woman's Journal,* the organ of the American Woman's Suffrage Association, Higginson denounced the tendency of polite society to lionize these decadent, often extravagant poets. He did not specify the nature of their transgressions, let alone the homoerotic tendencies of much of their work—he was, after all, addressing women as "the guardians of the public purity"—but the implication was clear enough. "Mr. Wilde may talk of Greece," Higginson pointedly observed, "but there is nothing Greek about his poems; his nudities do not suggest the sacred whiteness of an antique statue, but rather the forcible unveiling of some insulted innocence." And Higginson contemptuously dismissed the assertion that their poetry was "manly": "Each of these so called 'manly' poets has had his opportunity of action and waived it." Whitman, he suggested, should have volunteered to serve as a soldier in the Civil War, but having failed to meet that test, he "had best cease boasting about his imminent manhood." As for Wilde, Higginson asked, at a time when his native Ireland was in a state of near anarchy, "Is it manhood for her gifted sons to stay at home and help work out the problem; or to cross the Atlantic and pose in ladies' boudoirs or write prurient poems which their hostesses must discreetly ignore?"

Reading between the lines of such criticism, it is hardly surprising that Whitman sometimes questioned the meaning of his earlier poetry, written in a different climate more than a generation earlier, or that he reacted so vehemently to Symonds's questioning when Symonds was in effect suggesting that Whitman's adhesiveness was closer to the Englishman's definition of sexual inversion than to the poet's original meaning. Many later critics and biographers, uncomfortable with Whitman's sexuality, have seized on his letter to Symonds in order to downplay or deny his homosexuality. But the proponents of a positive view of homosexuality in the late nineteenth century and the gay liberation movement a century later claimed or reclaimed him, and rightly so. Adhesiveness was central to his art and to his life as he lived it.

There is no more exuberant expression in any language of the sheer joy to be found in the love of one man for another than, "When I Heard at the Close of Day." Nor is there any more powerful declaration of the rightness of such love and the necessity of proudly asserting it and bravely fighting for it, whatever the odds, than this:

As I lay with my head on your lap camerado,
The confession I made I resume, what I said to you and the open air I resume,
I know I am restless and make others so,
I know my words are weapons full of danger, full of death,
For I confront peace, security, and all the settled laws, to unsettle them,
I am more resolute because all have denied me than I could ever have been
 had all accepted me,
I heed not and have never heeded either experience, cautions, majorities, nor
 ridicule,
And the threat of what is call'd hell is little or nothing to me,
And the lure of what is call'd heaven is little or nothing to me;
Dear camerado! I confess I have urged you onward with me, and still urge you,
 without the least idea what is our destination,
Or whether we shall be victorious, or utterly quell'd and defeated.

The public and political message implied here was made explicit elsewhere. Adhesiveness was as central to Whitman's vision of America and its future as it was to his own life. As the United States sank into materialism and political corruption following the Civil War, Whitman wrote in *Democratic Vistas* of what his country could be and in a footnote suggested comradeship as an antidote to its present ills:

It is to the development, identification, and general prevalence of that fervid comradeship . . . that I look for the counterbalance and offset of our materialistic and vulgar American democracy, and for the spiritualization thereof. Many will say it is a dream, and will not follow my inferences; but I confidently expect a time when there will be seen, running like a half-hid warp through all the myriad audible and visible worldly interests of America, threads of manly friendship, fond and loving, pure and sweet, strong and life-long, carried to degrees hitherto unknown—not only giving tone to individual character, making it unprecedentedly emotional, muscular, heroic, and refined, but having the deepest relations to general politics. I say democracy infers such loving comradeship, as its most inevitable twin or counterpart, without which it will be incomplete, in vain, and incapable of perpetuating itself.

To Symonds in 1872 or to Ginsberg in 1972 the effect of such a declaration was electric because it was not merely neutral in tone and terminology, but positive; because it was not weak or apologetic or defensive, but strong and assertive; because it did not rely on the past, on what the ancients had done, for validation, but on itself, in the here and now, and on the future. It was, in a word, liberating. Symonds perhaps put it best. In a letter to Horace Traubel, Whitman's friend and literary executor, written only a month before the poet's death, Symonds wrote: "You do not know, & I can never tell anyone, what Whitman has been to me. Brought up in the purple of aristocratic school and university, provided with more money than is good for a young man, early married to a woman of noble and illustrious connections, I might have been a mere English gentleman, had not I read Leaves of Grass in time."

## Chapter 7

**Pioneers: Germany**

While Walt Whitman was perfecting his views of comradeship in America, from his first use of adhesiveness in his own special sense in the mid-1850s, through the publication of the Calamus poems in 1860 and his tending of the sick and wounded during the Civil War, to the publication of *Democratic Vistas* in 1871, a parallel process was going on in Germany. It too was largely the work of one man, Karl Ulrichs, but of a different type and in very different circumstances. Whereas Whitman had a poet's vision of what America could be, Ulrichs was involved on a practical level with the legal status of his kind in an emerging German nation. Like many, perhaps most, Germans of his generation—he was born in 1825—Ulrichs eagerly anticipated the apparently inevitable unification of his fragmented homeland; his concern was with the form unification would take. He feared and opposed the so-called *Kleindeutsch* solution to the problem of German unification, a narrow, predominantly Protestant, Prussian-dominated state, favoring instead the *Grossdeutsch* solution, an inclusive and broadly tolerant Germany incorporating the Austrian lands, with their large Catholic and Slavic populations. This is hardly surprising given his background as well as his sexuality. Though a north German Protestant, he was born far from Prussia, near the Dutch border. His father was a minor bureaucrat in the Hannoverian government, and Ulrichs himself studied law in preparation for a career in the civil service at the University of Göttingen in Hannover (where homosexuality as such was not illegal) and in Berlin, the capital of Prussia (where it was).

Nonetheless, it was probably in Berlin that Ulrichs came out sexually. The city had a thriving homosexual subculture, sufficiently active and visible at this time to be a source of concern to the police, and in at least one respect militaristic Prussia must have appealed to young Ulrichs, who had a weakness for men in uniform. In every other respect he had little use either for the military or for Prussia. He enthusiastically supported the revolution of 1848 and even applied for a post with the revolutionary Frankfurt parliament. Failing to get that post, he returned to his job in the Hannoverian civil service, where, however, he became increasingly frustrated and unhappy as the government retreated from the liberal constitution granted in 1848. Finally, in 1854, he resigned, possibly to avoid revelation of his sexuality, a public scandal, and likely dismissal.

Ulrichs then turned to literary pursuits, which he combined with his own brand of liberal nationalism. He joined the Young German Society, a pan-German cultural organization founded in 1858, and was appointed secretary when it changed its title to the All German Society a year later and took on a more overtly political tone. Ulrichs settled in Frankfurt and soon became active in the city's leading cultural society, the Free German Foundation for Science, Art, and General Culture. He supported himself, precariously, largely by writing for newspapers, and it was the combination of his journalism with his interest in national cultural organizations that brought him to the issue of homosexual rights. In the summer of 1862 Ulrichs reported on the All German Shooting Festival for his paper. The organizer of the festival, Johann Schweitzer, was active in a number of German workers' organizations as well as in the model for all later institutions linking sport with nationalism in Germany, the gymnast movement. Two weeks after the end of the shooting festival he was arrested on a morals charge, accused of having seduced an underage boy. Ulrichs, who had already come out to his family and was planning an essay on homosexual law reform for submission to the Free German Foundation, decided to intervene. He sent Schweitzer a legal brief for his defense (which was not used) and offered his newspaper an article on law reform (which was not published).

Given Ulrichs's natural stubbornness, if anything these reverses pushed him into even greater commitment to this new cause. For some time he had been groping toward a theory of the origins of homosexuality. Like Whitman, he was briefly drawn to the idea of animal magnetism, speculating that it might provide an explanation for same-sex attraction, but he soon abandoned that as cause rather than effect. By the end of 1862 he had worked out the basis of the intermediate- or third-sex theory that was to be at the core of his thinking for the rest of his life. Like Bentham before him, Ulrichs developed a new and neutral vocabulary. Like many of the nineteenth-century proponents of greater freedom and recognition for homosexuality, the classically educated Ulrichs drew on Greek mythology. His term for men attracted to other men was *Urning,* from the Uranian Aphrodite as described by Pausanias in Plato's *Symposium.* Ulrichs's central proposition was that the Urning constituted a distinct third sex, physically masculine but at least partially feminine in emotional makeup. This was biologically possible, he believed, because the physical and emotional development of the human embryo could follow different tracks. The sexual organs of the male and female embryo were virtually indistinguishable in the early stages of pregnancy, and the fully formed embryo of either sex retained the undeveloped characteristics of the other. The same, he argued, was true of emotional development, and in some cases, he concluded, while the body might develop in one direction, the emotional development of the individual might be in the opposite direction. The result was the Urning: a predominantly female personality in a predominantly male body (or, as he later acknowledged, vice versa).

Ulrichs first published his views under a pseudonym in two pamphlets in 1864. Critical and friendly commentary, further reading in the medical and scientific literature, and, above all, contact with a rapidly growing number of his own kind led him to revise and refine his theory in later pamphlets. Somehow he had to account for Urnings who were thoroughly masculine in their actions and appearance; for effeminate Urnings attracted to other Urnings and not, as he had originally supposed (and was himself), attracted only to thoroughly masculine men; and for Urnings who had a clear preference for either the active or the passive sexual role. Ultimately he elaborated a complex set of categories and subcategories ranging from masculine men to effeminate men; but the core of his theory remained unaltered.

The reaction, both positive and negative, was immediate. He had decided to publish largely in the hope of helping "my poor and . . . innocently persecuted comrades in destiny." The response from that quarter was gratifying. As the pamphlets filtered out through the subculture, letters of thanks and life stories poured back in, and his next three pamphlets, which followed within a year, were largely inspired by this moving evidence that he was not fighting for himself alone. The second group of pamphlets contained not only the first major refinements of his original theory but, in the first of them, a personal and confident declaration of his ultimate goal: "I am an insurgent. I rebel against the existing situation, because I hold it to be a condition of injustice. I fight for freedom from persecution and insults. I call for the recognition of Urning love. I call for it from public opinion and from the state." It was only in the last of these pamphlets that Ulrichs addressed the moral, in particular the biblical, objections to Urning love. Essentially he argued that since such love was inborn, it could not be deemed either unnatural or immoral. And as to the Bible, he denied that the authorities usually cited—Romans 1, Leviticus, and so on—were opposed to Urning love as such rather than to any perversions of heterosexual passion. In any case, like most nineteenth-century champions of same-sex love, Ulrichs was content to enlist a different set of authorities—the ancient Greeks and Romans—on his side.

All this was secondary, however, to establishing the authority of his own theory. If he could achieve that, then, he was certain, it would be possible to transform public attitudes towards the legal status of Urnings. For once it could be demonstrated that Urning love was inborn, then the persecution of Urnings would finally be seen as both futile and wrong. In these expectations Ulrichs was hopelessly naive, of course; the publication of his theories had precisely the opposite effect. He was expelled from the Free German Foundation immediately after he first aired his views to them. The police in Saxony seized copies of the first two pamphlets from his publisher, who was accused of obscenity and of promoting illegal acts. Though the cases were thrown out by the judge, and the pamphlets returned to the publisher, the authorities in neighboring Prussia acted more decisively, seizing and banning the pamphlets in Berlin and throughout Prussia. Ulrichs, who was as outspoken about politics as he was about sexual matters, was prosecuted for that as well. When Prussia defeated Austria in the Six Weeks War in 1866 and annexed Hannover, Ulrichs vehemently denounced the annexation, for which he was imprisoned briefly, his house searched and papers seized. Following his release from prison he left Prussian-dominated Hannover and settled in Bavaria, beyond the reach of the Prussian criminal code.

None of this deterred Ulrichs; quite the contrary in fact. Since Prussia now seemed destined to dominate Germany, the fight for the rights of Urnings was all the more important since in Prussia, unlike in much of the rest of Germany, sodomy was a crime. In 1865 he had proposed to the Congress of German Jurists a resolution in favor of decriminalization. The steering committee had refused even to put it on the agenda at that time but two years later agreed to let Ulrichs speak to the 1867 congress in Munich. Even before he reached the podium, however, the hall was in an uproar; he had barely gotten beyond protesting the earlier exclusion of his proposal and was only just beginning to touch on its substance when he was shouted down, with only a minority urging that he be allowed to continue. The chairman was unable to restore order, and Ulrichs finally left the platform, though he bravely remained very much in view during the rest of the congress. Shaken but still resolute, he published an account of his experiences at the congress and an updated version of his theory, in both cases under his own name, and sent copies of the latter to the judge and lawyers in a trial of four men for crimes against nature in the city of Bremen. Ulrichs took up the cause of many other defendants in sodomy cases, in Austria as well as in Germany, publicizing their plight and the often questionable tactics of the police and prosecution in his pamphlets and bombarding the authorities with petitions and legal briefs.

Ulrichs's most significant act of public intervention, however, came in 1869, when a commission charged with drafting a criminal code for the North German Confederation (of Prussia and its newly annexed territories) addressed the issue of the antisodomy laws. Ulrichs petitioned the commission "for the repeal of the legal punishment of nature," and he was far from alone in doing so. A number of jurists and a panel of doctors recommended decriminalization, seeing no reason to single out this particular form of indecency. Nor could the doctors, who, by the way, made a point of warning against the dangers of masturbation, see any reason to condemn homosexuality on medical grounds. As the by now considerably less naive Ulrichs feared might be the case, however, traditional morality—and the predominance of Prussia in the confederation—prevailed: the Prussian penalties were extended to the whole of north Germany on the grounds that "the people's consciousness of right judges these acts not only as vices, but as crimes, and the lawmakers must, in the face of this perception of right, justly hesitate to declare actions free of punishment, which in the public opinion happily are taken as worthy of punishment. To withdraw from the civil penal code the condemnation of such persons as have sinned in this way against the natural law, and to leave them to the moral law, would undoubtedly be blamed as a legislative mistake." The weight of public prejudice, in short, was allowed to determine law. This process was repeated following the incorporation of Bavaria and Wurttemberg into the German empire in 1871. Bavaria, which had had no antisodomy laws since the Napoleonic Wars, adopted the German imperial criminal code, including the antisodomy provisions of Paragraph 175, a number that was to become a symbol of a century of oppression and resistance of German homosexuals, through four regimes—imperial, Weimar, National Socialist, Federal Republican.

Following this final, devastating defeat of his hopes for Germany Ulrichs appears finally to have lost heart. He wrote little more on Urning love or on law reform; he no longer intervened in legal cases. Instead he turned to literary pursuits, and in 1880 he left Germany for Italy, where he lived out the last fifteen years of his life in obscure poverty. The only well-known person to seek him out during this time was John Addington Symonds, who had just completed his defense of sexual inversion and looked on Ulrichs as "one of the men I prized and respected most."

It is tempting to dismiss Ulrichs as a rather pathetic failure. He achieved none of his aims. His efforts to influence criminal law and judicial opinion ended in nothing. He left no disciples. In 1865 he drafted bylaws for an Urning organization that was never formed. In 1870 he published the first and only issue of a periodical for and about Urnings. His third-sex theory was occasionally cited in the medical literature, but usually only to be derided; like Whitman's, his ideas were overtaken and overwhelmed by the rise of medical interpretations of the origins of homosexuality. Even the designation he invented, *Urning,* was only briefly in vogue, replaced by *homosexual,* coined seven years later. Most of these failures, of course, were due to circumstances beyond Ulrichs's control, but his personality and tactics did not help. He was naive and had no sense of how to play politics; he was obsessive even in the face of overwhelming odds and prickly, overly concerned with his own status and credentials and quick to take offense.

On the other hand, perhaps these were qualities necessary in the pioneering proponent of an unpopular cause. A more politically astute, less driven, more easygoing man would probably never have done what Ulrichs did. Nor was it all a waste. He gave voice to many who had no voice, a sense of belonging to many who had felt totally isolated. As one of his many correspondents from all over Europe put it, "Thanks pours out to you from the hearts of those unfortunates, whom you have raised in their consciousness, whom you have rescued from the abyss of self-contempt. . . . The poor person who feels this fateful drive within himself, under the ban of world opinion until now, had to consider himself a trespasser of the laws of nature. Under this frightful consciousness all the energy of his soul was crippled. He has you to thank, if now, like awakening from a nightmare, he can breath again. You have given him back his self-respect." On a more practical level, through Symonds Ulrichs had tenuous links with the English pioneers of homosexual rights, while in his own country before the end of the century the periodical he had hoped to continue and the organization he had hoped to found had both come into existence, inspired in no small measure by his efforts.

The central figure in these achievements, but not an isolated figure like Ulrichs, was Magnus Hirschfeld. Like Ulrichs, he came from the professional middle class, though somewhat higher up the social scale—his father was a doctor—and less provincial in origin. Following in his father's footsteps, he trained as a doctor and quickly developed a successful practice. In 1896 he moved to Berlin and, in the same year, first took up the issue of homosexual rights, inspired by a patient who, on the eve of his marriage, shot himself because of his secret homosexuality. In a pamphlet entitled *Sappho and Socrates,* published under a pseudonym, he argued for the naturalness of homosexuality as simply one of the many possible permutations of human sexuality. His timing appeared to be excellent. The trial and imprisonment of Oscar Wilde had taken place the year before, shocking much of educated European opinion. Here, surely, was an opening for greater tolerance, and in the following year Hirschfeld, together with his publisher, founded the Scientific Humanitarian Committee (Wissenschaftlich Humanitares Komitee, or WHK) to press for greater understanding of homosexuality in general and for the repeal of Paragraph 175 in particular.

The first public act of the WHK was to get up a petition to the Reichstag urging repeal, but there the parallel with Ulrichs's efforts ends. Both in the nature of its backing and in its content Hirschfeld's petition displayed a political astuteness Ulrichs never developed. The petition did not come from an individual or small group, nor only or even primarily from avowed or suspected homosexuals; nor was it aimed at the general public. It was signed by and directed to the eminent and powerful: jurists, doctors, cultural leaders. And surprisingly quickly it won their support in large numbers; some two hundred signed the first petition, and thousands more the many subsequent ones. The tone was conciliatory, and the claims modest (though controversial in their underlying assumptions). It cited the growing body of expert opinion in favor of decriminalization and the absence of any ill effects in countries such as France, Italy, and the Netherlands, where there were no antisodomy laws. It stated as "virtually proven" what was in fact only a theory, that same-sex attraction was inborn and therefore neither unnatural nor blameworthy. It emphasized how many great men of the past had been "subject to feelings of this kind" and that the present law "condemns very many upright, valuable individuals, who already suffer enough at the hands of nature, to disgrace, despair, insanity or death." And finally it noted that by criminalizing homosexuality the law fostered criminal behavior, including both blackmail and male prostitution.

Because he regarded same-sex attraction as inborn and therefore not immoral, Hirschfeld, like Ulrichs, failed at first to address religious condemnation of homosexuality (a tactical error he soon corrected). Unlike Ulrichs, he rarely employed the language of individual rights or freedom of expression, especially if to do so might pose a direct challenge to generally accepted social norms. His aim was to persuade, not to defy, to win tolerance, if not acceptance, within society at large, not to assert a distinct Urning subculture. To these ends he consistently downplayed a number of inconvenient realities of that subculture in a vain search for respectability. The petition denied that either anal or oral intercourse was common among Urnings; when the WHK republished Ulrichs's writings it took care to omit references to specific sexual acts; and in his 1904 account of the Berlin subculture, based largely on personal investigation, Hirschfeld paid as little attention as possible to prostitution and promiscuity within the subculture, emphasizing instead the prevalence of long-term relationships and the convivial aspects of the homosexual bars and clubs. His careful distancing of himself and his work from the legacy left by Ulrichs implied no disrespect or fundamental disagreement. On the contrary, he revered his predecessor; indeed, in the spring of 1909, while on a visit to Italy, he made a pilgrimage to Ulrichs's last home and grave. Hirschfeld's concerns were tactical.

Hirschfeld took care not to become too closely identified with this one issue. Unlike Ulrichs, he never publicly avowed his own homosexuality, and however much of his time and energy were devoted to what was unquestionably his major cause and interest, he continued to pursue related interests in public health, alcoholism, and sexology in general. Indeed, he preferred, at least for public consumption, to place the WHK firmly (and safely) in the context of the wide variety of reform movements that were sweeping Germany toward the end of the nineteenth century. "It is no coincidence," he later recalled,

> that the Wandervogel movement and the first country boarding schools were founded during the same brief time span when . . . a number of sexual reform movements took shape. . . : the Society for Control of Venereal Disease. . . ; the movement for the protection of maternity, which took up the cause of unwed mothers and illegitimate children. . . ; the Scientific Humanitarian Committee. . . . And above all there appeared on the scene the pioneers, then called "radical," of women's emancipation. . . . It was also characteristic for the trend of the times that all of the strivings for natural modes of living and health increased their spread among the people during the final decades of the nineteenth century. Thus the first lodge against alcohol . . . was founded in Berlin in 1896. . . . I myself was actively involved in all these movements after settling in Berlin.

Above all, Hirschfeld was determined that the cause be pursued in an impeccably rigorous and scholarly manner. In his "quest for truth, justice and humanity," as the petition to the Reichstag put it, he preferred always to rely on "the current status of scientific knowledge" as his primary and most effective weapon. He adopted some of Ulrichs's terminology, particularly the designation *Urning*, and also his fundamental assumption that homosexuality was inborn, a function of embryonic development. However, he rejected the notion of a female personality in a male body and did not envision the individual as occupying a place somewhere on a male-to-female continuum. Gender identity, Hirschfeld believed, was the sum of a number of traits, physical and emotional, and any one of these might tend more toward the male or toward the female in any single individual; it was the mixture of contrary traits that produced the intermediate sex. The cause, he ultimately concluded, was hormonal, a function of differing glandular development and activity. To the extent that homosexuality could therefore be seen as the result of hormonal imbalance or deficiency, Hirschfeld was open to the proposition that it might be due to a congenital defect that, in turn, might be susceptible to medical treatment or cure. This was totally at variance with Ulrichs's view of the all but immutable nature of same-sex attraction.

However great the changes in his views on the origins and character of homosexuality, and however long he took to arrive at his fixed and final conclusions, Hirschfeld's methodology and public aims remained constant. When the WHK submitted its first petition in 1897, Hirschfeld was granted an interview at the Ministry of Justice, where he was advised that "the government's hands are tied until the public knows that your demands are a matter of ethics and not just some sexual or scientific whim. You must educate the public so that it will understand what's involved if the government does away with this paragraph [Paragraph 175]." Temperamentally predisposed to follow such a course in any case, Hirschfeld never abandoned it, despite many later frustrations and considerable pressure from colleagues and rivals. He cultivated dialogue and potential allies in all branches of the medical profession and in the emerging fields of psychology and sexology; both Richard von Krafft-Ebing and Sigmund Freud were among his correspondents and supporters of his efforts to repeal Paragraph 175. Hirschfeld lectured widely, and the WHK sponsored conferences and debates and distributed letters and copies of its petition to priests and ministers, to newspapers, to local government officials, judges, and prosecutors, as well as to members of the Reichstag and the higher civil service.

For nearly a quarter-century, beginning in 1899, the WHK published a *Yearbook of Sexual Intermediaries,* for which Hirschfeld invited contributions from critics as well as supporters. The yearbook published material in every relevant field—history, anthropology, law, medicine, and so forth—as well as reviewing works of fiction and nonfiction and reporting on the activities of the committee and the progress of its petition. Seeking to allay the fears and misapprehensions of the general public, in 1901 the WHK published and distributed a pamphlet entitled *What Should the People Know about the Third Sex?* Two years later the committee sent out questionnaires to groups of students and factory workers in the hope of developing reliable statistics on the frequency and character of homosexuality in the general population (as a result Hirschfeld estimated that 2.2% of the male population was homosexual, a far higher percentage than Ulrichs had dared suggest). Hirschfeld's magnum opus, *Homosexuality in Men and Women,* published in 1914, was based on thousands of case studies collected over the previous two decades from his own practice and information supplied by others, both at home and abroad. A teacher and advocate as much as, if not more than, a clinician, Hirschfeld was always conscious of the audience he hoped to influence and of the limitations within which he had to operate if he ever hoped to reach it. Nonetheless, while in this he was far more realistic than Ulrichs, in at least one respect he was no less naive. His motto was "Through Knowledge to Justice," and throughout his long career, almost to the eve of the Nazi era, he stubbornly held to the belief that he could, and would, triumph through reason and persuasion.

Despite or even because of his tone and approach Hirschfeld made enemies. He maintained a cordial professional relationship with Krafft-Ebing until the latter's death in 1902 but was denounced by many in the medical fraternity either because they disagreed with his theories or because they believed he was using—or misusing—science in the service of self-promotion, propaganda, and a political agenda. Hirschfeld ultimately fell out with Freud, who earlier had supported him, and Albert Moll, now virtually forgotten but regarded at the time as an expert on sexual deviance, became one of his most inveterate detractors. His insistence on discussing objectively and dispassionately what many on the right regarded as unmentionable and decadent aroused fear and hostility. Some of the students (but none of the workers) who received his questionnaire sued him for promoting obscenity—and won. He was savagely attacked in the Reichstag, particularly by members of the Catholic Center Party, and his agitation in favor of the repeal of Paragraph 175 was effectively countered by a social purity movement, centered in the Protestant churches, which, if anything, sought stricter enforcement of the laws against homosexuality and ultimately even their extension to include lesbians. In 1898 the national leadership of the purity movement answered Hirschfeld's petition with one of its own urging, "in the interests of the welfare of the German people, in the name of religion, morality and order," that Paragraph 175 not be weakened or repealed.

On the other hand, a substantial wing of the homophile movement regarded Hirschfeld's theories and tactics as woefully inadequate, offensive, and even dangerous. Inadequate in that Hirschfeld's rationalistic and scientific approach ignored and devalued the rich heritage of literary and artistic celebrations of love between men. Offensive to many in the movement who saw themselves as thoroughly masculine, not as partially feminine members of some intermediate or third sex. Dangerous because even in the hands of a homosexual advocate of freeing homosexuals from persecution, the theory that the Urning was the product of a distinct and different path of embryonic development opened the way to the conclusion that the Urning was the product of a genetic defect, nothing more nor less than a biological freak, able perhaps to arouse sympathy but not respect. These champions of what they preferred to call "chivalric love" or simply "love of friends" specifically rejected the terminology Hirschfeld employed—*Urning, homosexual*—as well as his methods, seeking instead their origins and justification not in modern science and medicine but in history and cultural tradition.

The leader of this increasingly separate movement within a movement was the political anarchist Adolph Brand, once a teacher, later the owner of a bookshop, and in 1896 (the year Hirschfeld published *Sappho and Socrates*) the founder of *Der Eigene,* the first long-lived homosexual magazine in the world. The magazine, like Brand himself, led an unstable existence. Begun primarily as a radical organ tinged with anarchism, it became a "journal of male culture" in 1898. Short of money, Brand ceased publication about the turn of the century, but *Der Eigene* reappeared in 1903 as a "journal for male culture, art and literature." When Brand was imprisoned for reproducing pictures of nude boys, publication ceased again, but it resumed briefly in 1906, only to be stopped until after World War I as a result of Brand's intervention in a major homosexual scandal that led to his imprisonment for the second time in less than a decade.

Initially an ally of Hirschfeld's and an active participant in the work of the WHK, by the end of the century Brand—and *Der Eigene*—had become among his most savage critics. In 1902 Brand founded a new homophile organization, the Gemeinschaft der Eigenen (variously translated as "Community of the Special" or "Community of the Other"), less as a rival to the WHK than as an alternative based on different assumptions about the nature and significance of love between men. Among the most active members of the Gemeinschaft were Wilhelm Jansen, a prominent figure in the German youth movement, Paul Brandt, a classical scholar who wrote a study of sexual morals in ancient Greece, Edwin Bab, who often wrote for *Der Eigene* and was one of the few doctors who supported Brand against Hirschfeld, and Elisar von Kupffer, also a frequent contributor to *Der Eigene* and the compiler of an anthology of homoerotic literature stretching back from the era of passionate friendships in eighteenth-century Germany through the Renaissance to ancient Greece and Rome. Along with Brand, however, the most important and influential member of the Gemeinschaft was Benedict Friedländer.

The chief theoretician of the Gemeinschaft, Friedländer was also an early member of Hirschfeld's WHK, but the differences between them were fundamental and ultimately proved unbridgeable. Whereas Hirschfeld was a rational liberal, deeply committed to scientific inquiry and education as the surest route to the understanding and the freedom of Urnings as a distinct category of beings, Friedländer might most accurately be described as a libertarian conservative, profoundly suspicious of the aims and methods Hirschfeld set such store by. Thus, Hirschfeld sought to ally his movement with a variety of other reform movements, including especially the feminists, and welcomed a wide range of supporters, including women, into the WHK. Friedländer and Brand, on the other hand, were elitists and deliberately kept the Gemeinschaft small and exclusively male; though both were married, they saw women as occupying an important but separate, clearly subordinate, largely private role in society as wives and mothers. Indeed, if Germany was to remain a strong and vital nation, it must, Friedländer believed, avoid the feminization of society already overtaking countries such as the United States, reawaken the waning tradition of passionate friendships between men that had been central to the national revival at the beginning of the nineteenth century, and adopt as a model for the training of young men the Greek ideal of highly eroticized relationships between adult males and youths. The members of the Gemeinschaft and contributors to *Der Eigene* were always a bit ambivalent, even somewhat prudish, concerning the role of sex in such relationships. They disdained the sex-centered Urning subcultures of the modern urban world, as well as the effeminate homosexuals Hirschfeld studied, as perversions of the ideal of manly affection, preferring to emphasize "the more spiritualized" aspects of love between men, between youths, and between the generations. However, Friedländer did acknowledge that in his ideal society "same sex intercourse of men [would be] tolerated" as an expression of the ideal.

Friedländer's "esteem for the beauty of youths" and his celebration of a male-dominated society infused with eroticism had nothing to do with Hirschfeld's painstaking research into embryonic development, his elaborate classification of different sexual types, his laborious collecting of survey data, and the dissemination of his own and other authorities' views in his yearbook and, ultimately, on the eve of World War I, in his massive *Homosexuality of Men and Women*. Indeed the two approaches were so antithetical that a break was inevitable. It came in 1906, when Friedländer seceded from the WHK, justifying his actions in a long, somewhat rambling memorandum in which he outlined his fundamental disagreements with Hirschfeld and urged others to join him. The repeal of Paragraph 175 was not, and should not be, the primary object of the movement, he argued; indeed repeal was almost irrelevant to its true purpose, which was to liberate the inclination, natural to many, perhaps most, men, to love and bond with one another, an inclination given free rein in the ancient world (and in many non-Western cultures) but suppressed in feminized Christian nations.

The medical researchers had, Friedländer admitted, performed one valuable service by removing the taboo on public discussion of same-sex love. But that was the end of their contribution, since the predominance of medical men in that discussion, their primary concern with the sexual dimension of love between men, and their commitment to the intermediate-sex theory predisposed the public to see same-sex love as a pathological condition confined to a small, abnormal minority rather than as a quality, potential in most men, whose sexual expression was only one component, and that not the most important component. So long, therefore, as Hirschfeld and his ilk dominated the movement for homosexual rights, Friedländer concluded, they would never achieve genuine freedom, since "with sicknesses one can have pity, of course, and act 'humanely' toward the sick, and even seek to 'cure' them; the individual rights of those alleged to be physically inferior will never be recognized." He believed that it was critical to approach the question "from the standpoint of natural rights as one of personal freedom," indeed as only one aspect of "the whole modern sexual freedom movement . . . [which] proceeds, consciously or unconsciously, from a protest against the ascetic morality of the

Middle Ages." Even on practical as well as philosophical grounds Friedländer believed that his approach was more likely than Hirschfeld's to result in greater freedom for same-sex love, as well as less frought with dangers in the pursuit of that goal: "Since we renounce in principle making propaganda for homosexual activity, viewing sexual matters rather as a private affair, and fight against Paragraph 175 on purely juridical grounds, and since that which we positively advocate is nothing other than male friendships and men's unions— our propaganda will be strictly legal and much safer from police intervention than that of Hirschfeld, which on the basis of its medical theory is forced to go into all kinds of sexual details openly in public."

This was not merely a theoretical disagreement. By the middle of the first decade of the twentieth century Hirschfeld's strategy, which had once appeared so promising, had reached a dead end. Hirschfeld could rightly claim that "one thing has been achieved, and it is not the least important thing. The period of passing the matter over in silence and disregarding it is past, for good. We now find ourselves in the midst of a period of discussion." He asserted that "the homosexual question has become a genuine question" but drew from that the overly optimistic conclusion that it had therefore become a question "which will continue to be discussed until it has been resolved in a satisfactory way." In fact, though the WHK was able to garner an ever greater number of distinguished signatories for its petition, there was only one major debate in the Reichstag on the reform of Paragraph 175, in 1905, and that ended in an overwhelming defeat for the reformers. The only significant support for a change in the law came from the Social Democrats, but their leader, August Bebel, had already become impatient with the gradualist tactics of the WHK and as early as 1902 had suggested the advisability of something more dramatic, such as giving wide publicity to prosecutions of homosexuals as a means of demonstrating the cruelty and inequity of the law. After the devastating defeat of 1905 even the most moderate supporters of reform realized that they had to rethink their methods. Brand, ever the proponent of radical courses, advocated revealing the homosexuality of prominent opponents and actually "outed" a leader of the Catholic Center Party. The WHK had earlier considered and rejected taking this "path over corpses," as the outing strategy was graphically called, but did discuss the possibility of a massive coming out by prominent Urnings all over Germany, who would turn themselves in to the police and demand that they be prosecuted. This proved impractical, of course, so the WHK, somewhat chastened, returned to its familiar strategy of recruiting prominent supporters and educating the general public.

Friedländer's belief in the efficacy of an alternative strategy was never properly tested. He died in 1908, before he could organize the challenge to the WHK that he had envisaged when he broke with Hirschfeld. The doctor and his committee were thereby left in command of the field, able to define the terms in which the issue of homosexuality was discussed and agitated within the subculture in early-twentieth-century Germany—dissented from, to be sure, but never seriously challenged. Nonetheless, *Der Eigene,* the Gemeinschaft, and above all Benedict Friedländer had defined an alternative if at times bizarre explanation and justification for same-sex love and sexual freedom. In Germany and elsewhere the discussion of what it meant to be homosexual and the struggle for homosexual rights was to be framed by these two conflicting traditions for much of the remainder of the twentieth century.

## Chapter 8

**Pioneers: England**

For all the differences between the pioneering prophets of the love between men in the United States and Germany—Whitman the visionary poet and Ulrichs the scholarly lawyer and pedant—they had important characteristics in common. Both belonged to the first generation of modern defenders and definers of homosexuality. Whitman was born in 1819, Ulrichs in 1825, and they came of age in the 1840s, a time of liberal ferment in both countries. The United States was a new and expanding nation that had yet to experience the tragedy of civil war; Germany was not yet a single nation but seemed destined soon to achieve unity through the will of the people rather than, as was to be the case, through blood and iron. Both Whitman's ebullient faith in a democratic society based on comradeship and Ulrichs's naive belief that prejudice and error could be righted by appeals to reason were born of the heady optimism of the 1840s, before the violent and sobering realities of later decades set in.

The men who laid the groundwork for the modern homophile movement in England, John Addington Symonds and Edward Carpenter, emerged in very different circumstances. Born in the 1840s, they came of age in the 1860s, when Whitman and Ulrichs were at their most active and when Germany and the United States were undergoing profound internal crises. Moreover, while Germany and the United States were both in the early stages of building modern nation-states, England was not only one of the oldest nation-states but already the most urbanized and most industrialized country in the world. Thus Whitman and Ulrichs understandably saw themselves as pioneers, not only because they were breaking new ground but also because they hoped to influence and shape the emergence of new or renewed societies. Symonds and Carpenter, on the other hand, saw themselves as almost the opposite, as critics of an established society, as confined within rigid norms that needed to be broken down. Whitman and Ulrichs ultimately arrived at not dissimilar views of their own and their countries' condition. But that was a product of disillusionment; Symonds and Carpenter began more or less where Whitman and Ulrichs ended up.

The Englishmen's acute consciousness of being sexual outsiders was largely responsible for this sense of frustration, of course, but not entirely. The 1860s was a pivotal decade in England, a time when the Victorian consensus established by their parents and grandparents came to seem too narrow and stifling to the generation of Symonds and Carpenter. However necessary the disciplines imposed on early Victorian society may have been during the transition from a predominantly rural, agricultural society to an urban, industrial one, that was no longer true by the mid-sixties. England had made that transition, and made it peacefully, avoiding the revolutions that had swept the Continent. England was a prosperous, relatively stable country with at least the rudiments of the institutions necessary to manage a complex modern society. It could afford to both broaden the base and loosen the restraints of that society. And it did. Urban working men were given the vote in 1867, and a more limited local franchise was gradually extended to women, who also increasingly demanded and won greater employment and educational opportunities and a more nearly equal status in law and marriage. From the issues of gender equality in and out of marriage it was but a short step to the discussion of issues of sexuality and of sexual fulfillment as something good in itself, quite apart from procreation. The doctrine of free love, scarcely mentioned since the late eighteenth century, was broached again, as were issues such as family planning and contraception. The Darwinian revolution and the questioning of revealed religion served to reinforce and validate what the sons and daughters of the mid-Victorians were moving toward in any case, the discussion of such matters apart from traditional morality, as practical questions of individual rights, scientific inquiry, and social policy.

Much in this climate of intellectual ferment spoke directly to Symonds's and Carpenter's concerns arising out of the nature of their sexuality. Unwilling and ultimately unable to live according to the sexual mores of Victorian society, both were intent on breaking out, on finding a means, as Symonds put it, of "self effectuation." They took very different routes toward that goal, however. Carpenter dropped out; indeed, much of his life can be read as a voyage away from the stultifying respectability in which he had been brought up. Symonds, on the other hand, was a successful, outwardly respectable man of letters, very much part of the cultural establishment, but for that very reason acutely conscious of the conflict between his inner and his outer self and determined somehow to resolve that conflict. Both were securely middle-class in background, Carpenter the son of a naval officer, Symonds the son of a doctor; both were well educated, Carpenter had been at Cambridge, Symonds at Oxford; and both took fellowships at their respective universities after receiving their degrees.

Thereafter their paths diverged. Carpenter abandoned his fellowship to devote himself to adult education in working-class communities in the industrial north of England. He also experimented with a variety of pursuits at or beyond the fringe of Victorian respectability: vegetarianism, manual labor, communal living, and Eastern mysticism. Eventually, in the early 1880s, he used a modest inheritance to buy some land at Millthorpe in Derbyshire, which he worked as a market garden; he became an ardent advocate of communitarian or cooperative (as opposed to state) socialism; and he published a long poem, *Towards Democracy,* a celebration of life, humanity, and freedom in somewhat Whitmanesque terms. Symonds's evolution could hardly have been more different. He too abandoned his fellowship, but he was forced to do so when a fellow student with whom he had become infatuated revealed some letters and poems from Symonds in a fit of pique. After that Symonds did some schoolteaching while gradually building a career as a successful essayist and amateur literary scholar and historian. Independently wealthy, he traveled extensively and lived much of the rest of his life abroad, in Switzerland and Italy, in large part because of poor health.

Symonds's and Carpenter's experiences of and attitudes toward their own sexuality were equally different, except in that both traveled long and difficult paths to self-acceptance and then set out to win tolerance and ultimately even social acceptance for homosexuality. What is more, both began the voyage of intellectual and sexual self-discovery by reading Whitman. Symonds discovered him in 1865, at the age of twenty-five, Carpenter in 1868, at twenty-four, and both were immediately all but transformed by the experience. Symonds first wrote to Whitman in 1871, enclosing one of his own poems; Carpenter wrote him in 1874 and crossed the Atlantic primarily to visit him three years later. Whitman may have liberated their thinking, as both readily acknowledged, but their actions were more problematical. Carpenter had had little or no sexual experience as a boy and seems to have repressed his natural attraction toward other men in early adulthood as well. Not until he stripped his life down to basics did he find "a few special friends. . . . Before that happened," "I was once or twice on the brink of despair and madness with repressed passion and torment." Finally, at the age of forty-five, on a railway journey in the winter of 1889–90, he met twenty-year-old George Merrill, the son of an engine driver, who was ultimately to become his sole companion for the rest of his life.

Symonds had an altogether more convoluted sexual history. He experienced a number of schoolboy crushes in his youth and at university, but they found only tentative physical expression (it was his writings, not his actions, that got him in trouble at Oxford). Indeed he was a bit of a prig in sexual matters. Passionate but pure friendships were one thing—he was thrilled by the discovery of the appropriate passages in Plato while at Harrow—but the rude and crude sexual experimentation of his schoolmates was another matter entirely. He was horrified by it. When another boy confided to Symonds that he was having an affair with the headmaster, Dr. Charles Vaughan, Symonds eventually told his father, who threatened a scandal if Vaughan did not resign immediately, which he did. After his own scandal at Oxford the younger Symonds desperately sought to remake his life and half forced, half persuaded himself into marriage, not as a cover for his true sexuality, but as an escape from it. All this fed into and fed on a simultaneous crisis in religious belief, and his health, never good, suffered badly, culminating in a nervous breakdown at the age of twenty-eight.

From this crisis, however, dated the beginnings of a long process of coming to terms with his sexual nature. He fell in love with a seventeen-year-old boy and took a teaching job at the boy's school simply in order to be near him. He confessed all to his wife, Catherine, and suggested to her a novel solution to the growing tensions in their marriage: if she would agree to a celibate marriage and let him seek sexual satisfaction "within the limits of good sense and taste" elsewhere, he would in every other respect be an exemplary husband and father. Remarkably, she agreed, and though that did not prevent similar crises later in their marriage, it did remove the element of deception—and self-deception. Yet, while Symonds no longer needed to hide his true nature, at least within his marriage, he—and surely Catherine—continued to be troubled and perplexed by it: "To have the imaginative and sensuous side of passion disconnected in one's nature from the rational enduring solid part of love, and never to feel the former in its truest sense for women, but only for dreams or the incarnations of dreams in male beings, selected for the moment, not thoroughly respected or believed in; is this common?" he asked himself.

It was another two years, and then only after the death of his father in 1871, before he began the painful process of integrating his literary career with his private passions by initiating his correspondence with Whitman and taking the first tentative steps toward writing a defense of ancient Greek pederasty. (In yet another parallel between Symonds and Carpenter, the death of the latter's father not only provided him with the means to purchase Millthorpe but appears to have liberated him in other respects as well, for it was soon followed by the first public declaration of his commitment to socialism and by the publication of *Towards Democracy*.) Symonds's sexual coming out was no less tentative. Not until he was thirty-six did he have the first of his many liaisons with young working-class men, culminating in a refreshingly uncomplicated affair with a Swiss sledge driver, Christian Buol, and a long and increasingly open relationship with a dashing Venetian gondolier, Angelo Fusato, who often accompanied Symonds on his travels, even to England, and was with him at his death in Rome in 1893.

That degree of openness was long in coming, however, and Symonds's early involvement in the homosexual subculture of London, while finally resolving one inner conflict, only increased his awareness of the contradiction between his inner and his outer self. He illustrated the nature of that tension perfectly in his memoirs, in an account of one of the pivotal experiences of his adult life, his first visit to a male brothel, while in London to deliver a series of lectures on Florence and the Medici. There he met a "brawny young soldier," with whom he arranged a private assignation that opened up a world of unforeseen possibilities: "That the physical appetite of one male for another may be made the foundation for a solid friendship, . . . that . . . even in that lawless godless place, permanent human relations—affections, reciprocal toleration, decencies of conduct, asking and yielding, concession and abstention—find their natural sphere: perhaps more than in the sexual relations consecrated by middle class matrimony. . . . From him I learned that natural male beings in the world at large were capable of corresponding to my appreciation of them. A dangerous lesson, perhaps." Meanwhile he was obliged to give his lectures: "Very dull lectures they were, for my soul was not in them; my soul throbbed for my soldier; and I had composed the lectures specially for what I most abhor, an audience of cultivated people. This is a paradoxical confession. I am nothing if not cultivated. . . . But in my heart of hearts I do not believe in culture except as an adjunct to life. . . . Passion, nerve and sinew, eating and drinking, the stomach and the bowels, sex, action, even money-getting—the coarsest forms of activity—come, in my reckoning before culture."

Determined to resolve these contradictions, to integrate his private and his public self, Symonds turned to writing on the subject of homosexuality. (Actually he rarely used the term *homosexual* or *homosexuality,* coinages he disliked, preferring Whitman's *comradeship,* the English variant of Ulrichs's *Urning, Uranian,* or either *unisexual love* or *sexual inversion.*) His first essay, *A Problem in Greek Ethics,* had been written some years before, in 1873, after his initial breakthrough. Essentially it was a description and defense of sexual inversion in ancient Greece, designed to demonstrate that it was natural, integrated into the social fabric, compatible with heterosexual marriage and the family, and based on love, not lust. Significantly, however, he did not publish it until a decade later, and then only in a private edition of ten copies for circulation among friends. Other references to the subject in his scholarship and criticism were cagily worded. At the end of the 1880s, however, he decided that he had to go further, and in 1889 he began two groundbreaking works. The first, a frank autobiography tracing his personal development and self-acceptance, was suppressed by his executors until the 1970s and only published in 1984. The second, *A Problem in Modern Ethics,* designed as a companion to his earlier essay, was a critical survey of contemporary views of homosexuality, favorable and unfavorable, in the medical and psychological fields and in imaginative literature, closing, inevitably, with Whitman. It was shortly after completing this essay that Symonds wrote his penultimate letter to Whitman, in which he pressed the poet unsuccessfully to reveal the hidden meanings of the Calamus poems. Not that Symonds himself was much more forthcoming; he clearly had no intention of exposing the essay or himself to public view. "If I were to publish it now," he told one of his daughters, "it would create a great sensation. Society would ring with it. But the time is not ripe for the launching of 'A Problem in Modern Ethics' on the world. The Ms lies on my table for retouches, & then will go to slumber in a box of precious writings, my best work, my least presentable, until its Day of Doom." Like his earlier essay, this too was published in a limited edition (of fifty copies) to be circulated among friends.

By this time, even so, Symonds felt driven to speak to a wider audience. He was frustrated and isolated by his own and others' inability to communicate directly and honestly about as fundamental an aspect of human nature as sexuality. What is more, he was encouraged by the response from the gradually widening circle of those who had seen the earlier essay and applauded his determination to pursue the subject. Perhaps the most touching reaction came from the literary critic and biographer Edmund Gosse. He and Symonds had been friends for fifteen years, but Gosse had always sidestepped the issue of his own sexuality. Now he came out to Symonds:

> I know of all you speak of—the solitude, the rebellion, the despair. Yet I have been happy, too; I hope you also have been happy,—that all with you has not been disappointment & the revulsion of hope? Either way, I entirely deeply sympathize with you. Years ago I wanted to write to you about all this, and withdrew through cowardice. I have had a very fortunate life, but there has been this obstinate twist in it! I have reached a quieter time—some beginnings of that Sophoclean period when the wild beast dies. He is not dead, but tamer; I understand him & the trick of his claws.

Such a letter almost demanded that Symonds persevere, but he was acutely conscious of his limitations as an authority and public spokesman. As a literary critic and historian, and himself a sexual invert (who was, however, determined to maintain his cover), he could easily be dismissed as a biased amateur. Clearly he needed a qualified and reputable ally, and in 1892 he found one in Havelock Ellis, England's first and leading sexologist.

Painfully shy and both physically and culturally isolated (in provincial Australia) for much of his adolescence, Ellis was drawn to the study of sex in large part as a way of compensating for his lack of youthful sexual knowledge and experience. But though socially and sexually a late developer, he was intellectually precocious. Before the age of thirty he had finished his medical training, established himself as a regular contributor of cultural criticism to major journals, and won acceptance in the most avant-garde circles of London intellectual life. His first important book, *The New Spirit*, published in 1890, a ringing endorsement of individual freedom, scientific inquiry, and rational social planning, placed him almost overnight in the forefront of the younger generation of left-wing intellectuals. That he singled out Whitman as one of the most important prophets of this emerging new spirit drew an enthusiastic response from Symonds, who, however, remained characteristically cautious concerning the meaning of comradeship in Whitman's poetry, a question he raised ostensibly only as a topic of mutual scholarly interest. But at least he had been able to broach the subject with Ellis; the basis for further discussion and, ultimately, collaboration had been laid.

At the same time that he was so quickly and successfully establishing his place and reputation in London's intellectual life, Ellis became involved in a couple of intense but decidedly odd relationships with women. The first, which ended in mutual frustration, sexual and otherwise, was with a South African novelist whose restless nature was the opposite of his relatively passive temperament. The second was a companionate, almost passionless marriage, at the age of thirty-two, to an ardent feminist whose sexual attraction to other women Ellis had intimations of even before the wedding and explicit knowledge of thereafter. It was largely because of this that his general interest in the study of sex first found concrete expression in a study of homosexuality.

Ellis and Symonds had corresponded on literary topics even before the publication of *The New Spirit,* and Ellis had met Carpenter, as he was to meet his own wife, at a meeting of the Fellowship of the New Life, one of the myriad idealistic social reform groups that sprang up in late Victorian England. Indeed Ellis later recalled that he was drawn to the subject of homosexuality not only by his wife's lesbianism but by his knowledge of the homosexuality of Carpenter and some of his other friends. In the summer of 1891, some months before his marriage, Ellis, having heard of Symonds's essays, wrote to him in Switzerland expressing the hope that they might have "the opportunity of talking over this question . . . [which] is one that constantly forces itself on one's attention." Symonds replied warmly, suggesting that the subject "ought to be scientifically, historically, impartially investigated." Ellis warned, and Symonds acknowledged, that their views might differ in important ways, but their interests and concerns were converging, and less than a year later, in June 1892, Symonds approached Ellis (through mutual friends) with the suggestion that they collaborate on a study.

A few months later, after a further exchange of letters, Ellis agreed, though with as much hesitancy as enthusiasm. His caution was justified; the collaboration was not an easy one. Symonds was pursuing a personal crusade. He was out to demonstrate that the medical literature was wrong and that homosexuality was not only inborn but a natural, nonpathological variant. Ellis, on the other hand, as a doctor and a heterosexual, was more impressed with the medical authorities, had no compelling personal agenda apart from intense curiosity about those close to him, and was concerned to maintain both his objectivity and his reputation. Even so, they were able to work out an uneasy division of labor that allowed their views and interests to coexist. Ellis wrote the scientific critique, making use of the material from Symonds's essay on modern ethics, while Symonds contributed his Greek essay. They collaborated in collecting case histories.

At this point Carpenter was brought into the project. Though Ellis had met Carpenter some years earlier, Symonds had only known him since early 1892, when they were introduced, indirectly but appropriately, through Walt Whitman. When Whitman was suffering his final illness, his soon-to-be executor wrote Carpenter asking him to pass on the news to others, including Symonds. From this developed a correspondence largely concerning Symonds's project with Ellis. However, because Symonds lived abroad much of the year, most of his role had to be conducted by mail. Indeed, he met Carpenter only once, and he never met Ellis. Before he could do so, and before the project was finished, Symonds, always in poor health, died at the age of fifty-three. Carpenter stepped in to help, but not very fast or very far. He contributed a case history and recruited others to do likewise. But Ellis was relieved to be free of a collaborator, especially one like Symonds—and possibly Carpenter, who did or might differ with him on the origins and medical aspects of homosexuality. Besides, Carpenter was striking out on his own.

Partly inspired by the Symonds-Ellis project, Carpenter produced four pamphlets on sexual and gender issues during 1894–95. The first was on the place of sexual love in a free society, the second on the role of women, the third on marriage, and the fourth on what he called "homogenic love" (a term he preferred to *homosexual* since it derived entirely from Greek roots, not a mix of Latin and Greek). Carpenter adopted Ulrichs's concept of an intermediate sex and the designation *Uranian,* though he rejected the notion of a woman's soul in a man's body, positing instead that everyone was a mix of masculine and feminine characteristics. Those who were at one extreme or the other—the effeminate man and the masculine woman—might, he admitted, conform to popular stereotypes in physical characteristics as well as behavior, but most Uranians, he argued, fell somewhere in between and were more or less indistinguishable from the general population. They were, in short, not as rare as people commonly believed, nor were they pathological or especially promiscuous. (Indeed, aware of the prejudices of a general audience, Carpenter insisted on the predominance as well as the superiority of the emotional over the physical in same-sex love.) He acknowledged that Uranians might be unusually prone to nervous maladies, but he guessed that that was due to their having to live a double life in a potentially hostile society.

Carpenter's central contention, however, was that Uranians were not made but born: "Sexual inversion . . . is in a vast number of cases quite instinctive, mentally and physically, and therefore twined in the very roots of individual life and practically ineradicable." And from this fact of nature, "that they exist, and have always existed," he drew his most challenging, his most original conclusion: "there is a strong probability that they have their place and purpose." Inevitably Carpenter reached back to the ancients and out to other cultures to support this contention, but it was, of course, the need to demonstrate the contribution the Uranians' "great genius for attachment" could make to modern society that most concerned him. Not only would homogenic attachments not add to the problem of overpopulation, he argued, but because they were outside the traditional institutions of home and family, they could contribute to a wider sense of social responsibility, to comradeship across class lines, and thereby to the democratization of society, to charitable work and the healing arts, to the peaceful resolution of social and political conflict, and above all to the education and socialization of the young. In the hero worship of a young boy or girl for another a few years older and in the protective response this evoked, in the loving care good teachers displayed toward their pupils and in the devotion returned, Carpenter believed, lay the foundation for a stable and humane social structure. He recognized that such natural sentiments could be abused and sullied, but that, he was certain, was due primarily to such relationships' being driven underground by a public ignorant of the great tradition and noble purposes of homogenic love.

With both Carpenter's *Homogenic Love* and Ellis's *Sexual Inversion* finished by early 1895 (a year before Hirschfeld's *Sappho and Socrates* in Germany), it seemed that the virtual absence of any serious discussion of homosexuality in England was about to end. But it was not to be. Both authors encountered insurmountable problems with potential publishers, who were suddenly fearful of being associated with such controversial works. Homosexuality was, it is true, one of the hot topics of the year in England, but not because of anything achieved by Ellis or Carpenter. Eighteen ninety-five was the year of the trial and imprisonment of Oscar Wilde.

# Chapter 9    Wilde

If Walt Whitman was the first iconic figure, the first saint, in the modern gay pantheon, Oscar Wilde—certainly no saint—was the first martyr. The trials and imprisonment of Wilde can be read as a purely personal tragedy, the product of the conjunction of the particular players involved, and the law under which he was prosecuted appears at first sight to have made it to the statute book almost by chance. But martyrs rarely come out of nowhere, and martyrdoms do not take place in a vacuum. Seen in context the persecution of Oscar Wilde has about it an air of inevitability. It was the obverse of—indeed the ultimate example of the reaction to—that opening up of Victorian England that produced Symonds and Carpenter, among so many others. The savagery of that reaction is in itself the best evidence of how deeply divided English society had become during the final quarter of the nineteenth century. Those who feared the breakdown of moral and social disciplines clung fiercely to traditional standards of behavior and did so with ever greater rigidity precisely because once generally accepted norms were being questioned and openly flouted.

Perhaps inevitably, sexuality, especially deviant sexuality, became one of the actual and symbolic battlegrounds of that cultural conflict, but although homosexuality ultimately emerged as a central issue, it was not so at first. As had happened both a century and two centuries before, homosexuality became caught up in a movement that had both wider, long-term causes and other, immediate ones, in this instance prostitution. In the 1860s the British government passed a series of Contagious Diseases Acts, which allowed the authorities in military garrison towns the power to order any woman suspected of being a prostitute to be tested for venereal disease. To the proponents of these acts they were commonsense public-health measures designed to protect the armed forces. To their opponents they were an outrage. A movement for their repeal sprang up almost immediately, led by one of the most formidable of the first generation of modern British feminists, Josephine Butler, who put together an extraordinary coalition comprising not only traditional moralists, who argued that state regulation of prostitution in effect condoned it, but also feminists, who saw prostitutes not as criminals but as victims of the masculine-determined double standard; social reformers, who saw them as victims of urban poverty; and civil libertarians, who feared arbitrary police power.

In the end this coalition proved more than sufficient to win the repeal of the acts, and, along the way, in 1873, Butler presided over the formation of an even more influential and enduring movement, the Social Purity Alliance. By the time the Contagious Diseases Acts were repealed, in 1886, there were hundreds of branches of the alliance as well as other similar societies, their members pledged to purity in word and deed. At the end of the 1870s revelations that English girls were being lured, tricked, or abducted into prostitution on the Continent led Butler to take up this even more explosive issue, and the white slave trade, as the newly emerging sensational press delighted in calling it, quickly became the focus of public hysteria out of all proportion to the reality of the problem.

It is tempting to dismiss the purity movement as only harmful or merely absurd. However, it did substantial good in raising public awareness of the sexual double standard and of the plight of poor women and, above all, in getting the age of consent raised. Moreover, Butler herself was no narrow-minded busybody. Far from being authoritarian, she believed that people should be led to act morally and responsibly through education and conviction. Perhaps inevitably, however, the coercionists took over, much as they had in the late eighteenth century, on the familiar grounds that at the very least sources of temptation should be removed and that even if people were not themselves virtuous, they should be compelled by law and relentless social pressure to act virtuously. So far as the achievement of their legislative agenda was concerned, that approach was vindicated by results. A year before the repeal of the Contagious Diseases Acts, the Criminal Law Amendment Act raised the age of consent and cracked down on procuring and prostitution. These back-to-back victories were largely the result of a carefully orchestrated campaign led by one of the founders of the new popular journalism, W. T. Stead, who arranged the procurement of a young girl as part of a lurid exposé of the sexual underworld provocatively entitled "The Maiden Tribute of Modern Baby-lon." Stead also played a central role in organizing a mass meeting in Hyde Park in the summer of 1885 at which the most militant and interventionist of the purity groups, the National Vigilance Association, was launched. In such an environment Parliament was all but stampeded into action.

It was at this point that the issue of homosexuality was introduced into the mix in the form of the infamous Labouchère amendment to the Criminal Law Amendment Act, which prescribed a punishment of up to two years in prison for "any male person who in public or private commits, or is a party to the commission of or procures or attempts to procure the commission by any male person of, any act of gross indecency with another male person." With this brief and simple clause tacked on to a piece of legislation directed at an entirely different target we enter a new era. By specifying private as well as public acts and by not specifying particular acts but criminalizing sexual con-tact between men in the vaguest terms, the amendment broadened the scope of the law considerably. No longer only the limited though often ill-defined of-fenses of sodomy or buggery but homosexuality and homosexuals themselves, very much in the modern sense as all-inclusive categories, were henceforth to be treated as criminal.

There is some question whether Henry Labouchère intended this—or, for that matter, what his intentions were—in proposing his amendment. He may have seen it as a wrecking amendment, designed to weaken or even defeat the Criminal Law Amendment Act as a whole. We know that he was skeptical about the very existence of the white slave trade and disliked the purity cam-paigners, whom he frequently attacked in his own muckraking journal. Hind-sight is especially misleading with regard to the thinking of those who sup-ported the Labouchère amendment at the time of its passage. While we are aware of the anguish and suffering it caused for nearly a century, not only could they not have foreseen its consequences but they were not given, nor did they take, time to consider the nature of the trap they were setting: the amendment was hastily drawn up and passed late at night with no debate in a nearly empty House of Commons.

That said, however, the amendment was accepted by the government, ruled in order by the speaker, and voted into law. In short, whatever La-bouchère's intentions may have been, the time was ripe. An attack on one form of sexual deviance—prostitution, especially of children—had prepared the ground for attacking another, in fact for a much broader and more viru-lent campaign. Stead's journalistic exposés, the Criminal Law Amendment

Act, and the founding of the National Vigilance Association were symptomatic of an irresistible tide in public sentiment in the summer of 1885. The purity campaigners were riding high, and few dared oppose them publicly, let alone successfully. I do not mean to suggest that the vigilance association was a creature only of its triumphant beginnings; it survived as an influential private watchdog of public morals up to World War I, and even beyond, working with the police and magistrates where possible but also acting to bring legal and moral pressure on its own, much as its predecessors in the late decades of each of the two previous centuries had done.

Homosexuality was only one of many targets for the purity crusaders, but it became an ever more important one as time passed, at least as central as the issue that had spawned the movement, prostitution, largely because the growth of the purity campaign coincided with the increasing visibility of homosexuality, not only through the works of Whitman, Carpenter, and Ellis but also, unfortunately, through a series of scandals. The first of these, really more a sensation than a scandal since the one prominent man involved, an aristocratic member of Parliament, died before the case came to trial, involved two flagrant transvestites, Ernest Boulton and Frederick Park, who went about London in drag and appeared as women in amateur theatricals. Charged with conspiring to commit a felony, they were acquitted for lack of evidence, and their brush with the law might therefore be dismissed as more amusing than serious, except for when it took place. They were arrested in 1870, as the social purity movement was hitting its stride, thus giving visibility to the homosexual subculture at just the wrong moment.

Far more serious, both because it occurred in 1884, as the purity movement was reaching its apogee, and because it involved high government officials, was the Dublin Castle scandal. Rumors of homosexual activity among English administrators in Ireland were picked up and published by two Irish nationalist members of Parliament, William O'Brien and Tim Healey, both of whom were delighted to be able thus to embarrass the British government. The highest-ranking official implicated in the article, the head of the Criminal Investigation Department, James French, immediately sued for libel. O'Brien countered by hiring a private investigator, who uncovered evidence of a homosexual network in Dublin involving both civilian and military personnel, some with aristocratic connections. Naming still more names, O'Brien invited additional lawsuits, but the plaintiffs, overwhelmed by an array of witnesses testifying to their sexual activities, lost and were themselves arrested and charged with conspiracy to commit buggery. The first set of trials ended in hung juries. At a second trial two of the most prominent defendants were found not guilty, but the second trial of Detective Inspector French again resulted in a hung jury, which might have been expected to end the matter. However, with a vindictiveness eerily presaging what was to happen to Oscar Wilde a decade later, the government persisted and won a conviction at a third trial.

Whether the Dublin Castle scandal contributed to the easy passage of the Labouchère amendment the following year—or, indeed to Labouchère's proposing it—is uncertain, but there were no such ambiguities surrounding the most sensational homosexual scandal prior to the Wilde case, the Cleveland Street affair. It began, pettily enough, with an investigation into the possible theft of a small sum of money from the Post Office in the summer of 1889. A fifteen-year-old Post Office messenger boy who came under suspicion because he appeared to have a good deal of extra spending money admitted under interrogation that he had earned it working in a male brothel at 19 Cleveland Street, as, he also admitted, did at least three other messenger boys (one of whom had the delightfully suggestive name Thickbroom). It was a lucrative sideline for these boys, who were especially admired within the homosexual subculture. One of the so-called Uranian poets, a schoolmaster who dedicated most of his poems to his pupils, was nonetheless aware of the charms of working-class youths:

> Smart looking lads are in my line
> The lad who gives my boots a shine,
> The lad that works the lift below,
> The lad that's lettered G.P.O.

Evidence from the boys as well as police surveillance of the brothel soon revealed the names of a number of prominent clients, including a member of the royal household, the keeper of the Prince of Wales's stables, Lord Arthur Somerset. Yet there were only two arrests, the first of an associate of the proprietor who had himself worked for the Post Office before being dismissed for improper conduct with telegraph boys, the second of a messenger boy, appropriately named Newlove, who had seduced and recruited the other messenger boys. Both pleaded guilty to the least of the charges against them and received relatively light sentences. As for the proprietor of the brothel, Charles Hammond, warned of the investigation by some of the boys, he fled the country. So too did Lord Arthur, who had ample time to do so (and to return to England and flee yet again) thanks to the indecisiveness of officials in a number of government departments, who were uncertain how best to proceed in such a potentially explosive matter—if, indeed, they should proceed at all. Only after months of delay, and with Lord Arthur safely out of the country, was a warrant for his arrest finally issued.

A few days later a young radical journalist who suspected a cover-up and had access to police sources published the first account of the affair to go beyond innuendo and name names and also suggested the possibility of collusion between the authorities and some of the prominent clients of Cleveland Street. He even hinted at the involvement of someone much closer to the throne than Somerset, no less a person than Prince Albert Victor, the duke of Clarence, familiarly known as Eddie, the son and heir of the Prince of Wales. (Prince Eddie, by the way, was suspected by some of being unusually busy at this time; he was suggested as a candidate for the role of Jack the Ripper, the great journalistic crime and sex sensation of the previous year, 1888.) Beyond wild rumors nothing more came of the account, and unfortunately for the journalist who broke the story, he had insufficient or incorrect evidence on one of those he named and was, therefore, successfully sued for libel. However, during the course of the libel trial much of the story behind the Cleveland Street scandal was revealed, along with a lurid picture of the homosexual underworld of London, most colorfully, if not always reliably, on the evidence of Jack Saul, a professional hustler and sometime housemate of Hammond. Saul achieved a kind of immortality as the subject and co-author of the most famous example of late Victorian homosexual pornography, *Sins of the Cities of the Plain: The Confessions of a Mary Ann,* but he was well past his prime by the time of the Cleveland Street scandal, having retreated back to the streets around Leicester Square where he had begun his career or to lesser brothels such as that on Cleveland Street. In his younger days he had worked the most exclusive homosexual clubs and parties, claiming, for example, to have known—in both senses of the word—all the principals in the Boulton and Park case.

Testimony of this sort, together with the government's handling of the case, opened up an irresistible opportunity for the more flamboyant adherents of the Liberal opposition to the Conservative government, both in the press and in Parliament. Labouchère, whatever his sentiments at the time he fathered the amendment that bears his name, was now in full cry at the evils of homosexuality. True to his reputation as a radical, he also denounced the government for discrimination on the basis of class in prosecuting only the least of those involved, while letting the titled and well connected escape.

Even more seriously, he accused the government of orchestrating a cover-up not only by allowing Lord Arthur Somerset to flee and by negotiating a plea bargain with those who were charged, thus avoiding an open trial, but also by deliberately employing endless delays and outright lies at the very highest levels in order to mislead and confuse the public, the press, and Parliament. For thus questioning the truthfulness of the government, Labouchère was briefly suspended from the House of Commons. The government likewise suffered no long-term damage; it was temporarily embarrassed but in no way shaken. For the principals in the case, Hammond and Somerset, there were lasting consequences: neither was ever able to return to England. Hammond had fled to France but was expelled after only three months. In Belgium and under constant surveillance, he used veiled threats to extract from friends of Somerset sufficient funds for first-class passages to America for himself and the boy who was traveling with him. As for Lord Arthur Somerset, after his final departure from England he traveled as far afield as Constantinople in a vain search for employment (and for freedom from occasional police harassment), finally settling on the French Riviera, where he lived quietly until his death in 1926.

Although it had no lasting political consequences, the Cleveland Street affair unquestionably widened the cultural divide in late Victorian England. For the purity campaigners it was yet more evidence that the country was in a moral crisis and that homosexuality was at the center of that crisis. For the homosexual subculture the Cleveland Street affair, coming so soon after the passage of the Criminal Law Amendment Act, was both a goad and a frightening portent. It was at its height, for example, that Symonds, at once angry and fearful, wrote *A Problem in Modern Ethics* yet dared not publish it. As he and others sensed, the time was ripe for a witch-hunt; the stage was set for something like the Wilde prosecution. Indeed, something like it may have been nearly unavoidable following the government's inept handling of the Cleveland Street affair. Pressed by the purity campaigners and by a conspiracy-minded popular journalism, the Liberal government of the early 1890s, which was as weak as its Conservative predecessor had been strong, was unlikely to be willing to incur the political risks involved in backing off from a morals prosecution, particularly of someone prominent and well connected. There is, in fact, compelling evidence that after Wilde's first trial ended in a hung jury, the government proceeded with a second trial for fear it would be accused of dropping the case because the names of two Liberal prime ministers had been mentioned in earlier proceedings, though only in passing and not in relation to the case. "I would [let Wilde off]," the solicitor general explained privately, "but we cannot, we dare not. It would at once be said . . . that owing to the names mentioned . . . we were forced to abandon it." Such reasoning, perhaps unlikely before Cleveland Street, was all but inevitable in its wake.

Wilde himself appears not to have recognized the warning signs, or if he did, he appears not to have heeded them. He was, in any case, inclined to tempt fate, to court danger, to defy convention. He often deliberately sought out sexual partners from the darker recesses of the homosexual subculture and then flaunted his relations with them in public: "It was like feasting with panthers," he recalled, "the danger was half the excitement." Wilde may well have believed that his wit and his fame would protect him; in fact, however, once he was wounded they worked against him, opening the way to his destruction. The story of Wilde's homosexual life can be told briefly, not only because it has been told so often but also because it was so brief, occupying only the last fifteen years—the final third—of his life. Whatever his early inclinations may have been, he almost certainly had no homosexual experience as a youth, either in school or at university. When he was in the United States at the age of twenty-seven he visited Walt Whitman, who, he recalled later, made no secret of his homoeroticism and kissed Wilde on the lips as they parted. But Wilde did not, at least not consciously or deliberately, cross the Delaware to Camden, New Jersey, in the role of sexual disciple, as Edward Carpenter had done five years before. Indeed, Wilde married shortly thereafter and fathered two sons in quick succession. There is no reason to suggest that he married as a cover, let alone, as Symonds had done, to escape from his true nature.

Wilde did not act on his underlying attraction to young men until he met Robert Ross three years later, and it was the very young but surprisingly sexually sophisticated "Robbie" who seduced the thirty-two-year-old Wilde, not the other way round. As Wilde's fame grew during the late 1880s, he gathered around him a circle of young aesthetes and became increasingly bold and flamboyant in his public behavior and in his writings, though he took care to maintain a certain ambiguity in both, for example, by not specifying the excesses reflected in *The Picture of Dorian Gray*. The fastidious Symonds, who had recently completed *A Problem in Modern Ethics* and hoped through cooperation with Havelock Ellis to project an image of a healthy and, if not respectable, at least respected homosexuality, was dismayed by the tone and tendency of Wilde's work and lifestyle. Symonds found *The Picture of Dorian Gray*—Wilde had sent him a copy—"unwholesome" and was disturbed by its "morbid and perfumed manner." "I resent the unhealthy, scented, mystic touch which a man of this sort has on moral problems," he wrote, "[and] am afraid that Wilde's work in this way will only solidify the prejudices of the vulgar." Had Symonds lived to see it, he would have been even more troubled by the next chapter in Wilde's life and by its role in undermining the work of Carpenter, Ellis, and himself: in 1892 Wilde began his stormy affair with Lord Alfred Douglas, "Bosie," the younger son of the marquis of Queensberry.

Bosie introduced Wilde to the homosexual underworld of working-class boys on the game, and together, and in competition with each other, they displayed their prizes in ever more inappropriate places. Through one of Bosie's friends Wilde met Alfred Taylor, a former public-school boy long since totally immersed in the homosexual subculture of private clubs and rent boys, who introduced Wilde to a number of his less savory sexual partners, young men who were more than willing to earn a bit extra through extortion or blackmail. Finally, and ultimately catastrophically, Bosie drew Wilde into his bitter feud with his father. When the pugnacious marquis accused Wilde of "posing as a sodomite," Wilde, at Bosie's urging, sued for libel. That this was an error all of Wilde's other friends agreed, but it did not at first appear to be disastrous. Indeed, under cross-examination Wilde scored point after point against opposition counsel with a quickness and wit that won the laughter and support of the spectators. It was a show quite on a par with either of his two plays then running in London theaters.

When asked if a certain book was immoral, he replied, "It was worse; it was badly written."

When asked whether a compromising letter he had written to Bosie might be deemed improper if written by someone other than an artist, he answered, "A man who was not an artist could not have written that letter."

When asked if another very flowery letter represented his ordinary way of addressing young men, he observed, "Everything I write is extraordinary."

When asked if one of the lads he had befriended was a newspaper vendor, Wilde expressed mock surprise: "It is the first I have heard of his connection with literature."

Apparently at an advantage, having been able to counter even the most embarrassing revelations, Wilde then made a fatal slip. When asked if he had kissed one of these boys, he replied flippantly, "Oh dear no. He was a peculiarly plain boy. He was unfortunately extremely ugly."

In that moment the whole case turned. Not only did the grounds for Wilde's libel action collapse but he was now open to prosecution under the

Criminal Law Amendment Act. Many of his friends urged him to flee the country, but stunned and indecisive, he remained in England, where he was arrested and tried. At the trial he showed flashes of his accustomed wit, despite damning evidence from a succession of the more disreputable young men with whom he had consorted. When asked why he had gone to Alfred Taylor's flat and if it was in a rough neighborhood, he replied, "That I do not know. I know it is near the Houses of Parliament." There were even instances when he directly challenged the prosecution: "Truth may be found, I believe, at the bottom of a well," he observed. "It is, apparently, difficult to find it in a court of law." And there was one remarkable, often quoted moment of eloquence. Asked about a poem by Bosie ending with the phrase "the love that dare not speak its name" and what that phrase might mean, Wilde answered:

> "The love that dare not speak its name" in this century is such a great affection of an older for a younger man as there was between David and Jonathan, such as Plato made the very basis of his philosophy, and such as you find in the sonnets of Michelangelo and Shakespeare. It is that deep, spiritual affection that is as pure as it is perfect. It dictates and pervades great works of art like those of Shakespeare and Michelangelo, and those two letters of mine, such as they are. It is in this century misunderstood, so much misunderstood that it may be described as the "Love that dare not speak its name," and on account of it I am placed where I am now. It is beautiful, it is fine, it is the noblest form of affection. There is nothing unnatural about it. It is intellectual, and it repeatedly exists between an elder and a younger man, where the elder has intellect and the younger man has all the joy, hope, and glamour of life before him. That it should be so, the world does not understand. The world mocks at it and sometimes puts one in the pillory for it.

As the prosecution had amply demonstrated, however, Wilde's relations with most of these youths had little to do with that kind of love, and the evidence from and about them was devastating. The trial ended in a hung jury, with perhaps only one holding out against a guilty verdict. The government, its attention fixed on public opinion and the possible political consequences of dropping the prosecution, determined on a second trial. Out on bail and hounded into hiding by the marquis of Queensberry, Wilde was again urged by his friends to flee the country but once more decided to stay, this time out of concern for those who had put up the money for his bail and legal expenses but also out of conviction: "I decided that it was nobler and more beautiful to stay," he wrote Bosie. "I did not want to be called a coward or a deserter."

Resigned to the near inevitability of his conviction, Wilde, like his friends, his counsel, and many of the spectators in the courtroom, was nevertheless shocked by the severity of the sentence—two years at hard labor—and by the tone with which the judge delivered it:

> The crime of which you have been convicted is so bad that one has to put stern restraint upon one's self to prevent one's self from describing . . . the sentiments which must rise to the breast of every man of honor who has heard the details of these two terrible trials. . . . It is of no use for me to address you. People who can do these things must be dead to all sense of shame, and one cannot hope to produce any effect upon them. It is the worst case I have ever tried. . . . I shall, under the circumstances, be expected to pass the severest sentence that the law allows. In my judgement it is totally inadequate for such a case as this.

The crowd outside the Old Bailey appeared to agree; there was, literally, some dancing in the streets. That night the marquis of Queensberry held a celebratory dinner.

The Wilde case had ramifications far beyond its impact on the principals. For Wilde, of course, it was a tragedy, in the true sense of that much misused term: a brilliant man brought down at the height of his fame and fortune by his own character flaws, the wrath of the public, and the weakness and vindictiveness of officialdom. He became a nonperson. Upon his arrest his name was taken off the marquee at the theater where *The Importance of Being Earnest* was playing, another of his plays was closed down, and his books were withdrawn by his publisher. After his release from jail in 1897 he went into exile in France, his health and spirits largely broken. Financially ruined, he died in poverty in Paris in November 1900, shortly after his forty-sixth birthday.

Less directly but no less certainly the Wilde case contributed to greater influence for the purity campaigners, leading to further legislation and to a corresponding timidity among their critics but also, and not least of all, to greater self-awareness and a sense of solidarity—as well as greater fear—within the homosexual subculture. According to Wilde's first biographer, Frank Harris, himself one of the great sexual libertines of the age, immediately following Wilde's arrest "every train to Dover was crowded, every steamer to Calais thronged with members of the aristocratic and leisured classes," fearing they might be next. What in fact came next was censorship. Carpenter's London publisher, already nervous about the radical tendencies of his writings, dropped him, and he had to fall back on an obscure socialist press in the north of England, which published *Love's Coming of Age*, containing his essays on women, sexual love, and marriage but excluding the essay on homosexuality, in 1896. Ellis had an even worse time of it. Problems finding a publisher for his joint work with Symonds on sexual inversion led to its being published first in 1896 in Germany (where it was generally well received in the scientific community, and especially by Magnus Hirschfeld). A new but somewhat shady London publisher was eventually found, and the first English edition appeared a year later. Symonds's family and his literary executor were appalled. Fearing that Symonds's reputation and the sales of his other works might suffer, they tried to buy up the entire printing. When a new edition appeared, much of Symonds's contribution and all references to his contribution were gone. The Greek essay was omitted, and his name no longer appeared anywhere in the text, in the footnotes, or on the title page. His connection with the subject of homosexuality had been made to disappear, not to resurface for nearly three-quarters of a century.

Even with these precautions Ellis had trouble; *Sexual Inversion* might be a work of science with most of the advocacy now excised, but its subject remained taboo. In the spring of 1898 an undercover detective, John Sweeney, purchased a copy of *Sexual Inversion* from a small bookshop owned by George Bedborough, who was then promptly arrested and charged with selling an obscene publication. *Sexual Inversion* was not the sole or even perhaps the primary target of the police. Bedborough was involved in a number of radical causes, including free love, secularism, and, of greatest interest to the authorities in the 1890s, anarchism. By linking sexual deviance to anarchism, and vice versa, Bedborough provided the police with an irresistible opportunity to besmearch both.

The shy and retiring Ellis, who feared that he too might be arrested, did nothing beyond consulting a number of lawyers. Others who were not at risk acted more decisively. A prominent anarchist founded a Free Press Defence Committee, for which he was able to recruit a diverse group of supporters ranging from Frank Harris to George Bernard Shaw, whom detective Sweeney dismissed as "a nice little gang of Secularists, Socialists, Anarchists, Free Lovers and others anxious to obtain a little cheap notoriety by defending Ellis's book on principle." A test case of fundamental civil liberties seemed to be in the making, but Bedborough, understandably wary of martyrdom, agreed to plead guilty and was let off with a small fine. As for Ellis, he was not charged, but his premises were searched and his pioneering work on sexuality was described by the judge at Bedborough's hearing as an obscene publication posing as a work of science, a characterization that, because of the guilty plea, went unchallenged by contrary evidence. Meanwhile, as the case was working its way to this unhappy anticlimax, Parliament passed the Vagrancy Act, which made soliciting for immoral purposes, by either sex, a crime.

Eighteen ninety-eight marked the end of the most virulent phase of public and official homophobia following the Wilde case. Thereafter the climate began to improve, both for the homosexual subculture and for the frank discussion of sexual matters. The fifth edition of Carpenter's *Love's Coming of Age*, published in 1906, was expanded to include his essay "Homogenic Love and Its Place in a Free Society." Two years later that essay and his other writings on the subject were published as *The Intermediate Sex*. As for Ellis, he persevered with his massive *Studies in the Psychology of Sex*, of which he had always viewed *Sexual Inversion* as only one part. The sixth and final volume, *Sex in Relation to Society*, was published in 1910, but in America, not England.

Equally significant was the founding on the eve of World War I of the British Society for the Study of Sex Psychology (BSSSP). The work of Hirschfeld in Germany was well known among English reformers and researchers such as Carpenter and Ellis, and the possibility of founding an organization comparable to the Scientific Humanitarian Committee, perhaps even as a branch of that committee, had already been canvassed in England before the meeting of the fourteenth International Medical Congress in London in 1913 provided what appears to have been the final impetus. Hirschfeld was one of the prominent speakers at the congress, and his presentation made appallingly clear just how far behind Germany England was in public and scientific knowledge of sexuality. The BSSSP, founded the following year, was specifically designed to correct this situation through public education as well as research, with the ultimate goal of bringing about needed reforms in medical practice and the law. Homosexuality was only one of the concerns of the new society; indeed, with militant feminism at its height in prewar England, the needs and equality of women naturally took precedence. But homosexuality was the primary concern of many of the society's members, who found in it a safe public forum in which to pursue their interests and the cause of liberation. Carpenter was its first president.

An even more dramatic illustration of the degree to which public and official hostility toward homosexuality had abated prior to World War I was provided by a court case eerily reminiscent of the first Wilde trial, even to the extent of involving some of the same principal players. In 1914 Robbie Ross was denounced as a sodomite by, of all people, Lord Alfred Douglas, acting with all the self-righteousness of a reformed sinner. Ross sued for libel, just as Wilde had sued Bosie's father almost two decades earlier. Despite impressive evidence and testimony mustered by Douglas in justification of his accusations, the jury could not—or would not—find for either party. Ross withdrew his suit, but as had been the case with Wilde, he was now vulnerable to prosecution under the Criminal Law Amendment Act. Yet no such prosecution followed, and Ross was able to keep his job, his friends, and his prominent position in society.

The extent of the change in public and official attitudes toward homosexuality, let alone in the lives of ordinary inverts, should not be exaggerated, however. Ross avoided disaster in large measure because he was more discreet than Wilde had been. Indeed, discretion remained the price, not for freedom or security for homosexuals, since potentially they had neither, but simply for being left alone. There was a small homophile organization in London at this time, but we know little about it since the identity of its members and all sensitive communications between them were kept secret. The Order of Chaeronea, as it was named, in honor of the battle in 338 B.C. in which the Theban band of warrior lovers fought and died in defense of Athens against Philip of Macedon, was founded in the 1890s, perhaps in the wake of the Wilde trials (which would certainly account for its obsession with secrecy). The founder of the order, George Ives, was directly influenced by Carpenter, whom he visited at Millthorpe, and therefore indirectly by Whitman. He also knew Wilde and, perhaps more intimately, Lord Alfred Douglas. In his public life he was a criminologist and advocate of law reform, as well as an active member of the BSSSP. Other members of the order also served in prominent positions in the BSSSP, including Laurence Housman, the brother of the poet A. E. Housman, as its chairman.

For these men the BSSSP represented the public face they dared not show as members of the Order of Chaeronea. Even coming out as far as they did was courageous; to have come out further could have led to their destruction or self-destruction. There were personal tragedies aplenty in the early years of the twentieth century, most of them played out in obscurity, but also a number of public homosexual scandals that did not end up as well as Robbie Ross's. A few were hushed up when the ramifications threatened to reach too high, others resulted in a jail term or flight abroad, and there were a number of possible or actual suicides. The most prominent of these was Major General Sir Hector MacDonald, a much-honored participant in Britain's colonial wars from Afghanistan to South Africa, who shot himself in a Paris hotel room in 1903 on his way back to his posting in Ceylon, where he was to face a court of inquiry into accusations of homosexuality.

Short of such personal catastrophes, avowed or suspected homosexuals and their defenders faced public humiliation, harassment, or ostracism. Ross may have escaped prosecution in 1914, but he was overwhelmed by the shame of the scandal and died five years later. Edward Carpenter, by far the most prominent defender of homogenic love in England, was subjected to frequent criticism, even from well-meaning friends and allies, for his obsession with sexual subjects in general and for possibly doing damage to the socialist cause by linking it with homosexual law reform. In 1908 he had to endure far worse: relentless persecution by a local purity campaigner. Carpenter's antagonist wrote pamphlets attacking his politics and sexuality, distributed them in the area around Millthorpe, and attempted to enlist the local vicar as an ally against him. Luckily for Carpenter, his long residence in the district and support from many of his neighbors, including the vicar, prevented things from getting out of control. He suffered no long-term humiliation or damage—apart from losing his seat on the village council.

That the purity campaigners still had clout as well as zeal, however, was demonstrated three years later by the appointment of Charles Brookfield as national censor of plays. The author of vulgar farces and having neither appreciation nor respect for the theatrical revolution of the preceding generation, Brookfield was an astoundingly inappropriate choice, so much so that the matter was raised in Parliament. His appointment was troubling in another respect: he had played an especially repugnant role in the downfall of Oscar Wilde. Especially repugnant because Brookfield owed much of his early success in the theater to Wilde, having written a popular spoof of one of Wilde's plays and acted in another. But some years earlier Wilde had caught Brookfield in a social gaffe, for which Brookfield apparently never forgave him. Hence, when the marquis of Queensberry began his campaign against Wilde, Brookfield volunteered his services as a supplier of information on Wilde's sexual escapades. He was rewarded for his efforts by an invitation to the marquis's celebratory dinner on the night of Wilde's conviction. Whether or not his contribution to the destruction of Oscar Wilde was regarded as a qualification for his new position, it clearly was not seen, as surely it should have been, as an insurmountable bar to his ability to judge plays fairly and dispassionately. There could have been no clearer signal that the forces of moral conservatism remained on the ascendant than the appointment of Charles Brookfield as arbiter of what was acceptable in the English theater.

That said, while it is true that the Wilde trial retained even into the second decade of the twentieth century some of the chilling effect it had clearly had immediately following his conviction, there were other, and to the purity movement unwelcome, consequences of his persecution. The vindictiveness with which Wilde had been pursued by the marquis of Queensbury and by the law, the conditions of his imprisonment with hard labor, and his exile and death following his release from prison were seen by a significant and growing body of opinion in England as a source of national shame and the perhaps inevitable result of public ignorance and moral hypocrisy. In considerable measure the founding of the BSSSP represented the institutionalization of that realization and the sense of purpose that sprang from it. As Laurence Housman wrote many years later, on the occasion of the dedication of a memorial plaque to Wilde on the centenary of his birth: "His unhappy fate has done the world a signal service in defeating the blind obscurantists: he has made people think."

Moreover, while Wilde's persecution had driven the late-nineteenth-century homosexual subculture back underground, as so often happens in such circumstances, at least some of its members found in their very separation from mainstream society a source of solidarity, as well as a source of grievance. To be sure, many, perhaps most, homosexual Englishmen who came of age before the 1920s grew up isolated, ill informed, and innocent, with little understanding of the nature of their own sexuality, let alone a sense of community with others like themselves. "I didn't know what homosexuality was," one man born in the year of the Wilde trial recalled. "How should I know? In those days they never spoke of it." Or as another contemporary put it, "I didn't realize the significance of it. I just did it. But I thought that married life . . . was the proper thing to do." On the minority who did see themselves as belonging to a distinct subculture the impact of repression was often precisely the opposite, however. The almost paranoid secretiveness of the Order of Chaeronea was one result of the persecution of Oscar Wilde, but the founding of the order was another. Havelock Ellis caught that new mood within the subculture perfectly. "The Oscar Wilde trial," he observed, "with its wide publicity, and the fundamental nature of the questions it suggested, appears to have generally contributed to give definiteness and self-consciousness to the manifestations of homosexuality, and to have aroused inverts to take up a definite attitude. I have been assured in several quarters that this is so and that since that case the manifestations of homosexuality have become more pronounced." As one of his correspondents put it, in a letter Ellis published in *Sexual Inversion,* "Reviewing the results of the trial as a whole, it doubtless did incalculable harm, and it intensified our national vice of hypocrisy. But I think it also may have done some good in that it made those who, like myself, have thought and experienced deeply in the matter—and these must be no small few—ready to strike a blow, when the time comes, for what we deem to be right, honorable, and clean."

## Chapter 10

**Degeneracy and Atavism**

The trials and imprisonment of Oscar Wilde were seen at the time and have been seen ever since as important symbolic events, and not only in the development of a sense of homosexual group consciousness and gay liberation. Wilde's persecution was simply one act in a greater cultural, social, even political drama. The increasing visibility and articulateness of the homosexual subculture was contemporary with and linked, or seen to be linked, to a variety of other challenges to mid-Victorian values and conventions: feminism, the free-love movement, secularism, socialism, and the like. Inevitably the forces of conservatism and respectability struck back, and the Wilde trials provided a perfect opportunity to do so. The prosecution denounced him not only as a sexual deviate but as a corrupter of youth—though the youths in question hardly needed lessons in corruption—and even as a threat to the social order in that he constantly consorted with those well below him on the social scale. That this was almost as serious a breach as his sexual offenses and certainly made them worse was an argument the prosecution clearly hoped the jury would find doubly persuasive. The presiding judge at the first Wilde trial certainly did. In his summing up he characterized Wilde's co-defendant, Alfred Taylor, who had introduced Wilde to many of his sexual partners, as belonging "to a class of people in whom it is difficult to imagine such an offense." The implication was unmistakable; if Wilde and Taylor would not—had not—set an example of respectability such as their social standing required, then society could and should make an example of them.

That suffices to explain most of what happened to Wilde and, in the aftermath of Wilde, to Carpenter and Ellis—most but not quite all. The ferocity of press commentary on Wilde would seem to indicate a deeper anxiety than the Wilde case by itself could have engendered, even with all the baggage that became attached to it. Very few in the press kept their heads, the most interesting and surprising example being W. T. Stead, whose white-slavery campaign ten years earlier had played a critical role in creating the climate for the passage of the Criminal Law Amendment Act. "The heinousness of the crime of Oscar Wilde and his associates does not lie," Stead argued,

> in its being unnatural. It would be unnatural for seventy-nine out of eighty persons. It is natural for the abnormal person who is in a minority of one. At the same time it is impossible to deny that the trial and the sentence bring into very clear relief the ridiculous disparity there is between the punishment meted out to those who corrupt girls and those who corrupt boys. . . . The male is sacrosanct; the female is fair game. To have burdened society with a dozen bastards, to have destroyed a happy home by his lawless lust—of these things the criminal law takes no account. But let him act indecently to a young rascal who is very well able to take care of himself, and who can by no possibility bring a child into the world, . . . then judges can hardly contain themselves from indignation when inflicting the maximum sentence the law allows.

Nor, according to Stead, was that the only example, or even perhaps the most glaring one, of British hypocrisy in such matters: "Another contrast is that between the universal execration heaped upon Oscar Wilde and the tacit universal acquiescence of the very same public in the same kind of vice in our public schools. . . . Public schoolboys are allowed to indulge with impunity in practices which, when they leave school, would consign them to hard labor." Though that was certainly an exaggeration—homosexuality, though notoriously rife in the public schools, was often savagely punished—such frankness, detachment, and recognition of the social and sexual double standard was exceedingly rare. For the most part the press overindulged itself in gleeful vindictiveness or haughty self-righteousness.

Long content, though with increasing bite and more than a touch of hysteria, to satirize Wilde as the symbol of limp-wristed aestheticism, the humor magazine *Punch* now savaged him mercilessly:

> If such be "Artists," then may Philistines
> Arise, plain sturdy Britons as of yore,
> And sweep them off and purge away the sins
> That England e'er such noxious offspring bore!

The *Westminster Gazette* excoriated his "unwholesome tendencies." The *Daily Telegraph* was satisfied that this "righteous sentence of the law" would serve as a warning to those—the young especially—seduced by certain "artistic tendencies of the time." "Open the windows!" it declared. "Let in the fresh air." The *Westminster Review* praised Queensbury for "throwing the search-light of justice upon that hideous circle of extensive corruption," while the *National Observer* declared, "There is not a man or woman in the English speaking world possessed of the treasure of a wholesome mind who is not under a deep debt of gratitude to" the pugilistic marquis "for destroying the High Priest of the Decadents."

The deep-seated anxieties revealed by the Wilde case were not confined to England; England simply provided the most dramatic example of a pattern common to much of the rest of the Western world. Public discussion and awareness of homosexuality increased substantially in continental Europe and the United States in the closing decades of the nineteenth century, as did public and official expressions of homophobia. The focus and impetus for much of this greater interest in homosexuality, as well as the rationalization for homophobia, were provided by the medicalization of homosexuality (along with much other socially deviant behavior formerly categorized as either criminal or sinful). The claims of medical science in the fields of sex and sexuality were not new, of course. The medical literature on masturbation stretched back to the mid-eighteenth century, and that on homosexuality, to the work of Johann Valentin Müller in the 1790s, but from the mid-nineteenth century on a steady stream of clinical and theoretical studies addressed the subject at length.

Particularly at first, much of this new work was, like Müller's, in the field of forensic medicine and as such was inherently unbalanced. Only those charged with or convicted of crimes were subjected to rigorous examination, with the purpose of establishing through physical evidence either that a crime had been committed or, more insidious, that a suspect conformed to a particular criminal type. This could lead to bizarre, even frightening results. The leading French authority in the field of forensic medicine, Ambroise Tardieu, was convinced by his study of hundreds of individuals that he could identify "true pederasts" by certain physical characteristics, that the anus of the passive partner and the penis of the active, for example, would be altered and shaped in predictable ways by habitual homosexual activity. By the time Tardieu first published his findings, in 1857, the ability to make such determinations had taken on an importance that it—and therefore Tardieu—probably would not have had a decade or more earlier. In the relatively liberal political and cultural climate of the 1830s and 1840s in France sexuality and gender roles were not necessarily seen as fixed or rigid categories, and both homosexuality and transvestitism were common themes of plays and novels. Following the revolution of 1848, however, in the conservative early years of the Second Empire, gender lines, like class lines, hardened, a process that both furthered and was furthered by the career of Tardieu.

Tardieu was troubled by the indiscriminate mixing of social classes in the homosexual subculture, which posed a threat to the social order as serious as, if not more serious than, the association of pederasty with other forms of antisocial, even criminal behavior such as prostitution and blackmail. Convinced by his researches that pederasty was far more common than was usually supposed, Tardieu was especially alarmed by the secretiveness of the subculture and by the ability of individual pederasts, despite their underlying inherent effeminacy, to pass undetected by society at large yet identify others of their kind. In dealing with what amounted to a sort of secret society it was therefore critically important to Tardieu that his fellow practitioners be ever on the lookout for "traces of the habits of pederasty in individuals charged with public offenses against decency; it must not be forgotten, in fact, that this legal qualification is almost the only one under which the repression of this shameful vice, when it is possible, can be effected." Short of recriminalizing sodomy in France, which Tardieu clearly would have preferred, rigorous enforcement of the laws against public indecency and meticulous inspection of those arrested in order to identify the habitual pederast were seen as the surest means of circumscribing the practice (and checking the spread of associated diseases).

Pederasty and the homosexual subculture were clearly ineradicable, but their visibility and their influence on society at large could be minimized, as was attempted, for example, by the outlawing of transvestitism in 1853 and by raising the age of consent to thirteen ten years later. But as in France in the eighteenth century, so a hundred years later, the primary weapon against sexual deviance was the identification and classification of the deviants themselves, a policy vigorously pursued by François Carlier, the head of the morals section of the Paris police force in the 1860s, whose exposé, *Les Deux Prostitutions: étude du pathologie sociale,* presented a lurid picture of the homosexual subculture and demonstrated how, even in the absence of adequate criminal penalties, the police could monitor and control that subculture through the time-honored French practice of accumulating files on known homosexuals and systematic harassment of their public activities. In support of such policies Tardieu contributed what appeared to be the full weight of objective scientific research. His views were therefore very influential; his

*Etude medico-légale sur les attentats aux moeurs* went through many editions and remained the standard work on the subject in France for more than half a century.

Tardieu's German counterpart and contemporary, Johann Caspar (a major influence on Ulrichs), was equally concerned with detecting signs of criminal behavior, but his standards were more rigorous, based on more intensive and extensive case studies. From his own observations, as well as close study of Tardieu's findings, Caspar concluded that the Frenchman's catalogue of signs was largely unscientific nonsense, born of prejudice rather than objective research. Caspar was also one of the earliest practitioners of forensic medicine to emphasize the congenital, inborn nature of most homosexuality. Tardieu, like most earlier authorities, viewed pederasty as simply one, though certainly one of the most serious, of the vices or perversions or unnatural acts or crimes to which the weak or impressionable could give way if they were living a licentious life, were subject to bad influences, or were insane. Indeed, Tardieu confessed his bafflement at the origins of homosexuality; "I do not claim to explain the inexplicable," he wrote, "and so penetrate the causes of pederasty." Caspar, on the other hand, while recognizing circumstantial homosexuality, born of chance or misfortune, believed that "in the majority of persons who are subject to this vice, it is congenital, or at any rate the sexual inclination can be followed back into the years of childhood like a kind of physical hermaphroditism."

This distinction between circumstantial, or acquired, homosexuality and congenital homosexuality, with far greater emphasis on the latter, was central to the thinking of a number of German researchers of the next generation, notably Otto Westphal and the most influential sexologist before Freud, Richard von Krafft-Ebing. Both men were introduced to the subject through the writings of Karl Ulrichs; in Krafft-Ebing's case Ulrichs sent him his early pamphlets in the 1860s after reading a statement by Krafft-Ebing calling for a criminal code based on science, not emotion. Westphal, in an article published in 1869 in the *Archive for Psychiatry and Nervous Diseases,* coined the phrase "contrary sexual feeling" to describe the condition of the true invert, in whom "normal"—that is, heterosexual—object choice was virtually absent, replaced by attraction to one's own sex. (This article has somewhat arbitrarily been deemed by some the first medical paper on homosexuality in the modern sense.) Krafft-Ebing, whose magnum opus, *Psychopathia Sexualis,* first published in 1886, was the most widely read and translated work of its kind in the nineteenth century, first wrote on the subject of homosexuality in the late 1870s. Over the years he elaborated a schema incorporating and classifying every known form of sexual deviation and abnormality, but while his views on the origins of homosexuality changed in the process—he ended up with a theory not unlike Ulrichs's, of female emotional and sexual attributes developing in a male body—his central assertion that most homosexuality had a congenital basis did not change.

From that assumption followed, or should have followed, a number of important conclusions. If the predisposition toward homosexuality was inborn, than that predisposition and to some extent homosexual behavior itself could hardly be labeled a sin or a crime since it was clearly not a matter of choice. For that reason Krafft-Ebing, like most sexologists and psychiatrists in Germany, supported the repeal of Paragraph 175 of the German criminal code, a position that won him considerable support from within the subculture, at least initially. But if it was not a sin warranting damnation or a crime warranting imprisonment, homosexuality could be labeled a sickness warranting medical or psychiatric treatment. The individual homosexual might not be responsible for his condition, either morally or legally, but both Westphal and Krafft-Ebing, like virtually all experts in the field, were convinced that homosexuality was indicative of an underlying pathology, the result of an inherited neurological or psychological condition. Krafft-Ebing concluded: "In almost all cases where an examination of the physical and mental peculiarities of the ancestors and blood relatives has been possible, neuroses, psychoses, degenerative signs, etc. have been found in the families."

Even in cases of acquired, or circumstantial, homosexuality, which Krafft-Ebing believed resulted from trauma or debilitation caused by sexual abuse or—that old standby—self-abuse, he was certain that it could not take hold in the absence of a hereditary taint of some sort. Although near the end of his life Krafft-Ebing did acknowledge the possibility that homosexuality might occur in otherwise normal men, his work as a forensic psychiatrist with the inmates of prisons or asylums predisposed him to see connections between homosexuality and other pathological conditions. Since few homosexuals had children, he did not contend that it was homosexuality as such or a predisposition toward homosexuality that was inherited. Rather, he viewed homosexuality as a symptom, along with all sorts of other conditions, such as criminal behavior, mental illness or retardation, or physical debility or deformity, of a more general phenomenon: hereditary degeneracy.

Degeneracy theory spoke to a wide range of obsessions and fears in the Western world at the close of the nineteenth century, and it influenced aspects of almost every ism of the era, from socialist plans for massive social reform, to imperialist dreams of rejuvenating the old societies of Europe through the exploration and settlement of new territory, to eugenics and proto-Nazi racial theories. The founding father of degeneracy theory was Benedict Augustin Morel, the chief physician in a provincial French lunatic asylum, whose *Treatise on Physical, Intellectual, and Moral Degeneration in the Human Species* was published in 1857, the same year as Ambroise Tardieu's seminal work in forensic medicine. Morel employed the religious image of the fall of man to illustrate his fear that modern man was in danger of degenerating because of the peculiarly modern, especially urban social conditions of crowding, communicable disease, poor nutrition, alcoholism, and the like. He believed that the average mental and physical capacities of the population in most Western countries were already measurably in decline and that such characteristics would or could be passed on from generation to generation in an ever-increasing downward spiral.

Such views cannot be dismissed as only a reflection of the now discredited but then popular and respectable belief in the inheritability of acquired characteristics, although that was central to his theory. After all, there is now persuasive evidence that undernourished, alcoholic, or drug-dependent mothers tend to produce children with lower birth weights and lower IQs. But whatever the scientific validity of Morel's theory, it spread like wildfire in the 1870s and 1880s, largely because it reflected and explained middle- and upper-class anxieties at the prospect of rapid industrialization and urban growth, with all of their attendant social problems, which seemed to be spinning out of control: slums, crime, poverty, poor public health and housing, and the growth of an underclass. Degeneracy theory also spoke to the particular fears of particular countries: to a France humiliatingly defeated by Germany in the Franco-Prussian War, now with a stagnant population; to an England fearful of becoming decadent and effete and unable to maintain its status as the world's greatest power in the face of competition from Germany and the United States; to a Germany new as a nation and surrounded by potential enemies, especially the hordes of Slavs to the east; to nativists in the United States alarmed at the late-nineteenth-century mass immigration of eastern and southern Europeans.

These at times almost paranoid obsessions with national rivalries and especially with the threat from other, possibly inferior peoples to one's own nation and culture point to another, related source of anxiety that was also rooted in the notion of hereditary taint. The fear in this case was not that frailties produced in modern man by modern social conditions might be passed on from generation to generation but that primitive, atavistic characteristics of earlier generations might survive in modern man. As Charles Darwin put it at the very end of the *Descent of Man*, published in 1871, "Man with all his noble qualities, . . . sympathy. . . , benevolence. . . , god-like intellect. . .—with all these exalted powers—Man still bears in his bodily frame the indelible stamp of his lowly origins." From this it was but a short step to the worst nightmare of the Social Darwinists: that it might not be the fit who would survive and dominate the future in civilized nations but the unfit, the misfits, who might simply outpopulate, and be allowed by a misguided humanitarianism to outpopulate, the fit.

The chief theoretician of this alarmist view of human nature was the Italian physician and criminologist Cesare Lombroso, whose study *Of Crime, Its Causes and Remedies* was first published in the 1870s, at the same time that the concept of contrary sexual feeling was gaining currency in Germany. Lombroso argued that the habitual or born criminal, like other social or sexual deviates, was a throwback, a survival from a more primitive stage in individual and social human evolution. His theory was by no means incompatible with degeneracy; on the contrary, the throwback was seen as peculiarly vulnerable to the ills of modern society. Atavism, in short, could open the way to degeneracy, and degeneracy could reveal atavism. As in degeneracy theory, so also and most emphatically in Lombroso's theory homosexuality was regarded as a clear sign and symptom of a hereditary taint, in this case of an atavistic survival. And from this proposition similar practical conclusions tended to follow: that homosexuality should not be stigmatized as a sin or punished as a crime, but treated as a pathological condition.

Just how serious a condition it was, and how dangerous to society, was a matter of widely varying opinions. Krafft-Ebing, for example, took a relatively detached view since his case studies of inverts quite often revealed them to be fully functional and socially acceptable in most other respects. "Sexual perverts," he observed, "in general by no means constitute the worst type of degeneration." Also, of course, true, or congenital, inverts were the least likely of sexual deviants to procreate, so that even if they were degenerates or throwbacks, at least their bloodlines were likely to end with them. That reassurance did not calm the fears of those who took a more alarmist view and believed that homosexual activity was likely to be associated with or to lead to other antisocial behavior. Nor were they convinced by the argument that because a hereditary taint had to be present in order for someone to become an invert, a normal person could not therefore be seduced or corrupted into homosexuality. The danger to the general population was that many apparently normal people carried a slight defect, a trace of an inborn taint, that might remain latent, virtually undetectable, and all but harmless if not provoked or excited.

The potentially weak had therefore to be protected from those who might corrupt them. (In essence this was little different from the old moralistic notion of the need to remove the temptation to sin dressed up in the medical/scientific language of degeneracy theory.) How best to protect the vulnerable and restrain those who might bring out their dormant deviances also was a matter of opinion. Proposals ranged from compulsory psychiatric treatment to incarceration (not in a jail, of course, but in a mental institution) to castration. Those who saw homosexuality as a sign of atavism, Lombroso included, tended to take the harshest view, that offenders must be isolated and society protected at all costs, while for those who saw homosexuality as a sign of degeneracy the nature of the treatment depended on how degenerate the individual was and to what extent a particular medical practitioner believed degeneration could be reversed or corrected.

These trends in the medical literature increasingly alarmed the late-nineteenth-century advocates of greater freedom and recognition for homosexuality and the homosexual subculture. They welcomed the support of many of the most advanced medical researchers in their condemnation of Paragraph 175 of the German criminal code and of the Criminal Law Amendment Act in England, but that, upon reflection, was small compensation for being labeled degenerate or atavistic. The problem for the nascent movement for homosexual liberation was that the medical authorities had such great and growing prestige that it was hard to challenge them. Ulrichs hoped to win their support, only to have his theories used as a building block of degeneracy theory. Hirschfeld was himself a doctor, indebted to the founders of serious research into sexuality such as Krafft-Ebing, and sought to enlist their contributions to his journal and their aid in his fight to repeal Paragraph 175. Symonds was no doctor and attacked them, often savagely, in his privately printed *A Problem in Modern Ethics*, but he recognized how little weight his views would carry unless they were linked to the work of a professional such as Havelock Ellis. But while reformers had to move with care in challenging the medical basis for categorizing homosexuality as a sign of degeneracy or atavism, they could attempt to refute it in practice by demonstrating in their own lives and through their own research and writings that homosexuals were

unlike other men only in their homosexuality, that they were otherwise as productive, creative, and socially responsible as anyone else—not degenerates,
not throwbacks—and that perhaps, as Whitman, Friedländer, and Carpenter
had in their different ways suggested, they might have a special, even unique
contribution to make to humanity.

That, to return to where we began, with Oscar Wilde, was perhaps the
main reason that Symonds so fiercely attacked Wilde: his dissolute life, his
open celebration of decadence, and his deliberate defiance of respectability
seemed to confirm the stereotype of the degenerate in the public mind. And
while it is tempting to dismiss Symonds as a stuffy old hypocrite, he had a
point, for surely one can fully comprehend the savagery with which much
of English society turned on Wilde only by taking into account the spread
among the general population of the ideas of hereditary taint and degeneracy
and the anxieties that fed and fed on such ideas.

## Chapter 11

**Purity and Impurity**

Although the medical profession and the categories it established rapidly came to dominate the late-nineteenth-century discussion of issues of sexuality and sexual deviance among the educated public, that only begins to answer what is surely the most frustrating question in cultural and intellectual history, namely, the extent to which such ideas influenced opinion in society at large. After all, Tardieu, Caspar and Westphal, Krafft-Ebing, Morel, and Lombroso were specialists writing primarily for an audience of specialists. To be sure, Krafft-Ebing was widely translated and widely read for many decades. But that in a way misses the most important point: like the theories of Freudian psychology later—and still—these ideas filtered down and out, often in simplified and debased form, into the general population and there had a long life.

When the author of this book was young, in the middle years of the twentieth century, habitual violent criminals were often called *throwbacks,* while homosexuals in particular, but also other sexual minorities, were commonly labeled *degenerates.* At the time I had no idea of the historical or intellectual origins and context of these terms, but their literal meanings and implications were clear and vivid enough. They provided a conceptual framework in which the greater visibility of the homosexual subcultures of the late nineteenth century could be understood and responded to. Two centuries or a century earlier the emergence of these subcultures had been perceived as a threat to moral order, to social order, or both. But to these concerns with public morals and public order a new concern was added in the late nineteenth century: that homosexuality might pose a threat to the public health. The conflicts and anxieties that culminated so dramatically in England in the trials of Oscar Wilde were played out in different but parallel ways in much of the rest of the Western world. The open discussion and spread of liberal views on sexuality and sexual deviance provoked a reaction that ultimately became linked with other social concerns, many of them couched in the vocabulary of degeneration and decline.

As in the early nineteenth century, so near its end, the Netherlands nearly perfectly reflected the conflicting trends in its larger neighbors. Ever since the imposition of the French criminal code by Napoleon in 1811, homosexual acts, as long as they took place between consenting adults in private, had not been illegal in the Netherlands, and all attempts to recriminalize homosexuality had been successfully resisted by the liberal majority in the Dutch parliament. That began to change in the final quarter of the century, when, as elsewhere in western Europe and the United States, growing concern with the problem of prostitution spilled over into increased awareness and alarm at other apparent threats to the moral fiber of the nation, such as pornography, drunkenness, and homosexuality. The homosexual subculture in major Dutch cities may indeed have become more active during these years; it certainly became more noticeable, or at least more noticed. There were lurid accounts of sodomitical meeting places in the sensational press, and the police force, larger and more professional than earlier in the century, felt both able and free to act against the subculture. Surveillance of well-known cruising spots—public urinals and parks, certain streets and canals—increased, as did, gradually during the 1870s and 1880s and dramatically in the 1890s and early 1900s, arrests for indecent homosexual acts in public, at least in Amsterdam. There were also more frequent raids on semiprivate meeting places such as coffeehouses, beer halls, and brothels, primarily, it would seem, as a means of controlling and intimidating the subculture but ostensibly in order to protect youths who might have found their way, or been seduced, into such places.

The laws protecting the young were also strengthened. As in England at the same time and France some years earlier, in 1886 the Dutch parliament raised the age of consent. Sexual relations with anyone under sixteen, even if in private and no compulsion were involved and even if the youngster initiated the contact, were made illegal. Supported by an active purity movement and backed by the major churches, both Protestant and Catholic, the 1886 law reflected the growing sentiment that the protections afforded to children should extend into adolescence. However, the law was not specifically directed against homosexuality; sexual relations with underage girls were included on the same terms, and an attempt to amend the law to single out unnatural acts was defeated. The distinction between the criminal and what most members of parliament agreed was reprehensible was kept; the former was punished, the latter was not.

It was a distinction the consensus in favor of which soon proved impossible to maintain. Both sides attacked it. Inspired largely by the work of the Scientific Humanitarian Committee in Germany, some individuals began to speak out in favor of objective research into sexual deviance and even genuine equality and acceptance for homosexuals, not merely toleration. Jacob Schorer, a jurist of noble lineage, argued for the naturalness of same-sex love. Lucien von Römer, a physician and historian also from an aristocratic background, studied with Magnus Hirschfeld and contributed a number of articles on the history of homosexuality to the yearbook of the Scientific Humanitarian Committee. He also published two scientific inquiries into the nature, development, and frequency of homosexuality. Arnold Aletrino, trained as a criminal anthropologist, broke with his mentor Lombroso to assert that homosexuality could occur in otherwise normal individuals. He also encouraged Jacob Israel de Haan, the author of the first Dutch homosexual novel, published in 1904, one of the earliest such works to appear anywhere in Europe. All four men were most active in the first decade of the twentieth century, and all four paid dearly for speaking out. De Haan lost his jobs as schoolmaster and journalist; Aletrino was savagely attacked for his views at the 1901 congress on criminal anthropology in Amsterdam; Schorer was denounced in parliament by many of his colleagues in the legal profession; and Römer submitted a dissertation on homosexuality to the University of Amsterdam in 1908, only to have it rejected as immoral and offensive.

To the coalition of conservative and religious political parties that won power early in the new century the public discussion and defense of homosexuality was intolerable. As the prime minister put it, "Now we have come so far that these ideas are not only expressed in secret, but also in public. I should like to ask whether . . . it is [not] finally about time to intervene." And intervene they did. Determined to assert traditional values against the center left, liberal and socialist opposition's continuing commitment to unfettered individual liberty and public neutrality in matters of private morals, the new conservative majority proposed a series of laws restricting abortion, birth-control information, brothels, pornography, and gambling. In 1911, despite vigorous opposition, the government pushed through a provision singling out homosexual (including lesbian) relations with minors and raising the age of majority for such offenses to twenty-one. The advocates of homosexual rights and freedom, led by Schorer and Aletrino, responded by founding a Dutch branch of the Scientific Humanitarian Committee, but clearly they were on the defensive. Had the Netherlands had a different legal history and not kept the French penal code, all homosexual acts would doubtless have been made illegal at this time.

No such restraints operated on the other side of the Atlantic. Although the death penalty for sodomy was gradually abolished throughout the United States during the nineteenth century, the antisodomy laws were often modernized and, as in England, broadened in the late decades of the century. Unfortunately for the denizens of the homosexual subcultures of America's burgeoning cities, sexual deviance could plausibly be linked, at least as symptom, perhaps as cause, to the ill effects of many of the developments that were transforming the country almost beyond recognition at breakneck speed. The Civil War had uprooted hundreds of thousands of young men from farms and small towns, thrown them together in an all-male society far from home and family, and exposed them to all sorts of temptations and alien influences. During the war and in the generation after it, America experienced unprecedented urban and industrial growth. By the end of the century the United States had surpassed Britain as the world's greatest industrial nation, and whereas in 1850 there had been only one city, New York, with a population of over 200,000, by 1900 there were nineteen or twenty. All these cities were more than populous enough to support a variety of subcultures, ethnic, cultural, criminal—and sexual. What is more, the process was made doubly unsettling by the waves of immigrants, mostly from unfamiliar places, who were diluting what had been an overwhelmingly northern European, Protestant population.

Respectable middle-class Americans of older stock were at once fascinated and horrified by these mushrooming subcultures, which, depending both on the nature of the subculture and the nature of the observer, became the objects of study, of reform—this was the Progressive era—or of repression. We therefore have a good deal of evidence of these subcultures, much of it, and in the case of the homosexual subculture most of it, highly colored negative evidence from the police, doctors, moral reformers, the sensational press, and other outsiders. By the early twentieth century, however, more sympathetic observers were at work. The earliest known defense of homosexuality by an American, *The Intersexes: A History of Similisexualism as a Problem in Social*

*Life,* was published in 1908. Not surprisingly, its author led a double life. As Edward Stevenson he contributed to many of the leading magazines of the day; as Xavier Mayne he wrote and published privately not only *The Intersexes* but also *Imre: A Memorandum,* probably the first American homosexual novel. *The Intersexes* ranged widely, including not only the usual references to ancient Greece and to famous homosexuals of the past but also a comprehensive overview of the modern literature on the subject and lively accounts of the subculture at home and abroad. The result was a massive work of more than six hundred pages. (Interestingly, believing that homosexuality was inborn and that scientific research would demonstrate this and thus ameliorate prejudice, Stevenson dedicated the book to Krafft-Ebing.) Non-Americans also contributed information on the United States: both Havelock Ellis and Magnus Hirschfeld published accounts based largely on firsthand material from homosexual correspondents.

From all of this, as well as from interviews and from recently discovered diaries and letters, it is possible to piece together a remarkably full picture of what was, after all, an illegal and largely subterranean world. Even at the time professionals in medicine and law enforcement, and to a degree the general public, were becoming aware of homosexual subcultures in their own backyards. In 1898 a Massachusetts doctor informed an audience of his colleagues "that there is in a community not far removed [presumably Boston]—and I am informed that the fact is true of nearly every center of importance— a band of urnings, men of perverted tendencies, men known to each other as such, bound by ties of secrecy and fear and held together by mutual attraction. This band . . . embraces, not as you might think, the low and vile outcasts of the slums, but men of education and refinement, men gifted in music, in art and literature, men of professional life and men of business and affairs." But it was New York, with its population of more than 3 million at the turn of the century, that received and still commands the most extensive coverage of its large and visible homosexual subculture—or, more accurately, subcultures, reflecting its great class and ethnic diversity. Middle-class "queers," as they were called and generally called themselves, had created a subculture recognizably similar to that of the later twentieth century, at least up until the beginning of the gay liberation movement. Of necessity, in order to preserve their social standing, they had to be discreet, acting and appearing like other men of their class in their everyday lives, revealing their sexual nature only in private. They therefore disdained flamboyant and effeminate inverts, who brought unwanted attention to homosexuality and with whom, in any case, they felt little kinship since for the most part they saw themselves as like other men except in their sexual desires.

For something different, something more adventurous, middle-class queers had to descend both socially and geographically to a different world, the ethnic neighborhoods of the Lower East Side. There most notoriously and in similar districts elsewhere in the city sexual deviance was at once both more open and more structured. In addition to male prostitutes, who plied their trade in the same streets and saloons as their female counterparts, there were a substantial number of boys and young men known to themselves and to outsiders as "fairies." Deliberately and often outrageously effeminate in manner, dress, personal grooming, speech, and nicknames, they congregated in a number of well-known saloons, partly for the sake of each other's company, partly in the hope of picking up a sexual partner, preferably men of unquestionable masculinity. The roles in such relationships—and sometimes they developed into lasting relationships—were carefully defined. The fairies assumed the passive, or female, role, servicing the sexual needs of their active, male partners. At a time when American cities had a huge surplus of unattached, working-class males—sailors, itinerant laborers, immigrants without families—such sexual encounters were tolerated, even accepted, and the men who sought or received the services of the fairies were not seen, and did not see themselves, as any less masculine so long as they remained the dominant partner. The fairies paid a price, of course: they forfeited their status as men. Indeed, their deliberate adoption of a feminine role and character meant that unlike the middle-class queers, they were not a challenge to anyone's notion of what it was to be a man, but that was the price they paid for toleration, though it also opened them up to derision and physical abuse.

Though the middle-class queers and the working-class fairies occupied what may seem like different universes within the same city, those differences are easy to exaggerate. The fairy subcultures were common in some ethnic neighborhoods, much less so and far less flamboyant in others. In any case, working-class youths, unlike their social betters, had no choice but to live their sexual lives largely in public; in the crowded tenement districts privacy was a luxury few could afford. Furthermore, while participation in the fairy subculture was the most common ticket of entry into the gay world for working-class youths, many left it after a short time, and many others rejected it completely. And even among those who immersed themselves in playing the fairy role to the hilt, it was often no more than that—a role, a style—rather than an accurate reflection or projection of how they viewed themselves. However, many fairies do appear to have seen themselves much as both the men they serviced and most outsiders saw them, not as men attracted to other men, but as in some sense truly feminine, as something close to Karl Ulrichs's idea of an intermediate sex, of a female personality in a male body. But the working-class youths who could comfortably pass in their own neighborhoods during the day, at work and among other men, but transformed themselves into fairies in the saloons along the Bowery at night defied, and defy, easy categorization either by themselves or by outsiders.

As for the middle-class queers, while many of them did see themselves simply as men loving other men and were lucky to have in the legacy left by Walt Whitman a strong affirmative voice in support, others, puzzled by their nature and groping for an explanation, acknowledged the possibility that they had a feminine component in their makeup. Many queers ventured below 14th Street, most often, perhaps, to take advantage of the free and easy sexual atmosphere and maybe pick up a fairy but sometimes to experiment with the role of fairy themselves. Thus, while in theory the fairy might explain his attraction to other men as due to an inversion of gender identity and the queer might see it only as a matter of sexual orientation or preference, in practice the distinction was far from clear, and queers may have disdained the flamboyant fairies not only because they had so little in common but also because they had too much in common for comfort.

The respectable middle-class queers had good practical reasons as well for being nervous about the proximity of the fairy subculture, for it was the fairy who fixed the stereotype of the homosexual in the public mind. The popular image of sexual deviance was created by press accounts of police raids and arrests, by sensational exposés of the social and sexual underworld, and by boiled-down versions of the medical literature. The response was exactly what one might expect. As in England, homosexuality became caught up in a wider campaign to regulate and control sexuality. And again as in England, this began with the issue of prostitution. During the Civil War the military and the medical profession cooperated to regulate prostitution, a policy they attempted to carry over into peacetime. The reaction was swift and devastating. A coalition of moral reformers and women's-rights advocates similar to the one that emerged contemporaneously in England but with some peculiarly American additions, such as former abolitionists who likened prostitution to slavery, defeated or reversed every effort to regulate and thus, in effect, sanction prostitution. The movement quickly developed into a broad-based social purity campaign involving both the temperance movement and many supporters of women's suffrage. Like most late-nineteenth-century movements for the reformation of manners and morals, it initially looked to education and voluntary cooperation from men willing to abandon the sexual double standard, but even more quickly and eventually more thoroughly than in England the American purity movement resorted to coercive measures.

The central and most notorious figure among the more fanatical purity campaigners was Anthony Comstock, a salesman and leader in the Young Men's Christian Association (YMCA) from Connecticut. He became obsessed with the suppression of obscenity as he defined it, and he defined it very broadly to include not only such things as sensational dime novels and lewd postcards but also serious sexual-advice manuals and the representation of nudity in the fine arts. At the head of his own New York Society for the Suppression of Vice and backed by most other leaders of the purity movement until even some of them felt he was going too far, he successfully pressed Congress and many state legislatures to pass stringent censorship laws, which he, as a postal inspector, vigorously enforced. Homosexuality was only one of many targets of the purity campaigners, and in the absence of major scandals such as the Cleveland Street affair or the trials of Oscar Wilde, it never was the focal point that it became in late-nineteenth-century England.

Even so, those who saw themselves as having a special responsibility for the training of youth, such as the leadership of the YMCA, became uncomfortably aware of the threat posed by homosexuality and began to move against it at about the turn of the century. Founded in the 1850s by evangelical Protestants, the American YMCA was closely associated with the moral purity movement after the Civil War. When, from the 1880s onwards, at the height of concern with degeneracy, the association made physical development a central aspect of its mission to develop the whole man—body, mind, and spirit—it was compelled to confront the possibility that this, coupled with the close male bonding and mentoring that had been at the heart of its mission from the beginning, could open the door to a variety of abuses, including homosexuality. Such anxieties were rarely directly expressed before the more open discussion of homosexuality became possible in the 1920s, but they were clearly reflected in the association's embarking on sex education in conjunction with its program of physical development, in its growing preference for married staff over the bachelors who had dominated the movement in the nineteenth century, and in its gradually increasing the role of women in its activities. Despite these precautions, however, "the very institutions established to help the YMCA shape men's physical needs and sex lives, the gymnasium and the dormitory, became the sites of rampant same-sex sexual activity."

Notorious as its reputation within the homosexual subculture became, the YMCA skillfully protected its wider public image. A major scandal in Portland, Oregon, in 1912 threatened that image. Eventually more then fifty men, many of them prominent in local affairs, were arrested and charged with "indecent and degenerate" conduct following a police raid prompted by reports of sexual contacts between adults and boys. But the association and the city's leaders closed ranks to prevent the situation from getting further out of hand. Aware of the problem even before the Portland scandal, the leadership of the YMCA, then and later, local and national, generally preferred to look the other way rather than risk negative publicity. The danger was contained. At the same time that the YMCA began to wrestle with the potential contradiction between its commitments to developing the male physique and ensuring that comradeship and admiration for the finely tuned male body did not find sexual expression, enforcement of antisodomy laws was markedly stepped up. In New York City in the 1890s there were on average as many arrests every year as there had been prosecutions during the entire first three-quarters of the century. However, a high proportion of these arrests were of adults who had sex with children, whose protection, primarily through laws raising the age of consent, was one of the chief goals and achievements of the social purity movement in the United States as in much of the Western world. And as with the protection of children, so also with the central issue of prostitution, by and large homosexuality was feared and attacked as a symptom of a larger crisis of moral and social degeneration that was threatening to consume America's urban jungles rather than as a critical issue in itself.

Ironically, one of the main reasons for this circumspection may have been the savage censorship laws that made the serious discussion of almost any controversial sexual subject difficult until well after 1900 and any but the most oblique or censorious reference to a subject as far from the mainstream as homosexuality rare even then. Edward Stevenson's *Intersexes* was not only published privately and under a pseudonym; it was also published abroad, in Italy, where Stevenson chose to live more than half his life. There was nothing in the United States comparable to the work of Carpenter and Ellis and the British Society for the Study of Sex Psychology in England or of Schorer and Aletrino and the Dutch branch of the Scientific Humanitarian Committee in the Netherlands, let alone of Hirschfeld and the parent Scientific Humanitarian Committee in Germany.

However, although Germany was the country in which the rational study and discussion of homosexuality was most advanced, it was also the home of a moral purity movement that singled out homosexuality for special condemnation and was, moreover, the setting for the most important homosexual scandal of the early twentieth century. Like its English and American counterparts, which often served as models for German organizations, the late-nineteenth-century German moral purity movement was a response to real or perceived threats to the family, and especially to women and the young, at a time of unprecedentedly rapid social and economic change. The earliest moral purity groups in Germany sprang up in the 1880s and were brought together under the umbrella of the General Conference of German Morality Organizations in 1890. From the League of the White Cross, whose young male members pledged to protect German womanhood and preserve their own chastity, to church and secular organizations aimed at proselytizing urban youths and suppressing prostitution and pornography, the purity campaigners saw themselves as fighting a desperate struggle against the roster of liberal reform movements with which Hirschfeld classed his own Scientific Humanitarian Committee: feminism, nudism, progressive education, and family planning, among others. Because the homosexual subculture and the Scientific Humanitarian Committee had such visibility in turn-of-the-century Berlin, homosexuality figured prominently on the agenda of the German social purity movement, certainly far more than in the United States, where the subject was rarely mentioned in polite society, or even in England, despite the string of homosexual scandals culminating in the trials of Oscar Wilde. In opposition to Hirschfeld's efforts to change public opinion and ultimately to change the law, the propagandists of the moral purity movement painted an alarmist picture of the dangers homosexuality posed to the moral and physical health of the nation, and in particular to impressionable adolescents. It was in the context of heightened public awareness of homosexuality and its potential danger that the Eulenburg scandal broke.

This scandal—or crisis, as it in fact became—is far less well known than the Wilde case; it is rarely mentioned in any detail or even at all in general or political histories of modern Germany. Yet its importance was enormous: it reached to the very highest levels of society and government and changed the balance of influence at the imperial German court in the years before World

War I. A Prussian aristocrat who did not fit the stereotype of the Junker class, to which he belonged, Philipp, Fürst zu Eulenburg, was a man of great refinement and artistic tastes. Although married and a father, he was unquestionably homosexual. He had a number of sexual liaisons with working-class men and perhaps also, though this is not certain, with a few intimates of his own class, but he felt most comfortable, as one of his friends put it, in "highly idealized effusive male friendships" of the kind that had been common in Germany early in the nineteenth century.

Eulenburg first met the future Kaiser Wilhelm II when the prince was in his late twenties and Eulenburg was in his forties. He quickly became the prince's friend and confidant and remained so after Wilhelm ascended the throne in 1888. Eulenburg gathered around him a circle of equally culturally inclined men, in whose company the Kaiser found a welcome escape from the military and bureaucratic aides who staffed his official court. Whether hunting in East Prussia, sailing on the royal yacht, or on brief excursions to Eulenburg's estate, once away from the capital this tightly knit group diverted themselves, and most of all the moody Wilhelm, with a variety of entertainments. There were amateur theatricals, musical evenings, bawdy sketches, practical jokes, and the occasional excursion into cross-dressing, all of these apparently quite innocent, if often rather juvenile. But since most members of the Eulenburg circle were homosexually inclined (though how much and in what way we will probably never know since the relevant evidence has largely been destroyed), rumors began to circulate about the nature of the circle and even about the Kaiser himself. So far as Wilhelm is concerned these rumors were almost certainly groundless. Given his uncertainty about his own capacities as head of state and commander in chief of the army and his acute sensitivity about his physical limitations (he had a wizened left arm), it is highly unlikely that he would have acted on or even acknowledged to himself any homosexual tendencies.

Whatever the actual or suspected nature of Eulenburg's relationship with Wilhelm, the extent of his influence, political as well as personal, was undeniable, and to many in and out of government it was unacceptable. The Kaiser rewarded Eulenburg with additional titles and ultimately with the sensitive diplomatic post of ambassador to Vienna. Eulenburg advocated a cautious rather than a forward foreign policy; he questioned the wisdom of imperial expansion and initially opposed the building of a large German navy. This did not mean that he was in any sense a liberal. On the contrary, he saw himself and his friends as upholders of an older, nobler traditional Germany against the crude materialism of the modern era. It was this sense of exclusiveness, of cultural superiority, as much as his views and influence on policy matters that incurred the wrath of his enemies, who saw Eulenburg and his circle as decadent and weak both morally and politically and therefore a danger to the strength of the German state and nation in more ways than one.

For all these reasons the widening circle of Eulenburg's enemies were determined to undermine him, and early in the new century they found their opportunity. Eulenburg and the Kaiser quarreled over the handling of the divorce of Eulenburg's younger brother, whose estranged wife had accused him of unnatural sexual practices. Suddenly vulnerable, Eulenburg soon found himself the target of nasty rumors that reached the ears of the Kaiser, as well as the object of direct threats to his career and reputation. His most dangerous antagonist was the muckraking nationalist journalist, Maximilian Harden, who early in 1902 published an article full of hints and innuendoes based on damaging information that he had been methodically collecting on Eulenburg's private life for some time. Later that year, pressed from all sides and suffering from nervous exhaustion, Eulenburg retired into private life.

That was not the end of the matter, however. Three years later, his health recovered, Eulenburg returned to government service and to the favor of the Kaiser. He did so at a critical moment, just as Germany was about to suffer an embarrassing diplomatic setback at the hands of Britain and France in the crisis arising out of French penetration of Morocco. Unable to drive a wedge between the partners in the newly formed Anglo-French entente and thereby compel France to make major concessions, Germany emerged from the Morocco crisis appearing weak and isolated. In the inevitable search for scapegoats that followed, Eulenburg was a perfect target. Known to have conciliatory views on foreign policy and to have influence with the Kaiser, Eulenburg was also open to the suspicion of a role in the crisis bordering on treason. The first secretary in the French embassy in Berlin, Raymond Lecomte, was an occasional member of Eulenburg's circle; the two met as the crisis was building and may have met at other times during the crisis, although that and what took place at these hypothetical meetings is a matter of conjecture. Eulenburg's enemies had no such doubts. They were certain that he had passed sensitive information on to the French, and led by Maximilian Harden, they were determined to destroy him.

Harden's chosen weapon was Eulenburg's sexual history. This was a tactical decision on Harden's part since he himself was relatively liberal on the issue of homosexuality, having met Magnus Hirschfeld and publicly supported the repeal of Paragraph 175 of the criminal code. On the other hand, he shared the general prejudices of the time that homosexuals were weak and effeminate, duplicitous and cliquish, and while Harden almost certainly did not realize the likely ramifications of what he was doing when he began his campaign to root out the Eulenburg circle, his use of homosexuality to do it touched a sensitive nerve in public opinion. The rapidity and avidity with which other newspapers took up the cry only makes sense to the extent that Eulenburg and his circle, like Oscar Wilde a decade earlier, were seen as symptoms of decadence, degeneration, and decline. Harden himself got caught up in the frenzy. What began as a political maneuver designed to get rid of Eulenburg quickly became a paranoid obsession. "In 1908 I first learned," he later wrote,

> of the terrible propagation of homosexuality, felt clearly . . . "the leveling effect of the common efforts of the forbidden through all classes," in the mound of threatening letters from cities near and far, in the signs of comradeship which is stronger than that of brothers in an order of freemasons, and holds more tightly together, which links together a band beyond the divisions of belief, state or class. . . . Everywhere men of this tribe sit, in courts, in high positions in the army and navy, in ateliers, in the editorial rooms of large newspapers, in the chairs of merchants, teachers and even judges. All united against the common enemy.

The witch-hunt was on.

Harden's opening shot, delivered late in 1906, was a threat to Eulenburg and his friend and companion Kuno Moltke, the military commandant of Berlin, to expose their "abnormal sexual instincts." Moltke was especially vulnerable. Like Eulenburg's brother, Moltke was divorced by his wife on account of his homosexuality, and though that was not cited publicly at the time of their separation, she did provide damning evidence to Harden, which the journalist was now prepared to use. When Harden renewed his attack early in 1907 and the Kaiser, informed of the escalating campaign, demanded to know why Eulenburg and Moltke had not acted to clear themselves, they had to respond. Under increasing pressure Eulenburg initiated an investigation of his conduct by a local (and presumably friendly) prosecutor, resigned from the diplomatic service in June, and retired to his estate. Also in June, Moltke began libel proceedings against Harden, having resigned his commission a month earlier. Harden was acquitted, much to the dissatisfaction of the Kaiser and the government, which overturned the verdict on a technicality, instituted state proceedings against Harden, and won.

Since the local investigation of Eulenburg had, to no one's surprise, produced nothing, it seemed early in 1908 that both he and Moltke had escaped, their reputations sullied but not destroyed. Yet at that moment the situation was already beginning to spin out of control. As a harbinger of things to come, in between the two Moltke-Harden trials the editor of *Der Eigene,* Adolph Brand, entered the fray, alleging that no less a person than the German chancellor was homosexual. Unable to substantiate his accusations, Brand was sentenced to eighteen months in jail. Harden, meanwhile, despite his legal reverses, was more determined than ever. He deliberately set himself up for yet another libel trial, this time in a friendlier jurisdiction, at which he presented fresh evidence of Eulenburg's homosexuality. Since Eulenburg had testified at both the Brand and second Moltke trials that he was not homosexual, he was immediately arrested and charged with perjury. But before his trial in the summer of 1908 was finished Eulenburg suffered a collapse and was ruled unable to continue; and when an attempt to retry him was made the following year, the same thing happened again. Though Eulenburg was thus able to escape conviction, his career and his personal reputation were ruined, as were those not only of Moltke but of half a dozen others whose names had come up in the trials or in the press. One even committed suicide. Another member of Eulenburg's circle suggested that Eulenburg should do likewise, though he doubted his old friend was man enough.

The consequences of the Eulenburg scandal were many and serious. The nature of the scandal and the destruction of his dearest friend shook the Kaiser and contributed to a breakdown he suffered late in 1908. The Kaiser also suffered politically by his association with the Eulenburg circle. His judgment was called into question, and that helped precipitate the worst peacetime political crisis of his reign, following an indiscreet interview with an English newspaper. The nature of his regime also changed. The Kaiser's military advisers were principal players in the effort to destroy Eulenburg. The chief of the military cabinet, for example, supplied Harden with incriminating information while at the same time urging the Kaiser to demand full disclosure. When the dust settled the military advisers were in the ascendant, with virtually no effective civilian check in place at court. At a time of mounting anxiety over national weakness and humiliation this was an especially dangerous development.

It almost need not be added that this same climate of opinion was disastrous for the homosexual rights movement in Germany. And the leaders of that movement only made matters worse. Not only did Brand launch his ill-conceived allegations against the German chancellor but Hirschfeld made a disastrous misjudgment by agreeing to appear in the Harden libel trials as an expert witness for the defense concerning the nature of Moltke's sexuality, which he suggested at the first trial was psychically if not physically homosexual. Presumably Hirschfeld believed that he could inject an element of rational scientific analysis into the controversy and perhaps establish his Scientific Humanitarian Committee as an arbiter in such matters. If so, he was hopelessly naive. The scandal was driven by political motives and public hysteria. He should have realized that any involvement with it could only damage him and his movement. And it did. Eulenburg attacked Hirschfeld for besmirching "one of the finest German virtues, . . . the capacity for friendship," by suggesting the possibility that "every friendship is suspect of 'dirty' sex." The press was even more savage. Newspapers of every political persuasion condemned Hirschfeld, if for nothing else, for treating the unmentionable as a fit subject for rational public discussion.

Hirschfeld and Harden responded by backing off from their earlier characterization of Moltke's sexuality, acknowledging that it was difficult to distinguish between passionate friendship and homosexuality. But the damage had been done. Hirschfeld was now open to attack for being inconsistent and irresponsible, or lacking in the courage of his convictions, and many members and friends of the committee, frightened by the bad publicity or, indeed, any publicity at all, withdrew their support. The fiasco also undermined the Scientific Humanitarian Committee, already weakened by its recent defeat in the Reichstag, by reinforcing the determination of the Gemeinschaft der Eigenen to break with Hirschfeld and his methods. The damage was even more extensive. As the press and the public tired of the scandal and became concerned at how it was tarnishing Germany's image at home and abroad, there was a natural tendency to turn on the purveyors of scandal. Maximilian Harden himself became an object of attack, and unfortunately, he, like Hirschfeld, was a Jew. At a time when Germany was experiencing a crisis of national self-confidence it proved all too easy to fan the flames of anti-Semitism.

That, however, was a secondary and accidental aftershock of the Eulenburg scandal. More immediately and directly affected was the German youth movement, which suffered through a major sex scandal of its own shortly before World War I. Indeed, with the subject of homosexuality very much in the air and increasingly openly discussed, institutions for the training of the young, particularly but by no means only in Germany, inevitably became the subjects of public scrutiny and concern. Inevitably because once the potential of a sexual dimension in such institutions was admitted, that very possibility raised the two issues surrounding homosexuality that modern society found, and still finds, most unsettling: the sexual component in relations between friends and comrades, which calls into question the nature of masculinity, and the sexual component in relations between generations, which contradicts the modern tendency to enhance the protection of children and to deny or circumscribe childhood sexuality.

# Chapter 12    The Cult of Youth

The Eulenburg scandal in Germany, like the Wilde trials in England, at once reflected and heightened the fears of degeneration and decadence that were such a potent ingredient of respectable middle-class opinion at the turn of the century. The answer, the antidote to what was often likened to an infection, was to strengthen those institutions that instilled the manly virtues—physical, mental, emotional, and moral. But that was a more complex task than it seemed. As in the movements for national regeneration a century earlier, lurking in the shadows were dangers and contradictions, uncomfortable questions that could not be avoided. What was manliness? Was it possible to foster virility without fostering sexuality? Could comradeship and intense personal loyalties be celebrated without countenancing the sensual expression of that comradeship, those loyalties? For the single-sex schools and youth groups charged with training young men for the single-sex pursuits of national defense, taming the frontier, and expanding and governing far-flung empires these were profoundly disturbing questions. The very institutions designed to counter degeneracy might in fact be incubating it. Thus it was no accident that as these institutions were reworked or founded to further the manly ideal, anxiety about the possible corruption of these institutions and that ideal rose commensurately.

Nor was this the only contradiction. Increasingly vocal segments of homosexual subcultures in a number of countries themselves subscribed to the manly ideal. Ulrichs and others might posit the existence of an intermediate sex, and Wilde and others might attempt to blur traditional gender roles, question accepted notions of masculinity, and celebrate androgyny, but Brand and Friedlander in Germany, Carpenter in England, and those who defined themselves in the language of Walt Whitman rejected the idea of an intermediate sex and viewed homosexuality or, at the very least, homoeroticism as simply a variation on the norm, but well within the range of the normal. Symonds compared sexual inversion to color blindness; others, wishing to avoid any implication of disability, compared it to left-handedness. And Symonds attacked Wilde precisely on the grounds of his being unwholesome and effete, while Brand broke with Hirschfeld in part on the issue of whether effeminate homosexuals should be included in the movement. On the one hand fearful of being painted with the brush of degeneracy and on the other hand intent on enlarging the meaning of masculinity to include homosexuals, they embraced the ideal of manliness. But they did so, of course, in a manner certain to heighten the anxieties of heterosexual advocates of manliness. For to the question whether one could divorce virility from sexuality, they answered not only that one could not but that one should not. And as to the possibility that comradeship might find sexual expression, that, they argued, could well constitute the fullest realization of comradeship. A few radical homosexual theorists actually said such things openly, and some others entertained such thoughts in private, but even that was rare. Much more common were what would now be called "closeted" homosexuals, who found idealized romantic but probably nonphysical outlets for their homoerotic feelings in the service of all-male institutions such as schools, youth groups, or the military.

In the English-speaking world no institution better—or more notoriously—sums up the problems inherent in the attempt to instill the manly virtues in the young male than the English boys' boarding or public school. There had always been sexual activity in these schools, of course. Put a few hundred adolescents together in a self-contained world, and there will be sexual activity; and if all of those adolescents happen to be of the same sex, there will be same-sex sexual activity. Nor were sexual scandals at these schools unique to the late nineteenth century. Revelations about older boys abusing or seducing younger boys, followed by expulsions, surfaced periodically, as, less often, did incidents of masters seducing—or being seduced by—their pupils, followed by sudden, usually unexplained resignations. The mysterious departure of Charles Vaughan from Harrow in 1859 is, now that we know the full story, perhaps the most dramatic example, but there were others. The two best-known cases, the subject of much speculation at the time, both involved masters at Eton, William Johnson and Oscar Browning. Both were brilliant teachers who sought to expand the narrow confines of the Victorian curriculum, and both were popular with their pupils, whose emotional as well as intellectual development they oversaw with almost obsessive interest. Johnson, best known as the author of the Eton boating song, also wrote sentimental poetry and inadvisably passionate letters to and about the boys he doted on, including a future prime minister, Lord Rosebery. In 1872 he suddenly and without explanation left the school he had served for a quarter-century, never to return. He changed his name to Cory and so far as Eton was concerned became a nonperson; though the textbooks he had written remained in use, his name was removed from the title page.

Three years later a similar fate befell Oscar Browning, who had been one of Johnson's pupils at Eton. Always ready to deal with the personal problems of his pupils, Browning took on a few students for particular attention, usually boys who were as notable for their looks as for their intellect. Of all his favorites the future Lord Curzon, who was later to serve as viceroy of India and as foreign secretary, was the most famous, and it was their intimate friendship that started the process that led to Browning's dismissal. Browning and the headmaster differed on nearly everything, from curriculum to discipline, but it was almost certainly suspicions about the nature of Browning's personal relationships with his students that precipitated the final break. After leaving Eton, Browning retreated into a fellowship at Cambridge and finally into self-imposed exile in Italy, both places where he could pursue his private life with an openness and characteristic boisterousness that had been impossible at Eton. Indeed, despite the suspicions of his enemies, it is unlikely that he indulged himself sexually with his students; he had far too strong a sense of his own responsibility and of their vulnerability. In any case his sexual tastes appear to have run to working-class youths, for many of whom he acted as patron; he had a special fondness for sailors.

Nonetheless, Browning's frankness about his own attraction to his students, along with his unusual willingness to help them understand and channel their adolescent passions, equipped him perhaps uniquely to comprehend the underlying erotic content in relations between the boys and between the boys and their teachers in the hothouse atmosphere of the English public school, or indeed of any single-sex institution devoted to the training of the young. Symonds certainly thought so. After completing his essays on Greek and modern homosexuality, Symonds wrote Browning suggesting that he take up the issue and in particular address the question whether exposing impressionable adolescents to the alien sexual attitudes of the ancients might possibly be harmful or at least confusing. Unfortunately, Browning declined Symonds's suggestion, though, as his biographer noted, he was always ready to discuss such questions with "a strange mixture of pagan enthusiasm and moral fervor," which was one of the hallmarks of the classically educated Victorian homosexual.

By the time of Browning's dismissal from Eton many English public schools were in the grip of something approaching sexual panic. It was a recent development. In the early Victorian era the great old public schools had been reformed, and a host of new ones founded, to embody the twin principles of godliness and good learning, and when school reformers referred to vice and immorality, they usually meant not sex but lack of discipline, dishonesty, or even drunkenness. As the public-school ideal was gradually secularized later in the century sports and physical fitness were elevated to a prominent position in school life. Indeed, sports came to be seen as a necessary component in intellectual development—the healthy mind in a healthy body—and in building moral character through team spirit and a sense of fair play. The process began well before the late-nineteenth-century concern with degeneracy, which, of course, served to redouble the emphasis on sports and physical development but also contributed to a heightened underlying anxiety about the growing emphasis on sports. As the physical development of boys became a central concern of the public school, so too, and in direct proportion, did their physical purity.

The perennial battle against the dangers of masturbation was taken up with renewed vigor in midcentury, spurred on by dire warnings from the medical profession, most notably and influentially in William Acton's *The Function and Disorders of the Reproductive Organs, in Childhood, Youth, Adult Age, and Advanced Life, Considered in their Physiological, Social and Moral Relations,* first published in 1857. The book rehearsed the familiar catalogue of the inevitable consequences of self-abuse: physical weakness, isolation from society, slovenliness, and intellectual sluggishness. "Such boys," he concluded, "are to be seen in all stages of degeneration, but what we have described is but the result towards which they all are tending." The following year one of the most popular nineteenth-century novels of public-school life, *Eric, or Little by Little,* took up the issue of schoolboy immorality in no less apocalyptic terms. The precise nature of the awful practice into which the impressionable boy might be lured was never specified, but it was almost certainly masturbation, not homosexuality.

Well before the end of the century, however, homosexuality had largely though never entirely displaced masturbation (if only because of fears that one practice might lead to the other) as the primary source of anxiety about immorality in the public schools. Headmasters and school chaplains delivered lectures and sermons against usually unspecified vices, thus only confusing many of the younger boys while probably whetting the curiosity of the older ones. Dormitories were patrolled at night, students were enlisted to spy on one another, doors were removed from lavatories, and the number of supervised activities was increased so that boys would have less time to themselves. Sports were regarded as especially beneficial since they could tire out the boys. However, some schools decreed that bare legs should not be exposed during sports lest that provoke the lusts that strenuous physical exercise was designed to exhaust. In perhaps the most extraordinary example of the lengths to which some schools would go, at Wellington the headmaster, E. W. Benson, later archbishop of Canterbury, personally supervised the placement of wire entanglements on top of cubicle walls.

Benson was somewhat ahead of his time—he was headmaster in the 1860s—but others soon caught up with him. By and large the growing hysteria closely paralleled the social purity movement and reached its peak in the 1880s and 1890s. So great was the concern that euphemisms were often dropped in favor of more or less frank discussion and denunciation of any sort of erotic, let alone sexual, relationship. Perhaps the saddest result was the suppression of the sort of intense and innocent romantic friendships between boys and between boys and their teachers that had been characteristic of the early Victorian era (just as growing self-awareness had dampened such relationships between adults a century before). Such friendships had earlier been encouraged by schools as helpful in socializing younger boys and instilling a sense of responsibility in their elders, and they were often celebrated in the early novels of schoolboy life, such as *Tom Brown's Schooldays*. And while these novels warned against the dangers inherent in such friendships, what they singled out was the vulnerability of hero-worshipping younger boys to evil influences not even by implication of a sexual nature (though there is one small hint of it in *Tom Brown's Schooldays*). Such innocent indulgence of passionate friendship could hardly survive in the age of the Labouchere amendment, the Cleveland Street and Wilde cases, and the writings of Havelock Ellis; both parents and those who ran the schools became too knowing, too self-aware.

Once the genie of adolescent homoeroticism had been let out of the bottle, the late Victorians were left with few options other than to celebrate it or to attempt to suppress it. Most, of course, chose to do the latter, but some few more or less openly sought to depict the love of boys and the loves of boys as the highest and noblest forms of love. A not insubstantial poetic subgenre emerged, reaching its peak in the early 1890s, extolling the beauty of adolescent boys and wistfully recalling the intense but fresh and innocent passions of youth. The heyday of what have come to be called the Uranian poets was brief, lasting only from the late 1880s until the persecution of Oscar Wilde sent them scurrying for cover. They did not resurface until more than a decade later, and then more cautiously and largely shorn of the "sensuous, dreamy, Greece-haunted and luxurious ideas of the Aesthetic school, and the over-handled images of Antinous and Ganymede, seen through a Renaissance gauze." Their existence as something approaching an identifiable group would likely have been ephemeral in any case. Their audience was, to say the least, a highly specialized one, and they were entirely dependent on a handful of publications for encouragement and support. Two were short-lived student magazines at Oxford, one of which, the *Spirit Lamp*, was edited for a time by Lord Alfred Douglas, while the other, the *Chameleon*, contained in its first and only issue the poem by Bosie in which he coined the phrase "the love that dare not speak its name," as well as a series of epigrams from Wilde, later to be used against him at his trials.

Beyond the confines of Oxford the Uranian poets could count on support from only two magazines, and then only when they had sympathetic editors. Charles Kains-Jackson, who, like a number of the Uranian poets, was later a member of the Order of Chearonea, was made editor of the *Artist* in 1888 and transformed the magazine, gradually at first, more openly by the early 1890s, making it the major outlet for the Uranian poets. In 1893 one of his contributors, Joseph Gleeson White, became editor of the *Studio*, a magazine slightly more cautiously Uranian in its sympathies. He had earlier established an informal holiday retreat for the Uranian poets at his home on the south coast of England. The other unofficial Uranian resort was at Falmouth, on the southwest coast of Cornwall, which provided the nearest that England could boast to the sort of Mediterranean setting that the classically educated Uranian poets so often sought to evoke in their writings.

The central figure in Falmouth was not a poet but an artist, Henry Scott Tuke, who specialized in paintings of naked or at least shirtless boys frolicking, working, or simply contemplating one another in, on, or by the sea. At first he relied on classical themes as the vehicles and justification for painting the young male nude, but gradually and with the encouragement of friends and patrons, including John Addington Symonds, he abandoned all references to other times and places in favor of a sunlit world of perpetual summer peopled with boys forever young. Tuke was solicitous of his youthful models, who were always local boys, not professionals. Although some of them lived with him for a time, the boys' families appear to have trusted him completely, and there was never a hint of scandal. Even after they married, as most of them did, Tuke remained their friend and patron. Though Tuke exhibited regularly at the Royal Academy, and many of his paintings were bought for public collections, the Uranians understandably thought of him as their painter. Both the *Artist* and the *Studio* praised his work, and private collectors snapped up most of his paintings, more than one of which, along with some of his models, served as inspiration for poetry.

This poetry, like most Uranian poetry, was pretty awful: mawkishly sentimental, effusive variations on an endlessly repeated theme. One example, inspired by what is perhaps Tuke's best-known painting, *August Blue,* should therefore more than suffice:

> Stripped for the sea your tender form
> Seems all of ivory white,
> Through which the blue veins wander warm
> O'er throat and bosom slight,
> And as you stand, so slim, upright
> The glad waves grow and yearn
> To clasp you circling in their might,
> To kiss with lips that burn.
>
> Flashing limbs in the waters blue
> And gold curls floating free;
> Say, does it thrill you through and through
> With ardent love, the sea?
> A very nymph you seem to be
> As you glide and dive and swim,
> While the mad waves clasp you fervently
> Possessing every limb.

And so on for another three stanzas.

Although it took the persecution of Oscar Wilde to stifle the Uranian poets, they were already in trouble before that. Indeed, what were generally seen as their excesses contributed to the savagery with which Wilde was hounded by his enemies. The most blatantly pederastic of the issues of the *Spirit Lamp* edited by Lord Alfred Douglas earned him a stern rebuke from the university authorities; the *Chameleon's* one issue contained so much provocative material (in particular a story entitled "The Priest and the Acolyte") that it received unfavorable notice in publications outside of Oxford; and early in 1894, a year before the Wilde trials, Kains-Jackson was fired from his post as editor of the *Artist.* Perhaps as a cause, perhaps as a result, of his being fired, he published a sort of Uranian manifesto in the last issue of the magazine under his control. Entitled "The New Chivalry," it called not for the "exaltation of the youthful female ideal," as had been the case in "the early and imperfect civilization" of the Middle Ages, but for "the exaltation of the youthful masculine ideal" in an "adult and perfect civilization."

Kains-Jackson's updated romantic medievalism was shared by others in the Uranian fraternity, especially those who were drawn to the trappings and ceremonial of Roman Catholicism or High Church Anglicanism or indeed to a less superficial commitment to those churches. But the more common inspiration, of course, was classical, with the usual cast of characters—Adonis and Ganymede, Hylas, Narcissus and Hyacinthus—standing in for modern boys, endowing their brief adolescence with a suggestion of timelessness (and not incidentally providing the poets who sang their praises with a degree of cover). Virtually all of these poets were themselves former public-school boys. A few were schoolmasters, by far the most prolific being John Gambril Nicholson, who was later a member of the Order of Chaeronea and also served as an officer of the British Society for the Study of Sex Psychology, one of whose founders, George Ives, also dabbled in Uranian poetry. Nicholson became involved in passionate friendships with some of his students and dedicated collections of his poems to his particular favorites. This troubled Symonds, who admired the poetry but, doubtless recalling his own earlier passion for a schoolboy as well as the fate of Vaughan at Harrow and Cory and Browning at Eton, felt that Nicholson should resign his post if he continued to write in the same vein.

Most of the Uranian poets, and not only those among them with responsibilities for the young, faced similar actual or potential conflicts between their private predilections and their public careers and reputations. Apart from the recklessness with which a few of them promoted the Uranian sensibility in the years before the Wilde trials, for the most part they tended to resolve the dilemma by staying quietly within their own circle, publishing their slim volumes of poetry privately and identifying themselves on title pages only by initials or with a pseudonym. Much of what they wrote was never published, just circulated among friends and patrons, through whom it often reached the public schools themselves, where it helped to define an often intense homoerotic subculture.

On the official level, of course, the schools moved firmly in the opposite direction. Romantic friendships became more and more suspect, were discouraged, then banned, then punished. Older and younger boys were not allowed to consort, and in some schools teachers were subject to strict rules about having boys alone in their rooms. According to the diplomat and author Harold Nicolson (who, like his wife, Vita Sackville-West, was homosexual, as his son later revealed in a remarkable dual biography of his parents), the result of this policy of repression was that "the authorities in their desire to deprive us of all occasion for illicit intercourse, deprived us of all occasion for any intercourse at all. We were not allowed to consort with boys not in our own house. . . . In addition, one was deprived of all initiative of action or occupation. . . . We had thus no privacy and no leisure. . . . And the vices which this system was supposed to repress flourished incessantly and universally, losing in their furtive squalor any educative value which they might otherwise have possessed." The intense attachments of adolescence continued to be acknowledged but were redirected away from other individuals to the community—to the residential house, to the team, to the school, and beyond the school to nation and empire.

The English public schools were venerable institutions—or new ones aping the venerable—compelled by changing values and circumstances to alter the ways in which they channeled the energies and passions of their adolescent charges. But late-nineteenth and early-twentieth-century England spawned new institutions and movements that were even more specifically dedicated to fostering the manly virtues in growing boys and therefore no less concerned with protecting their budding manliness from corruption. Boys' clubs and youth organizations sprang up all over England, but far and away the most important example was the Boy Scouts, founded by Robert Stephenson Baden-Powell. A public-school product and later a professional soldier, Baden-Powell served the empire in the African wars of the 1890s, in India, and as one of the heroes of the Boer War. However, he rightly regarded his greatest achievement as the founding of the Boy Scouts.

Though the Boy Scouts now purports to be a nonpolitical movement devoted to promoting camaraderie and healthy outdoor activities, they were, and were intended to be, a good deal more than that, at least in their origins. More perhaps than any other institution in early-twentieth-century England the Boy Scouts was the product of late-nineteenth-century anxieties about national competitiveness and national and racial degeneration and decline. Such anxieties reached their peak in England following the Boer War, during which an alarmingly high percentage of recruits were found to be physically unfit for military service. The flood of articles, books, and reports by governmental commissions that followed these revelations concluded, almost without exception, that the physical—and by implication moral—condition of the urban masses of England was seriously at risk as a result of earlier neglect. The Boy Scouts was founded in 1908 as a means of national regeneration, to teach healthy habits to children ignorant of basic hygiene, to instill discipline and encourage a sense of social responsibility in boys to whom these were almost alien concepts, to act, as Baden-Powell put it, as a "character factory." Far from being apolitical, the Boy Scouts was intended to be socially conservative, protomilitary, nationalistic, and proempire. The organization was a training ground designed to reshape the whole boy—socially, physically, and morally. The handbook of the movement, *Scouting for Boys,* written by Baden-Powell, included advice on everything from personal hygiene to handicrafts and originally included a long section entitled "Sexual Continence" (expurgated and tidied up by its publisher), in which Baden-Powell warned in dire terms of the evil effects of masturbation.

Of homosexuality, on the other hand, there was no mention, even obliquely, which is hardly surprising since Baden-Powell was almost certainly homosexual in his inclinations. That these inclinations remained no more than that and were deeply repressed not only in practice but in self-knowledge seems highly likely. He married and had children, but he married late; and his closest, almost inseparable companion throughout his early adult life was his best friend. He always preferred the company of men and boys to that of women, and he took great care to warn the scouts against the dangers of becoming too involved with the opposite sex, or "girlitis," as he called it, a malady he neither understood nor was subject to himself. In the all-male world of the army he became unusually close to the men under his command, so much so that it was a source of comment. He often struck up friendships with young recruits, even though this was seen as suspect not only for reasons of discipline but also because of growing awareness of homosexuality in the military dating from even before the affair of Cleveland Street (where a number of underpaid guardsmen had offered their services, a practice for which certain regiments had since become notorious). Baden-Powell liked to watch scouts and soldiers bathe naked but found female nudity distasteful even in art. We know of one occasion when he poured over a collection of photos of naked boys taken by a former classmate who had become a teacher at his old public school.

It is not easy to determine how self-aware Baden-Powell was. He distinguished between what he called "sentimentalism" in scoutmasters, which he applauded, and actual sexual contact, which he condemned severely. And that probably comes close to defining his view of himself. He recognized his own and others' attraction to men and boys and thought it natural, even healthy, so long as it was chaste. He gave advice to those who were troubled by their sexual feelings and wrote of the need to achieve "that deeper form of subordination of one's desires." There is some fragmentary evidence of possible contacts abroad, in North Africa, a traditional haven for repressed northern Europeans, and also with social inferiors back home, another venerable English tradition, but that evidence is far from conclusive. It is also almost beside the point. Here was a man who felt threatened by sexuality, as his views on masturbation and on women attest. The Boy Scouts, like the army, offered a perfect solution by providing constant close proximity to attractive young men and boys without the conflicts involved in actual sexual contact.

Baden-Powell was far from alone in dealing with his sexuality in this manner. One of the curiosities of late-nineteenth-century British imperial and military history is the strikingly high percentage of the greatest empire builders who married late or not at all and surrounded themselves with coteries of notably—and it was noted—handsome young men or took an avid interest in the training of boys. Whatever their particular predilections may have been, and however open or repressed (usually the latter), such men inhabited, and chose to inhabit, virtually all-male worlds. The roster of names is long and illustrious: James Brooke, the first raja of Sarawak; General "Chinese" Gordon, the hero of the Taiping Rebellion and the martyr of the siege of Khartoum; Field Marshal Kitchener, conqueror of the Sudan; Cecil Rhodes, prime minister of South Africa and founder of Rhodesia; H. M. Stanley, of Stanley and Livingstone. It would be absurd—though tempting—to suggest that the British Empire, as well as the Boy Scouts and dozens of other youth organizations, was built as a vast exercise in the sublimation of homosexual drives, but the pattern is striking.

While the all-male late-nineteenth and early-twentieth-century English institutions designed to instill manliness and the manly ideal managed to keep their homoerotic tendencies more or less invisible (at least to the noninitiate among their contemporaries, if not to us) and therefore kept social anxieties about such matters largely below the level of consciousness, the same was not true in Germany. There the youth movement was rocked by a major scandal involving accusations of homosexuality, one of its chief propagandists extolled homoerotic attachments as central to the ethos of the movement, and, inevitably therefore, public anxiety about the sexual implications of the youth movement surfaced as it never quite did in England. The major German youth organization, the Wandervogel (literally, "migratory bird"), was founded in Berlin in 1901, seven years before the English Boy Scouts, in direct emulation of the national revival movement in Germany a century earlier. It was unlike the Boy Scouts in being a movement primarily for middle-class boys who desired to escape the confines of bourgeois urban life, rather than a middle-class-inspired movement to uplift lower-middle- and lower-class boys. It was like the English Boy Scouts, however, in targeting teenagers and celebrating youth, in promoting comradeship and group identification, and in stressing fitness and a return to nature. But it also differed from the Boy Scouts in being subject to constant splits over questions as diverse as its political implications, its structure, and, not least of all, its potential for sexuality.

In the wake of the Eulenburg scandal the leadership of the movement became increasingly sensitive to the issue, and in 1910 William Jansen, one of the cofounders with Adolph Brand of the Gemeinschaft der Eigenen and a wealthy patron of the Wandervogel, was thrown out of the movement, accused of pederasty. Whatever the truth of the matter, there was plenty of suggestive evidence against him. Looking to ancient Greece as a model, he idealized the young male body and had introduced nudism and nude bathing into his local Wandervogel group. Following his resignation from the Wandervogel, Jansen, together with Hans Blüher, a young group leader who had introduced him to the movement, founded a rival body, the Jungwandervogel, which was more clearly erotic in its emphasis on intense male bonding. Two years later, in 1912, Blüher, still only in his twenties, made the implicit explicit in his startlingly frank history *The German Wandervogel Movement as an Erotic Phenomenon.* Drawing on sources as diverse as Plato, Sigmund Freud, and Benedict Friedländer, Blüher asserted that not only did most young males go through a period of erotic attachment to other boys but a significant number remained inverts throughout their lives; "the typus inversus is a primary phenomenon, not a deviation nor a traumatism, that is to say no pathological phenomenon," he wrote.

It therefore followed that an erotic, even potentially sexual component in youth movements, both between boys and between boys and group leaders, was both inevitable and natural—indeed at the core of such movements—and that it was not those who extolled it, such as Jansen, but those who feared and sought to repress it who were warped. Yet Blüher himself was troubled and ambivalent about the sexual dimension in such relationships. He acknowledged the possibility and early on saw his ideas as sufficiently compatible with the work of the Scientific Humanitarian Committee that he got Hirschfeld to write a foreword to his book. But they soon fell out. Blüher was disturbed by the intermediate-sex theories of Hirschfeld and disgusted by the effeminate homosexuals and others he termed "degenerates" who peopled the homosexual subculture Hirschfeld sought to decriminalize. To Blüher, as to Brand and Friedländer, such decadents represented the antithesis of that manly homoeroticism in which genital sexuality played at most a minor role, which not only informed the youth movement but served other critically important and irreplaceable social functions. Male bonding, Blüher believed, provided a basis for much that was creative and necessary in the building of nations and civilizations; it was a model of social organization complementary to but beyond and in certain important respects above the family.

Blüher occupied an extreme position within the German youth movement, and not only in the youth movement. An ardent nationalist (and anti-Semite), he continued to expound his views on the erotic and male communities into World War I and postwar Germany, seeing in the army and the paramilitary groups of the 1920s, as he had in the prewar youth movement, both examples and models of his ideal. Yet, while he went further, and was more explicit, than almost anyone else in promoting that ideal, he was far from alone in early-twentieth-century Germany in seeing the erotic element and male bonding as central to the training and socialization of the young. At the other end of the political spectrum, Gustav Wyneken, a socialist, pacifist, and pioneer of progressive education, believed that an erotic relationship between students and teachers, however sublimated, was, and should be, at the heart of a good education. An advocate of a distinctive youth culture, he hoped to bring all the elements of the splintered youth movement together under the aegis of a single broad-based organization, the Free German Youth, which staged a mass meeting on the Hohe Meissner, a mountaintop near Kassel, in central Germany, in October 1913.

Much of this was more than a little suspect to solidly respectable middle-class Germans, who had no objection to youth groups that hiked in the mountains every summer but wanted nothing to do with a distinct youth culture, especially if it was tinged with homoeroticism. The Jansen scandal and Blüher's writings had tainted the whole movement in the eyes of many conservatives; it was even denounced as a homosexual front by one Bavarian legislator. That was nonsense, of course, but though a gross distortion, it was a distortion of a reality: any movement devoted to the propagation and celebration of manliness is almost certain, ironically, to have a strong homoerotic element, implicit or explicit, and to attract the homoerotically inclined into its ranks. The late-nineteenth-century homosexual emancipation movement might welcome that reality, usually privately, occasionally and especially in Germany publicly, while most heterosexuals suppressed or simply denied the connection—and still do. Only very rarely has it been treated matter-of-factly. One instance of such treatment appeared, surprisingly, in the English *Journal of Education* early in the 1880s. In a flurry of letters that followed an article in the journal on sex in the public schools, one Old Etonian approached the issue with common sense, even humor, and only an occasional bow to conventionality:

> I have in my mind's eye a list . . . of those who at my school were unfortunately conspicuous . . . in this particular manner; . . . and what ought I to find was the case with them now? . . . Why, of course I should . . . have to point to mental and physical wrecks, men who have dragged hitherto a miserable existence, preys (not martyrs) to consumption and atrophy and insanity; or else to outcasts from all good society. Now, what do I find? That those very boys have become Cabinet Ministers, statesmen, officers, clergyman, country gentlemen, etc.; that they are nearly all of them fathers of thriving families, respected and prosperous.

The anonymous correspondent even suggested that in some cases the practice might serve a valuable social function:

> Every old public school boy knows what is meant by "spooning." . . . It exists in all large schools, and I contend it would be wiser to regard the habit with contempt than with horror. A friend of mine—a peer, the Lord Lieutenant of his county, and the father of a public school boy—told me that when he was at school he was "taken up" (as it is called) by boys bigger than himself, and petted—he supposed because of his good looks; that before he received such notice he was an "untidy, slovenly little ruffian," and that he dated his conversion to gentlemanly habits and refined manners from the time when he was so patronized.

Such detached and unhysterical observations were rare, to say the least. For most people, now as then, the issue was too sensitive and disturbing to be treated so coolly.

# Chapter 13    Forster and Gide

Less than a year after Gustav Wyneken presided over
the meeting he hoped would lead to the unification of the major German
youth organizations, his aspirations were overtaken and destroyed by the outbreak of World War I. Like their contemporaries in all the European bel-
ligerents, most of those who gathered at the Hohe Meissner presumably saw
military service during the following five years, and many, perhaps a majority,
were wounded, gassed, maimed for life, or killed. And surely virtually all of
them lost family or close friends and comrades in the war. For many of those
who served in World War I the innocent idealism of the prewar world seemed
impossibly distant by 1919, hopelessly naive and quite beyond recapture. The
leaders and thinkers and the organizations and institutions they had looked to
with hope and respect before the war often now appeared at best to be irrelevant, at worst as having contributed to the horror.

Members of the homosexual subcultures of Europe and those who sought
or were pressed to speak for them were as deeply shaken by their experience
of the war as any group, in fact more so than most, since the war raised fundamental questions about what it meant to be a man and the terrible price
that traditional notions of manliness could exact; about comradely affection,
the intensity of it and the pain of its loss; about the beauty of youth and its
ultimate fragility. Those within the homosexual subculture in the first generation of the twentieth century—both those who fought and those just too
young to fight—who addressed, and often felt compelled to address, these
questions appeared to themselves and still appear to us far closer to the late-
twentieth-century gay rights movement than to their immediate forbears
among the nineteenth-century precursors of homosexual emancipation.

For those of a slightly older generation, those who had reached middle
age by 1914 and therefore did not fight, World War I was not so decisive a

discontinuity. They were inclined to see themselves less as cut off from their elders than as enabled to take a new perspective by standing on their elders' shoulders. If only as a useful corrective to the tendency to see World War I as a cataclysmic dividing line, it is worth pausing before considering those who did come out of the war to look more closely at their parents' generation, which, because it had already created virtually all the seminal works of modernism before 1914, tended to see the war not so much as an initiator of change as an often brutal winnowing process that closed off certain options while opening up others. Among the advocates of homosexual emancipation many of the pioneering figures in Germany—Hirschfeld, Brand, Wyneken—belonged to that generation and were to provide continuity as well as revealing contrasts between Wilhelmine and Weimer Germany.

Elsewhere, among the major writers of fiction on homosexual themes in this generation two in particular stand out, one French, one English, both for their intrinsic importance and because they make an especially interesting comparison. Both were born in the late nineteenth century (one in 1869, the other a decade later), so that both were in or approaching middle age in 1914 and already well established as writers. Both lived well into the twentieth century, until after World War II. Both were avowedly homosexual (at least to themselves and to their friends), and for both their sexuality was at the core of their personal philosophy. Both wrote frankly of their sexuality on the eve of World War I, but they took different routes in navigating the difficult course between their private and their public selves, between what they wrote and what they published. Yet both were to directly influence the defining of the character of the gay subcultures of the twentieth century. The Frenchman was André Gide, the Englishman E. M. Forster.

Gide was born in 1869 into a comfortably middle-class family. After the death of his father when he was only eleven, André was brought up by his overly strict and emotionally inhibited mother. A sickly and timid child and a Protestant in a Catholic country, Gide saw himself as different from other boys, as an outsider, from an early age. He had a troubled sexual history, and the working out of the contradictions in it, both in practice and in his writings, was one of the central themes of his life. He remained a virgin until the age of twenty-four, when, far from home and in the relative freedom of an alien culture, he was seduced by an Arab boy in Algeria. But that was a source more of anguish than of satisfaction, and it was followed by a near nervous breakdown. Only on his second visit to North Africa in 1895 did he begin to accept his sexual nature. The agent of this was none other than Oscar Wilde, who was in North Africa with Bosie enjoying the reputation of the Arab world in such matters. Gide had first met Wilde in Paris four years earlier; now Wilde took him in hand, to a bar where Gide saw a boy who intensely attracted him. Wilde, sensing what Gide dared not express, asked if he wanted the boy. When Gide replied that he did, Wilde immediately arranged it. This gift of sexual liberation from a sexual libertine was of incalculable importance to the young Gide, for he was not yet ready to make such a breakthrough on his own. "The great pleasure of the debauchee is to debauch," he observed of Wilde in his autobiography. And of himself he wrote: "No doubt, since my [earlier] adventure . . . there was not much left for the Adversary to do to complete his victory over me; but Wilde did not know this, nor that I was vanquished beforehand—or, if you will, . . . that I had already triumphed in my imagination and my thoughts over all my scruples. To tell the truth, I did not know it myself; it was only, I think, as I answered 'yes,' that I suddenly became aware of it."

Although Gide now felt free to acknowledge his desires to himself and to act on them, he also still felt the need for cover, for respectability, not merely for the sake of outward appearances but also to ensure his internal stability. The year was 1895; Wilde returned from North Africa to England and to disaster. Gide was horrified and retreated into marriage, with a cousin who had earlier turned him down. It was a curious marriage, nonsexual yet affectionate, and on the side he cruised the streets of Paris for boys. There was, in short, a virtually complete separation of domestic affection from sexual pleasure, a gap he did not bridge until late in World War I, when, at the age of forty-eight, he began a love affair with a boy thirty-one years his junior, Marc Allegret.

For Gide the process of bringing together his private and his public selves was no less long and difficult. Though he had hinted at the subject in some of his earlier work, he first wrote explicitly about homosexuality in the wake of a series of scandals and tragedies culminating in the Eulenburg case in Germany. The scandal got a good deal of coverage in France, much of it self-congratulatory. It was, after all, taking place in hated Germany, and the French were heartened to find what were generally taken to be signs of decadence in their past and likely future enemy, in whom, many commentators assured their readers, the vice of homosexuality was far more common than among the French. A few observers approached the subject more dispassionately, treating homosexuality as simply one variant in the enormous range of sexual possibilities open to humankind, and it was this juxtaposition of a new open-mindedness with surviving prejudices that prompted Gide to take up the issue.

He did so in the form of a series of dialogues between a defender and a detractor of homosexuality entitled *Corydon,* a title taken from a poem by Virgil. Although Gide began *Corydon* in 1907, he was slow to publish it. He printed a private edition of twelve copies for circulation among his friends in 1911, expanded and completed it in the early stages of his affair with Marc Allegret, and printed another private edition of twenty-one copies in 1920. Not until 1924 did he finally oversee the publication of a public edition, and then only because of further encouragement and further provocation. The encouragement came from the writings of Freud, which he read in the early 1920s and found not so much an "awakening" as an "authorization." The provocation was Marcel Proust's novel *Sodom and Gomorra,* published in 1921, which reflected and in large measure endorsed the medical view of homosexuality as a pathological condition. This was hardly surprising since both Proust's father and his brother were doctors and his father had studied under Ambroise Tardieu. As Proust indicated in a letter to Gide, he was well aware that his "attempt at objectivity . . . will render the book particularly hateful. . . . The enemies of homosexuality will be revolted by the scenes I shall depict. And the others will not be any more pleased at seeing their ideal of virility presented as the consequence of a feminine temperament."

Gide accepted the risk of publishing *Corydon* largely in order to counter what he saw as Proust's neurotic vision of homosexuality, and he cleverly made the protagonist of his dialogues, Corydon, a doctor. His little book was first of all a plea for acceptance and understanding, but emphatically not for the toleration of something sick. Rather Gide sought toleration for something well within the range of normality, which, he argued, was far wider than society usually allowed for. Since most societies tended to define as natural what was merely customary, his aim was to expand the definition of the natural to fit the variety of human experience instead of narrowing experience to conform to a restricted definition. Many of the early dialogues in *Corydon* were therefore devoted to demonstrating the naturalness of homosexuality based on its persistence despite society's efforts to eradicate it and to imprint people heterosexually; the sexual habits of other species, which he discussed at excessive length; the celebration of male beauty that was central to the artistic achievements of classical art in ancient Greece and Renaissance Italy; its occurrence in many cultures past and present, with ancient Greece once again put forward as the most compelling example. Indeed Gide celebrated the Greek ideal of intense friendships between adolescent youths or of intimate nurturing relationships between older and younger men (or boys), the latter being his own personal preference.

Gide was scarcely an isolated figure among French writers in his sexual tastes. The brief and stormy affair between the poets Paul Verlaine and Arthur Rimbaud early in the 1870s, which began when Rimbaud was seventeen, is certainly the most famous because the most melodramatic example; Roger Peyrefitte's lasting relationship with one of the young actors in the film version of his first novel is possibly the most startling since the boy was only twelve when they first met in 1963. Peyrefitte was also instrumental in instructing the older but more closeted novelist Henri Montherlant how best to pick up boys on the streets of Paris. After Montherlant moved to the south of France they conducted a frequent correspondence, much of it devoted to their shared sexual tastes. There is a long and rich tradition, not only in modern French literature but in photography and the cinema, celebrating the often androgynous beauty of the young male, as well as passionate friendships and, since World War II, notably in the writings of Peyrefitte, overtly sexual relationships between boys and between adults and adolescents. The taboos that inhibited the discussion and depiction of adolescent sexuality in English-speaking countries, isolating the Uranian poets and their successors from the rest of the subculture, operated only intermittently in France, where homosexuality as such was not illegal and the age of consent was set at thirteen (at least until after World War II). "This leads," in the view of one critic, "to a much greater sense of sexuality as a spectrum of related interests than is the case in Anglo-Saxon culture. Accordingly, Gide and Peyrefitte make it plain that they see themselves as homosexuals, of the subspecies 'pederast,' a term which they use without any negative connotations."

Caution was necessary nonetheless, if not in fiction and memoirs then certainly in practice. Provisions of the criminal code penalizing affronts to public decency, incitement to debauchery, and corruption of young persons under the age of twenty-one remained in force and, though theoretically neutral so far as gender or sexual orientation was concerned, were often used to suppress homosexual activity. In France as in many other Western nations such laws, as well as laws regulating prostitution, were actually strengthened in the early years of the twentieth century. Police raids on bars, hotels, baths, and active cruising areas, especially those known to attract the young, were by no means uncommon, and the private sexual activities even of the wealthy and well born were not immune. In 1903 the twenty-three-year-old Baron

Adelsward-Fersen was arrested and convicted of debauching the young by photographing a group of (apparently quite eager) local schoolboys in the nude in his apartment. The case was widely publicized, and he fled to the island of Capri, already well established as a haven for expatriate homosexuals, notably the English author Norman Douglas and the German industrialist Alfred Krupp (who had committed suicide the year before after his sexual exploits were revealed by a left-wing newspaper). For Gide, adherence to the Greek ideal of mentoring love relationships between mature and adolescent males served not only as a justification—or rationalization—but as much-needed cover for his personal predilections.

Certainly his idealized vision of homosexuality did not correspond with his own promiscuous sexual history, which was more accurately reflected in the memoirs of his early life, *If It Die,* which, not incidentally, had a publishing history similar to that of *Corydon.* Written before World War I and at first only privately published for circulation among his friends, *If It Die* was finally published in the mid-1920s, two years after *Corydon.* It is surely no accident that these years of literary coming out also coincided with a sharp leftward turn in his politics following a trip to French Equatorial Africa during which he became increasingly critical of the exploitation of France's colonial subjects. From the mid-1920s on, particularly through the publication of his journals but also, for example, in his account of a visit to Soviet Russia in 1936, he deliberately blurred the distinction between his private and his public self, between his sexuality and his politics.

Gide paid a high price for his frankness. Most of his friends urged him not to publish *Corydon,* and some of them broke with him after he did. Nor were even other members of the homosexual subculture necessarily happy with the result. What Gide had begun before World War I as a defense of homosexuality in general, with a predisposition in favor of what he called "normal pederasty," he completed in the final dialogues, written near the end of the war, and in the preface, written in the early 1920s, with a far more assertive championing of pederasty, to the virtual exclusion of other forms of homosexuality. Sexual relations between adult males were largely ignored, and effeminate homosexuals or inverts were dismissed contemptuously; he singled out Proust for having too readily accepted the intermediate-sex theories of Magnus Hirschfeld. Gide had practical reasons for taking this approach. In 1917 France, its population stagnant, had already lost more than a million men in the war. Gide felt compelled to demonstrate that homosexuality would not endanger population growth, the family, the nation's martial spirit, or its moral fiber. "I can think of no opinion more false," he asserted, "and yet more widely held than that which considers homosexual conduct and pederasty as the pathetic lot of effeminate races, of decadent peoples." He cited the ancient Spartans, Eulenburg's Germany (a clever though risky tactic in France), and that favorite among classically educated homosexuals, the Theban band of warrior lovers as proof that sexual bonding among young males not only would not diminish but might enhance military prowess. Hoping to allay fears about the effects of homosexuality on population and public morals, Gide suggested that for most young men sexual relations with other adolescents or older men represented only a phase, a necessary outlet for surplus adolescent sexual energy and certainly preferable to the seduction of respectable girls or a resort to prostitution. Thus, Gide concluded, respect for women and for the family would be preserved, and most young men would sooner or later abandon pederasty for marriage and fatherhood.

This was hardly a line of argument likely to appeal to his fellow homosexuals. Nor was it even consistent with the earlier dialogues in *Corydon* or, indeed, with his own sexual history, since he, like his protagonist, was a lifelong pederast. Nor, even more to the point, did it satisfy his critics, who not only seized on these inconsistencies but, far from being mollified by Gide's attempts to accommodate his views to the concerns of moralists and demographers, dismissed them as unconvincing or simply offensive. He was accused of trying to have it both ways by asserting that sexual morality was culturally determined, while at the same time arguing for the universal value of Greek pederasty. His long disquisition on homosexuality in animals was criticized as equating what was natural with what was good or desirable. None of his critics accepted Gide's contention that adolescent homosexuality was no bar to later heterosexual fulfillment, and almost without exception they stressed that for all his talk of the heroic qualities of male sexual bonding, homosexuals were to some degree weak and effeminate. Homosexuality might not be illegal in France, but the almost universally and often viciously negative response to *Corydon* demonstrated just how great the gulf was between legal tolerance and social acceptance.

Gide had few illusions about the reception *Corydon* was likely to receive. Furious at the tendency of critics to gloss over or deny the sexual dimension of the relationship between Rimbaud and Verlaine, Gide early on resolved "to make a posthumous masquerade impossible in my case by using my writings from now onwards." Publication was another matter, however, but the decision to publish, once made, took on the character of a moral obligation and was irreversible. "However dangerous that truth may be," he explained, "I hold that the falsehood that covers it is even more dangerous." That the publication of the truth might also be a heroic act certainly occurred to Gide. In the opening pages of *Corydon* he lamented the lack of martyrs to the cause. There were victims aplenty—he cited four, two British, two German: Wilde, MacDonald, Krupp, and Eulenburg—but they were not martyrs since "they all denied—they always will deny. . . . It's a surrender to public opinion to establish one's innocence by disavowing one's life. Strange! we have the courage of our opinions, but never of our behavior. We're quite willing to suffer, but not to be disgraced."

Contemplating whether he might have the courage to be disgraced, Gide concluded that it was likely he did not: "I would probably lose courage and deny everything, just like my predecessors." But that was written at the very beginning of *Corydon,* when its possible publication was a distant prospect at best. In finally publishing it Gide did indeed demonstrate that he had the courage of his opinions; and in publishing his memoirs two years later, with their frank depiction of his early sexual history, he finally demonstrated the courage of at least some of his behavior. An interesting measure of just how great Gide's courage was in persisting with his self-revelatory publications is that when the much younger Jean Cocteau published an openly homosexual autobiographical novel four years after *Corydon* and two years after *If It Die,* he did so anonymously.

As for the inconsistencies and contradictions within *Corydon* and between his own life and the ideal as represented in *Corydon,* that did not trouble Gide unduly. We are all of us bundles of contradictions and paradoxes, he believed, and the gap between the ideal and the actual is an important part of what makes us human. Of himself Gide once wrote, "I am merely a little boy having a good time compounded with a Protestant Minister who bores him." The way to reconcile such conflicting aspects of oneself lay, he was certain, not in suppressing one in favor of the other, or in a vain attempt to fuse incompatible elements, but in establishing equilibrium, in being truthful about oneself to oneself, to one's friends, and finally, he realized, to the wider world. At the time of Gide's death, in 1951, an English critic summed up this aspect of his character and contribution especially well, saying that Gide was able "to transmit through his writings . . . not life's greatness . . . but life's complexity, and the delight, the difficulty, the duty of registering that complexity and of conveying it. . . . He is the humanist of our age. . . . He had also, and above all, a belief in discovering the truth and following it. . . . Gide had not a great mind. But he had a free mind, and free minds are as rare as great, and even more valuable at the present moment."

The Englishman who wrote that and, in the early stages of the Cold War, placed such a high value on a free mind and singled out Gide's pursuit of the truth for special praise was E. M. Forster, whose life paralleled Gide's often remarkably closely but whose discovery and following of his own truth took a very different course. Forster was born in 1879, ten years after Gide. Like Gide, he lost his father when he was young, and again like Gide, he was brought up by a devout evangelical Protestant mother. They differed, however, in that Gide tended to revolt against maternal authority, whereas Forster and his mother remained close, sometimes suffocatingly so. Like Gide, he was comfortably middle class and inherited a substantial private income, and like most members of his class in England, Forster was sent away to school. A sickly child, as was Gide, he had a strong sense of being different from other boys and from an early age recognized his own homosexuality. Forster was miserable at school, and it was only after he went up to Cambridge in 1897 that he finally began to find himself both personally and intellectually—but not sexually. His upbringing, reinforced by the recent and terrible object lesson of the destruction of Oscar Wilde, placed almost insuperable obstacles in the way of entering into anything more overtly sexual than the occasional romantic friendship such as he had had at school and had at Cambridge with his closest friend, Hugh Meredith. The Apostles, the most exclusive intellectual circle at the university, to which Forster was elected in his final year, occasionally discussed homosexuality—the open airing of controversial topics being the central credo of the society—but it was all very theoretical and for Forster seemed likely to remain so.

And remain so it did, for a long time. Forster desperately wanted physical love but almost despaired of achieving it. After leaving Cambridge he briefly resumed his affair with Meredith, but that appears not to have gone beyond kisses and caresses. The real breakthrough came, again as with Gide, far from home, in North Africa. During World War I Forster volunteered for Red Cross work in Egypt where (shades of Whitman) he met a streetcar conductor, Mohammed el Adl, with whom, after much hesitation and mutual cultural misunderstandings, he had his first fully satisfying sexual encounter. For Forster the comfortable relationship that soon developed between them was a passage not only through a sexual barrier but also through barriers of color and class. For the rest of his life he preferred a similar pattern of sexual relations, sometimes with non-Europeans, usually with men of the working class.

Inevitably these involved misunderstandings and misadventures, in part because of the social and cultural gulf between Forster and most of his sexual partners, in part because he was prone to look for love even in casual encounters. The results were sometimes painful but sometimes, as he recognized, the stuff of comedy. Shortly after the war he accepted a position as secretary to a young Indian maharaja. Increasingly sexually frustrated, Forster made advances toward one of the palace servants, but news of his indiscretion leaked out, and he confessed all to the maharaja and offered his resignation. The maharaja, far from wishing Forster's dismissal, entered into the game of finding his valued secretary a suitable partner and a time and place for them to meet. His only caution to Forster was not to assume the passive role sexually, as that would cost him respect from other members of the palace hierarchy.

On his return to England Forster met and gradually became a close friend of a young and promising writer, Joseph Ackerley, whose promiscuous sexual escapades in an ultimately vain search for, as he put it, "the Ideal Friend" he recorded in one of the most readable memoirs of the period. Ackerley introduced Forster to a new sexual world. Determined to overcome Forster's late Victorian reserve in such matters, Ackerley drew him into his own circle of artists and writers and later into the pleasures of casual sexual encounters with young men of the working class—sailors, bus conductors, the unemployed, and that traditional standby of London homosexual life and legend, guardsmen. By the end of the 1920s, however, Forster had grown tired of such encounters. "I am not romantic, not like you," he wrote Ackerley, "at least not anymore. I like these flowers, and life would be lovely if a new one sprouted every day, but I have learnt how they wither." Luckily for Forster, fate combined with his own hunger for something more stable to open the way to one of the most important relationships of his middle years, with a policemen, Bob Buckingham, whom he met at one of Ackerley's parties. The exact nature of their relationship, that is, how far it went beyond affection, is uncertain, but it survived Buckingham's marriage and remained a central ingredient in both men's lives until well after World War II.

Satisfactorily coming to terms with and acting on his sexual self-knowledge took Forster more than thirty years, from the time of his friendship with Hugh Meredith at Cambridge, through his Egyptian idyll with Mohammed el Adl, to his lasting relationship with Bob Buckingham. The no less difficult problem of integrating his private sexual life with his profession as a writer, let alone with the public dimension of that profession, he never solved to his satisfaction. His first and most fully worked out attempt at addressing the issue, his only novel on a homosexual theme, *Maurice,* was, interestingly, written before his personal sexual breakthrough in Egypt. It was, in fact, a fantasy about what he wanted but had not yet had—and feared he might never have. Looking back from the intense early stages of his affair with Mohammed el Adl, he wrote, "I was writing the latter half of *Maurice.* I now know so much more. It is awful to think of the thousands who go through youth without ever knowing. I have known in a way before, but never like this."

The circumstances of the novel's inspiration were decidedly unusual, the literary equivalent of Wilde's intervention in Gide's sex life, only in Forster's case the agent of change was Edward Carpenter. In 1913, feeling almost desperate "in my loneliness," Forster traveled north to Millthorpe to sit at the feet of the then nearly seventy-year-old prophet of the "Love of Comrades," who

> seemed to hold the key to every trouble. I approached him . . . as one approaches a savior. It must have been on my second or third visit to the shrine that . . . he and his comrade George Merrill combined to make a profound impression on me and to touch a creative spring. George Merrill also touched my backside— gently and just above the buttocks. I believe he touched most people's. The sensation was unusual and I still remember it, as I remember the position of a long vanished tooth. It was as much psychological as physical. It seemed to go straight through the small of my back into my ideas, without involving my thoughts.

Immediately afterwards the whole of *Maurice,* "the general plan, the three characters, the happy ending for the two of them, all rushed into my pen." The central figure, Maurice, an unexceptional middle-class young man, unexceptional, that is, except in his sexual orientation, is drawn into an intense but asexual affair with a fellow Cambridge student from the upper classes, Clive. Through this relationship, clearly modeled on Forster's own with Hugh Meredith, Maurice realizes his own true nature, while Clive ultimately rejects his homosexuality in favor of marriage and respectability. Maurice then suffers agonies of self-doubt until, at last, he finds sexual and personal fulfillment with a young man of the working class, Alec Scudder, Clive's gamekeeper.

*Maurice* is very far from being Forster's best novel. Parts work well, but much of it is simplistic wish fulfillment, written out of a need to resolve immediate problems not only sexual but professional. He had published four complexly plotted and psychologically penetrating novels about Edwardian English society in only six years but had then suffered an acute case of writer's block. His initial inspiration as a writer having played itself out, he came face to face with the fact that there was an area of his own personality he could not write about for publication. He hoped, even expected, that by writing *Maurice* he could work through that block. In practice it had the opposite effect. He now realized that he had said all he had to say about heterosexual society. He wrote only one more novel, *A Passage to India,* but that grew out of his personal experience of India and dealt more with cultural than with sexual ambiguities. For the rest—and he lived until 1971—he wrote essays and reviews and a number of erotic short stories on homosexual themes. The earliest of these, written before he began *Maurice* and intended, as he put it, "not to express myself but to excite myself," he later burned, an act he soon regretted. He wrote more such stories after World War I, and they survived, to be published after his death. These stories, along with *Maurice,* he circulated among his friends but never seriously considered publishing during his lifetime. He made major revisions in the novel as late as 1960 and asked of himself then, as he must have done many times before, whether, though he believed *Maurice* was publishable, it was worth the risk.

The answer was always the same: no, it was not. To what extent Forster's career as a writer might have been different had he answered differently, whether closing the gap between his public and his private self might have freed him, are questions that cannot be answered. But it is legitimate to ask why, unlike Gide, he decided not to publish, and especially so after Gide himself did take that risk. Some of the difference undoubtedly was due to the differing legal status of homosexuality in France and England. Forster felt that the state of English law made *Maurice* more unpublishable because the novel had, as he was determined it should have, a happy ending. "If it ended unhappily," he later observed, "with a lad dangling from a noose or with a suicide pact, all would be well. . . . But the lovers get away unpunished and consequently recommend crime." A happy ending was not only illegal in England but, he felt, unlikely. As he concluded in 1960, the upper-class magistrate, "Clive, on the bench, will continue to sentence Alec in the dock." Maurice, Forster noted cynically but realistically of the English system, "may get off."

The contrast between England and France should not be exaggerated, however. While the mid- to late 1920s was something of a golden age for gay and lesbian subcultures in France, public disdain and official disapproval set clear limits to what would be tolerated. In 1924, the year *Corydon* was finally published, the first French homosexual periodical, *Inversions,* was closed down for offending public morality. And when the founders of *Inversions,* Gustave-Leon Beyria and Gaston Lestrade, responded by bringing out another journal, *L'Amitie,* they were tried (in camera) and imprisoned, Beyria for ten months, Lestrade for six. Unfortunately for them, Beyria, a clerk, and Lestrade, a postal worker, lacked the social status or literary credentials that might have protected them from prosecution. Not that Gide got off unscathed. *Corydon* was often savagely attacked for crossing the line, and Gide was never admitted to the Académie Française. He too paid a price, and he was at serious risk of having to pay more.

That he was willing to do so and Forster was not was, in the end, probably due more to personal differences, including their differing views about the nature of their homosexuality, than to differences in their legal status as homosexuals. For Gide, going public, revealing the truth about himself, was perhaps the only way of attaining the internal equilibrium he so valued, of resolving the conflict between the little boy and the Protestant minister within, of closing the gap between the public and the private self. Forster saw his problem differently, as one of peeling away a succession of inhibitions. First and by no means the least of these were inhibitions of family. When Ackerley urged him to follow Gide's example, Forster replied, "But Gide hasn't got a mother." Beyond that, he had to overcome religious, class, racial, and, above all of course, sexual inhibitions, initially by admitting his orientation to himself and to friends and then by acting on it. His personal motto was, "Only connect," and he once wrote that his "defense at any last judgment would be that I was trying to connect up and use all the fragments I was born with." Yet in the end he proved unable or unwilling to break through the final inhibition against public acknowledgment and make the ultimate connection beyond himself and his immediate circle. He certainly considered doing so. As late as the age of eighty he reworked parts of *Maurice,* wrote an afterword explaining its origins and significance, and circulated it among a newer, younger generation of friends. But in the end he concluded that it could not be published in his lifetime, if ever.

Apart from personal shyness one of the main reasons that Forster never "came out" publicly may have been that he had a way station between the personal and the public in a supportive network of friends. He valued the ability to make and keep friends above any other human attribute. "The central preoccupation of his life," according to his official biographer, "was friendship. . . . He believed—literally, and as more than a sentimental cliché—that the true history of the human race was the history of human affection." The first and most famous circle of friends in Forster's adult life was the Bloomsbury group. Because so much has been written about them since the 1960s, it is all but impossible now to view them dispassionately. But that is under-standable. The leading lights of Bloomsbury—the novelist Virginia Woolf, the artists Vanessa Bell (Virginia Woolf's sister) and Duncan Grant, the critics Clive Bell (Vanessa's husband) and Roger Fry, the publisher and political writer Leonard Woolf (Virginia's husband), the historian and biographer Lytton Strachey, and the economist John Maynard Keynes—are as intriguing as they were important. Like Forster, almost all the male members of Bloomsbury had been at Cambridge, and again like Forster, most had been elected to the Apostles, whose creed of rational and unfettered discussion most of them carried into their post-Cambridge lives and personal relations. They lived in the same, then somewhat dowdy Bloomsbury section of London, often in the same buildings. They stayed with one another in their country cottages, and despite quarrels, marriages, infidelities, breakups, and affairs, they continued in this manner for years. Small wonder that there was a revival of interest in Bloomsbury in the 1960s; they appeared to be a model of what the uncon-ventional communal life could be.

Above all, the Bloomsberries, as they called themselves, remained friends and valued friendship. Thus, it hardly mattered, at least not for long, that some married and some did not, that some had affairs—often with other members of the group—and some did not, that some were straight, some were gay, and some were bisexual. Duncan Grant established something of a record, having affairs at one time or another with Strachey, Keynes, and Vanessa Bell, with whom he fathered an illegitimate daughter. Of those who were gay or bisexual the two most famous were Strachey and Keynes. They were close friends but sexual rivals. Twice Strachey met a likely young man, wrote lyrical letters about him to Keynes (and almost everyone else), and in-troduced him to Keynes, only to have him stolen by Keynes. To Strachey such reverses were the stuff of tragedy; actually his love life was more like farce. His much-advertised sudden and intense passions usually ended in disaster, at least until his last major affair, which worked well, by his quixotic standards, despite a twenty-year difference in age. Keynes, with his public ambitions and increasingly prominent role in government and economic policy, had to be more circumspect, but as he put it to Strachey, "So long as no one has anything to do with the lower classes or people off the streets and there is some discretion in letters to neutrals, there is not a scrap of risk, or hardly a scrap." Keynes was correct. None of the Bloomsberries, not even the impul-sive Strachey, got into trouble due to their homosexuality. Their social status, together with a degree of discretion, protected them. Keynes himself had a number of homosexual affairs, almost always, in accordance with his advice to Strachey, with younger members of his own class, until he married at the age of forty-two.

The contrast between Strachey and Keynes is perfectly illustrated by their respective biographies. The official life of Keynes made no mention of his homosexuality, which is hardly surprising since it was published in 1951. Michael Holroyd's massive *Lytton Strachey,* published in the late 1960s, placed his subject's sexual history at the center of his life story and in doing so marked a significant breakthrough in biographical writing. Not surprisingly, it also sparked considerable controversy, some efforts at suppression, and a few threatened lawsuits. A more recent and equally voluminous study of Keynes, by Robert Skidelsky, could therefore hardly avoid the subject, which he treats judiciously though perhaps with insufficient emphasis (at least in comparison with Holroyd, who may give it too much).

Whatever their difference and rivalries, Strachey and Keynes remained friends. Personal loyalty and mutual support were among the chief hallmarks of Bloomsbury and perhaps its most attractive characteristic. Certainly it was this quite as much as intellectual companionship that attracted the often shy and awkward Forster. He was not a constant member of the Bloomsbury group. He sometimes found the inner circle of Bloomsberries arrogant and intimidating, and as a group they often were; it was their besetting sin. But even as a group they provided Forster with a haven that he could enter and leave at will, and as individuals they were of inestimable value. With most of them he could be open about his sexuality and share his otherwise carefully secreted homoerotic writings. To Forster's surprise it was the often caustic Strachey who was most enthusiastic about *Maurice,* though Strachey did take Forster to task for his fastidiousness in treating the sexual relationship between Maurice and Alec: "I really think the whole conception of male copulation in the book rather diseased—in fact morbid and unnatural." Forster, who, unlike Strachey, had yet to have a real sex life, reluctantly agreed, and Strachey became one of Forster's confidantes and one of his best audiences for his homoerotic stories. Virginia Woolf was especially fond of Forster, and he of her, though as she rightly sensed, he always held back a little from her, perhaps simply because she was a woman, and he always resisted letting her read *Maurice.* Leonard Woolf intervened at critical moments of self-doubt for Forster, encouraging him to keep writing. Vanessa Bell helped him find a flat in Bloomsbury when he felt he had to get some time away from his mother. Roger Fry painted his portrait, taught him to appreciate modern art, and helped him find a French translator for *A Passage to India*. And it was primarily through the Bloomsberries that Forster met many of his later, younger friends.

The importance to Forster of this complex network of relationships cannot be overemphasized. In a 1938 essay entitled "What I Believe" he declared, "If I had to choose between betraying my country and betraying my friends, I hope I should have the guts to betray my country." Forster never had to make such a choice, of course, but having shared with the Bloomsberries their opposition to World War I and, like so many Europeans in the 1930s, not quite trusting his country, he decided to limit his trust to his friends. Had the law in England been different, as it was in Gide's France, he might have acted differently—but perhaps not.

# Chapter 14    Conclusion to Part 2

If André Gide in France and E. M. Forster in England can serve in some measure as representative of those in the pre–World War I generation of intellectuals, straight or gay, who were able to make the transition to the postwar world more or less gracefully, their German contemporary Magnus Hirschfeld typified a no less important element of continuity, the tendency of early-twentieth-century reformers to enlist the experience of World War I in support of their own agenda of social, political, or, in his case, sexual reform. Like many reformers of his generation, Hirschfeld rejected the notion of the war as a cataclysmic dividing line. "No matter how catastrophic the changes of the World War were," he wrote, "we must regard these alterations as a continuation of previous developments. To be sure, the dimensions of the change were now raised to the realm of the fantastic, but they were nonetheless connected with conditions existing before the war." In his view the war had removed or at least weakened the restraints on processes that had been building momentum since the late nineteenth century.

Hirschfeld's contribution to realizing the promise thus opened by the war was, to say the least, unusual: he wrote a *Sexual History of the World War.* In it he dealt not only with obvious subjects such as prostitution and rape (or allegations of rape in enemy propaganda) at or near the front, promiscuity and adultery back home, and the spread of venereal disease on both fronts but also with the erotic dimensions, however disguised or sublimated, of war hysteria, nursing, men in uniform, espionage, and, most complex of all, the heightened sense of physical being in the face of possible imminent death. The chapter on homosexuality was more tendentious than descriptive; in the guise of sociological scholarship Hirschfeld was content to make a few crucial points. Urnings, he argued, were as patriotic as heterosexuals, despite their persecution in peacetime; many Germans who had fled the country to avoid prosecution under Paragraph 175 returned to serve their fatherland. Far from being effeminate cowards, homosexuals were as brave as their heterosexual comrades, or even braver, since, having no wives or children, they tended to identify more closely with the group. Like the ancient Theban band of warrior lovers, they fought all the more fiercely beside their comrades, even though, unlike the Thebans, they had to keep secret the true meaning of that comradeship. Homosexual officers, though severely punished if found out, were especially solicitous of the welfare of their troops and could count on their loyalty in return.

Yet, Hirschfeld reassured his readers, though the comradeship so valued and celebrated in war often had a homoerotic component, and the homoerotic shaded almost imperceptibly into the sexual, those who were not constitutionally homosexual could not be "infected": "While it is perfectly true that the normally constituted person can occasionally have homosexual relations, it is totally untrue to conclude that in this way they can become homosexual. . . . Where there is no homosexual constitution, there is no homosexual seduction." At least as patriotic, brave, and loyal as their heterosexual fellow soldiers, and of no danger to their morality, Urnings in uniform had, Hirschfeld asserted, demonstrated their worth to their countries beyond any doubt or prejudice. Only those homosexuals of "feminine constitution" had been unfit for military service, but such men had proved ideal recruits for the medical corps and, echoing Walt Whitman, for tending the sick, the wounded, and the dying. The practical lesson was obvious: repeal Paragraph 175 and similar laws punishing homosexuals.

The actuality of homosexuality in wartime was a good deal subtler than Hirschfeld's account would suggest. There is a wealth of literary evidence that the unique and uniquely intense experience of life in the trenches awoke many to the homoerotic side of their nature, often only for the duration, sometimes for life. Homoerotic rather than homosexual, by and large, because the crowded conditions of trench life and military discipline did not lend themselves to overt sexual activity. But the very conditions of static trench warfare that militated against sexual relations encouraged intense comradely relationships between equals and solicitous, protective relationships between older and younger soldiers and between officers and the men under their command. If this seems reminiscent of English public schools or of the prewar youth movements of England and Germany, that is no accident. The homoerotic poems and memoirs of World War I read like extensions of passionate schoolboy friendships or the cult of youthful male beauty that were such common themes of the poetry, paintings, and—a new contribution—photography of the aesthetic movement at the turn of the century.

But with the coming of war these themes took on added poignancy, for not only were youth and youthful beauty and passion fleeting and ephemeral, now life itself might be extinguished at any moment. To be sure, prewar Uranian poetry had often included images of boys dying. That, however, was romantic fantasy. Now they were dying in fact, and horribly, by the tens of thousands. Thus, the images of homoerotic poetry and art remained familiar: youths bathing, a favorite and recurrent theme dating back to Walt Whitman; youthful saints and martyrs, the naked Saint Sebastian shot full of arrows most commonly; brave young medieval knights or boys, real or mythological, from classical antiquity—Hyacinthus, whom Apollo loved and killed by accident, or the favorite of the emperor Hadrian, Antinous, who drowned at the peak of his youth and beauty. But during the war the tone changed, from a wistful sense of loss to growing anger at the terrible waste of young life, from longingly extolling the beauty of idealized, etherealized youth to identifying with and speaking for real, very mortal flesh-and-blood young men.

In particular there were a number of English poets who wrote in this new vein, and of these Wilfred Owen was perhaps the most direct, the most unforgettable. Owen died at twenty-five from machine-gun fire a week to the day before the armistice in November 1918. Well before that he had come to empathize with those under his command to a degree that is only faintly suggested by the homoerotic poetry he composed, very much in the Uranian tradition, in his youth before the war. Because of his overwhelming feelings of identification with his men, a month prior to his death Owen, who had been sent home suffering from shell shock, requested to be returned to the front. "I came out in order to help these boys," he explained, "directly by leading them as well as an officer can, indirectly by watching their sufferings that I may speak for them as a pleader can." From that degree of personal identification with the young cannon fodder of World War I there was no going back to the refined and sentimental prewar Uranian poetry. The images of vulnerable flesh torn to pieces or slowly bleeding to death simply canceled out the earlier images. Owen himself canceled them out, deliberately excising the soft and pastoral from his depictions of young men dying. In an early version of a poem recounting the transportation of a badly wounded soldier away from the front he wrote:

If you could hear, at every jolt, the blood
Come gurgling from the froth-corrupted lungs,
And think how, once, his head was like a bud,
Fresh as a country rose, and keen, and young.

In the final version the reference back to a fresh-faced youth in a rural setting
is gone, a casualty of the war as surely as the dying soldier himself:

If you could hear, at every jolt, the blood
Come gurgling from the froth-corrupted lungs,
Obscene as cancer, bitter as the cud
Of vile, incurable sores on innocent tongues,

Those who could not accept or adjust to this change in sensibility, particularly those of an older generation who were most deeply committed to a
vision of an Arcadian, classically inspired homoeroticism, were simply left behind, living anachronisms in a postwar world that saw them as slightly embarrassing or merely irrelevant. One of the most interesting of these survivors,
from an era that seems more distant than it in fact was, was Baron Wilhelm
von Gloeden, a pioneer in the use of photography as a medium of homoerotic
art. Born into a wealthy aristocratic family in 1856, Gloeden developed tuber-
culosis in his early twenties and left Germany for the healthier climate of Italy.
There he settled in Sicily, in the coastal town of Taormina (still well known as
a gay resort, a reputation Gloeden himself did much to establish). He purchased a villa and staffed it with locals, including a fourteen-year-old boy
whom he nicknamed Il Moro, "the moor," because of his dark skin, who remained his servant and companion until Gloeden's death half a century later.

Gloeden's life of easy self-indulgence came to an abrupt end in 1888, when
financial support from his family back in Germany stopped; his stepfather,
having offended the kaiser, lost his estates and fled the country. Gloeden now
had to support himself, and to do so he took up photography, to which he
may have been introduced by his cousin, Wilhelm Plüschow, who had earlier
settled in Rome and was also to specialize in homoerotic subjects. Gloeden
gradually established himself as a photographer of local scenery and local
color for the tourist trade. Soon he was able to afford to resume his old way
of life and to indulge his real artistic interest, the photography of adolescent
boys, naked or scantily clad, sometimes with wreaths or garlands in their hair,
posed next to a classical ruin or set against the stunning scenery around Taormina, sometimes in a tableau, sometimes alone, sometimes just a pair of boys,

suggesting with a look or touch, but never more than suggesting, the possibility of pleasures to come. It proved a remarkably successful formula. Travelers from north of the Alps came to Taormina—where, as Keynes advised Strachey (speaking of Tunis, but the same would have been true of Sicily), the cost of "bed and boy" was cheap—and returned home with idealized, classicized photographic mementos of their stay by the shores of the Mediterranean. The roster of visitors to Gloeden's villa and the underground network of patrons who ordered his photographs from as far away as the United States were truly impressive.

Gloeden prospered until the outbreak of World War I, but when Italy joined the Allies, he chose to return to Germany rather than face internment as an enemy alien. At war's end he returned to Taormina, where he sequestered himself in his studio the first night, poring over old photographs, sobbing uncontollably at the sight of those of his former models killed in the war. He soon resumed his prewar way of life, including his photography, but it never brought its former rewards. In the aftermath of the war his art seemed too elegiac and effete, even somewhat absurd. The leading German photographer of homoerotic subjects between the two world wars was not Gloeden but the much younger Herbert List. Whereas Gloeden had invited his audience into an unreal but reassuring neoclassical world peopled with soft and beautiful, languid and passive adolescent youths playing at being ancient Greeks and Romans, List confronted his audience with surreal images of boys photographed from odd angles with stark lighting in often bizarre settings. And even when the props and settings were classical, the boys were modern boys placed not in but against, in contrast with, a distant and ultimately irretrievable cultural inheritance.

Luckily for Gloeden, the final disastrous blow to his world was not delivered until after his death in 1931. Five years later, as part of a purity campaign, the fascist police invaded his villa, smashed hundreds of photographic plates, arrested Il Moro, to whom Gloeden had left his estate, for possession of pornography, and seized the remaining photographs as evidence. Remarkably, Il Moro was able successfully to defend himself and the artistic merit of Gloeden's work. He was released, along with the remainder of the photographic plates, and lived quietly in Taormina until his death following World War II. The photographic plates, dispersed for safe keeping, were largely forgotten until the easing or successful legal challenges to censorship laws combined with the rise of the modern gay rights movement to allow for the republication of these artifacts from a different and seemingly distant past.

Gloeden was far from alone among those in his generation who, deeply imbued with a classically inspired vision of the ideal homosexual life, found the years after World War I inhospitable. A near contemporary and, like Gloeden, an expatriate, Edward Perry Warren, perfectly exemplified their dilemma and their ultimate inability to escape it. The son of a wealthy Boston manufacturer, he was very much the odd boy out in his childhood, interested from an early age primarily in art, poetry, and dressing up. He had a number of crushes on his classmates at school and college, but these apparently proved more frustrating than satisfying, and it was only after he graduated from Harvard and left America for England that he finally found a world in which he felt at home. Not that Warren was a unique figure in late-nineteenth-century Boston; far from it. The city was at the epicenter of the aesthetic movement in the United States, which, like its model and counterpart in England, was suffused with homoeroticism. The philosopher George Santayana; the head of the Boston Public Library, Theodore Dwight; the photographer F. Holland Day; the artist John Singer Sargent; the architect Ralph Adams Cram; and the pioneer collector of Americana Henry Sleeper were among the more or less certainly and predominantly homosexual members of the overlapping circles centered on Beacon Hill, Back Bay, Harvard, and the North Shore that largely constituted the Boston renaissance.

Warren knew many of these men but was never a full-fledged member of any of these circles, perhaps because, as one historian has tentatively suggested, he "was effeminate by the standards of masculine conduct of his era." Negotiating the difficult terrain within the homosocial world between conduct and appearance, between participation in the homosexual subculture and wider social acceptance, may well have been more difficult in nineteenth-century America than in England, at least until after the Wilde trials. And Warren settled in England long before that, early in the 1880s, when Wilde, whom he had made a point of meeting during Wilde's tour of the United States, was only just beginning his meteoric rise. In any event, the sheltered, all-male setting of an Oxford college suited Warren perfectly, and he spent much of his later life attempting to replicate a like environment for himself and his friends. He wrote a novel of homoerotic fulfillment in a college setting that was similar in many respects to the Cambridge chapters of Forster's *Maurice*. But unlike Forster, he did not have to reach beyond the university or down the social scale to an Alec Scudder to satisfy his protagonist's romantic yearnings. Like his fictional alter ego, Warren found the great love of his life, John Marshall, in college, and a few years after they left Oxford Warren purchased a country estate, Lewes House, where they lived surrounded by friends, many of them from their college days, until Marshall married in 1907.

Warren's ambitions extended beyond the creation of a perfect personal life for himself and Marshall at Lewes House. He also hoped to realize in modern times a semblance of the Greek ideal of homosexuality, to educate modern society and particularly his native country in Greek aesthetics and values, and above all to reassert the centrality of the masculine ideal as a model of social organization in contrast with the soft, feminized culture of the modern Christian West. Hence what was to prove his greatest and only lasting achievement: his amassing on behalf of the Boston Museum of Fine Arts of one of the great collections of classical art of the nineteenth century. Hence his proposal, never realized, to found a college at Oxford dedicated to the study of Greek language and culture. Hence his sponsorship of promising local boys, one of whom he adopted. And hence what he regarded as his greatest achievement, a long essay entitled *The Defense of Uranian Love*. It began promisingly with an account of how a shy, sensitive boy might come to recognize his true nature and ultimately mature into an adult capable of acting as a loving guide and mentor to youths like himself, clearly a role Warren wished someone had played for him and one that he wished he in turn might play for others. It is a genuinely touching passage because so personal and so deeply felt. Unfortunately, the essay then descends into a turgid exposition of the glories of Uranian love in ancient Greece and the need to revive not only the ideal but its practice in modern times, especially in the education and training of the young.

Sadly, Warren, like Benedict Friedländer, who put forward similar views at roughly the same time in Germany, could not see beyond these classically inspired models. Both men were unable to conceive of any means of accommodating their sexual nature to the modern world except through reproducing some version of the Greek ideal. Perhaps luckily for Friedländer, he died before World War I. But Warren lived on, and his ideas, eccentric even at the turn of the century, appeared truly bizarre and quite beside the point in the harsh light of postwar Europe. Warren himself sensed the change. He rightly thought of himself as the last of the aesthetes, and though he had been made an honorary fellow at Oxford and enjoyed living part of the year in his old college, like Gloeden in postwar Taormina, he sometimes felt out of place in 1920s Oxford. He was comfortable, even perhaps indirectly influential, with the neo-aesthetes but was dismayed by the influx of women and did not quite know what to make of the new crop of students, often battle-hardened veterans, let alone they of him. Many in the younger generation of undergraduates rejected the aesthetic tradition as hopelessly prewar and looked on Warren and his ilk as quaint anachronisms. What Warren could never fully acknowledge but even his official biographer recognized was that "there is in the modern world no place which can be or probably should be the home of the Greek idea."

Even the language that had been the vehicle of the Uranian sensibility began to fall into disuse following the war, a process hastened by the gradual decline in the importance of classical education. The term *Uranian* itself, despite its wide acceptance early in the century, was displaced by the clinical terms *homosexual* and *homosexuality,* and the once common references to figures from Greek and Roman history and mythology gradually disappeared during the interwar years as the near obsession the pioneers of homosexual self-definition had had with classical precedents lost its grip. That obsession, puzzling though it seems now, served an important purpose, however, giving those who sought to redefine homosexuality and the homosexual subculture from within two indispensable tools: a common vocabulary and a legitimizing past. What to later generations of readers seem frustratingly opaque references to obscure passages in Greek and Roman literature were to classically educated Victorian homosexuals a sort of coded language, at once private and universal, accessible to those in the know, rich in relevance to their own circumstances and aspirations, and international in character. That this vocabulary was drawn from classical antiquity not only distanced, even to a degree freed, the writings of Ulrichs, Friedländer, Symonds, Gide, Warren, and others from the oppressive categories of religious and legal discourse but lent their work a measure of respectability, placing it in a cultural tradition that could not be dismissed out of hand. As late as the early nineteenth century homosexuality and the homosexual subculture had been defined entirely negatively by outsiders. A century later that was no longer the case. A few articulate, even daring men within the subcultures of western Europe and the United States had begun the process of defining themselves, and it was for the most part the classical heritage, however misinterpreted or wishfully interpreted, that had allowed them to do so.

There were, however, dangers in their tendency to return constantly to the Greek example. What was unquestionably an inspiration could also be a constraint, limiting their ability to come to grips with the reality of the modern world. John Addington Symonds certainly felt this. One of the reasons he so admired Whitman was that Whitman appeared to be free of dependence on classical precedents. As for the notion that the practice of Greek love could be revived in nineteenth-century conditions, Symonds dismissed that contemptuously, saying that it "finds no place in modern life and has never found one." Indeed, what most struck him was the cruel contradiction between the ideal vision of manly love in the classical literature assigned to impressionable schoolboys and the furtive, often sordid reality of homosexuality in modern times. The susceptible youth, he declared, burdened by "the weight of law and custom," finds the work of Plato "maddening because it is stimulating to the imagination; wholly out of accord with the world he has to live in; too deeply in accord with his own impossible desires." E. M. Forster wrote *Maurice* in part in the hope of resolving or transcending that contradiction. "I wrote it," he explained to a friend, "neither for my friends or the public but because it was weighing on me. . . . Now I do feel that I have created something absolutely new, even to the Greeks."

Although Forster could never bring himself to publish *Maurice,* he was determined that it should be, and remain, a modern story. After he loaned the manuscript to Christopher Isherwood early in the 1930s, he worriedly asked the young novelist, "Does it date?" To which Isherwood replied, "Why shouldn't it date?" Indeed, he recalled, "the wonder of the novel was that it had been written when it had been written; the wonder was Forster himself, imprisoned within the jungle of pre-war prejudice, putting these unthinkable thoughts into words." That those thoughts, if not their setting, should remain fresh dictated Forster's later revisions. The original ending had the two lovers, Maurice and Alec, escaping into the wilds and living as woodcutters. Improbable as that seemed even before the war (though clearly inspired by Edward Carpenter's life with George Merrill), it was absurd, even laughable, in "the transformed England of the First World War." It belonged, Forster explained, "to an England where it was still possible to get lost. There is no forest or fell to escape to today, no cave to curl up in, no deserted valley for those who wish to be left alone." For Forster such references to an Arcadian ideal served as an inspiration but not as a model. Indeed he often used the classical inheritance as the starting point for his humorous stories on gay themes, such as "The Classical Annex," in which an adolescent boy is magically joined to a Roman statue of an athlete, there to be blissfully buggered for eternity.

By the likes of Edward Perry Warren, Benedict Friedländer, or Wilhelm von Gloeden no such levity would have been tolerated. They took the Greek ideal of homosexuality deadly seriously, not merely as an inspiration but as a model to be imitated in modern life. And if modern life and the Greek ideal should prove incompatible, they had the patience and the faith (and the money and the social position) to wait and work for the realization of their dream, as well as to live it as best they could themselves. World War I put an end to that illusion and to their hopes. The Uranian sensibility, a delicate and ephemeral phenomenon at the best of times, could not survive the war. The vision, so central to the Uranian idea of ancient Greece, of sexual innocence lost and long forgotten but perhaps, just perhaps, not lost irretrievably was mortally wounded in the trenches of the western front. So much youth and beauty wasted, so much comradeship cynically exploited, robbed that vision of its idealism, rendering it almost cruel. Those who, like Gloeden and Warren, continued to cling to that vision were left, irretrievably, behind. Others, like Gide and Forster, took what they needed from the Uranian tradition and moved on. As for the war and postwar generations, they were freed, violently to be sure but freed nonetheless, to redefine their sexuality in modern terms.

Part 3

## Organizing a Subculture

## Chapter 15

**Between the Wars**

The Uranian tradition of harking back to ancient Greece as a justification, an inspiration, even as a model for homoeroticism in the modern world, a tradition that had played a central role in the emergence of defined and articulate homosexual subcultures in the nineteenth-century West, would in any event have suffered a decline in the twentieth century as the influence of classical education declined. But the horrors of World War I all but killed the Uranian sensibility, making it seem irrelevant, overly sentimental and effete, indeed little short of obscene, set against the harsh realities of the modern industrial world.

Not that more generally acceptable views of masculinity, even including the cult of unselfconscious manly athleticism, untainted by anything as offensive to respectable society as homoeroticism, fared much better. After all, it was just such hearty English public-school boys and German and English youth leaders who most enthusiastically rushed to fight for their countries, only to be slaughtered by the tens of thousands. Not surprisingly, then, there was in the 1920s in almost all the belligerent nations a conscious revolt not only against military values but against conventional notions of masculinity, which were seen by many as having contributed to the war itself and certainly to war fever. Especially in England it became fashionable for young men of college age—that is, military age—regardless of their ultimate sexual orientation to dabble in homosexuality. There is scarcely a memoir of anyone who went to Oxford or Cambridge in these years that does not mention this as central to the temper of the times. According to the journalist and academic Goronwy Rees,

It would be fair to say that, as in Strachey's Cambridge, so in Oxford in the 1920s and early 30s homosexuality was . . . at once a fashion, a doctrine and a way of life, and, as with the Apostles, exercised an influence which extended far beyond the boundaries of the university. It could be said that no more people were affected by it than are today [Rees wrote this in 1968] addicted to marijuana, LSD or Flower Power, and the comparison would be just, because homosexuality was very largely the particular form which the revolt of the young took at the universities at that time. But the effect of a cult on an institution or a society is not limited to the number of its actual adherents, any more than the influence of Catholicism is limited to those who go to Mass.

It is an apt comparison since those who, like Rees, went on after university to live heterosexual lives were undoubtedly affected in their thinking. It is surely no accident that it was members of his generation, young in the 1920s, who in middle age recommended and then enacted laws decriminalizing homosexual relations between consulting adults in private. Indeed Rees was himself a member of the Wolfenden Committee, which recommended decriminalization. On those who remained or became predominantly homosexual after leaving university, as well as on nonuniversity men drawn into their circles, the effect of college-age sexual experience was, of course, both greater and more immediate. For many of the "Bright Young Things" of the mid- to late 1920s, Brian Howard and Harold Acton perhaps most notably, their thinly disguised homosexuality was a central ingredient in a carefully cultivated public persona—witty, sophisticated, irreverent, a touch Wildean. These neo-aesthetes were able to set the tone for much of London society, the theater, and the world of fashion, but even then they were known, and now they are remembered, if at all, primarily for their style and as the inspiration for the most flamboyant character, Anthony Blanch, in Evelyn Waugh's evocation of Oxford in the 1920s in *Brideshead Revisited.* Acton, Howard, and company remain quaintly archaic figures, as trapped in their decade as any of their prewar counterparts.

A college generation is short. The Acton era at Oxford was immediately followed by the Auden era, and the change was both sudden and dramatic. Noel Annan, in his collective biography of his own generation, put it well: "When Auden went up to Oxford . . . homosexuals were aesthetes. Auden . . . was not an aesthete. He had no wish to be an Oxford Wit . . . his homosexuality was not an adornment of his nature but a routine expression of his attitude to life. Homosexuality had become normal." To him and to others in his circle the frivolousness of many of their only slightly older contemporaries was disturbing. Christopher Isherwood wrote of Brian Howard, "What was inexcusable was that he used [his talent] so seldom. His self indulgence was babyish; he was one of the most fascinating and dangerous babies of his generation." To Isherwood and his friends, all of whom ultimately dropped their masks, the issues raised by their homosexuality were or at least became serious matters, involving nothing less than a questioning of traditional notions of masculinity, and of the place of homosexuals in society, that appeared to imply, indeed almost to demand, a new gay sensibility. And the term *gay* is here appropriate, for the tone is recognizably modern. It was members of this generation who began to define the terms, if not yet the terminology, of a distinctively twentieth-century gay subculture. They deliberately rejected the conventions of prewar homoeroticism in favor of something more open, more direct, more self-accepting, more frankly sexual; they were no longer dependent on historical precedents or classical allusions but consciously of their own time.

They are therefore an especially important generation in the history of homosexuality but also, as an acutely self-aware postwar generation, especially fascinating. Born between roughly 1902 and 1912, what they had most obviously in common, in addition to their sexuality, was that they were too young, often only just too young, to fight in World War I. Mixed in with the relief they must have felt was a sense of survivors' guilt. After all, their fathers, uncles, older brothers, older friends, and schoolmates had fought, had died. Many also felt that they had missed the great event of their lifetime. Thus, they had to come to terms both with their sexuality and with the war they had missed. Those who most clearly set the tone, both in stating their dual problem and in resolving it, in England belonged to a small group of young writers, all of them major figures: Christopher Isherwood, born in 1904, W. H. Auden and John Lehmann, both three years younger, and Stephen Spender, the youngest of the group, born in 1909.

All of them went to school or university together or met shortly thereafter, all were more or less openly gay, and all decided in their early to mid-twenties to leave England because of its social and sexual constraints and puritanical censorship of new writing and art. But they went not to England's wartime ally France (to which their elders and mentors in Bloomsbury, as well as most American expatriates, automatically looked) but to Germany, the home of their former enemy, where homosexuality was illegal but, despite Paragraph 175, there was an extraordinary openness about sexuality and relatively little censorship. There had been exceptions before the war to the preference for France among English and American homosexual artists and writers. The American painter Marsden Hartley always felt more at home in "essentially masculine" Germany than in "utterly feminine" France. He first went to Germany in 1912, and the death of a young German officer whom he loved early in the war inspired his first major series of paintings. Hartley returned to Germany after the war, even as late as the first year of the Nazi era. For him, as for the Isherwood circle, postwar Germany was almost irresistibly attractive. Hamburg, Vienna, and above all Berlin in the 1920s were open cities. Before Hitler came to power Berlin had as many as a hundred—some estimates placed it far higher—bars, cafes, restaurants, dance halls, and the like, catering to a gay or mixed clientele, most of them located to the east or south of the city's historic center, from the fashionable area near the Alexanderplatz to the seedier neighborhoods around the Hallesches Tor. Every imaginable taste and type was provided for, and most places of entertainment specialized, though a few of the larger or more upscale establishments attracted a wide range of customers, including the curious out to see for themselves something of Berlin's notorious nightlife. As Isherwood put it, "Berlin meant boys."

There were at least a couple dozen periodicals, some short-lived, others lasting into the early 1930s, including not only Brand's *Der Eigene* and the publications of the Scientific Humanitarian Committee (although the important yearbook of the committee had fallen victim to the great inflation of 1923) but popular weeklies and monthlies full of pictures, gossip, news, stories, and personal ads, representing a variety of gay organizations or aimed at readers with specialized sexual interests. There were recreational and sporting clubs and societies with exclusively gay memberships, gay theater groups, and mainstream plays and films on gay themes. The lesbian subculture of Berlin was scarcely less visible and almost as variegated, with each of its major and lesser categories served by a wide assortment of bars and social clubs concentrated primarily in districts southwest of the city center. Like its gay male counterpart, and for that matter a distinct category of transvestite bars and cabarets, the lesbian demimonde became something of a tourist attraction. All in all, gay or lesbian, there was to be nothing like it again until New York and San Francisco in the 1970s, and certainly there had been nothing like it before.

When Ernest Hemingway visited Berlin in the 1920s he was disgusted by its decadence, but that was just fine so far as the expatriate English homosexuals were concerned. As Spender saw it, young Americans went to Paris in the 1920s to escape prohibition, while young Englishmen went to Berlin to escape prudery. "For them drink, for us sex," as he pithily summed it up. And sex they got. Three of these four venturers into the homosexual subcultures of central Europe—Isherwood, Spender, and Lehmann—wrote memoirs, or memoirs thinly disguised as novels, with each other as principal characters. Inevitably all of these works, set in the late twenties and early thirties, are shadowed by the impending horrors of Nazism, but that lengthening shadow served in their recollections largely as a counterpoint to the brighter, happier world that preceded it or even as a dramatic backdrop for their personal adventures. All of these memoirs were celebrations of the liberating power of sex, indeed of promiscuous sex, and especially, of course, of homosexual sex. Lehmann perhaps put it best. Weighing the pros and cons of being gay, he set against "the guilty feeling of being a misfit, . . . the absence of family and physical succession, [and] the danger of being pursued by the law" two major advantages: the greater freedom to leave a bad relationship and "that inversion, moving vertically through society rather than horizontally, can give the homosexual a far greater experience and understanding of his fellow men than the 'straight' young man, marrying into his own class and staying in it, can ever have."

Lehmann might have added that what was true of barriers of class was equally true of barriers of nationality. This was hardly a new discovery, to be sure; the pioneers of homosexual self-definition had consciously been breaking through the barriers of class and nationality for more than half a century. What differentiated Lehmann and his friends from their predecessors was that what Forster before them and Symonds before that were groping toward, sometimes hesitantly and defensively, the young men of the 1920s grasped with both hands and without apology. That they and those with whom they had sex might, had they both been a few years older, have been trying to kill each other only heightened the exhilarating feeling of freedom from convention they all felt and reinforced the sense they all had of a different loyalty, a loyalty to what Isherwood called "his tribe."

Isherwood's story is especially instructive, since he was based in Berlin, at the center of events in Germany, and also especially moving, since he faced most directly the issues of how to come to terms both with his sexuality and with the possibility or reality of war and, beyond that, of how to resolve and make sense of the complex relationship between the two. When Isherwood went to Berlin in 1929 he happened to rent a room next door to Magnus Hirschfeld's institute, where he was immediately subjected to the old man's passion for the classification of sexual types, introduced to some of those who were being studied or counseled by Hirschfeld or his staff, and shown around the institute's museum, in which evidence of human sexuality in all its variety, from the most loving to the most bizarre, was on display. Isherwood found all of this embarrassing, disquieting, and often a little absurd. He saw "the silly solemn old professor with his doggy mustache, thick peering spectacles, and clumsy German-Jewish boots" as a figure of fun. Yet when André Gide visited the institute and assumed a condescending manner, Isherwood suddenly realized that "he loved Hirschfeld, . . . [that] they were all three of them on the same side, whether [he] liked it or not. And later he would learn to honor them both as heroic leaders of his tribe." But that was in the future, and it was not the serious side of the subculture in Germany that was then his primary interest; far from it. His excuse for being in Berlin was to write, his means for doing so was to teach English (supplemented by a small stipend from a gay uncle back in England), and his purpose was to explore the bar scene, where he spent his evenings. His particular favorite, the Cosy Corner, specialized in working-class boys out to make a few marks or, if they were lucky, to meet a friend and patron; this was, after all, the beginning of the Great Depression.

After many brief encounters, one on-and-off affair, and frequent changes of address, in March 1932, less than a year before Hitler came to power, Isherwood met Heinz Neddermeyer, "a slim boy of about seventeen with large brown eyes," with whom he quickly and gratefully settled into quiet domesticity. It could not last. Within weeks of Hitler's appointment as German chancellor in January 1933 Isherwood's apolitical private world started to disintegrate. Suddenly, as Spender put it, "everything became politics." Determined to get out of Germany as quickly as possible, Isherwood was equally determined to take with him not only Heinz but, at considerable potential risk to all three of them, an employee of Hirschfeld's institute who was also a Communist. As it turned out, the border crossing was uneventful, and he and Heinz went on to Greece, stopping in Vienna only to visit John Lehmann, and then by way of France to England. There too Heinz encountered nothing worse than the usual formalities. However, when his entry permit expired, he had to return to Germany, from which, this time on his own, he again had no difficulty leaving once Isherwood had sent him the money for the trip. It was not Nazi Germany but democratic England that first circumscribed Heinz's freedom of movement.

The immigration officer at Harwich became suspicious of the youth, whose passport identified him as a domestic servant, who might illegally seek employment in England, whose money had been supplied by Isherwood, whose relationship with Isherwood was, to say the least, unusual. Heinz was refused entry. Auden, who had gone with Isherwood to meet the boat, sized up the situation and the offending official immediately: "As soon as I saw that bright eyed little rat I knew we were done for. He understood the whole situation at a glance—because he's one of us." So Isherwood had no choice but to join Heinz on the Continent, where they wandered from country to country depending on whim or on their ability to obtain visas for Heinz. There were some good times, particularly during visits from Forster and Bob Buckingham, from Spender and his companion Tony Hyndman, from dissolute Brian Howard and his equally dissolute German working-class companion of the moment, and from Auden, in various major European cities from Amsterdam to Lisbon. But caught between England, where they could not go, and Germany, where they dared not, it was only a matter of time before the exigencies of European politics pressed in on them inescapably. In March 1935 Hitler repudiated the disarmament clauses of the Treaty of Versailles and re-instituted the military draft. If and when Heinz was called up, he would have to return to Germany or else never be able to return, unless he could change his citizenship. Heinz's draft notice finally caught up with him in mid-1936. Frantically Isherwood tried to find Heinz a new nationality, but with no luck, and Heinz, expelled from various countries as undesirable, was told by a lawyer that he would have to go back to Germany and apply for a visa to Belgium. He did so, but, visa in hand, he was arrested as a draft dodger in May 1937, tried for that and for homosexual offenses, and sentenced to six months in jail, one year of labor service, and two years in the army.

Heinz's finally being forced back to Germany pushed Isherwood decisively toward opting out of Europe and the impending European war, which now seemed inevitable. The process of separation had begun in 1934, when Heinz was refused entry into England. Isherwood had gone to the Continent to be with Heinz, but his leaving England had been as much emotional as physical. As he wrote in his memoirs, "The England of Nearly Everybody had rejected Heinz. Before long he [here referring to himself] would be rejecting their England." Five years later there was now the real possibility that England would go to war with a Germany for which Heinz would be fighting. That posed a conflict of loyalties between love and duty beyond anything the gay poets of World War I had had to face:

> Suppose, Christopher now said to himself, I have a Nazi army at my mercy. I can blow it up by pressing a button. The men in that army are notorious for torturing and murdering civilians—all except for one of them, Heinz. Will I press the button? No—wait: Suppose I know that Heinz himself, out of cowardice or

moral infection, has become as bad as they are and takes part in all their crimes. Will I press the button, even so? Christopher's answer, given without the slightest hesitation, was: Of course not. . . . Suppose that army goes into action and has just one casualty, Heinz himself. Will I press the button now and destroy his fellow criminals? No emotional reaction this time, but a clear answer, not to be evaded: Once I have refused to press that button because of Heinz, I can never press it. Because every man in that army could be somebody's Heinz.

The dilemma that Isherwood had been forced to confront ever since "everything," even the most personal matters, "became politics" he had finally resolved by subordinating the political to the personal. Although, as he recognized, this was a highly idiosyncratic conclusion, he was not alone in contemplating it; Forster's declaration, published the previous year, that if compelled to chose between his country and his friends, he hoped he would have the courage to chose his friends, was essentially similar.

Isherwood had another, no less provocative reason, or some might say rationale, for turning his back on the coming European struggle, a reason that, though less individualized, also grew out of his sexuality. Once again it was a matter of loyalties. Like everyone else on the left in the 1930s, he was willing to ally with almost anyone against fascism. But his first loyalty, he realized, was to his tribe, and because of that he could not declare solidarity with the Communists, since in the Soviet Union, as in Nazi Germany, his tribe was persecuted: "[He] had done his best to minimize the Soviet betrayal of its own principles. After all, he had said to himself, anti-homosexual laws exist in most capitalist countries, including England and the United States. Yes—but if Communists claim that their system is juster than capitalism, doesn't that make their injustice to homosexuals less excusable and their hypocrisy even viler? He now realized he must dissociate himself from the Communists, even as a fellow traveler."

Neither for Isherwood nor, indeed, for the Soviet Union had this always been so. World War I had ended throughout most of central and eastern Europe in revolution, and with revolution had come the hope, the promise, of freedom not only political but also social, cultural, even sexual, and nowhere more so than in conjunction with that greatest of wartime revolutions, the revolution in Russia. Distinct and vibrant homosexual subcultures in Russia's major cities, comparable to those that had emerged in western Europe a century or more earlier, were little more than a generation old at the time of the revolution. Before that there had been individuals in public life and in the arts known or rumored to be homosexual—Gogol and Tchaikovsky perhaps most famously—as well as all-male institutions for the training of the young rumored to be hotbeds of sexual activity. Legally attitudes toward homosexuality sometimes reflected, sometimes ran counter to, developments in western Europe. Homosexuality in the military had been punishable since the reign of Peter the Great, but for the civilian population only since 1832. The penalty for anal intercourse between men was the loss of all civil and property rights and exile to Siberia for up to five years, and perversion of a minor was even more severely punished.

However, these laws appear to have been enforced rarely, and "homosexuality never served as a vehicle for symbolic politics, as it did in England and Germany during the same period." Even so, it was debated in late-nineteenth-century Russia in much the same terms as in western Europe. Conservatives insisted that as a degenerative condition likely to infect others, especially in modern urban settings, or as depraved behavior against which the weak must be protected even from themselves, or simply as conduct "the criminality of [which] is deeply rooted in the popular consciousness" homosexuality must remain a crime. To liberals such as the prominent jurist Vladimir Nabokov, father of the future novelist, this constituted a violation not only of individual rights but of the fundamental principle that laws should not be made or applied arbitrarily. Drawing on Feuerbach, Aletrino, Hirschfeld, and Ellis, he argued that however repugnant he or others might find homosexuality, the function of the law was not to punish private vices, still less to single out this particular vice for special condemnation simply on the basis of prejudice. A summary of his views on homosexuality was published in the yearbook of the Scientific Humanitarian Committee in 1903, the same year that Russia promulgated a revised criminal code.

The new code reflected the general trend toward the secularization of law and government institutions in Russia but stopped short of making an absolute distinction between public and private acts in sexual matters. Anal intercourse between men remained a crime, but no other homosexual acts were penalized, and all references to bestiality and to moral condemnation were omitted. Even before the adoption of the new criminal code, the liberalizing reforms of the 1860s had, by the end of the nineteenth century, created a cultural climate that propelled Russia to the forefront of European modernism, and at the heart of this movement was a circle of artists and writers, many of them more or less openly homosexual, centered around Sergei Diaghilev and his avant-garde magazine, *World of Art,* founded in 1898. Diaghilev is best remembered as a ballet impresario (and the sponsor and lover of the great dancer Nijinsky), but he was in fact a brilliantly successful backer of artists of all types—composers, painters, writers.

Of the writers one of the most remarkable and certainly the most openly homosexual was Mikhail Kuzmin. Born in 1872 into a provincial family of Old Believers, he moved with his parents to St. Petersburg in early adolescence and in his early twenties to Egypt and then to Italy. As with many northern Europeans of his own and earlier generations, his Mediterranean sojourn was a source of sexual as well as artistic awakening and the subject of much of his later writing. On his return to St. Petersburg in 1904 he was introduced into the Diaghilev circle, and two years later, following the revolution of 1905, which briefly all but ended censorship, he published an openly homosexual novel, *Wings,* in Russia under his own name. That in itself was a remarkable achievement. After all, his American and French contemporaries, Edward Stevenson and André Gide, both of whom first wrote on homosexual themes at the same time, either published in a foreign country under a pseudonym or dared not publish except for private circulation for more than a decade. Moreover, like the nearly contemporary E. M. Forster's *Maurice* (which was never published during its author's lifetime), *Wings* had a happy ending, with the young peasant hero, having accepted his sexuality, going off with his older, better-educated lover. (By contrast, the first Russian lesbian novel, published a year later, ended in tragedy.)

Not that Kuzmin always fared well with the czarist government, let alone the critics, literary or political. Some of his later works were seized by the authorities, and he and other openly homosexual and lesbian writers were savagely attacked not only by conservative commentators but also by some on the left who accused them of confusing sexual freedom with freedom in a wider sense and of pursuing individual sexual expression to the exclusion of social reform and the group discipline necessary to remake society. Nonetheless, when the Bolsheviks seized power late in 1917, they abolished the czarist criminal code, including its antihomosexual provisions. The Soviet criminal code that replaced it, promulgated in 1922 and amended in 1926, left sexual relations between consenting adults in private beyond the reach of the law.

Advocates of sexual law reform in the rest of Europe looked to this as an enlightened model, and nowhere more so than in Germany. There also the war ended in a revolution that appeared to hold out the promise of similar reforms. On the evening of the abdication of the kaiser in November 1918, with the sound of sporadic gunfire from various parts of the city audible in the background, Magnus Hirschfeld spoke to a crowd in front of the Reichstag, hailing the republic and the advent of socialism. And justifiably so, it seemed, since the Social Democrats, who presided over the transition to a republic, had been the only party openly to support the repeal of Paragraph 175 before the war. But the German Social Democrats, unlike the Russian Bolsheviks, were intent on legitimacy, on constitutional, not violent, change, which meant that old laws, even bad laws, would not be arbitrarily stricken from the books but would have to be changed by normal legislative processes. Had the Social Democrats had a clear majority in the new parliament, perhaps Paragraph 175 would have been repealed, but they did not. They needed the support of other parties, and one of those they depended on was the Center Party, a Catholic party, which had been an outspoken opponent of homosexual law reform before the war. Thus, decriminalization was sacrificed to political necessity. This was, of course, only one of many compromises, deals, and retreats the early Weimar government felt it had to make for the sake of a stable transition to a democratic republic. But the cost was high. The government weakened or alienated its support among many of what should have been its natural constituencies.

For Hirschfeld the cruelest indication of how unrealistic his early high hopes for the new republic were, and how quickly dashed, was the fate of the landmark film *Anders als die Andern* (Different from the others). Sponsored by the Scientific Humanitarian Committee, the film tells the story of a violinist, played by Conrad Veidt, who is loved by two women but loves another man. Tragically, the violinist is denounced by a blackmailer and sentenced to a term of imprisonment under Paragraph 175. He commits suicide. His young lover is at first determined to follow him but is dissuaded by a doctor, Hirschfeld playing himself, who urges him instead to devote his energies to the repeal of the antihomosexual laws. The film premiered in Berlin in May 1919, with Hirschfeld appearing in person to introduce it to the audience. Although it was widely shown in Germany and Austria, a number of cities banned the film, and Hirschfeld, hoping to counter mounting criticism, invited government officials and politicians to a series of special screenings at his institute. Nonetheless, on the recommendation of a panel of psychiatrists, the film was banned nationwide in the summer of 1920, just over a year after its release.

There were compensations. It was also in the immediate postwar period that Hirschfeld met the much younger Karl Giese, who was to be his colleague and companion until Hirschfeld's death in 1935. Professionally, although he never abandoned the agitation for reform, his disillusionment with the new regime led him to seek satisfaction elsewhere, primarily in the scientific and research dimensions of the issue. In 1919 he founded the Institute for Sexual Science, where homosexuality could be studied and homosexuals counseled as part of a broad-based concern with sex and sexuality—historically, clinically, and scientifically. It was the first institution of its kind in the world, predating the Kinsey Institute in the United States by a generation. Hirschfeld also played a central role in founding an international sexual reform movement. In 1921 he convened the first Congress for Sexual Reform, which was attended by specialists from most Western nations in fields as diverse as eugenics, family planning, law reform, and sex education. Later in the decade he oversaw the creation of the World League for Sexual Reform, which sponsored congresses in Copenhagen, London, Vienna, and Brno. Following the Vienna congress, held in 1930, Hirschfeld embarked on a world tour, hoping to advance the cause not only in the United States, where he spent three months, but outside the West and beyond the realm of specialists. Although he always sought to keep his institute and the congresses committed to scientific inquiry and rational advocacy above and apart from politics, by the early 1930s that was no longer possible. Even as early as the 1930 Vienna congress the nonpolitical stance of the league had come under attack as naive. Wilhelm Reich, one of the most radical of sexual reformers, argued that the real issue was "whether the political relations of a given state or social system permit the practical implementation of scientific knowledge—in other words whether or not social reform is actually possible under existing conditions." Reich's conclusion was that it was not, and he quit the league to found his own German Association for Proletarian Sexual Politics.

Tensions of this sort within the sexual reform movement were hardly new. Hirschfeld had been challenged by the Gemeinschaft der Eigenen before the war, and similar divisions appeared in the early 1920s. But in the immediate postwar years differences of opinion led to a division of labor, not, as happened a decade later, to an open split. Hirschfeld simply devoted himself almost entirely to the work of his institute and the World League and into the concoction and promotion of an anti-impotence compound, a commingling of private business with his work as counselor and scientific researcher that confirmed the worst suspicions of his enemies and troubled even many of his allies. Meanwhile the leadership of the active reform movement shifted to a younger generation, led by Kurt Hiller, and to new organizations, such as Hiller's Action Committee, founded in 1920. Though in certain respects a peculiarly German phenomenon, the Action Committee faced problems symptomatic not only of what was after all the first wide-ranging movement for homosexual liberation in history, in Germany in the 1920s, but also of the modern gay liberation movement, which emerged half a century later, namely, of how to protect and advance the interests of an unpopular minority. Hiller was impatient with the lack of results from the earlier sexual reform movement and disillusioned with the failed revolution of 1918 in Germany, which to him, as to many on the left, had compromised too much and changed too little. Although he had been active in Hirschfeld's Scientific Humanitarian Committee since 1908 and was a member of its governing board after the war, sexual reform was only one aspect of Hiller's concerns; he aimed at nothing less than a thorough recasting of German society to bring it back to its spiritual roots and true nature. Temperamentally an activist—he coined the term in German in 1915—he became a pacifist and a vocal opponent of militarism during the war.

Yet, while he detested the narrow prudery and materialism of the bourgeoisie, Hiller was no democrat either in his politics or in his autocratic leadership of the Action Committee. Fearing the tyranny of the majority, he believed in the unfettered development of the individual and that society must be guided by its natural leaders. He was, therefore, very much concerned with the training and formation of elites, which brought him into contact with theoreticians of the youth movement and educational reform such as Hans Blüher and Gustav Wyneken. Like theirs, his social theories were clearly influenced by his sexuality (though, like Hirschfeld, he was careful not to openly acknowledge it, at least not until late in life, after World War II), and his sexuality, coupled with his elitism, determined the nature and strategy of his activism. Convinced that sexual reform would never be achieved by democratic means—the masses, he was certain, were too prejudiced for that—he hoped to effect change by persuading those interests and individuals who wielded the greatest power and influence in German society. And that, in turn, required transforming the homosexuals' status as a persecuted minority from a disadvantage into an advantage, a process that required mobilizing the homosexual community's intense self-awareness, its feelings of solidarity, and its moral claims as a persecuted group. Hiller's insight into the peculiar problem of the homosexual rights movement—or that of any similar minority—derived as much from his Jewishness as from his own sexuality.

The purpose of Hiller's Action Committee was to create the needed sense of community and solidarity among homosexuals, regardless of their social class, their political affiliation, or their views on the nature of homosexuality. Representatives of the Scientific Humanitarian Committee, of the breakaway Gemeinschaft der Eigenen, and of purely social organizations and clubs were all welcome. At one point Hiller even contemplated a mass coming out as a way of transforming public perceptions of homosexuality. Nothing came of that, of course, and even the solidarity born of revolution and of disillusionment with its results proved impossible to maintain. There were simply too many groups with too many divergent views for a united movement to survive in the absence of a shared sense of persecution. And that one crucial element was lacking. Not only in Berlin but in virtually every city of any size in Germany the homosexual community had its bars and other meeting places, its organizations and publications, and above all increasing confidence that it would by and large be left alone.

The history of the leading homosexual social organization is symptomatic. The German Friendship Association was founded shortly after the war to serve the needs of ordinary people, in contrast to the research-oriented Scientific Humanitarian Committee or the elitist and culturally oriented Gemeinschaft der Eigenen. It had weekly meetings, published a newspaper, sponsored dances and other social events, founded branches throughout Germany, and held annual delegates' conferences. At first the association was militant, publishing news of the Scientific Humanitarian Committee, cooperating with the Action Committee, and as late as its second annual delegates' conference, in 1922, calling for an activist role by its members. A year later, however, following a change in leadership, it retreated from political activism into a predominantly social role. Ironically, just as the society, under the direction of Friedrich Radszuweit, was shifting its focus away from militancy, he changed its name to the League for Human Rights. The new title notwithstanding, the league's primary purpose was to provide entertainment, recreation, and information for its members through clubs in major cities and a variety of magazines aimed at different segments of both the gay and lesbian communities.

Radszuweit did not abandon opposition to Paragraph 175—the league offered legal assistance to its members who were arrested—but although the antihomosexual laws remained on the books and a danger to individuals, and there were periodic attempts at censorship, they were perceived as less and less of a serious threat to the subculture as a whole and to the organizations and publications that competed, often fiercely, for recognition as its champions. Hirschfeld's dream of orderly progress toward public and official enlightenment, let alone Hiller's vision of raising the consciousness of a minority and, through that, of wider social elites, disintegrated into a welter of subgroups, each with its own interests, and finally was overwhelmed by the unprecedented freedom and openness the subculture enjoyed in Germany in the 1920s. "Except for a few minor cliques," Hirschfeld lamented in 1927, "homosexuals are in reality almost totally lacking in feelings of solidarity. In fact, it would be difficult to find another class of mankind which has proved so incapable of organizing to secure its basic legal and human rights."

Hirschfeld and Hiller were, therefore, compelled to change their tactics. Unable even to get the issue before the legislature, in 1925 they joined with six other, mostly nonhomosexual groups to form a Coalition for the Reform of the Sexual Criminal Code in the hope of winning the repeal of Paragraph 175 as part of a package of reforms. The coalition published its proposals in 1927, and the issue was taken up by a Reichstag committee two years later. Although the Social Democrats, Liberal Democrats, and Communists were able to put together a bare majority of fifteen to thirteen in the committee in favor of repeal, their recommendation never reached the full Reichstag. The committee vote took place on 16 October 1929. The crash of the American stock market thirteen days later pushed all other issues aside. Reform of the sexual criminal code was tabled as Germany began its descent into economic depression, political chaos, and finally totalitarianism.

For unpopular minorities the situation began to worsen quickly, well before the Nazis came to power. As a Jew as well as an advocate of homosexual rights, and because of his prominent role in the prewar Eulenburg scandal, Hirschfeld had long been a popular target of the far right and had been threatened and even physically assaulted a number of times in the turbulent early 1920s. One reason why Hiller had assumed a leadership role in the reform movement was to decrease its identification with Hirschfeld. So dangerous had the situation become by the early 1930s that after he completed his world tour, Hirschfeld dared not return to Germany but, hopeful that the storm would pass, stayed in neighboring countries, where he was when Hitler came to power and embarked on the systematic persecution of homosexuals. The contrary and widely accepted impression that Nazism and homosexuality were closely linked was, and is, due almost entirely to the undoubted and often flamboyant homosexuality of the leader of the Nazi storm troopers, the SA, Ernst Röhm, which then and later led some propagandists, writers, and filmmakers to illustrate the depravity of the Nazis by impugning their sexuality. Thus, simply to cite one of many possible examples, the mystery writer Ross MacDonald early in his career wrote a spy story in which he characterized the Nazis in lurid terms: "I thought of Röhm, the homosexual chief of the SA, whom Hitler murdered with his own talented hands in the blood bath of 1934. I thought of the elegant Nazi boys I had seen in Munich with their lipstick and their eye shadow and their feminine swagger and the black male guns in their holsters. I thought of the epicene white worms which change their sex and burrow in the bodies of dead men underground."

In fact the National Socialists were virulently homophobic from the first. When Adolph Brand sent questionnaires to all political parties in 1928 requesting their views on sexual law reform, the Nazis responded, characteristically:

It is not necessary that you and I live, but it is necessary that the German people live. And it can only live if it can fight, for life means fighting. And it can only fight if it maintains its masculinity. It can only maintain its masculinity if it exercises discipline, especially in matters of love. Free love and deviance are undisciplined. Therefore we reject you, as we reject anything which hurts our people. Anyone who even thinks of homosexual love is our enemy. We reject anything which emasculates our people and makes it a plaything for our enemies, for we know that life is a fight and it's madness to think that men will ever embrace fraternally. Natural history teaches us the opposite. Might makes right. And the stronger will always win over the weak. Let's see to it that once again we become the strong! But this we can only do in one way—the German people must once again learn how to exercise discipline. We therefore reject any form of lewdness, especially homosexuality, because it robs us of our last chance to free our people from the bondage which now enslaves it.

Not that the issue of homosexual law reform in Germany was a simple matter of left versus right, supporters united against opponents. Four years earlier, in 1924, when a serial killer who specialized in street kids and male hustlers was tried and executed, it was revealed during the trial that he had been employed as a police informer. The police commissioner in Hannover, where the murders took place, was Gustav Noske, a Social Democrat who in January 1919 had led the suppression of a Communist uprising against the Social Democratic–dominated government. Here was an opportunity for the Communists to take revenge, and in press attacks on police handling of the murder case Communist papers slung as much mud as possible, demanding at one point that "the police be purged of monarchist, sadist, homosexual, and fascist elements."

This was hardly compatible with official Communist Party policy, which called for the repeal of Paragraph 175 as part of an overall program of sexual reform, but the sordid details of the case, together with the divisions the trial revealed within the Communist Party and between the Communists and other parties of the left were dangerous portents for the future. Not only was the Nazi path to power eased by left-wing divisiveness but the support for homosexual rights from most elements of the left opened them to criticism and finally to repression as a danger to national morals and discipline. It is hardly surprising, therefore, that from the moment the Nazis came to power homosexuals, along with Jews and Communists, were prime targets. Hitler was appointed chancellor of Germany on 30 January 1933. On 23 February the Prussian minister of the interior issued a directive suppressing public houses used for "immoral purposes . . . especially in the case of establishments which serve as the haunts of people who indulge in unnatural sexual practices." On 24 February the public display and sale of obscene material was banned "in the interests of the moral renewal of the German people." On 7 March Kurt Hiller's apartment was searched. On 23 March Hiller was arrested. (He was sent to the Oranienburg concentration camp but was released after nine months and fled Germany along with another inmate who was to remain his lifelong companion.) On 6 May Hirschfeld's institute was invaded by a group of right-wing students, complete with brass bands, followed by a squad of storm troopers. Files and books—some twelve thousand in all, the finest library of its kind in the world—were destroyed or carried off. On 10 May the seized material, along with a bust of Hirschfeld, was consigned to a huge bonfire. Shortly after Hitler came to power, Karl Giese managed to sneak some valuable files out of the institute and out of Germany. He then returned to Berlin, where he witnessed the sacking of the institute, after which he joined Hirschfeld in Switzerland. Thus came to an end the remarkable pioneering German tradition of the scientific study of sex and the world's first movement for homosexual rights. The official Nazi persecution of homosexuals had begun.

What opened the way to the application of systematic terror against the homosexual subcultures of Germany was the purge a year later of the storm troopers and their leader, Ernst Röhm, the only member of the Nazi leadership who was unquestionably homosexual (and possibly a visitor to Hirsch-feld's institute at one time). Though used as a justification for the purge, the elimination of sexual deviants from the movement was not its real purpose. Indeed, Hitler had dismissed earlier complaints about the morals of the storm troopers, noting that the SA was "not an institution for the moral education of genteel young ladies, but a formation of seasoned fighters." That, indeed, had become the problem. Once in power Hitler no longer needed street bullies, "seasoned fighters," especially not when the army and the business interests he was courting feared them. The SA had become a liability, and in June 1934 Röhm and his circle were murdered. His homosexuality was used as an ex post facto justification. Hitler now declared himself in favor of a "pure and cleanly" SA that every mother's son could join without fear of corruption.

While for Hitler that was largely a rationale, for the chief architect and beneficiary of the purge, Heinrich Himmler, it was not. Himmler was ob-sessed by hatred and fear of homosexuality and used his power as head of the now unchallenged SS (*Schutzstaffel*) and later, from 1936, of all police forces in Germany to wage a campaign of repression and finally of extermination. Later in 1934 the intent to commit a punishable homosexual act, not merely the act itself, was made illegal. In 1935, a year to the day after the Röhm purge, Paragraph 175 was broadened to include "any sex offense between males," not, as before, "only . . . intercourse-like acts." Thereafter it was no difficult task to add to the list of offenses, loosen the rules of evidence in prov-ing a case, and increase punishments. In the autumn of 1936 Himmler estab-lished a special Reich Office for Combating Homosexuality and Abortion within the newly reorganized Reich Criminal Police Bureau. These, along with racial mixing, he regarded as the greatest dangers to the survival of the Aryan race, the last by polluting it, the first two by depriving it of babies. Other categories of sex crimes and offenses against public morality were handled by other departments. The new department placed ever increasing pressure, through ever more detailed instructions, on the provincial police to track and crack down on sex offenders. Local authorities were encouraged to make use of regular surveillance and, if necessary, preventive detention of known offenders, authority for such aggressive methods having been broad-ened as early as February 1934. In addition, the now centralized police au-thority in Berlin relied on reports from all over Germany to amass a nation-wide file on habitual homosexuals, especially those thought to be corrupters of youth, homosexual prostitutes, and abortionists. Working in close conjunc-tion with the Reich Office for Combating Homosexuality and Abortion, the

Gestapo, which had had a similar department since 1934, carried out raids on actual or suspected homosexual meeting places such as bars, parks, railway stations, and the like.

Had the ultimate results of his obsessions not been so horrible, many of Himmler's policies would now seem almost laughable. Sexual prude though he was, he wanted his purebred SS men to father as many children by as many women as possible, in or out of marriage. Fearful that living in an all-male environment might lead his SS men to succumb to homosexuality (he had read Hans Blüher's writings on the youth movement and was duly horrified), Himmler provided prostitutes. He favored not punishing, even to some degree encouraging, homosexuality in occupied non-Aryan lands since it would weaken them further. Thus, penalties similar to those in Germany were extended to the Germanic Dutch, while homosexuality was often overlooked among the French or the Poles, unless, of course, they might seduce and morally corrupt their German near neighbors or occupiers. We have a full account of one such liaison between a Polish boy, Stefan K., and a German soldier, Willi, which ended in tragedy—concentration camp for the boy, an unknown fate for the soldier—when the boy, desperate for news of his departed lover, wrote him a compromising letter.

At least Stefan K. survived. Many others, including perhaps his German soldier, did not, and had Himmler's intentions not encountered practical difficulties, far more homosexuals would have joined the millions of others viewed as threats to German strength and racial purity—Jews, Gypsies, many Slavs, Jehovah's Witnesses—in the death camps. In a speech to the SS two weeks before setting up the special Reich Office for Combating Homosexuality and Abortion he described homosexuality as "a symptom of racial degeneracy destructive to our race. We have returned to the guiding Nordic principles that degenerates should be exterminated." Himmler was far from alone in using the issue of homosexuality as a weapon. Others, out of belief or opportunism, raised it as a means of discrediting non-Nazi youth groups, the Catholic Church, and old-line army officers. But it was Himmler who brought fanaticism to the task. The peak period of persecution lasted from late 1936, when the special Reich Office for Combating Homosexuality and Abortion was established, until 1940, when the exigencies of war provided some protection, at least for the occasional though not for the repeat offender.

The traditional distinction in the application of the law between habitual homosexuality on the one hand and circumstantial or casual homosexual contact on the other had been eroded by the broadening of the legal definition of homosexual offenses and the ever increasing power of the police since the Nazi seizure of power. But that distinction took on renewed importance once Germany was at war, especially in the military, with its concern for maintaining a proper balance between discipline and its insatiable demand for additional manpower. In practice this meant treating the one-time offender or victim of seduction relatively leniently and returning him to military service after appropriate punishment, while those who "acted out of a predisposition or an acquired and clearly incorrigible drive" would be discharged from the military, imprisoned, and subject to preventive detention, perhaps in a concentration camp, thereafter.

According to police records, during the peak years some twenty-five thousand were convicted of homosexual offenses under Paragraph 175. If that estimate is correct, the number for the entire Nazi period is somewhere between fifty thousand and sixty thousand. But even this estimate understates the extent of the Nazi persecution of homosexuals. The Reich Office for Combating Homosexuality and Abortion had dossiers on at least half again as many men and boys, and the statistics of those actually convicted included only civilians, Germans, and those convicted in accordance with normal judicial procedures. The military conducted its own only somewhat less zealous campaign (there were some seven thousand convictions in the army during the war). Homosexuals in occupied countries were subject to persecutions of varying severity, depending on the vagaries of occupation policy and the extent of cooperation from local authorities (the Dutch police were frustratingly unhelpful, for example). And the number of those arrested for other crimes but subsequently labeled homosexual or who found themselves the victims of arbitrary arrest and imprisonment or of surveillance restrictions amounting almost to house arrest will never be known for certain. Early on, homosexual offenders generally served their sentences in civilian jails, but as the intensity of persecution increased, commitment to a concentration camp after or even in place of a jail term became commonplace, especially for repeat offenders and those regarded as incorrigible. Members of the SS and police guilty of homosexual offenses were subject to the death penalty.

Of conditions in the concentration camps much has been written. Homosexual offenders had to wear pink triangles, in some camps they were housed separately, and in most they were subject to special humiliation and brutality, often being assigned to the worst work details. Cures (including, most commonly, castration) were sometimes attempted, and homosexuals were disproportionately used in medical experiments. Looked down on by the other inmates, homosexuals, as a diverse group socially and ethnically, had less of a sense of unity than racial, religious, or political prisoners:

> Because their subculture and organizations outside had been wantonly destroyed, no group solidarity resulted inside. Since outside they were regarded as effete, they were given no tasks of self-administration inside. Since outside every contact was regarded as suspicious, they did not dare even to speak to one another inside. . . . Since they were generally regarded as worthless, their fellow prisoners had a lower regard for them. . . . It is frequently reported that lively contacts could be observed amongst other categories, going even so far as sexual relations. In contrast, the pink triangle wearer became an object of suspicion if he so much as spoke to another.

Circumstantial sexual relations between the wearers of other insignia aside, intimate relationships between homosexual inmates did develop in the camps despite the odds against them. Many of those who survived did so largely through the emotional and physical support provided by a companion. But "if one lost his 'friend' through sickness or death, you could see it was all over," the commandant of the Sachsenhausen concentration camp and later Auschwitz recalled. "Many committed suicide. The 'friend' meant everything to these creatures in this situation. On several occasions two friends committed suicide together." Young, attractive individuals might survive by becoming the lovers of the Kapos, those inmates who ran the barracks, or of German guards, but that was the opposite of helpful to the group as a whole and, in any event, appears to have happened rarely, despite the impression left by a handful of novels and memoirs. It was not the youngest, presumably sexually most desirable homosexual inmates who survived longest but those in their late twenties, who had perhaps better honed their survival skills in the wider world. The opposite impression, the myth, "that homosexuals were able to save their lives by offering pederastic services . . . is a further example of that stigmatization which was not only imported from society into the camp but has also now crept into historical writing on the camps." Indeed, regardless of age, no non-Jewish group of inmates had a higher death rate. In all, at least fifteen thousand homosexuals died in the camps, which may not seem like a lot, but that it does not is perhaps more than anything else a comment on a century accustomed to counting its victims in the millions.

The status of lesbians in the Third Reich was less certain. Although one of Himmler's underlings, a lawyer who wrote a book widely used in the SS on the evils of homosexuality, wished to criminalize lesbianism, and the possibility was considered, it was never made illegal. Even so, there were cases of individual women arrested for other crimes or on trumped-up charges but apparently really arrested and certainly treated especially brutally because of their sexual orientation. Such cases were rare and random, however, examples of the arbitrary nature of the Nazi regime rather than the result of a coherent policy. That, of course, did not make the fate of those women caught up in the system any less horrible. In one case five lesbians were taken to a POW camp, where the prisoners were allowed to rape them and were rewarded for doing so with rations of liquor.

Nazi Germany was not alone among totalitarian states in savagely repressing homosexuality. In a change of policy so, too, did the Soviet Union. The liberal atmosphere of the immediate postrevolutionary years in sexual matters, as in so much else, did not survive very far into the 1920s. Abroad, the Soviet Union cultivated and retained its progressive image. Magnus Hirschfeld toured Russia at the invitation of the Soviet government in 1926, and the Soviet delegates to the congress of the World League for Sexual Reform in Copenhagen two years later could still boast of the forward-looking nature of Soviet policy. Back home, however, the situation had already begun to deteriorate. Chronic residential overcrowding, together with the nationalization or closure of the bars and bathhouses that had been at the center of the pre-Soviet homosexual subculture, pushed men in search of sexual partners out into the streets and parks and public toilets, depriving the subculture of its cohesiveness and depriving its members of privacy, either as individuals or as a group, even during the period of official toleration in the 1920s.

Decriminalization did not mean acceptance, however; far from it. Membership in the cultural elite, traditionally a fairly safe haven for Russian homosexuals, provided fewer and fewer guarantees of open sexual self-expression. Even as prominent a figure as Kuzmin, who had supported the revolution and enjoyed considerable latitude in the early 1920s, found it increasingly difficult to get his work published and was subjected to mounting criticism, not yet directly for his homosexuality, but for his political views and class background. Thus, the Soviet about-face, the recriminalization of homosexuality, should not have come, as it did to so many, as a complete shock. Under the new law, promulgated in 1933 and put into effect early the following year, sexual relations between men carried a penalty of up to five years at hard labor, with commensurately longer sentences for the use or threat of force or for sexual relations with a minor or subordinate. This was followed in 1935 by equally repressive (and dangerously vaguely worded) measures against pornography and in 1936 by the outlawing of abortion.

It is ironic that these changes in Soviet policy toward homosexuality coincided with the beginnings of the Nazi campaign, but that accident of timing should not be allowed to obscure the differences between the two totalitarian regimes on issues of deviant sexuality. The Nazis condemned homosexuality and pornography as threats to German morals and the German race, while the Soviets viewed them as subversive of socialism. Since socially deviant behavior of all sorts, not only homosexuality, as they saw it, was a product of decadent capitalist society and would therefore disappear under socialism, those in whom deviant behavior persisted after a generation of socialism had to be, in the words of the Soviet commissar of justice, Nikolai Krylenko, "remnants of the exploiting classes" who "in their vile secret dens are often engaged in another kind of work, the work of counter revolution."

Whatever the ideological differences underlying Nazi and Soviet persecution of homosexuals, there was little basis on which to choose between them so far as European liberals were concerned, let alone for those whose loyalties were primarily personal or, as with Isherwood, to his tribe. Under these circumstances his decision to turn his back on Europe and go to America early in 1939, less than eight months before the outbreak of war, made sense of a sort. It may not have been the right decision—he was severely criticized for it—but it was neither easy nor cowardly. Nor, of course, was it a common decision. Isherwood was accompanied by Auden, who wished to escape the confines of family, friends, and the literary life of England and who disliked the relentless intrusion of politics into his life and his art. The others in their circle stayed and served their country each in his own way during World War II.

Spender had had to confront a series of personal dilemmas not unlike Isherwood's, but he managed to reconcile his conflicting loyalties, or, more accurately, to separate them out, and not allow disillusionment in his personal dealings to immobilize him in the public sphere. When he settled down in London in 1933, after his own experience of sexual liberation during brief sojourns in Hamburg and visits to Isherwood in Berlin, Spender embarked on a long affair with a young, lower-middle-class, unemployed former soldier named Tony Hyndman (Jimmy Younger in Spender's memoirs). He moved in with Spender, became his secretary, and, as so often occurs in such unequal relationships, in Spender's words, "lived my life, not I his." Three years later, with both of them feeling confined by their relationship, Spender decided they must live apart, and shortly thereafter, much to everyone's surprise, he married.

By this time the Spanish Civil War had broken out, and Spender threw himself into the republican cause to the extent of joining the Communist Party and speaking and writing on its behalf. Tony Hyndman did likewise but went Spender one better by joining the International Brigade to fight in Spain. Despite his earlier experience in the British army, Tony turned out to be no warrior. He disobeyed orders, questioned the authority of his Communist superiors, and was horrified by his first taste of battle; although removed from combat duty, ultimately he deserted. Spender was appalled, not least at what he was convinced was his part in what had happened: "Someone I loved had gone into the war as a result of my influence and of my having abandoned him," he later wrote. Accepting a newspaper assignment from the *Daily Worker,* Spender rushed to Spain, partly to see the war for himself but mostly to help Tony. Before Tony deserted, Spender had a reasonably sympathetic reception; thereafter he could only plead frantically that Tony be sentenced to prison rather than face a firing squad.

He succeeded. After serving time in a prison camp and in jail Tony was repatriated to England. Nonetheless, Spender's experiences in Spain—his dealings with the political commissars in Hyndman's unit, who laced their rigid party line with innuendoes about the nature of Spender's relationship with Tony, and his gradual realization as he traveled through republican territory that the Communists were prepared to sacrifice everything, not only the individual but their allies and ultimately even the truth to the cause—all this began a process that ended with his leaving the Communist Party. But he did not abandon the antifascist cause, which, precisely because it was in danger of falling under Communist control, needed the active participation of "an effective number of those who are as scrupulous in their personal behavior, judged by personal standards of loyalty and honesty and affection, as by their outer devotion to it."

Spender was accompanied on the first of his visits to Spain by T. C. Worsley, a former schoolmaster who had recently turned to journalism, whose fictionalized account, in *Fellow Travelers,* of the complex relationship between Spender and Hyndman and between them and a wider circle of friends, their relatives, and sexual partners, many of whom also went to Spain, captures perfectly the ways in which in the 1930s the personal was projected into politics and the political impinged on the personal. Spender (Martin Murray in the novel) is the central character of *Fellow Travelers,* and what most impressed Worsley about him was his clarity of vision, his ability to cut through confusion and contradiction, his ability to "divide himself in two," particularly in his efforts on behalf of Tony Hyndman. On the one hand he recognized the legitimacy of the political commissars' point of view concerning Tony's actions, "yet he manages not to let that interfere with his fixed intention of getting [Tony] out." Indeed, "he was terrifically tough with them and wasn't in the least put out by their accusations and sneers." As one of the characters in the novel put it, Spender did not let himself be immobilized by indecision; "he just goes for what he wants."

Like his more famous friends, Worsley had also traveled to Germany in search of sexual liberation, though somewhat belatedly. With the help and encouragement of one of his former pupils he had his first fully satisfying homosexual experience with a young hustler named Heinz (they all seemed to be named Heinz) in Munich. When he arrived in Germany Worsley feared he might have left things too late. It was the summer of 1934, and Hitler had been in power for more than a year; indeed, he had only recently purged Ernst Röhm. Luckily for Worsley and for Heinz, as well as for the denizens of the bar where they met, the personal—the sexual—had not yet become fully political, even in Germany. For Isherwood, however, it already had, as it soon would for Spender and for Worsley, for Auden and for Lehmann, for those like Tony Hyndman they had been able to save and protect, but also, and with far more serious consequences, for the Heinzes left behind.

Postscript: Isherwood's Heinz survived. After serving in the German army during the war, on both the eastern and western fronts, he returned to Berlin, married, and raised a family. Isherwood visited him there in 1952, twenty years after they had first met.

## Chapter 16

**The Making of a Lesbian Subculture**

No less a product of the interwar years than what one historian labeled the Auden Generation was the vibrant international lesbian subculture centered in Paris, which flourished up until the beginning of World War II. A remarkable phenomenon in itself, it was all the more extraordinary because virtually unprecedented. Up until that time there had been little or nothing for lesbians comparable to the increasingly well defined and self-defined male homosexual subcultures that had begun to emerge a century or more earlier in northwestern and then in central Europe. The primary reason for the difference is clear. It was not until the 1920s, or perhaps shortly before World War I, that the modern feminist movement, a late-nineteenth-century phenomenon, bore fruit, and the emergence of a distinct lesbian subculture is inconceivable apart from feminism. Indeed, lesbianism may arguably be scarcely less productively studied as an aspect of women's history than as part of the history of homosexuality.

As the historical study of romantic relationships between women is broadened in scope and pushed further and further back in time that judgment will have to be revised and refined, as indeed it already has been, but probably not fundamentally altered. An excellent case in point is Emma Donaghue's study of relations between women in eighteenth-century England, *Passions between Women*. Thanks to Donaghue's book we now know far more—and what is of greater importance, it is clear that people at the time knew far more—about loving, highly erotic, even possibly or probably sexual relations between women than we would have thought possible even a few years ago. Not only has she unearthed a substantial body of new material but, simply by pulling together known but scattered references, she has altered our perceptions of the erotic lives of women together. There is a rich store of poems, novels, and diaries to draw from, as well as accounts of scandals full of gossip and innuendo. Much of this material was written by men, but a good deal of it was written by women, and while many of the men clearly intended primarily to excite or shock their audience or to denigrate women, others were simply puzzled, and some—as well, of course, as many women writers—displayed a genuine if cautious appreciation for such relationships.

Some women sought to rival men, even to the point of passing as men, sometimes for the sake of serving in the military or getting a job normally closed to women but not infrequently in order to be able to marry another woman. Others chose spinsterhood, proudly though usually privately asserting that the love of another woman was superior to the love of a man. (That dichotomy—like or equal to, versus different from or even superior to, men— echoes throughout the whole subsequent history of lesbianism and of feminism.) A variety of explanations were offered for erotic attachments between women. Some self-appointed experts (men, of course) thought lesbianism might be the result of a physical abnormality such as an enlarged clitoris, while others argued the reverse, that sexual relations between women might produce physical abnormalities. Like male homosexuality, lesbianism was often blamed on seduction or some other, usually childhood trauma. And there were a few who speculated that it might be in a person's nature. Certainly the vocabulary was there and in use. The words *lesbian* as both noun and adjective and *Sapphic* as a reference not to the poet Sappho but to passions between women, along with a number of more pejorative and insulting labels and a few slang terms, such as *Tommy* (perhaps related to *tomboy*), were fairly commonly understood in eighteenth-century England.

Yet, while it is now clear that there were many such loving relationships between women and a significant number of small circles of women in such relationships and, moreover, that the phenomenon was fairly widely known, there is no evidence for anything like a developed subculture. Donaghue attempts to get around this, first by denigrating the idea of a subculture as "implying subordination, minority interests and inferiority" and then by suggesting that there were lesbian subcultures after all, that there were "lesbian communities, a lesbian culture that permeated British culture, its parties, institutions and homes." Contradictions aside, much of what she argues is unconvincing. Of course a subculture is subordinate and a minority interest. It is those things by definition, which does not mean, however, that it is inferior. As for her positive claims for a lesbian culture, to say, on the basis of the evidence she presents, that it permeated British culture and institutions is too strong, and to suggest that it had communities is misleading at best. That had to await the emergence of an organized feminist movement in the late nineteenth century. Before then lesbian women lived out their erotic lives as individual couples or in small, isolated groups that, precisely because of the status of women, were never able to aspire to the scope and scale of male sodomitical subcultures. Our knowledge of them necessarily remains fragmentary, often dependent on second- or thirdhand sources, innuendo, gossip, and guesswork.

The most important, indeed almost the only exception was in eighteenth-century France, at court and in Paris. There, among the aristocracy and in the world of high fashion and the arts romantic friendships between women were an accepted part of the Paris social scene and a frequent subject of literature. Such relationships were often approved of even by men, either as a prelude and training ground for marriage or as an outlet for married women who might otherwise be unfaithful with other men. Romantic friendships between women were much less suspect than similar friendships between men were already becoming in the eighteenth century. Most of the women openly involved in intimate relationships with other women were from the upper classes, many of them in arranged marriages, which allowed them to retain some financial and personal independence. Much of Parisian social life was centered on salons run by such women, who often flaunted their affection for other women to the point of public gossip. Lower down the social scale there were major scandals in the 1770s involving actresses who were, or were thought to be, notoriously open in their sexual lives, so much so in one case that a leading actress in the Comédie-Française lost her job and was only reinstated at the request of the king. Paris was unique, however, in its development of a rich and distinctive feminine culture of which lesbianism was an acknowledged, at times notorious part. Moreover, much of what was written about Parisian high society was wildly exaggerated, the stuff of rumor and scandal rather than reliable reportage. The French philosophes, for example, played up female as well as male homosexuality at court and in the aristocracy as signs of decadence in the upper classes, and their attacks on the church often included thinly veiled insinuations concerning the sexual doings in monasteries and convents.

No other city in Europe, not even London, came close to matching Paris in its incorporation of romantic friendships between women into the social fabric of urban life. Indeed, the most remarkable example of such a relationship in Britain occurred not in London but in, of all places, a remote corner of rural Wales. In 1778 two socially prominent and independently wealthy

Irish women, Lady Eleanor Butler and the much younger Sarah Ponsonby, eloped from Dublin and settled in the village of Llangollen. Although they wore men's clothes and shared a bed, they gradually won local acceptance. At one point a newspaper hinted at lesbianism in their relationship, and they consulted Edmund Burke about the possibility of instituting a lawsuit. He wisely advised against it, they dropped the matter, and there was remarkably little other gossip in view of their prominence. Over the years they developed a circle of friends and admirers that would have been the envy of the most sophisticated London hostess. They corresponded with or were visited by many of the leading figures of the English Enlightenment, including Josiah Wedgewood, Walter Scott, and William Wordsworth, as well as Burke. Byron included them along with famous male couples such as David and Jonathan, Pylades and Orestes, and Nisus and Euryalus as examples of same-sex couples to emulate.

Lesbianism was not, of course, restricted to the upper classes or to women partly outside the class system, such as actresses. We know of a group of lesbian working women in Amsterdam in the 1790s, but only because they got caught up in the final wave of repression of homosexuality in the eighteenth-century Netherlands and were charged and convicted of committing lewd or unnatural acts. No less hidden from view, and even more intriguing, was the not inconsiderable number of women who passed and lived as men for at least part of their adult lives. While most of them did so in order to be able to serve in the military, to be near a husband or lover in the army, navy, or merchant marine, or out of economic necessity—they were drawn overwhelmingly from the lower classes—a significant minority did so in order to be with another woman. Whether they passed as men primarily to disguise a socially unacceptable relationship or in part because as women attracted to other women they saw themselves as men in women's bodies is uncertain (and the subject of hot debate among historians). The social and legal response to such women was equally ambiguous. In theory sexual relations between women violated both biblical and, in some countries, legal injunctions against sodomy. In practice the authorities did not quite know what to make of relationships that not only rarely came to light but did not exactly fit the usual definitions of sodomy. In the Netherlands, where recent research has revealed a rich sample of women passing as men for a variety of reasons, those who did so for the sake of marital or sexual relations with other women were condemned by the courts and by public opinion more, it seems, for the act of deception and for assuming the status of a man, for fraud and for violating gender roles in short, than for any sexual act. Thus it was often only the woman who had assumed a male identity who was punished, usually by exile, which, of course, ensured that the couple would be separated.

The more individual instances we discover of erotic relationships between women in the early modern era, the more we come up against the limitations of what can be known about such relationships. With few exceptions they existed in private and usually in isolation since most women did not command the financial resources, the physical mobility, and above all the social networks available even to the illegal male sodomitical subcultures of major European cities. Aristocratic ladies who sought escape from arranged marriages in the company of other women, middle- or upper-middle-class women who had the independence of mind and means to chose spinsterhood and life with other women over marriage, actresses and other bohemians who dared to flout social convention by more or less openly displaying their romantic attachment to other women—such women were few in number and exceptional in their social status or as individuals, which, indeed, is why we know of them at all.

Clearly more went on among women who were more representative of society at large, but of their lives we know, and will always know, next to nothing apart from the occasional carefully veiled reference in letters or diaries. As for the women who passed as men, fascinating though they are, they were the most exceptional of all. Surely very few women had the inclination, let alone the audacity, to attempt it, and it is worth noting that by definition those we know of with few exceptions were those who failed in the attempt and were discovered by accident, by betrayal, or after death. Much of the information we have on these women comes from court records, but that too makes them unusual, more akin to male sodomites than to other women. Although lesbianism was illegal in a number of European countries, it was rarely prosecuted. Thus, we lack for women the most extensive sources of information we possess on male homosexuality before the nineteenth century, skewed though these sources are.

This does not mean that lesbianism was accepted or condoned. In France, where it was most common, or at least most commonly known and discussed, it was talked of with derision, distaste, and ridicule. It was generally tolerated, at least within certain bounds, largely because it was not taken all that seriously. All the writers of religious tracts on sexual morality, all the commentators and administrators of laws regulating sexuality, and all the medical experts on sexual behavior were men, as were all the early advocates of homosexual liberation, who wrote about women, if at all, as an afterthought or as subordinate or marginal. And whatever the differences between them, almost all of these men had in common an appalling ignorance about female sexual response. They did not, by and large, assume that women were passive and lacking in sexual desire, as is often thought (though some Victorian medical professionals clearly did think so). On the contrary, many accepted authorities believed that eroticism in women, once aroused, was at least as powerful as, if not more so than, in men. However, they generally took a phallocentric view, that women responded to sexual stimulation from the male, and from that it followed that whatever two women might do together, they could not have real sex.

That smug assumption could work in practice to protect lesbian women from public and legal condemnation. In Scotland in 1811, for example, when a schoolgirl accused two of her schoolmistresses of lesbianism, they sued for libel and won, in large part because the court accepted the argument of their lawyers that they had been accused of a crime "so utterly abandoned that it is totally unknown and even doubtful that it can exist." Even those who were less naive in such matters tended to assume that meaningful sexual response was only possible as a result of penetration. Significantly, on the infrequent occasions when lesbianism was punished, it was the use of some object by one women to penetrate another that was most severely condemned (just as in the case of male homosexuality to be penetrated was seen as the worst offense). Once again, as with cross-dressing, it was the violation of accepted gender roles that the authorities found most disturbing. However, since women could only violate their accepted sexual role through the use of artificial means such as a dildo, there was a tendency to ignore the possibility or even to deny it, at least so far as respectable women were concerned. Foreigners or others, such as actresses, who were considered disreputable might be suspected of such behavior, but it was assumed—or hoped—that women of one's own class or country were immune even to the thought, let alone the act. In the Scottish case this presumption also worked in favor of the accused, who were well-respected schoolmistresses, and against their accuser, who was illegitimate and half Indian. Thus it is hardly surprising that the Labouchere amendment of 1885, which criminalized all forms of homosexual contact, was directed only at men, primarily because lesbianism had never been against the law in England but also because it was an alien, almost unthinkable concept to most Victorians, including, apparently, the queen herself.

In order for sexual relations between women to emerge from the shadows and for that in turn to contribute to eroding the conventional wisdom about female sexuality, the status of women would first have to change. Educational opportunities for women at both the secondary and in some measure at the university level increased substantially during the latter half of the nineteenth century in most Western countries. At the same time, the enfranchisement of women was for the first time seriously considered and fought for, and with some success at the local and even at the national level, primarily in the English-speaking world and Scandinavia. Finally and perhaps most importantly, the range of occupations open to middle-class women expanded enormously, not only in traditional areas such as teaching, nursing, and charitable work but in such rapidly growing sectors of the economy as retailing and secretarial and clerical work. Even before the end of the century these trends had combined to create conditions in which significant numbers of middle-class women had the personal and financial independence to chose to live their own lives outside of marriage and, if they so wished, to enter into romantic friendships with one another.

So common and so accepted did such relationships become in late Victorian England and the northeastern United States that there was even a name for them: Boston marriages. They were central themes of a number of novels of the period, notably Henry James's *The Bostonians,* and the subject of much social commentary, favorable and unfavorable, as an aspect of the late-nineteenth-century fascination with the liberated, New Woman. Many women from socially prominent families (including James's sister Alice) found personal fulfillment only after entering into such relationships, sometimes following a bad marriage or while—or after—playing their expected role as caregiver to an aging parent or other relative. A few sought and were able to assert their independence from traditional roles and relationships throughout their adult lives and were fortunate in having a number of the most important American women authors of the time—Katherine Lee Bates, Amy Lowell, Willa Cather—as champions and role models, perhaps the most articulate and inspiring of whom was Sarah Orne Jewett.

In 1877, in her late twenties, Jewett published a novel, *Deephaven,* extolling romantic friendships between women and citing the ladies of Llangollen as an ideal. Shortly thereafter she met Annie Fields, with whom, after the death of her own father and Annie's husband, she entered into what one later literary critic called "a union—there is no truer word for it," which lasted until Jewett's death in 1909. This was by no means Jewett's only such relationship. From adolescence until very near the end of her life, when she took the young Willa Cather under her wing, she sought out and cultivated such loving friendships. As for E. M. Forster, "friendship occupied perhaps the first place in her life," as Cather put it. For marriage, on the other hand, she had no use at all, at least not for herself or for women like her; it would be too confining, stunting, stultifying. "But the growth of true friendship," she pronounced at the beginning of her most famous novel, "may be a lifelong affair." Of critical importance to her as her many passionate friendships clearly were, it was her union with Annie Fields that remained the central relationship of Jewett's adult life. They lived apart for some months every year. Jewett would retire to the family home in Maine so that she could write undisturbed, but even then she and Annie Fields wrote to each other almost every day. The rest of the year they spent together in Boston society and literary circles or traveling abroad.

Jewett was fortunate in her companion in this respect. Annie Fields, through her late husband James, who had been the publisher of the *Atlantic Monthly,* had ready access to upper-middle-class American society and to the inner circles of the Anglo-American literary establishment. Like Margaret Fuller a generation earlier, who had translated a collection of love letters between two German women and written her pioneering feminist tract, *Women in the Nineteenth Century,* in the supportive environment of the Transcendentalist circle, and like the ladies of Llangollen, to whom Fuller as well as Jewett looked as models, Jewett was able through her extensive contacts to avoid the social isolation that must have been the lot of most unmarried women living in committed relationships with other women in what was, after all, still a man's world. That was beginning to change by the time Jewett met Annie Fields. Not only were there more such relationships, because more women were in a position to effect them, but there was, really for the first time, an institutional setting for them in the schools and colleges for women that had sprung up over the preceding generation. Their teaching staffs were made up primarily of unmarried women, many of them in Boston marriages, and the young women they trained graduated into a network of contacts and support unavailable to their mothers' or earlier generations.

Jewett's contemporaries were fortunate in another respect. Like the ladies of Llangollen, they lived at a time when there was a name, and an honorable one, for intimate loving relationships between women. Romantic friendships in the late eighteenth century and Boston marriages a century later were generally looked upon by society as embodying the noblest sentiments. The language of passionate love in the letters, diaries, and poems of so many of these women and even the physical expression of their affection in hugs and kisses were an inspiration to many other women and the subject of indulgent, if often condescending, commentary from men. Only rarely did anyone suggest or ask the question that immediately occurs to the post-Freudian observer: to what extent were these relationships sexual in nature? The answer is that in most cases we shall never know. It is probable that very often they were not. Surely many women internalized the prevailing misconceptions about female sexuality, as well as Victorian notions about female purity. But even where relations were sexual, the partners were saved from the imputation of it—even in their own minds, perhaps—by these very misconceptions, combined with society's assumptions concerning what respectable middle-class women—and Boston marriages were very much a middle-class phenomenon—as opposed to women of the lower classes would do or even know about.

What was true of adult women was even more the case with girls. Concern about intimate friendships among schoolboys, which were a source of anxiety in the late nineteenth century, did not yet extend to girls. Adolescent crushes were considered perfectly normal, even charming, and certainly temporary. Such assumptions did not begin to change until after the beginning of the new century, yet within a generation thereafter they took a turn of 180 degrees. As late as the years immediately before World War I such relationships, adult and adolescent, were assumed to be nonsexual without evidence to the contrary; but by the late 1920s the reverse was commonly the case. The more effusive passages in diaries, letters, and memoirs of earlier generations of unmarried women began to be read—and edited or suppressed—with a new self-consciousness by a new generation, and girls' schools now followed boys' schools in discouraging such friendships. The modern notion of lesbian relationships had finally surfaced, a century or more after similar views about male homosexuality had become commonplace.

What changed the prevailing assumptions about the nature of romantic friendships between women was the growing body of medical literature on sexual inversion, which fed on and fed into growing alarm about the challenge that the New Woman of the late nineteenth century and the feminist movement in education, politics, and the workplace posed to traditional notions of the proper role of women. This comes through clearly in the writings of two of the most widely read pioneering sexologists, Richard von Krafft-Ebing and Havelock Ellis. Krafft-Ebing viewed lesbianism as more or less the mirror image of male homosexuality: one of many possible outward manifestations of a hereditary taint and a sign of possible degeneration. He categorized lesbians according to their degree of masculine appearance and behavior, and his criteria were as much—or more—social than sexual. Of the most extreme type, he noted, "The masculine soul heaving in the female bosom finds pleasure in the pursuit of manly sport and in manifestations of courage and bravado."

One might expect Ellis to have been more sympathetic both because of his early association with Symonds and because his wife was lesbian. And he was more sympathetic, up to a point. Like Krafft-Ebing, he believed that in most cases of lesbianism there was a congenital predisposition, though he did not characterize it as a taint, let alone as a sign of degeneracy. He was, however, persuaded that most inverts came from neurotic backgrounds. Ellis was more sophisticated than most of his predecessors in his understanding of female sexual response and of what women could actually do sexually. Nor did he think lesbianism was rare, certainly not much less common than male homosexuality. Many of the most illustrious women in history were, he acknowledged, lesbian, but he attributed that to an unusually large masculine component in their makeup, to which he also ascribed the greater tendency toward violent crime in lesbian than in heterosexual women. Although he rejected some of the more absurd ideas about the physical and personality characteristics of lesbians—some nineteenth-century doctors still held that the clitoris in lesbians could develop into a kind of pseudo penis—Ellis nonetheless accepted much of the conventional wisdom about the supposed masculine temperament of the true lesbian and even some of the sketchy evidence for physical signs and differences such as the underdevelopment of some parts of the body and the overdevelopment of others. Ellis was equally ambivalent about feminism. While he supported women's demands for emancipation, he feared that single women out in the world, unconstrained by traditional sexual morality, would find sex where they could, including with one another. Thus, he concluded, "while influences of the modern movement cannot directly cause sexual inversion . . . they develop the germs of it, and they probably cause a spurious imitation" since "the congenital anomaly occurs with special frequency in women of high intelligence who influence others."

Many in the older generation of feminists were hurt and angered by the sexualization of their romantic friendships with other women, which they saw as robbing those relationships, in their own and in society's eyes, of their innocence and nobility and narrowing people's understanding of the richness of human relationships in general. As one retired Wellesley College professor put it in 1937, "A woman's life in which sexual interests have never existed is a life neither dull, nor empty, nor devoid of romance." Others rationalized the sexual aspect of their romantic friendships by placing it in a wider context, belittling its importance, and distancing themselves from those for whom sex was central: "Our lives were on a much higher plane than those of the real inverts. While we did indulge in our sexual intercourse, that was never the thought uppermost in our minds." Many younger women involved in such relationships went a step further, accepting the sexualization of those relationships and, for that matter, the congenital view of the sexologists that lesbianism was in most instances inborn.

Given the baggage that was often attached to the congenital theory—the suggestion of a hereditary taint, even of degeneracy—this may seem surprising. For male homosexuals the congenital view, despite its negative associations, served an important purpose: it bolstered the argument for decriminalization. But lesbianism was rarely illegal and even more rarely punished. Lesbians accepted the congenital theory for entirely different reasons. It allowed, even compelled, them to confront their sexuality as previous generations of women drawn to other women had been unable or unwilling to do. "I considered myself without shame," one of the most prominent figures in the Paris lesbian subculture between the wars, Natalie Barney, declared; "albinos aren't reproached for having pink eyes and whitish hair; why should they hold it against me for being a lesbian? It's a question of Nature. My queerness isn't a vice, isn't deliberate, and harms no one." Moreover, the congenital theory could be employed by lesbians as a useful weapon against the subordination of women. It bolstered the argument that some women were inherently different from any stereotypical view of women in that they were to some degree masculine in nature, and that such women had a right to demand autonomy, indeed a nonsubmissive, nonsubordinate role so far as men and male dominated society were concerned. Thus, lesbians could serve—in fact already had served—as a vanguard for the rights of women in general. As a leading German lesbian feminist put it in 1904, "The homosexual woman is particularly capable of playing a leading role in the international women's rights movement for equality. And indeed, from the beginning of the women's movement until the present day, a significant number of homosexual women assumed the leadership in the numerous struggles and, through their energy, awakened the naturally indifferent and submissive average women to an awareness of their human dignity and rights." This was an argument based at least as much on feminism as on sexuality, a mixture of motives and priorities that posed no problems for lesbian feminists but did pose a problem, and still does, for nonlesbian feminists.

It should come as no surprise that the new radical lesbian feminism first surfaced in Germany. Magnus Hirschfeld welcomed lesbians into the Scientific Humanitarian Committee almost from its beginnings, and there appear to have been at least the rudiments of distinct lesbian social organizations before World War I. There was unquestionably a surge of lesbian writing, not only poetry and fiction celebrating love between women but also speeches and pamphlet literature calling for tolerance and equality. In novels and poetry the tendency was still to stress the nobility and purity of such relationships, very much in the tradition of romantic friendships, and to make few, if any, references to sexuality, and those vague. However, lesbians did play an important though largely unacknowledged role in the German feminist movement. Indeed, emboldened by the support of the Scientific Humanitarian Committee, lesbians challenged feminists to back their cause. At the 1904 annual conference of the Scientific Humanitarian Committee one openly lesbian speaker castigated the women's rights movement for its indifference: "Considering the contribution made to the women's movement by homosexual women for decades, it is amazing that the large and influential organizations of the movement have never lifted a finger to improve the civil rights and social standing of their numerous Uranian members."

Radical feminists and some elements within the homosexual rights movement in Germany were forced into closer association following the Eulenburg scandal when, in 1909, a draft penal code drawn up for consideration by the Reichstag proposed that Paragraph 175 be extended to include the criminalization of sexual relations between women. Early in 1911 Magnus Hirschfeld was invited to speak to a meeting of the Bund fur Mutterschutz und Sexualreform (perhaps best translated as League for the Protection of Motherhood and Sexual Reform), which then passed a resolution condemning the proposed change in the law. The league had been founded in 1904 out of concern for the plight of unwed mothers, and its leader, Helene Stöcker, though not herself lesbian, believed that both women's rights and sexual freedom were indivisible, as well as inextricably linked, and that an attack on lesbianism was therefore doubly dangerous and could not be ignored by feminists any more than it could be by Hirschfeld's Scientific Humanitarian Committee. Later in 1911 Stöcker and Hirschfeld joined forces to sponsor an international congress on motherhood and sexual reform.

Stöcker's willingness to link the two movements—she was made a director of the Scientific Humanitarian Committee in 1912—along with her sexual libertarianism, set her apart from the mainstream feminist movement in Germany, which was primarily concerned with more traditional women's issues—employment, the franchise, marriage law—while on controversial sexual matters such as prostitution and pornography it often allied with the moral purity movement. As much out of repugnance as for tactical reasons, even most left-wing German feminists wanted nothing to do with an issue as sensational as lesbianism. Stöcker and her allies remained on the fringe. And what was true of Germany was certainly true elsewhere. In England, for example, where the women's suffrage movement employed unprecedentedly radical methods, the leaders of the movement were careful to avoid any association with sexual radicalism, let alone lesbianism, even though some of the most active suffragettes were unquestionably lesbian.

It was not until after the war, and in considerable measure because of conditions arising out of the war, that openly lesbian subcultures or subcultures powerfully influenced by lesbianism emerged, not on the fringe, but at the center of social and cultural life in Western Europe and the United States. There had been a few precursors. One of the most remarkable was a mid-nineteenth-century expatriate community in Rome centered around Charlotte Cushman, an actress who often played male roles. She fostered a distinguished group of American and British women writers and artists, notably the sculptors Harriet Hosmer, Edmonia Lewis, and Emma Stebbins, who lived, often with each other, and worked in deliberate defiance of, or at least indifference to, the expectations of respectable society back home. Very few circles of unmarried women could afford to be so openly unconventional in dress and manners, let alone in romantic attachments, and even where women did gain admission to bohemian and artistic subcultures they generally did so as a subordinate minority. Even in prewar Bloomsbury, despite the centrality of Virginia Woolf and her sister Vanessa Bell, it was the men who by and large dominated the group, including its sexual character, homosexual as well as heterosexual: Strachey and Keynes more than Virginia Woolf or Vita Sackville-West.

In the 1920s the mix was different. The manpower needs of World War I had drawn women into a variety of occupations in public service and private employment hitherto closed to them, and while most women left or were pushed out of such jobs after military demobilization, many stayed on, and many others resented their relegation to traditional roles. Nor were their primary traditional roles of wife and mother any longer necessarily available to them. The decimation of a generation of young European men in the war ensured that many hundreds of thousands of women would never marry. They would have to work in the world and find love where they could. Thus, the increasingly sophisticated understanding of female sexuality, which was one of the chief legacies of the late-nineteenth-century sexologists, combined with the unique circumstances of women after World War I to give to lesbians and to lesbianism a prominence and a public and self-awareness without precedent.

Distinct lesbian subcultures emerged in a number of European and American cities, but nowhere more dramatically or more influentially than in Paris. There two remarkable women, both American, both writers, both openly, or fairly openly, lesbian, and both independently wealthy—Natalie Barney and Gertrude Stein—founded rival salons. Both had settled in Paris at the beginning of the century, and both, after brief but important affairs, had established their lasting love relationships before World War I, Stein with Alice B. Toklas, Barney with the American artist Romaine Brooks. Stein was remarkably attuned to the most innovative trends in modern art and had begun to build an important collection and a growing reputation as a patron and collector even before she embarked on her own innovative literary career. However, her first novel, *Q.E.D.*, which was also her most sexually revealing, was not published until after her death. She had an affair in 1905 with Etta Cone, an old friend from Baltimore, who also acted as Stein's typist and secretary, much as Toklas was to do in later years. The most important legacy from this brief liaison was that Stein introduced Etta and her sister Clarabel to Matisse and Picasso, thus inaugurating one of the great collections of early modernist painting, the Cone collection, now in the Baltimore Museum of Art. Shortly thereafter, in 1907, Stein met Toklas, who was to remain her companion until Stein's death thirty-eight years later.

Even though possessed of a dominant personality the equal of Stein's, and the author of several books of poetry, random reflections—*Pensées d'une Amazone*—and memoirs, Natalie Barney saw herself less as a creative writer than as a patron of others: the matron saint of Lesbos, one of her biographers called her. In 1904 she and the first of her protégé lovers, the poet Renée Vivien, traveled to the island of Lesbos, where they hoped to found a Sapphic school of poetry. However, they quickly became disillusioned with modern Greece. Vivien decamped for Constantinople to meet another of her lovers; Barney returned to Paris, where she discovered that in her salon and in her garden, complete with a small Doric temple dedicated to friendship, she could more nearly realize her ideal. She welcomed the leading male writers of the day to her salon but felt a special obligation to foster creativity in women. In 1927 she founded the Académie des Femmes to support and publish aspiring women authors. Barney's affair with Vivien, whom she had met in 1899, established the pattern for many of her later relationships. It was a stormy affair. Neither woman was faithful to the other. Indeed Barney always felt free to indulge her taste for sexual promiscuity, urged her friends to do likewise, and, unlike Stein, was quite open about her sexual orientation. Nevertheless, she and Vivien remained close until Vivien's death from anorexia in 1909. Thereafter Barney had a succession of affairs, including her long but far from monogamous relationship with Brooks.

As expatriates, and rich ones at that, Stein and Barney were able to live their lives largely independent of French society's standards and dictates. As Barney put it, "Paris has always seemed to me the only city where you can live and express yourself as you please." However, if only as a useful corrective to the notion that France was unusually tolerant of sexual deviance, it is worth noting that their French contemporaries, including some of their French lovers, enjoyed no such immunity, not even during the years around the turn of the century, when lesbianism enjoyed a certain vogue in Paris. Liane de Pougy, the most famous courtesan of the Belle Époque, had great difficulty finding a publisher for her autobiographical novel recounting her affair with Barney. As for Colette, by far the most important and influential French writer on lesbian themes of her generation, she suffered ostracism for her frankness and for her violation of social norms. The lesbian subject matter of her early Claudine novels, published in the first decade of the century and partly written by her husband, were considered acceptable so long as they appeared under his name, but not when it was revealed that they had been written by a woman. And in 1907, shortly after her divorce from her first husband, when she appeared with the marquise de Belboeuf, "Missy," in a pantomime with strong lesbian overtones, the performance was stopped by the outraged audience, and Missy was advised by the police not to take part in similar performances.

Colette's *Le Pur et l'impur,* which, in the words of one recent critic, "is undoubtedly the most important French text on lesbianism and on women's sexuality in general in the first half of the century," and as such has often been compared to *Corydon,* "was either ignored or treated as a bizarre excrescence" when it was published in 1932. The reason, one suspects, is that it was so challenging, ranging widely over a variety of types of lesbian relationships, from the most stridently separatist (which, Colette noted, often aped the patriarchal values they were in revolt against) to tender, mentoring relations between an older and a younger woman, some of her examples drawn from her imagination, others—Renée Vivien, the ladies of Llangollen—from life or history. Yet, while lesbian relationships were at the core of *Le Pur et l'impur,* they were not treated in isolation either from heterosexuality or from male homosexuality. Rather, they were seen as points on a "spectrum of human sexuality," as among the range of possibilities open to those who were open to them. The challenge for Colette, as for all her characters, real or fictional, a challenge almost impossible to meet, was to find and maintain a proper balance between emotional fulfillment and sexual passion, and between the parties themselves, whatever their differences in age or social status. Hence her admonition to readers that the book "will speak sadly of pleasure." Colette regarded *Le Pur et l'impur* as her most important work, but it received little attention compared with that received by her less controversial writings until the emergence of a new generation of lesbian authors and of feminist scholarship in France in the 1960s and 1970s. During the interwar years the most influential and most noticed writers on lesbian themes were the Anglo-American expatriates.

Both Stein and Barney were well established before World War I in their domestic arrangements, as patrons of the arts, and as hostesses, invitations to whose at-homes—Stein's on the Rue de Fleurus, starring the avant garde of modernism, Barney's on the Rue Jacob, more likely to hark back to the Belle Époque of the turn of the century—were already prized. But it was only after the war, with the arrival in Paris of a younger generation, that they took on almost legendary status as central figures in the international culture of the lost generation of the 1920s, and scarcely less prominently of a distinctive lesbian subculture. Among the new arrivals were Sylvia Beach, who opened an English-language bookstore that became a major gathering place for the Anglo-American expatriate community (her lover, Adrienne Monnier, ran a French-language bookstore nearby); Janet Flanner, whose letters from Paris, written under the pen name Genet, were a staple of the *New Yorker;* and Djuna Barnes.

If any one of these women can be said to have exemplified the popular image of the lost-generation expatriate, it was Barnes. Raised in a family that more or less defined the term *dysfunctional*—a dominating grandmother, a dilettantish and openly promiscuous father, a downtrodden mother—Barnes may have been raped as a child, probably by a friend of her father's, possibly (her own accounts differed) by her father himself, a traumatic event to which, she told one confidante, she ascribed her lesbianism. In 1913, in her early twenties, she left home to embark on a career in journalism and live in Greenwich Village, where she quickly became very much a part of the political, literary, and sexual avant-garde. Although she had a number of affairs with men throughout her life, her sexual preference apparently was always for women—she told one of her Paris friends that she thought women were better in bed—both in New York and in Paris, to which she was sent as a correspondent by *McCall's* magazine in 1921. It was there that she met the American expatriate artist Thelma Wood, ten years her junior, with whom she lived, Barnes faithfully, Wood always with an eye out for other partners, for eight years. Wood's final infidelity was the inspiration for Barnes's finest work, the bitter and brilliant novel *Nightwood*.

Most of Barnes's close male friends in the expatriate community, such as the artist Marsden Hartley and the writer and publisher (of her works among others) Robert McAlmon, were gay or bisexual. However, Hartley claimed to have seduced Barnes, who did have an affair with the very much younger and bisexual Charles Henri Ford shortly after her breakup with Thelma Wood. They met in New York during one of Barnes's frequent visits to the United States, and Ford then came to Paris in part in the hope of gaining Gertrude Stein's sponsorship for his novel of homosexual life in New York, *The Young and Evil*. Stein was delighted with the novel, which appeared to show her literary influence, but that was a source of tension between Ford and Barnes, who disliked Stein. Barnes's on-again, off-again affair with Ford lasted nearly two years and was ended by Barnes after she discovered she was pregnant by someone other than Ford. She returned to Paris from Tangier, where they had been vacationing, and had an abortion. The money for the trip was supplied by Natalie Barney, the first of a number of generous patrons who were indispensable to Barnes, especially after she, like Thelma Wood before her, descended into alcoholism. Barnes repaid Barney for her early support with the *Ladies Almanack*, a witty and bawdy satire on Barney and the women in her circle, Romaine Brooks and Janet Flanner among others, all but one of them lesbian.

To Barney and perhaps to many of those in her circle, as to the members of the Gemeinschaft der Eigenen in Germany, attraction to others of their own sex did not mean that they saw themselves as belonging to some ill-defined intermediate or third sex. On the contrary, Barney remained thoroughly feminine and, like Benedict Friedländer, looked to the classical inheritance, not to biology, as an explanation and as a model for a sexuality that both saw as inborn, to be sure, but entirely normal and healthy, and far more common that modern society was willing to recognize. Barney made an appearance as just such a proud and confidant lesbian as a character, Valerie Seymour, in the most important lesbian novel of the interwar period, Radclyffe

Hall's *The Well of Loneliness:* "Placid and self assured, [she] created an atmosphere of courage; every one felt very natural and brave when they gathered together at Valerie Seymour's. There she was, this charming and cultivated woman, a kind of lighthouse in a storm swept ocean. . . . Here was no mere libertine in love's garden, but rather a creature born out of her epoch, a pagan chained to an age that was Christian."

Barney was exceptional, however. Many in this remarkable group of lesbian women in Paris in the twenties (as well as slightly older ones in Berlin before the war) tended to accept the definition of themselves as in some measure masculine women possessed of masculine attributes, largely because they were trying to break into a male-dominated culture but also because the categories in which their sexuality was discussed, categories established by the late-nineteenth-century sexologists, clearly demarcated the sexes in terms of what were generally accepted as appropriate appearance and behavior. In the words of a German lesbian feminist, "The homosexual woman possesses many qualities, inclinations, and capacities which we ordinarily consider masculine. . . . She is, like the average man, more objective, energetic, and goal oriented then the feminine woman; her thoughts and feelings are those of a man; she does not imitate man, she is inherently similar to him." Reflecting this view of and by themselves, lesbians in the interwar years frequently adopted a male appearance in clothes, haircuts, and mannerisms, and often their relationships aped heterosexual marriage, with one partner clearly in the role of husband, the other acting as wife, in conformity with the so-called butch/femme stereotype. The category of mannish lesbian was in part imposed from outside, by heterosexual society, but was also adopted as a means of self-definition, as a way of acknowledging and dealing with their sexual nature, and not least of all as a political strategy, as a way of carving out a distinct place for lesbians in particular and women in general.

This was certainly true of the novel that became emblematic of lesbianism between the wars, *The Well of Loneliness,* published in 1928, and of its author, Radclyffe Hall. A near contemporary of Stein and Barney, Hall was born into an upper-middle-class family in England and came into a considerable inheritance at the age of twenty-one. Very much the mannish lesbian in dress and manner all of her life, even in childhood, when she assumed a male name for herself, Hall was nonetheless understandably slow to approach the subject in her writings. In an earlier novel, *The Spirit Lamp,* published in 1924, she painted a sympathetic portrait of the older generation of new women, the forerunners, the pioneers, as she called them, who, if they had the courage, chose a career and romantic friendships with other women over the often stifling security of heterosexual marriage and conventional social expectations. Essentially it was a feminist, not a lesbian, novel. *The Well of Loneliness* was another matter entirely. Its subject was the second generation of new women, and it confronted, as the earlier novel—and the earlier generation—had not, the issue of sexuality between women. And it did so in the language and categories of congenital sexuality: the mannish lesbian, the man in a woman's body, and so forth. Hall even got Havelock Ellis to write a scientific foreword to the novel. Hall's protagonist (it is tempting to say hero since she adopted a man's name, Stephen Gordon, and a man's demeanor) sensed her differentness from early childhood, and though the issue of sexual orientation was handled discreetly, it was unmistakable.

So unmistakable in fact that copies of the book, which was published in Paris, were seized in England under the Obscene Publications Act. The lawyer for the publisher attempted to weasel his way out from under the act by all but denying the sexual nature of the relationship at the heart of the novel, but Hall would have none of that. In her view it was better to have it judged for what it was and banned. Which it was. Thereby, despite the novel's suppression, indeed almost because of it, she had achieved one of her goals, the recognition of lesbianism. Some years earlier, in 1921, Parliament had considered making lesbianism a crime on a par with male homosexuality but had not done so, largely on the grounds that publicity should not be given to an act that most women had never even heard of. After the trial and the banning of *The Well of Loneliness* that argument was no longer tenable; lesbianism had been named and discussed.

However, Hall and others in that remarkable generation of lesbian women paid dearly for such recognition. By stressing the congenital nature of her lesbianism, that it was the result of an accident of nature, she hoped to gain understanding and sympathy. "I wrote the book from a deep sense of duty," Hall told her publisher. "I am proud indeed to have taken up my pen in defense of those who are utterly defenseless, who being from birth set apart in accordance with some hidden scheme of Nature, need all the help that society can give them." But to elicit that sympathetic response Hall deliberately made her protagonist at times a rather pathetic and lonely victim. This was probably a tactical error. It won condescending pity from liberal reviewers but only disdain for such a pitiful figure from more conservative critics, and it infuriated many lesbians, then and since. Although Vita Sackville-West joined Forster and Leonard and Virginia Woolf and dozens of others in protesting the suppression of *The Well of Loneliness*, she thought the novel quite inadequate, while her lover, Violet Trefusis, hated it, as did Romaine Brooks.

Indeed, *The Well of Loneliness* remains a subject of often bitter controversy among lesbian critics, some praising it for its boldness in asserting that lesbianism is a "neutral and natural sexual variation," while others, stressing the negative associations of the congenital view of homosexuality, assert that it "further morbidified the most natural impulses and healthy views." To the extent that it did the latter the novel was oddly at variance with the life of its author, which was quite unlike that of her ultimately lonely and self-sacrificing protagonist. Hall was successful as an author, occupied a prominent position in the international lesbian subculture of the 1920s (she and her lover, Una Troubridge, were both caricatured in Djuna Barnes's *Ladies Almanack*), and had a couple of long and far from self-sacrificing relationships, one with a women much older than herself, the other with a women somewhat younger, both of whom were married when Hall met them. Nonetheless, Hall and many other lesbians of her generation, by emphasizing the inborn masculine component in their nature, often in an exaggerated manner, while they undoubtedly enhanced their sense of self-definition, did so at a price. By and large they cut themselves off from heterosexual women, split feminism, and alienated most men. The interwar lesbian subculture ended up not unlike the heroine of *The Well of Loneliness*, self-aware—which was no small achievement—but isolated.

Perhaps a majority of lesbian women of that generation did not have much choice in the matter other than to define their sexuality as they did. As one feminist scholar put it, "For bourgeois women, there was no developed female sexual discourse; there were only male discourses . . . about female sexuality. To become avowedly sexual, the New Woman had to enter the male world, either as a heterosexual on male terms or, [like Hall, Stein, et al.], as a lesbian in male body drag (the mannish lesbian/congenital invert). Feminine women like Alice B. Toklas and . . . Una Troubridge could become recognizable lesbians by association with their masculine partners." There was another respect in which a number of the most prominent members of the interwar Paris lesbian subculture also ended up even more clearly in a dead end, although they did have other options open to them. Both Stein and Barney had political associations with the far right, Stein along with Hall sympathetic to fascism, Barney unusual in expressing approval even of Nazism. No generalizations about the sources and nature of their political views apply across the board, but there were some suggestive similarities between them, as well as contrasts with those who often passionately differed from them politically. By and large the most ardent feminists, whatever their sexual orientation, tended to be on the left, and certainly some of the most remarkable members of the lesbian feminist Paris subculture were vocally and actively antifascist. Sylvia Beach remained in Paris after the war began and helped a number of people escape from occupied Europe; when the United States entered the war, she was interned for a time as an enemy alien. Janet Flanner, for all her attempts to remain the detached observer, even after detachment could fairly be called escapism, ultimately dropped her pseudonym and under her own name urged commitment to the fight against Nazism. She left for the United States shortly after war was declared but returned to Europe as a war correspondent and to Paris after the war. However, there were exceptions to the feminist-leftist connection. Barney, for all her extreme right-wing sympathies, was also a feminist.

Another generalization that holds true for the most part is that those of independent means, who most feared the threat of Communism to their wealth and status, were also the most inclined to be drawn to fascism. This was certainly true of Barney, who was immensely rich, and of Stein and Hall, both of whom had inherited considerable fortunes. But once again there were exceptions. Another possible explanation, which, unfortunately, cannot be measured but may well have been even more significant, has been suggested by the feminist literary historian Shari Benstock. In her view the susceptibility of Barney, Stein, Hall, and others to fascism was very likely directly linked to their self-image and their self-realization as lesbians. In deliberately rejecting the traditional feminine roles of wife and mother, and ambitious to break into the center of a male-dominated cultural avant-garde in Paris, they almost necessarily assumed pseudomasculine, dominant roles for themselves in their salons and in their private relationships. Whether this rendered them unusually open to the lure of fascism is another matter. But attracted to fascism they undoubtedly were, and both Barney and Stein managed to have quite comfortable lives in fascist-dominated Europe. Both left Paris when the Germans invaded, Stein for unoccupied Vichy France, Barney for Mussolini's Italy. Both returned after the war, Stein to die in 1946, Barney to resurrect her salon, although it never had the same luster. All in all, it was a sad afterword to a remarkable chapter in the history of lesbianism and of feminism in general.

# Chapter 17    Homosexuality and Psychiatry

Auden and Isherwood were far from alone in turning their backs on Europe and emigrating to the United States on the eve of World War II. They were, in fact, part of a mass exodus that began with the Nazi rise to power and accelerated during and after the devastation of Europe by total war. The result was a decisive shift in the center of gravity of Western civilization across the Atlantic, not only economically, diplomatically, and militarily but in the arts and humanities and in the natural and social sciences, including the study of human psychology and sexuality. Among the emigrants were many of the leading disciples of the founder of modern psychoanalysis, Sigmund Freud. The intellectual revolution he fathered, like the political revolutions in Russia and Germany at the close of World War I, held out the promise of liberation to many, but in the hands not so much of Freud as of his followers it became a source of bitter disillusionment to sexual minorities, and to many individuals among them nothing short of a catastrophe.

Although Freud's first major work dealing with homosexuality, *Three Essays on the Theory of Sexuality,* was published in 1905, it was not until after World War I that his theories superseded those of the leading late-nineteenth-century sexologists, published a decade or more earlier, to become, often in a simplified and more judgmental form, the new orthodoxy of the psychiatric profession. It took somewhat longer for his ideas to filter down to the educated public and achieve the status of a sort of conventional wisdom, defining concepts and even the specific language in which human sexuality has been discussed ever since. So far as the general public was concerned this was a more extended process, stretching into the post–World War II era; the great, three-volume biography that set the seal on Freud's place as one of the seminal minds of the twentieth century was not published until the 1950s.

Freud was, however, a contemporary of the men whose theories concerning sexuality his own ultimately displaced. Only sixteen years younger than Krafft-Ebing, he was three years older than Havelock Ellis and twelve years older than Magnus Hirschfeld. He died in London only four years after Hirschfeld, in the same year as Ellis, as a Central European Jewish intellectual refugee from his now Nazified home city of Vienna, three weeks after the outbreak of World War II. Yet, while he was very much a part of the generation that founded the scientific study of sex, many of his ideas were radically different from those of the other pioneering sexologists. One of the common denominators of most of the early sexologists, whether they saw homosexuality as within the range of the normal or as a pathological condition, was their tendency to see it as inborn and largely immutable. This was as true of Krafft-Ebing's view of homosexuality as the outward sign of a hereditary taint or Lombroso's concept of atavism as it was of Ulrichs's or Hirschfeld's theory that homosexuals constituted a third or intermediate sex.

Freud rejected this. He believed that one was born bisexual, with an undifferentiated sex drive, and that sexual orientation was developmental, sorted out as one grew, largely in the early years. He noted that although most people end up as heterosexual, a homosexual phase along the way, usually during adolescence, is common. The puzzle for Freud was how to explain the minority whose homosexuality was not a phase but a long-term partial or even exclusive orientation. From his clinical experience he concluded that homosexuality was an adaptive response to traumatic events or unresolved conflicts about the individual's sexual feelings and drives, particularly in relation to one's parents, especially the mother. The effect of such a trauma might be to stop the usual development toward heterosexual object choice, to deflect it or even to cause a regression back into homosexuality. This was a complex process, and Freud identified at least four main scenarios in early sexual development that could lead to homosexuality (not just, in the case of boys, the smothering mother and absent father of pop psychology). And even then he did not entirely rule out some element of biological predisposition. But that was a long way from any theory of a third or intermediate sex. Freud was positing a wide range, a spectrum, of developmental outcomes, of possible resolutions of inner conflict, of pragmatic responses to the problems inherent in growing up; there was nothing fixed or immutable about it.

The proposition that homosexuality was a sign of degeneracy was especially incompatible with Freudian theory. After all, Freud believed that we are all born bisexual and that all of us, even those who end up exclusively heterosexual, retain some homosexual feelings. Moreover, not only clinical but ordinary observation easily disproved any necessary link with degeneracy. Freud found no correlation between homosexuality and any other signs of physical or mental degeneration. On the contrary, he was struck by how many of the greatest and most gifted figures in history were bisexual or exclusively homosexual, and he wrote individual studies of a number of them, including Michelangelo and Leonardo da Vinci.

Although homosexuality was not a sign of degeneracy in Freud's view, the question whether it might nonetheless be termed a pathological condition troubled him. He refused to call it a sickness and carefully distinguished between inversion and perversion, with homosexuality as such being the former but not the latter. On the other hand he did believe that sexual pleasure, though good and important in itself, was not an end in itself, that it was biologically intended to serve the purpose of procreation and that heterosexuality was therefore the norm from which homosexuality was a deviation, and exclusive homosexuality an unfortunate deviation. However, he acknowledged that it was unfortunate as much if not more because of social condemnation than because of the homosexual condition itself; hence his strong public support for the repeal of Paragraph 175 of the German criminal code and other similar laws. Moreover, he greatly valued the homosexual or homoerotic component in the human personality, believing it to be an important element in one's capacity for close friendship, camaraderie, and the "general love of mankind." Thus, he concluded, while exclusive homosexuality might be a source of social and personal dysfunction, its sublimation had undoubtedly produced some of mankind's greatest cultural achievements and, through a heightened sense of identification with others like oneself, a disproportionate contribution to the social good.

Not surprisingly, Freud's views on the efficacy and value of therapy for homosexuals were also both cautious and balanced. Therapy might be able to awaken the dormant or repressed heterosexual component in the homosexual, but not if the homosexual drive was deep and only if the motivation was strong. That, however, was rarely true in his experience. Most homosexuals sought treatment because of "external motives such as social disadvantage" and, since their homosexuality in itself was a source of pleasure, were rarely internally motivated to change. Late in life Freud wrote perhaps his best-known, certainly the pithiest, summary of his views on homosexuality in general and the prospects for therapy in particular in a letter to an American mother concerning her homosexual son. "Homosexuality is surely no advantage," he wrote,

> but it is nothing to be ashamed of, no vice, no degradation, it cannot be classified an illness; we consider it to be a variation of the sexual function produced by a certain arrest of sexual development. Many highly respectable individuals of ancient and modern times have been homosexuals. . . . It is a great injustice to persecute homosexuality as a crime, and cruelty too. . . . By asking me if I can help, you mean, I suppose, if I can abolish homosexuality and make normal heterosexuality take its place. The answer is, in a general way, we cannot promise to achieve it. In a certain number of cases we succeed in developing the blighted germs of heterosexual tendencies which are present in every homosexual, in the majority of cases it is no more possible. . . . What analysis can do for your son runs in a different line. If he is unhappy, neurotic, torn by conflicts, inhibited in his social life, analysis may bring him harmony, peace of mind, full efficiency whether he remains a homosexual or gets changed.

That, one might conclude, would have been the end of the matter, at least so far as Freud's self-proclaimed followers were concerned. Not so, since the letter reflected two openings in Freud's thought for another, less compassionate, less tolerant, less modest, more judgmental, and more interventionist view: the phrases "arrest of sexual development" and "normal heterosexuality."

Freud's use of the term *normal* was often ambiguous. Clearly it implied more than simply the statistical norm, but he was so deeply schooled in other cultures, ancient and modern, that he always remained wary of applying norms of psychosexual development from the modern West as more than points of reference and comparison. Similarly with the concept of arrested development, it might in his view deprive the individual of some of the richness of sexual and family life, but not necessarily to the extent of crippling personality or inhibiting the individual's ability to function productively in other respects. Many in the second generation of Freudians abandoned such distinctions. The normal patterns of psychosexual development in the modern West were increasingly upheld as standards not merely of comparison but for judgment. The cultural relativism of Freud all but disappeared. And while the definition of the normal was being narrowed, the concept of arrested development was broadened to the extent that it was seen as entailing a general stunting and distortion of personality development. The adult homosexual, it followed, was deeply troubled and functionally impaired.

Perhaps inevitably, Freud's belief in constitutional bisexuality was a casualty of this new way of thinking. What that meant in practice was that homosexuality was viewed no longer as representing the survival of a natural component that came to dominate only because the heterosexual component was stunted but rather as an unnatural distortion of normal heterosexual development. Thus, Freud's carefully maintained distinction between inversion and perversion was blurred, even abandoned. Homosexuals were increasingly seen as so consumed by their condition as to be incapable of sublimating it into creative activity and of being so narcissistic as to be antisocial and incapable of real love of others, both conclusions being, of course, the exact opposite of what Freud had believed. The idea of the homosexual who was in other respects healthy and well adjusted all but vanished, and there was less and less recognition of variety within the homosexual population. Freud's elaboration of many different routes to homosexuality, and therefore of many different types of homosexual, gave way to monocausal explanations and hence to the notion of *the* homosexual and *the* homosexual personality.

Such sweeping conclusions were often based on small samples of individual patients in therapy or of prisoners or institutionalized patients, without any kind of control group of well-adjusted homosexuals, the implicit and sometimes explicit assumption being that the latter did not exist. Freud had warned that analysts were unlikely to see those satisfied with their inversion. It was a warning all too few in the second generation of his followers heeded. They saw deeply disturbed people who happened to be homosexual and tended to conclude that they were disturbed because they were homosexual and therefore that all homosexuals were deeply disturbed. The broad and often vicious terms in which many leading psychoanalysts characterized homosexuals in purportedly objective articles in major professional journals is startling in retrospect. Even before Freud's death, and with increasing frequency during and after World War II, less and less sympathetic interpretations of homosexuality found their way into print and into therapy, to become by the 1950s a new orthodoxy in much of the profession. An article in the *Psychoanalytic Review* in 1943 confidently asserted that "suffering, unhappiness, limitations in functioning, severe disturbances in interpersonal relationships, and contradictory internal tendencies . . . are all present in the homosexual."

Such views not only went largely unchallenged for nearly two decades—at least among analysts—but hardened over time. Edmund Bergler, a self-appointed but for some years widely accepted authority on male homosexuality, had worked briefly with Freud in Vienna before emigrating to the

United States in 1938. He was obsessed with the subject, and eventually his views became so extreme that he was regarded as an embarrassment by other analysts. He was convinced that adult homosexuals were intent on and capable of seducing and ensnaring adolescent boys into a homosexual orientation and that homosexual fashion designers deliberately tried to make women look unattractive. Even in his major work on the subject, *Homosexuality: Disease or Way of Life?* published in 1956, he was unable to disguise his loathing. "I have no bias against homosexuality," he wrote, "[but] homosexuals are essentially disagreeable people . . . [displaying] a mixture of superciliousness, false aggression, and whimpering, . . . subservient when confronted with a stronger person, merciless when in power, unscrupulous about trampling on a weaker person." By the time he wrote that, Bergler had already begun to lose his credibility, but even a decade earlier, in an article in *Psychiatric Quarterly,* he had noted "the great percentage of homosexuals among swindlers, pseudologues, forgers of all sorts, drug purveyors, gamblers, pimps, spies, brothel owners, etc."

There were even more extreme views. Abram Kardiner, in a chapter entitled "The Flight from Masculinity" in his book *Sex and Morality,* after remarking that "the common judgment that homosexuality is a form of antisocial behavior is not altogether unwarranted," went on to compare the homosexual's hatred of women to the Nazi hatred of the Jews and to note the "predilection of the Nazi hierarchy for homosexuality." Even more extraordinary was the assertion of William Silverberg, published in the journal *Psychiatry,* that "the passive homosexual is trying to extinguish the race" and that therefore "society is justified in its violent feelings toward him and . . . in taking steps against him." Similar, only slightly less lurid commentary was common in the major professional journals, most of it, and certainly the most savage, directed against male homosexuality. But lesbianism did not escape notice, particularly when it could be linked to feminism. The most alarmist critics and psychiatric professionals echoed but went even beyond the cautionary tone of Havelock Ellis's warning that the modern feminist movement could "develop the germs" of sexual inversion in women to argue, as Frank Caprio did in *Female Homosexuality: A Psychodynamic Study of Lesbianism,* published in 1954, that "the new freedom that women are enjoying serves as a fertile soil for the seeds of sexual inversion."

What was perhaps even more disturbing than the imprimatur given to such opinions by their publication in leading professional journals was that those who uttered them were treating homosexual and lesbian patients, patients they generally disliked, for a central aspect of their personality that the analysts despised. Many of these patients no doubt internalized the homophobia of their therapists. Those who had the self-possession to sense their therapists' hostility and resist simply confirmed the professional view that homosexuals were devious and antisocial. This was not objective treatment; it was the application of prejudice masquerading as science. Fundamentally it was little different from the old notions of homosexuality as a sin, a crime against nature, or a sign of degeneracy, only now dressed up as psychoanalytic theory.

It would be grossly unfair to tar the entire psychiatric profession with the same brush. The most doctrinaire revisionists had their greatest influence in the United States, but many even there and a far greater proportion of those who remained in Europe continued to adhere to the more accepting and questioning views of Freud. Others outside the profession, notably Alfred Kinsey, approached the issue of sexuality from a different direction, through the collection of statistics and personal interviews. But Kinsey—of whom much more later—was attacked where he was not ignored by most analysts. The predominant view, at least in the United States, was summed up by Irving Bieber in a massive and influential study published in 1962, which, though it avoided the hysterical tone and *ad hominem* arguments of the extremists, was closer to them in its theory and practical conclusions than to Freud. Although he acknowledged the existence of dissenting opinions, including Kinsey's, Bieber stated flatly and without equivocation that "all psychoanalytic theories assume that adult homosexuality is psychopathologic," that "heterosexuality is the biologic norm and that unless interfered with all individuals are heterosexuals," that "a homosexual adaptation is a result of [quoting one of the most influential of the revisionists, Sandor Rado] 'hidden but incapacitating fears of the opposite sex,'" and that "the homosexual adaptation is an outcome of exposure to highly pathologic parent-child relationships and early life situations" and is definitely not inborn.

Ten years earlier the American Psychiatric Association (APA) had classified homosexuality as a sociopathic personality disturbance in its *Diagnostic and Statistical Manual,* and not until the end of the 1960s did the profession soften its position, and then not by much. In 1968 homosexuality was reclassified as among the "non psychotic mental disorders." The official psychiatric designation of homosexuality as a mental disorder throughout the 1950s and 1960s was influential well beyond the confines of the profession, in shaping public attitudes. Even those who rejected the designation were compelled to start from the categories it established, and it is still enlisted in support of the agenda of those who, for whatever reason, wish to decry homosexuality, despite the decision to remove it from the APA list of mental disorders in 1973 (a decision from which, however, more than a third of its members dissented in a referendum). The labeling of homosexuality as a mental disorder had no less profound consequences within the subculture. For many years many homosexuals internalized the revisionists' views of themselves (as their predecessors had often internalized their being labeled as sinful or unnatural), and it was against this orthodoxy and in response to it that the gay liberation movement emerged and fought.

It is, therefore, of no small importance to understand why the psychoanalytic theory of homosexuality changed and developed as it did in the hands of the second generation of Freudians during the critical middle decades of the twentieth century. A clinical psychologist and literary scholar, Kenneth Lewes, has suggested provocatively, "that the historical trauma of the war was one cause of this shift in opinion . . . the attack on liberal institutions by Fascism resulted in a reaffirmation of bourgeois values, especially those of an American variety. . . . It is as if psychoanalysis, having found refuge in a new homeland, sought to demonstrate its relief, gratitude, and worthiness by subscribing to and by lending its weight to the consolidation of American values and institutions. This led to a narrowing of the more nearly cosmopolitan European stance of the early Freudians."

This is a compelling argument. Many of those who brought psychoanalysis to America were Central European Jews who had left their homelands not by choice but literally to save their lives—from the Nazis, from war, from the Holocaust. The world they left behind was being destroyed, their relatives persecuted and murdered, civilization as they knew it consumed. Theirs was a bunker mentality, a circling of wagons in defense of traditional values and institutions and of the land that had given them refuge. In practice that often meant overlooking the faults and limitations of those values and institutions and of that country. It also meant attacking anything that appeared to corrupt, threaten, or even question them. Nor was it only against the hell they had recently left that they were closing ranks. The nation they had fled to for shelter was in the throes of upheaval during and after World War II. Consciously or unconsciously they threw in their lot with the social and sexual status quo.

## Chapter 18

**False Starts and New Beginnings**

With the exception of one exceptional individual, Walt Whitman, and one important social institution, the Boston marriage, the United States played at best a supporting role in the emergence of homosexual subcultures in the nineteenth century and in shaping attitudes toward deviant sexuality. In constructing the laws and customs and social movements that touched on such delicate matters Americans replicated, sometimes closely, sometimes at a distance, those of Europe. The social purity, social hygiene, and eugenics movements of the late nineteenth and early twentieth centuries were essentially American versions of foreign models, and the introduction of franker and more permissive attitudes toward sex was largely achieved through the influence of the works of Havelock Ellis or Freud (if, that is, they were available at all, even on the restricted shelves of libraries). By the standards of continental Europe Americans were sexually naive.

That certainly was the impression of the future novelist Julian Green, born of American parents but raised in France, who came to the United States in 1919 to attend the University of Virginia. "There were many of us," he recalled, "who retained it [our innocence] at this university, unlike the European ones where the notion of virginity merely raised a smile. . . . In France or Germany, scarcely two days would have gone by without my being given all necessary elucidation, but in America at that period it was all very different." Thus, an innocent himself, Green had to work his own agonizingly slow passage toward sexual self-acceptance, torn as he was between his spiritual and carnal impulses, his devout Catholicism and his irrepressible attraction to what one of his professors called "the shame of Antiquity, by which I mean boy-love." Once the reticent Green made a few close friends, they were, surprisingly, able to help by referring him to the appropriate writings of

Symonds, Carpenter, and Ellis (whose case studies showed Green that he "was no longer alone"). Unfortunately, Green did not say how and where these students in a small southern college town got ahold of these books or had even heard of them, but clearly America was catching up.

Indeed it was in the 1920s that the social foundations were laid for a peculiarly American approach to sexuality. Earlier than in Europe the United States developed a mass consumer society, a mass-based youth culture, and a relatively emancipated status for women, but while these changes had a profound effect on heterosexual mores and behavior in everything from the portrayal of sex in popular culture to dating patterns in high school and college and the incidence of premarital sex, they hardly touched on or were touched by the homosexual subculture. It would be forty or fifty years before that subculture became an important part of American consumer society. The emancipation of women was a necessary foundation of the Boston marriage, but that was an elite institution available in practice only to women of independent means and high social status. As for the male homosexual subcultures, they developed later than in northwestern Europe and, as a phenomenon almost exclusively of rapidly growing major cities, were viewed by many as alien importations even as late as the early years of the twentieth century.

Nonetheless, following World War I, and in large measure because the war cut across class, ethnic, and geographical boundaries, homosexual subcultures in the United States were also transformed, growing in size and number, becoming less isolated, and rising more nearly to the surface of national life. During the war, not only were hundreds of thousands of young men inducted into the armed forces but, as had not been the case during the Civil War, women in large numbers were recruited into the war effort, and many young Americans served abroad, where they encountered unfamiliar sexual laws and customs. Far and away the most fascinating evidence of how a homosexual subculture could emerge even in a relatively small city where there was a military presence was provided by an official investigation undertaken shortly after the war into "immoral conditions" in the naval port of Newport, Rhode Island. The conditions revealed were a curious mix of patterns and attitudes that are still to be found in the modern gay subculture with others irretrievably from a different era. That this window into a normally closed world was even opened was due to the commander of the local naval base, who, having heard reports of an active subculture involving some of his sailors, dispatched young, good-looking decoys from the base, all of them volunteers, to investigate. And investigate they did, some with considerable enthusiasm.

What they uncovered was an extensive, well-established, and highly structured subculture. As a resort as well as a naval base Newport had links to the Boston and New York subcultures. There were known cruising areas, bars and restaurants with a predominantly homosexual clientele, and above all the YMCA; and the subculture was organized around a group of sailors known as the gang. While none of this would strike anyone familiar with the late-twentieth-century gay world as especially remarkable, the social structuring and role-playing within the Newport subculture, though still recognizable and by no means absent even after Stonewall, appears to have been unusually well defined, even rigid, in retrospect. At one extreme there were openly effeminate men called—and self-styled—fairies who assumed a passive or feminine role in sexual and social relationships. At the other end were straight sailors, including the decoys, who occasionally went to parties or cruising areas and whose image—and self-image—as straight was not questioned so long as they took the dominant or masculine role in sex. Strikingly unlike anything in the post-Stonewall era was a middling group who hung out with the gang and took male lovers but were not identified even within the subculture as queer since they adopted the male role and were called "husbands." All these highly articulated gender roles were assigned and accepted in a manner more suggestive of Ulrichs or early Hirschfeld than of the gay subcultures of the later twentieth century. Another curious aspect of the scandal, an indication perhaps of how ignorant even educated opinion was about homosexuality, is that the language of the medical and psychoanalytical literature had not yet filtered down even to the subculture, let alone to the authorities. The categories and terminology used by all participants, even in court, was colloquial: *queers, fairies, trade,* and so on.

These neat categories within the subculture could and did break down, however. Some husbands in long-term relationships crossed or at least blurred the lines, as did some of the navy decoys who got carried away with their assignments, often took the initiative in their encounters with fairies, and began all too obviously to enjoy their work, much to their own and the navy's later embarrassment. Indeed, the very fact that the decoys had volunteered began to raise uncomfortable questions up the chain of command. What finally killed the operation was accusations by decoys against a respected Episcopalian clergyman, Samuel Kent, of too tender—that is, unmanly—solicitude for sailors up to and including sexual advances. The church hierarchy counterattacked, denying that Kent had had sexual contact with any of the sailors, supporting his Walt Whitmanesque tenderness toward young servicemen, and castigating the navy for training decoys to solicit sexual favors in the first place. Tried twice, once on state, once on federal charges, Kent was acquitted.

The navy was not so lucky. The full extent of the Newport operation was revealed in court, and the issue entered the arena of public debate and partisan politics. The Republican-controlled Senate Navy Committee investigated and condemned the Democratic-run Navy Department and in particular the young assistant secretary of the navy, who had authorized the Newport operation, Franklin Delano Roosevelt. Well before the scandal had escalated to that level, however, it had revealed a subculture, a network far more extensive than anyone in or out of that subculture had imagined. Indeed, even before Samuel Kent was drawn into the mess, it had become obvious that the operation was getting out of hand, and wiser heads had already begun to move to suppress it. As the chairman of the naval court of inquiry put it, "If your men don't knock it off they will hang the whole state of Rhode Island."

Even more directly a product of events growing out of World War I was the founding of what was, so far as we know, the first homosexual rights organization in the United States, the Chicago Society for Human Rights. Its founder, the German-born Henry Gerber, served in the army of occupation in Germany after the war. While on leave in Berlin, he discovered the city's homosexual subculture and conceived the idea of founding an organization in America in imitation of the similarly titled league in Germany. His aim was through self-education and public education to win medical and legal backing for a more enlightened approach to homosexuality and to demonstrate the respectability of the great majority of homosexuals. He failed miserably; neither Gerber himself, apparently a difficult man, nor the Chicago homosexual subculture, let alone the city authorities, was ready for anything so radical. In 1924, following his return to the United States, he managed to scrape together a sufficient number of supporters to found the society, but only barely. The membership never comprised more than a handful of men, all of them working class, and Gerber was able to produce only two issues of the society's newsletter, *Friendship and Freedom,* which he wrote and financed himself.

The society was able to get a charter without difficulty, but when the police and then the press were informed that it was an organization of homosexuals, Gerber's premises were searched in the middle of the night, without an adequate warrant, and he was arrested along with two other members. The charges against him were thrown out because of the illegal search, but Gerber was broke, fired from his job at the post office, humiliated, and labeled a pervert. What is most striking about this sad story, apart from the abusive and repressive policy of the police, the sensation seeking of the press, and the legitimate inhibiting fears of those who declined to join the society, is the indifference Gerber encountered within the Chicago subculture. It was a large and active subculture that had grown substantially since the war, but its members demonstrated no interest in translating their increasing vitality into political action. The Chicago Society for Human Rights was an isolated historical curiosity and would remain so for another two decades.

Though still without any lasting organizations dedicated to advancing the status of sexual minorities and well behind western Europe in the scientific study of homosexuality—the American medical literature did at least address the subject, but only to condemn it in the most traditional terms—the United States in the 1920s nonetheless had thriving homosexual subcultures more extensive and more visible than ever before. The end of the war provided gay men and lesbians who had served in the military or in the civilian war effort with a unique opportunity. Many did not return home but settled in major cities, often congregating in well-defined substantially or even predominantly homosexual neighborhoods. Formerly confined to the more disreputable districts, such as New York's Bowery, visible homosexual subcultures surfaced in no longer fashionable areas, where modest rents, merchants anxious for custom, and the ignorance or indifference of the residents of more respectable neighborhoods provided a substantial degree of support and protection. Such neighborhoods, together with the cities' entertainment districts, certain parks and city blocks, theaters and hotels, restaurants, cafeterias, and speakeasies, became the regular haunts of local residents and hustlers or of uptowners or out-of-towners in search of a bit of entertainment or perhaps of a point of entry into the gay world for themselves. Such openly homosexual enclaves were more diverse socially than their predominantly working-class counterparts a generation earlier and far more flexible in the sexual roles their inhabitants were willing to play. This was especially the case in the most private of homosexual meeting places, the bathhouses. As public baths became both less fashionable and less necessary than early in the century, many began to rely almost exclusively on a gay clientele and were to remain central institutions of the subculture until the onset of AIDS.

Identifiably gay neighborhoods developed in virtually every major American city and in many smaller ones, but New York inevitably led the way. Both Greenwich Village and Harlem became national bywords for cultural and sexual bohemianism in the 1920s. There had been a homosexual fringe in the Village since early in the century, but it was not until after World War I that a steady influx of what one local newspaper called "short haired women and long haired men" into the area created a distinct subculture with its own restaurants and clubs, including a few for lesbians and run by women, and its own social events, especially the lavish balls that were one of the hallmarks of gay New York in the 1920s. Harlem fostered an equally open and equally notorious homosexual subculture. A predominantly black area only since shortly before the war, as the final destination of many southern blacks in the great northward migration during and after the war Harlem quickly became the metropolis and cultural center of black America and a magnet for those of both races in search of the unconventional beyond even what Greenwich Village had to offer. Much of the feel and flavor of the exotic in 1920s Harlem was provided by the gay subculture, by the lives and lyrics of many of the greatest blues singers, the public displays of cross-dressing (in both directions) and the popularity of female impersonators, elaborate drag shows, a Harlem specialty, and above all New York's biggest and most lavish gay ball, the Hamilton Lodge Ball.

The public fascination with the more flamboyant manifestations of the gay subculture peaked in the early 1930s, when stage shows and nightclub acts of, by, and about "pansies" but aimed at a general audience proliferated in the theater district of midtown Manhattan, as well as in the Village and Harlem. These shows and the gay presence in the entertainment business, of which, it was emphasized, they represented only the tip of the iceberg, were frankly, if archly, reported for what they were in gossip columns and the tabloid press. The pansy craze would not have lasted very long, however, even had the authorities been willing to let it run its course, which they were not. It was a craze, after all. Nor did it indicate a broadening acceptance of homosexuality. The gay chic of the late twenties and early thirties certainly reflected a questioning of rigid late Victorian definitions of masculinity and propriety, but by emphasizing the most outlandish aspects of the subculture, it also provided a reaffirmation of the outside observer's own masculinity and essential respectability. Like the interwar representation of the Negro male as essentially unmanly, the caricature (and self-parody) of the typical homosexual as an effeminate fairy dealt with a visible and unavoidable social reality by distancing it, rendering it nonthreatening, even absurd, and therefore as something not to be taken seriously.

Nongay residents of Greenwich Village or Harlem and of similar districts in other cities could not dismiss their gay near neighbors so easily. Certainly they did not appreciate outsiders' identification of their districts with social and sexual license, let alone homosexuality. However, since both neighborhoods had grown up as havens for outsiders, the one cultural, the other racial, they were uneasy about coming down too hard on sexual nonconformity, though religious leaders, especially in Harlem, were often outspokenly critical of the subculture. Moreover, some of the most prominent figures in the art world of the Village and in the Harlem Renaissance were, or were reputed to be, gay, including the artists Charles Demuth, who painted often quite explicit scenes of gay clubs, bathhouses, and cruising areas, the most daring of these done in his later years for private circulation, and Marsden Hartley, whose homoeroticism surfaced in his paintings only in carefully coded visual language. Both artists appear to have internalized stereotypical views of homosexuals as effete and effeminate, and perhaps in compensation, both were fascinated by men in uniform, Demuth by sailors, Hartley by soldiers. The many Harlem writers more or less well known even at the time to be homosexual—Alain Locke, Claude McKay, Conlee Cullen, Langston Hughes, Richard Nugent—were generally no less conflicted and secretive about their sexuality. McKay, in his novel *Home to Harlem*, was unusually frank in depicting the nightlife of Harlem, gay and straight, and many black intellectuals criticized him for it. Nugent was even more unusual in writing stories that deal openly and comfortably with homosexual themes.

The blurring of the boundaries between the straight and gay worlds, not only in bohemian enclaves like Greenwich Village but in urban American society at large, was reinforced by a peculiarly American phenomenon, prohibition. By making the public consumption of alcohol illegal, prohibition not only made it a daring and defiant act but pushed it underground into close association with other illicit activities and groups, including the gay subculture. The criminalization of immoral behavior, which had been readily acceptable to respectable middle-class citizens so long as it involved others—prostitutes, the denizens of working-class saloons, homosexuals—was resented and resisted when it was directed against their own sources of pleasure. Indeed, the enforcement of public morals became a logistical impossibility once it was no longer only gay bars and other disreputable establishments that had to be policed but every speakeasy and every nightclub. Largely be default (reinforced by well-placed bribes) the gay subculture was allowed to thrive.

Not that the authorities did not attempt to suppress it. Urged on by the late-nineteenth-century purity groups, which had been reinvigorated by World War I (but gradually lost public support during the Roaring Twenties), the police occasionally raided gay clubs, speakeasies, and bathhouses. Twice during the 1920s New York passed legislation specifically directed against homosexuals. In 1923 the disorderly conduct laws were amended to include the solicitation of "men for the purpose of committing a crime against nature or other lewdness." Four years later, when Mae West announced her intention of bringing a play about the gay subculture to Broadway, the legislature hastily amended the obscenity laws to ban any play "depicting or dealing with the subject of sex degeneracy, or sex perversion." Such legislation did little to stem the tide; it merely diverted it into other channels. The pansy craze did not peak for another three years. Not until after the repeal of prohibition were the authorities able to regain substantial control over the gay subculture.

With the end of prohibition the protective cover the criminalization of alcohol had provided for other illicit activities also came to an end. The homosexual subculture once again found itself isolated on the wrong side of the law. The authorities' most useful weapon in regulating undesirable activity was stringent liquor licensing laws, which were passed throughout the country following the repeal of prohibition. The powers granted to licensing boards were often vaguely defined, as were the grounds on which a liquor license could be revoked. Thus, any bar that served a disreputable or potentially disorderly class of patrons—and homosexuals were regarded as both—risked losing its license, and bar owners, fearful of being driven out of business, became, in effect, the allies of the police and licensing boards in driving the gay subculture from place to place and deeper underground.

While it was strict liquor licensing, coupled with vaguely worded disorderly conduct statutes, that made suppression of public gay subcultures possible during the 1930s, much of the impetus was provided by the Great Depression. As the country sank deeper into economic disaster there was a reaction against what came to be seen as the excesses of the hedonistic 1920s and even a tendency to blame at least some of the worsening social crisis on those excesses. For critics who saw the Depression as a failure not only of the national economy but also of national discipline, even of national moral fiber, the gay subculture of the 1920s, increasingly visible and increasingly willing to flout conventional standards of behavior, was a perfect target. Even before the end of the pansy craze the tide had begun to turn. In New York in 1930 the police embarked on a systematic campaign to clear the streets and clubs of midtown Manhattan of the most easily identifiable homosexual elements. As the trade paper *Variety* predicted, accurately as it turned out, "If the cops have their way the effeminate class will hereafter confine its activities to the Village and Harlem."

Similar sweeps were carried out in cities all across the country, but nationally the most dramatic example of the renewed commitment to traditional values and the relegation of those that did not fit to a position beyond the pale was censorship, or, more accurately, self-censorship, in order to avert outside interference, in the motion-picture business. The Motion Pictures Producers Association sponsored a code of moral conduct as early as 1930, but it lacked teeth until, in 1934, under intense pressure from the Catholic Church, the producers reluctantly agreed to the creation of the Production Code Administration. (Interestingly, this coincided with the moves toward stricter enforcement of public morals in both Soviet Russia and Nazi Germany.) The code's prohibitions were sweeping. It banned the representation in films not only of "sex perversion or any reference to it" but also of miscegenation, incest, venereal disease, abortion, drugs, and the use of sexually explicit language and even the mildest of profanities.

Even without censorship and systematic suppression gay and lesbian subcultures would have shrunk during the Depression. In hard times sexual self-expression became for many a luxury they could scarcely afford. This was especially true for lesbian subcultures, which were newer and smaller than the gay male subcultures to which they were often only an appendage. The meeting places that catered to lesbians often simply withered away, as the hard-won professional advancement and economic independence of middle class-women succumbed not only to the Depression but also to a traditionalist reaction to early-twentieth-century feminism. For many lesbian women this meant a return to something akin to the Boston marriages of their grandmothers' generation.

If only because they were more numerous and better established, the institutions serving gay men were more likely to survive. Many bars and bathhouses closed, but at least in larger cities a few managed to hang on. Nonetheless, homosexual subcultures virtually everywhere were maintained primarily through private contacts, even in neighborhoods where they had formerly been an important public presence; by the late 1930s they were less visible than they had been since before World War I. Which is not to suggest that though more cautious and discreet they necessarily lacked either vibrancy or style, at least in a major metropolis such as New York. On the contrary, as the Depression deepened, many of the expatriates of the 1920s, straight and gay, ran out of money and were forced to return home, a reverse migration reinforced by the growing number of political refugees from Europe. Hardly typical but certainly prominent among the returnees was the remarkable—and remarkably handsome—trio of the poet and novelist Glenway Wescott, the publisher and later director of publications at the Museum of Modern Art Monroe Wheeler, and the photographer George Platt Lynes. Wescott and Wheeler had met and become lovers in 1919, while Wheeler was an undergraduate at the University of Chicago. In 1927 the twenty-year-old Lynes met Wescott and Wheeler in New York and promptly fell in love with Wheeler. Despite these amatory complications, the three remained close for the rest of their lives.

Although they first met in the United States, all three spent much of the late 1920s and early 1930s in Europe. Lynes first visited Paris at the age of eighteen, when he was introduced to Gertrude Stein, and it was a member of her circle who suggested he look up Wescott and Wheeler. They, in turn, had already settled in Villefranche, on the French Riviera, where they lived for a time in the same hotel as Jean Cocteau and one of his succession of youthful protégé lovers. A year after meeting Wescott and Wheeler, Lynes followed them, first to Villefranche and then to Paris, where, as in Berlin and more discretely in New York and especially London during these same years, gay male subcultures experienced something of a golden age. Though never quite as open or extensive as its Berlin counterpart, and apparently rather less separate and specialized, the gay male subculture of Paris catered to a wide range of types and tastes, from annual fancy dress balls and the elegant bars (and utilitarian pissoirs) off the Champs Élysées to the more flamboyant venues of Montmartre and the mixed working-class dance halls near the Place de la Bastille. For Wheeler, Wescott, and Lynes Paris represented what Berlin provided their English contemporaries, a degree of personal and sexual latitude not available back home. And as with Isherwood and company, their expatriate adventure was cut short by events beyond their control. After five years of traveling together throughout Europe, quite a few brief affairs on the side, and much to-ing and fro-ing across the Atlantic, the reality of the Great Depression finally began to catch up with them. In 1933 Lynes, virtually penniless, was forced to return permanently to New York. Wescott and Wheeler followed a year later, and shortly thereafter they moved in together, Lynes and Wheeler sharing a bed, while Wescott had his own room, now and then having sex with Lynes when Wheeler was away, a potentially unstable threesome that nonetheless lasted nearly a decade.

Through their connections with other writers and publishers, artists and museum directors, they occupied a prominent position in American cultural life from the mid-1930s on. Among their closest friends were a similar trio, the artist Paul Cadmus and his lover Jared French, whom Cadmus had to share after 1937 with French's wife, Margaret Hoening. Cadmus and French lived and traveled abroad until 1933, when poverty forced them to return to the United States, where they found employment as artists for the Works Progress Administration (WPA). They met Wescott, Wheeler, and Lynes through Lincoln Kirsten, a central figure in introducing modern art and dance to the American public. He and Lynes had been at prep school together but had not been close. "I didn't like him at all," Kirsten later told a friend. "He got all the good looking football players." Their friendship developed later, after they began to establish their professional reputations, one as an artist, the other as an impresario. They and the others in the circle in which they moved painted, photographed, wrote about, published, or exhibited each other or each other's work, often with remarkable generosity.

Yet, for all the support these men gave one another, and despite their deserved eminence in their respective fields, all felt constrained to lead double lives, to hide, sometimes almost frantically, their sexuality, to separate their public and their private selves almost completely. Even with their heterosexual colleagues in the cultural establishment there was an unspoken policy of "Don't ask, don't tell." And by and large both they and their colleagues observed the prohibition. Even Lynes, who had always been more open about his sexuality than almost anyone else in the group, moved with caution. He made his public reputation as a portrait and fashion photographer, and his photographs of male nudes that were published in the United States were legitimized by being cloaked in the trappings of mythology. His more explicitly erotic celebrations of modern male beauty were circulated privately among friends and published, if at all, abroad and anonymously. The largest collection of these photographs was amassed by Alfred Kinsey for his institute archives.

If this degree of discretion was necessary even in New York and even among the cultural elite, the climate elsewhere was markedly less supportive. In smaller cities not only were there few, if any, gay or even mixed bars and restaurants but there were no sources of information and no role models. For many, perhaps most, homosexuals in all but the largest cities, finding some sort of sexual and emotional fulfillment was a matter of luck or perseverance—a chance encounter at the local YMCA, a furtive visit to the bus station or park, where, according to one's straight friends, the "fags" hung out, a trip to the nearest big city. Merle Miller, one of the first writers to publish in the early, heady post-Stonewall years of gay liberation a frank account of his own sexual history, was lucky to discover the men's room in the local railway station in his hometown in Iowa, "where odd, frightening things were written on the walls. . . . And where in those days there were always boys in their teens and early twenties who were on their way to and from somewhere in freight cars. Boys who were hungry and jobless and who for a very small amount of money, and sometimes none at all, were available for sex; almost always they were. . . . That was the way it happened the first time. The boy was from Chicago, and his name was Carl. He was seventeen, and I was twelve and the aggressor. I remember every detail of it; I suppose one always does."

For the adolescent Miller it was a question of getting it where one could. But that hardly constituted entry into the gay subculture. In Marshalltown, Iowa, there was nothing that could properly be called a subculture. There, as in most of the rest of the country, the social networks that had been the mainstay of the subculture in the 1920s had been fragmented and driven deep underground by the Depression, censorship, and official policies of repression. Against this the subculture had no effective defense. At a time when social action took precedence over private or individual rights the total absence of an organized movement for homosexual rights was a critical weakness. Even among homosexuals, and certainly by outsiders, sexual freedom was viewed as a matter of personal self-indulgence, not, as had been the case in pre-Nazi Germany and would again be the case in post-Stonewall America, a political cause.

So nearly complete was the eclipse of visible interwar homosexual subcultures in the United States that later generations of gay men and lesbians were all but unaware of their existence until a group of younger historians, led by George Chauncey, brought them to light. Interesting historically as they are, therefore, the subcultures of the early twentieth century were only very tenuously a source of the post-Stonewall gay rights movement, which had its more immediate origins in the peculiar conditions of World War II and the early postwar years. Like earlier wars but on an unprecedented scale, World War II transformed much of American society, not only ending the Great Depression and laying the foundations for world economic predominance but also permanently altering the status of women and African Americans. No less dramatically affected but deliberately overlooked until many years later were the circumstances of gay men and lesbians.

The war created a vast, floating population of young people suddenly exposed to life in the barracks or aboard ship, as well as to leave or liberty or war work in big cities at home or overseas. For many of those, whatever their sexual orientation, who for the first time had the freedom to discover themselves this almost sufficed to compensate for the disciplines and dangers of wartime military service. And for those, such as many, perhaps most, homosexuals, who felt out of step with the mores and assumptions of the society they had grown up in, it could be truly liberating. Indeed, in the highly structured environment of army or navy life self-discovery might seem safer: in the erotically charged but essentially asexual world of barracks or shipboard horseplay and teasing; in the frustrations and temptations—and loneliness—of living under intense pressure in a single-sex environment; in the tendency of many soldiers and sailors to pair off as buddies; in the enforced physical intimacy of sharing a tent or a lower berth on a train or a bed in an overcrowded hotel; in the prevalence of drag shows as entertainment for the troops. Barracks or ship could also provide a safe haven, intimate yet in a way anonymous, to which to return after tentative forays into the gay subculture of strange cities. "The army is an utterly simplified existence for me," a young soldier wrote a gay friend back home. "I have no one to answer to as long as I behave during the week and stay out of the way of the M.P.s on weekends. If I go home . . . how can I stay out all night or promote a serious affair?"

What is more, the dangers of military service in wartime legitimized and enhanced the value of sexual experimentation, making it more exciting, more urgent, more something to be pursued for its own sake and for immediate gratification. No one has captured that better than Quentin Crisp, whose life as a much put upon, outrageously flamboyant and promiscuous fairy in prewar London was transformed by the arrival of American troops in Britain in 1942:

Then suddenly, into the feast of love and death that St. Adolph had set before the palates of the English—parched these long dark twenty five years— Mr. Roosevelt began, with Olympian hands, to shower the American forces. This brand new army of (no) occupation flowed through the streets of London like cream on strawberries, like melted butter over green peas. Labeled "with love from Uncle Sam" and packaged in uniforms so tight that in them their owners could fight for nothing but their honor, these "bundles for Britain" leaned against the lamp posts of Shaftesbury Avenue or lolled on the steps of thin-lipped statues of dead English statesmen. As they sat in the cafes or stood in the pubs, their bodies bulged through every straining khaki fiber towards our feverish hands. Their voices were like warm milk, their skins as flawless as expensive

India rubber, and their eyes as beautiful as glass. Above all it was the liberality of their natures that was so marvelous. Never in the history of sex was so much offered to so many by so few.

The military authorities, counseled by doctors and psychiatrists, recognized and, however reluctantly, accepted the inevitability of some degree of situational homosexuality in a single-sex institution under the peculiar strains of wartime conditions. What they were determined to exclude was the true or habitual homosexual, but that distinction and the problems involved in enforcing it led inevitably to contradictory policies. In 1940, in conjunction with the peacetime draft, the military adopted psychiatric screening. One of the chief proponents of screening, Henry Stark Sullivan, was himself homosexual and believed that homosexuality in itself should not bar a potential recruit from military service. However, in 1941 homosexuality was categorized as a disqualifying deviation by all branches of the military. But that only served to raise a series of practical problems: how to tell who was who, what to do with those homosexuals who slipped through the net and were inducted, how to prevent potential recruits from lying about their sexuality in order to avoid military service or get a discharge.

At the induction stage some psychiatrists made subtle use of the most up-to-date psychoanalytic theory to identify and weed out homosexuals, while other, more backward practitioners looked for stereotypical outward signs of effeminacy. At least one questionnaire about occupational choices included such categories as dancer and interior decorator. Many doctors, pressed for time, simply asked, "Do you like girls?" and many others turned a blind eye, especially after America entered the war and manpower needs allowed for less choosiness. Similar motives led the military, in 1943, to distinguish officially between incorrigible and circumstantial homosexuality (in much the same way and at much the same time as did the German enemy), with the occasional offender being counseled and kept in the service. As for malingerers, the military, over the objections of psychiatrists, opted for the deterrent effect of informing the rejected recruit's draft board of the nature of his disqualification. Those already in the service were deterred from either practicing or faking homosexuality by the creation of a special, readily identifiable discharge category and by the denial of veterans' benefits. Although such discharges could be personally devastating, the policy was initially adopted as a reform supported by psychiatrists. Previously, homosexual acts had been punished by imprisonment; now they were treated as a medical problem. Ironically, that made the punishment of homosexuals easier since discharges required no court-martial, only a hearing, and could involve latent as well as active homosexuals. Thus, while the number of convictions for forcible sodomy, which remained a crime, fell, the number of men discharged as "sexual psychopaths" rose rapidly, totaling nearly ten thousand for the duration.

For lesbian women the stakes were rarely so high. Not only did relatively few women serve in the military but the military authorities did not become concerned with lesbianism until late in the war. The vast majority of women remained civilians, and for those among them who were sexually drawn to other women the conditions of employment in wartime, frequently in jobs that had been male preserves, were peculiarly congenial. With most young men in the service, many women worked, socialized, and lived in a single-sex environment, often in crowded apartments or boarding houses, which allowed women who might otherwise never have acted on, or even acknowledged to themselves, their erotic attraction to other women to experiment. For those women who did enter the military, and for the army and navy as well, the experience was equally unprecedented. In earlier wars women had served only as nurses; now they supplied the personnel for a wide range of support services. Inevitably perhaps, as was the case with effeminate men who were disproportionately assigned to noncombat duties as, for example, medics, cooks, or clerks, servicewomen were often categorized in accordance with preconceived notions of appropriate gender behavior. The most masculine in appearance or demeanor were the most likely to become drill sergeants or to be assigned to the motor pool.

Even so, lesbians in the service were generally protected from anything more serious than stereotyping by the military's inexperience in dealing with women and by the lack of knowledge about lesbianism, which was not, in any case, thought to be covered by the antisodomy laws. Only after an embarrassing scandal at a WAC training center in Georgia—the discovery of some love letters from a sergeant to a private—were regulations tightened and lesbians excluded from the service on the same basis as homosexual men. In practice, however, the personnel needs of the military, together with the reality of who was already in the service, continued to provide protection. Thus, when General Eisenhower requested WAC sergeant Johnnie Phelps to ferret out lesbians in her battalion, she replied: "Yessir. If the general pleases I will be happy to do this investigation. . . . But, sir, it would be unfair of me not to tell you, my name is going to head the list. . . . You should also be aware that you're going to have to replace all the file clerks, the section heads, most of the commanders, and the motor pool." Eisenhower, who was to deal less benignly with a similar situation during his presidency, rescinded the order.

More than a few lesbians and a great many more gay men were not so lucky. Yet, despite the occasional purge by an overeager commander, despite many individual experiences of cruelty, ignorance, and prejudice behind stockades, on psychiatric wards, or before hearing boards, and despite all the attempts of the military to weed out vice in the services and in the civilian worlds that impinged on them, patrolling the entertainment districts of cities near military bases, declaring questionable hotels and bars off-limits, and the like—despite all this, homosexuality had become visible in a way that could not be undone. Tens of thousands of young men and women had had to confront it, at least in others, perhaps in themselves, and many who had grown up with a crippling sense of isolation discovered during the war that they were not alone, that there were innumerable others like themselves, and places to meet, and places to live where they could be themselves. Not the least of the many unintended consequences of World War II in America was the reinvigoration of gay subcultures, reversing the trends of the 1930s. Gay bars proliferated during the war, and gay neighborhoods grew following demobilization; gay communities emerged from the war with a clearer sense of their size and identity than ever before.

The military itself contributed to the change, inadvertently of course. Through a combination of its manpower needs and the influence of psychiatry it had been compelled to revise its policies toward homosexuality, distinguishing between habitual and circumstantial homosexuality, replacing a penal with a medical approach, and even adopting more objective language, dropping the term *sodomists* in favor of *homosexuals*. Moreover, the discharge policy allowed psychiatrists for the first time to study large, randomly selected groups of ordinary homosexuals, not patients or prison inmates. The majority of psychiatrists used the opportunity to seek confirmation for their preconceptions and looked for common physical or emotional traits, very much as their predecessors had done, in the hope of identifying various homosexual personality types. The methods and results could be absurd. At one military base doctors tested the gag reflex with tongue depressors in supposed malingerers as well as admitted homosexuals on the theory that while the malingerers would gag, those who had performed fellatio would not.

A minority of doctors and psychiatrists, however, concluded that homosexuals could not readily be typed and that homosexuality did not necessarily entail any psychological impairment or inability to contribute to the military or to society at large. Such views flew in the face of the emerging psychoanalytic orthodoxy and were largely overwhelmed by it, but studies of this type were ultimately to contribute to overthrowing that orthodoxy, and the very fact that the issue was being openly dealt with and its extent coming to be recognized by psychiatry, the military, and ordinary soldiers and sailors changed the way in which homosexuality and, for that matter, sexuality in general were discussed. The late 1940s and early 1950s saw an interest in and frankness about sexual matters that would have been inconceivable but for the experience of World War II, and the leading advocates of more liberal policies toward homosexuals within the military furthered the process.

In his study of the role of psychiatry in wartime, published in 1948, Dr. William Menninger subscribed to the prevailing view that adult homosexuality was the result of "an arrest of psychosexual development" and that homosexuality was in itself a "pathological" condition. Yet, when he turned to discussing his own and other professionals' direct experience with homosexuals, he showed considerable detachment and understanding. He inveighed against the "general [American] attitude of condemnation and intolerance" that "is shared even by many physicians"; he undoubtedly and, one suspects, deliberately shocked his readers by suggesting that the wartime army, as an all-male institution, was "in a technical, psychiatric sense . . . fundamentally a homosexual society"; and he contradicted one of the central popular and psychiatric assumptions about homosexuals when he pointed out that "for every homosexual who was referred or came to the Medical Department, there were five or ten who never were detected." His conclusion: "Those men must have performed their duty satisfactorily, whether assigned to combat or to some other type of service." What is more, these views carried the imprimatur of semiofficial government policy, since Menninger had served as chief consultant in neuropsychiatry to the surgeon general of the army during the war.

In the same year Doctor Alfred Kinsey's study *Sexual Behavior in the Human Male* appeared. It is almost impossible to overestimate the impact of this work. Overnight it made the United States the center of the scientific study of sex and changed the manner and methodology of such studies. Its conclusions were not distorted by reliance on case histories or information from patients in therapy. Kinsey's statistics were based on questionnaires gathered from a large, random sample of ordinary people. (Unfortunately, his report on women, published five years later, was based on a far smaller sample and was not accorded the same authority or fame.) Magnus Hirschfeld had attempted to gather some statistics, but on nothing approaching the same depth and scale. The public response was immediate and totally unexpected. A dry, scholarly book made up largely of statistical tables, of which only five thousand copies were printed initially, ended up selling a quarter of a million.

Kinsey's findings permanently altered the way sex was thought about. The incidence of everything from masturbation to extramarital sex was far higher than previously thought, but no statistics were more startling than those on male homosexuality. All earlier estimates, from those of Ulrichs on, had been little more than educated guesses, and all had been low. Kinsey's survey found that 37 percent of males from adolescence on had had at least one homosexual experience to orgasm, that 10 percent had been more or less exclusively homosexual for at least three years, and that 4 percent had been exclusively homosexual throughout their lives. No previous observer had arrived at figures anywhere near as high as these, and Kinsey himself doubted his own findings at first. But checking and rechecking produced similar results whose implications were astonishing. As Kinsey noted dramatically, if the 37 percent figure was correct, "that is more than one male in three of the persons one may meet as he passes along a city street," and that could be any city street. "Whether the histories were taken in one large city or another, whether they were taken in large cities, in small towns, or in rural areas, whether they came from one college or from another, a church school or a state university or some private institution, whether they came from one part of the country or from another, the incidence data on the homosexual have been more or less the same."

The practical conclusions to be drawn from these figures were potentially very radical, and Kinsey, in matter-of-fact prose that made his arguments all the more telling, relentlessly pursued them to their logical conclusions, conclusions that challenged orthodox views and policies in fields as diverse as education, law, medicine, and religion. In view of his findings, he argued, "it is difficult to maintain that psychosexual reactions between individuals of the same sex are rare and therefore abnormal or unnatural, or that they constitute in themselves evidence of neurosis." Psychiatrists, he noted dryly, "might very well reexamine their justification for demanding that all persons conform to particular patterns of behavior." So too, Kinsey suggested, should the official guardians of public morals, since "the police force and court officials who attempt to enforce the sex laws, the clergymen and business men and every other group in the city which periodically calls for the enforcement of the laws—particularly the laws against sexual 'perversion'—have a record of incidences and frequencies in the homosexual which are as high as those of the rest of the social level to which they belong." Charitably, Kinsey concluded that "it is not a matter of individual hypocrisy which leads officials with homosexual histories to become prosecutors of the homosexual activity in the community. They themselves are the victims of the mores, and the public demand that they protect those mores. As long as there are such gaps between the traditional custom and the actual behavior of the population, such inconsistencies will continue to exist."

In his own attempt to close that gap Kinsey sought to explode many of the most common myths about homosexuality. If, as his findings indicated, 37 percent of sexually mature males had had at least one homosexual experience to orgasm and 4 percent were exclusively homosexual, then 33 percent were in some measure bisexual, occupying a position, and not necessarily a fixed one, on a scale from completely heterosexual to completely homosexual. That being the case, any attempt to define or discover physical or emotional traits of the homosexual type or personality was futile. And while Kinsey acknowledged that most homosexual relationships were unstable, he attributed that, not to anything inherent in homosexuality, but to the lack of supporting institutions, such as marriage, and to the corrosive and divisive effects of social disapproval.

In this, of course, Kinsey was acting far more as social critic than as scientific observer, but his ability—and willingness—to enlist the apparatus and status of the latter in support of his comments as the former gave his opinions unusual weight. At the end of his chapter on homosexuality Kinsey, in his capacity as both statistician and critic, took on those who wished to eradicate homosexuality either through treatment or through isolation. Disingenuously, he noted:

> Whether such a program is morally desirable is a matter on which a scientist is not qualified to pass judgment; but whether such a program is physically feasible is a matter for scientific determination. The evidence that we now have on the incidence and frequency of homosexual activity indicates that at least a third of the male population would have to be isolated from the rest of the community, if all those with any homosexual capacities were to be so treated. It means that at least 13 percent of the male population . . . would have to be institutionalized and isolated, if all persons who were predominantly homosexual were to be handled in this way.

But even if that were possible, desirable, and accomplished, he argued, even "if all persons with any trace of homosexual history, or those who were predominantly homosexual, were eliminated from the population today, there is no reason for believing that the incidence of the homosexual in the next generation would be materially reduced. The homosexual has been a significant part of human sexual activity ever since the dawn of history, primarily because it is an expression of capacities that are basic in the human animal." No one had ever been able to make such a statement with such authority ever before.

The Kinsey report was not the only or even the earliest major publishing event for gay men in the immediate postwar years. The late 1940s witnessed a major breakthrough in gay fiction in the United States. Hitherto novels on homosexual themes had usually been deliberately ambiguous; and the less ambiguous, the more likely it was that they would portray the gay subculture as either sinister or campy, but certainly as alien, and that the central characters would end in tragedy or self-immolation. Incidental homosexual characters in other novels were usually treated as pitiful or comic figures. All that began to change with the publication of Gore Vidal's *The City and the Pillar* in 1948 and John Horne Burns's *Lucifer with a Book* in 1949. And there were others as well, so many in fact that a *New York Times* reviewer complained of "a groaning shelf" of homosexual novels. Vidal was especially open in treating his central character and clear in his purpose. "I set out," he wrote in an afterword to a later edition, "to shatter the stereotype by taking as my protagonist a completely ordinary boy of the middle class and through his eyes observe the various strata of the underworld." It was a daring thing to do even then, and Vidal paid for his courage and combativeness: the *New York Times* boycotted his work for years thereafter. (The novel was given a more respectful reception abroad and won him recognition from some of the grand old men of the European gay literary establishment. Gide sent him a copy of *Corydon,* and Forster invited him to Cambridge and confessed that he had written a somewhat similar novel.)

Vidal and Burns felt able to take the obvious risks to their present reputations and future careers because they had credentials. They had served in the war, and they had written war novels (Burns's *The Gallery* contained a landmark gay bar scene). They could not be dismissed as effeminate weaklings or typed as merely gay writers. They also had a supportive milieu in postwar New York, whose gay subcultures had resurfaced during the war, reinvigorated by European émigrés and later by demobilized servicemen. The number of major gay writers who grew up in or fled to New York in these years is extraordinary: James Baldwin, Truman Capote, Allen Ginsberg, Tennessee Williams. Small wonder that all of them felt increasingly free to take risks and write more or less openly about matters their predecessors in the 1930s had generally confined to diaries, correspondence, and privately circulated poetry and fiction, much of which remained unpublished until the 1980s.

Another sign of the times was the publication in 1951 of Donald Webster Cory's *The Homosexual in America,* the first book published in the United States by an avowed homosexual about homosexual life in the United States. Cory was a pseudonym and a play on words (Don Cory/Corydon), but his purpose was unambiguous. The book was in part a "spiritual autobiography," in part an introduction and guide for "straight" society to the "gay" world (terms he employed). As the former it demonstrated how he had come to peace with himself and his nature; as the latter it was a plea, but in no way whining or begging, not for mere tolerance but for understanding and ultimately acceptance. "The homosexual," he concluded, "desires freedom of expression, aspires to recognition for his temperament without discriminatory attitudes or punishment, and will find all these possible only when he is able to proclaim his true nature."

Cory was not content merely to challenge the heterosexual majority in its prejudices toward and treatment of the particular minority to which he belonged (or, indeed, toward minorities in general, with which he constantly drew parallels). The book was also aimed at homosexuals, to answer their questions and doubts, to give them as members of the most secret and therefore most fragmented of minorities an escape from isolation, to encourage self-acceptance and a sense of solidarity. In much of this Cory was very forward looking, but the book also shows it age. There was, for example, a long discussion of whether gays should enter into heterosexual marriage. Indeed, much beyond self-acceptance he dared not go, either for himself, as his use of a pseudonym attests, or in advising others. The most he felt able to recommend in closing was that people come out to trusted relatives, friends, and colleagues in the hope of changing public opinion one person at a time, although he recognized that this was a far from adequate answer to the great dilemma of the homosexual minority as he had stated it in his opening chapter: "Until the world is able to accept us on an equal basis as human beings entitled to full rights of life, we are unlikely to have any great numbers willing to become martyrs by carrying the burden of the cross. But until we are willing to speak out openly and frankly in defense of our activities, and to identify ourselves with the millions pursuing these activities, we are unlikely to find the attitudes of the world undergoing any significant change."

A tentative step toward confronting that dilemma had already been taken, however. In November of the previous year, 1950, five men had met at the home of Harry Hay in Los Angeles, and out of that meeting grew the first substantial and lasting homophile organization in American history, the Mattachine Society. Hay was thirty-eight years old when he founded the society, but he had been active in radical causes since his youth, despite, but often in conscious revolt against, his respectable middle-class upbringing. During the Depression Hay had earned a precarious living in a variety of jobs, but his great love was the theater, and it was in 1933, while working in one of Los Angeles's little-theater companies that he met—and had a brief affair with—the young Will Geer, who introduced him to the Communist Party, political activism, and left-wing street theater.

Hay had been sexually active even longer. Discounting preadolescent experimentation at the age of nine with a boy three years his senior, Hay's first, eagerly sought sexual encounter was with a sailor on the beach at Santa Barbara. Though he looked and acted much older, Hay was only fourteen at the time. It was, he jokingly recalled, his first experience of "child molestation" in that "as a child I molested an adult until I found out what I needed to know." Hay entered into a sustained affair three years later with a much older man, Champ Simmons, who educated him in the ways and vocabulary of the subculture (all sorts of euphemisms were used but not the terms *gay* or *homosexual*) and provided his young partner with a link to the past: one of Simmons's former lovers had been a member of the Chicago Society for Human Rights.

As an undergraduate at Stanford Hay led an active sexual life, frequenting the bars and cruising areas of San Francisco. He even came out publicly at college, a daring, even reckless thing to do in the early 1930s. Back in Los Angeles he settled into a pattern of casual sexual encounters interspersed with more lasting affairs. On Hollywood Boulevard, then as now a major cruising ground, he hung out with gay friends, picked up other pedestrians, or was picked up by car cruisers, some of whom provided useful contacts in the film and theater world. But Hay was never able to break into the inner circle of the Hollywood gay subculture, centered on such legendary figures as the director George Cukor. The Los Angeles gay subculture of the 1930s was as fragmented, as cliquish, and necessarily as discreet as its counterparts in other cities. When one of Hay's regular sexual partners, George Oppenheimer, a screenwriter with whom he occasionally collaborated, was invited to a party for the producer Irving Thalberg, Oppenheimer cut short any hopes Hay might have had of accompanying him. "I'm sorry," he said, "but you're too obvious."

Hay's intellectual curiosity about homosexuality dated back almost as far as his earliest sexual experiences. At the age of eleven he happened on a copy of Edward Carpenter's *The Intermediate Sex,* which later powerfully influenced his faith in the positive worth and potential for comradeship of homosexuality, a faith that was ultimately to find expression in the Mattachine Society. Unfortunately for Hay, his politics and his sexual inclinations were in conflict. At the time when he was becoming more and more deeply involved in the work of the Communist Party and in myriad popular-front groups in Los Angeles, the Soviet regime embarked on increasingly repressive, puritanical policies, including the recriminalization of homosexuality. For Hay this presented an impossible dilemma that could only be resolved by either quitting the party or abandoning his promiscuous homosexual lifestyle.

By the late 1930s every influence in his life was pushing him toward the latter course, a course that even seemed likely to include marriage. No longer the carefree youth, he was an adult with adult responsibilities. Family and friends expected him to settle down; indeed, many of his gay friends had themselves already married. He broke off two intense and potentially lasting love affairs, in part over political differences. When he sought medical advice, he was referred to a psychiatrist who suggested, "Maybe instead of a girlish boy, you're looking for a boyish girl." At this point Hay was willing to convince himself that that was indeed the case; after all, marriage, as he later remarked, was the "casting couch for society." He soon contrived to meet a young woman he had seen at political demonstrations, who appeared to fit the bill. Anita Platky was unusually tall, slender, and athletic, a handsome rather than a beautiful women, and passionately left-wing. Only five months separated their first meeting from their wedding in the fall of 1938, and, revealingly, immediately after they were introduced he formally applied for Communist Party membership.

What Hay, in common with probably most gay men who married, must have feared was that marriage had not resolved so much as buried his dilemma. He did try. He cut himself off from his gay friends; he and his wife moved to New York (returning to Los Angeles shortly after the United States entered World War II); they even adopted two children. But only a few months after their marriage Hay began cruising the streets and parks again in search of quick sexual release, and within two years he had embarked on a series of more lasting affairs. The first of these was with a medical student in New York, who introduced him to Alfred Kinsey, then in the early stages of his research into male sexuality. Kinsey took Hay's sexual history, which certainly did nothing to detract from the dramatic impact of his final statistics. By the late 1940s Hay had been compelled to realize that "somehow or other my [life] as a heterosexual, a pseudo heterosexual, was coming to an end," that the "relentless differences between me and the world of my choice had grown imperceptibly into an unscaleable barrier."

Confronted with a dilemma as intractable as the one that had led him to abandon his homosexual way of life in favor of marriage and a commitment to the Communist Party a decade earlier, Hay gradually came to the conclusion that the only way out was to redirect his passion for political activism into the service of homosexual rights. He took his first step in that direction almost by chance. On the evening of 1 August 1948 he attended a party to which he had been invited by a gay friend whom he had met while out cruising in one of the city's parks. Earlier that day he had signed the candidacy petition of the Progressive Party candidate for president of the United States, Henry Wallace, and Hay arrived at the party infused with even more than his usual political enthusiasm. He suggested organizing homosexual supporters of Wallace, and while most of the other partygoers treated this as a joke, a few took him more or less seriously, and eventually they came up with the ambiguous but suggestive title Bachelors for Wallace.

Encouraged, Hay then broached the idea of a permanent homosexual rights organization. Once again the response was mostly skeptical or dismissive, but the few positive comments were enough to send him home determined to proceed. He stayed up the rest of the night composing a prospectus for what at this stage he called the International Bachelors Fraternal Order for Peace and Social Justice. Unfortunately for Hay, in the sober light of day even those who had expressed some enthusiasm for his idea at the party were unwilling to act, at least not until he could enlist some prominent heterosexuals as sponsors. Yet when he approached a number of professional men outside the gay subculture, they all agreed that the initiative had to come from homosexuals themselves. Hay therefore shelved his plans for nearly two years.

In July 1950 Hay met and fell in love with the young Rudi Gernreich, later to achieve fame as one of the leading fashion designers of the sixties and seventies, who acted as the catalyst in the founding of the Mattachine Society. He provided Hay with the personal support he had hitherto lacked, and it was Gernreich who suggested that Hay approach Bob Hull, one of the students in Hay's adult education classes. Hull, in turn, asked Hay if he might bring his roommate, Charles Rowland, and his lover of the moment, Dale Jennings, over to discuss Hay's cherished and much reworked prospectus. The five men met on a hillside near Hay's home on 11 November 1950 and formed the nucleus of what was later to become the Mattachine Society. They called themselves by a variety of names at first, most commonly the Fifth Order, until one of them, probably Hull, thought of the Mattachine, a suitably obscure reference drawn from Hay's classes to masked medieval dancers. "We took the name Mattachine," Hay recalled, "because we felt that we 1950s Gays were also a masked people, unknown and anonymous, who might become engaged in morale building and helping ourselves and others, through struggle, to move toward *total* redress and change."

The foundation of the Mattachine Society transformed all their lives, but no one's more than Hay's. He informed both his wife and his mother of his homosexuality and of his commitment to the new society. (In reply to his speculation about what his late father might have thought of his son's homosexuality, Hay's mother simply replied, "Your father knew Cecil Rhodes.") Within a year Hay and his wife had divorced and he had severed all ties with the Communist Party and with many of his political comrades. The Mattachine Society was his new and sole obsession. Since not only Hay but two others of the original five had been Communist Party members, the society inevitably reflected party doctrine in its ideology and to some extent in its structure. They defined homosexuals as a distinct cultural minority schooled in the values of the dominant heterosexual culture but not, of course, able to fit into that culture except at great personal and social cost. They therefore saw the first task of the new society as raising consciousness, not, as in the Communist Party, of class, but of sexuality, and through increased self-awareness as a group to instill pride and solidarity and ultimately to inspire political and social action. One of the impediments to a changed consciousness was negative terminology, and Hay, like Bentham, Whitman, Ulrichs, and so many others before him, was determined to employ only neutral or positive language. After much discussion the founders came up with the term *homophile,* only to be told by the Austrian-born Gernreich that the term had been used in Germany before the war.

In order most effectively "TO UNIFY, TO EDUCATE, TO LEAD," as its statement of missions and purposes put it, the society launched discussion groups as the core of its early activities and its primary means of recruiting new members. The induction ceremony for new members was deliberately solemn and impressive, and all members were asked to fill out a detailed questionnaire on their personal and sexual history, from family background through their coming out to any encounters they may have had with the law, and the nature of their present sexual activities and relationships. In the spring of 1951 the society issued its statement of purposes, and at year's end the founders established a front organization, the nonprofit Mattachine Foun-

dation, with Hay's mother and female relatives of another member as it officers, thus effectively screening the identity of the society's officers. The timing was fortunate since the foundation was able to provide protective cover
when the society took its first step into activism early in 1952.

In February one of the founders of the society, Dale Jennings, was arrested
on a morals charge in an especially blatant case of police entrapment. The
Mattachine Foundation created an ad hoc Citizens Committee Against Entrapment to distribute fliers in gay neighborhoods, bars, and cruising areas
and to raise money to hire a lawyer to fight the case. At the trial Jennings
courageously admitted his homosexuality but denied the charges against him.
His lawyer was able to trap the arresting officer in a lie, the jury deadlocked,
and the charges were dropped, an almost unprecedented outcome. Elated by
this unexpected victory for a high-risk strategy, the leaders of the society embarked on ambitious plans to expand their membership and were rewarded
with an enthusiastic response from within the gay community, not only in Los
Angeles but in cities throughout California from San Diego to San Francisco.
Of perhaps even greater significance, two of the founders, Jennings and Rowland, took the bold initiative of founding what proved to be the first successful magazine for a gay audience in the United States, *One*, the premiere issue
of which appeared in January 1953.

A similar mixture of daring and caution was reflected in the organizational
structure of the Mattachine Society. It was modeled in part on the Communist Party, in part on secret fraternal orders such as the Masons. Strictly
hierarchical, the society's lowest level, the first order, comprised discussion
groups, or guilds, while the highest level, or fifth order, was reserved for the
founders, who exercised ultimate authority. The division of each of the lower
orders into individual cells allowed, in theory, both for secrecy and for infinite
expansion. Each cell was supposed to split in two once it reached a certain
size. As for secrecy, that was one of Hay's (many) obsessions, and he at least
never wavered in his commitment to it. He did not reveal Rudi Gernreich's
central role in founding the society until after Gernreich's death in 1985. Individuals were allowed to remain anonymous if they chose, the cellular structure of each order and the hierarchy of orders meant that it was possible to
control contacts within the society both horizontally and vertically, the early
meetings of the fifth order were deliberately moved from place to place, and
invited guests were met in neutral locations and then taken to the meeting
place. If much of this seems paranoid, it was not; the founding of the Mattachine Society coincided with the rise of McCarthyism, among whose prime

targets were homosexuals and homosexuality. As Hay later recalled his motives when he first conceived of what was to become the Mattachine Society: "The postwar reaction, the shutting down of open communication, was already of concern to many of us progressives. I knew the government was going to look for a new enemy, a new scapegoat. It was predictable. But Blacks were beginning to organize and the horror of the holocaust was too recent to put the Jews in this position. The natural scapegoat would be us, the Queers. They were the one group of disenfranchised people who did not even know they were a group because they had never formed as a group. They—we— had to get started. It was high time."

# Chapter 19    Reaction

*McCarthyism* long ago entered the political lexicon as a convenient shorthand term for the politics of anti-Communism in the post–World War II United States. In a way that is unfortunate, since it personalizes and thereby confines something far wider than Senator Joseph McCarthy, politics, or anti-Communism. It was, in fact, only part of a broad traditionalist social and political reaction to actual, threatened, or perceived changes in wartime and postwar America, changes of which the increasingly visible gay subculture of the 1940s was an especially disturbing example to conservatives. It was no accident that the reemergent gay subculture grew up in close association with the bohemian subcultures of New York and Los Angeles, nor that Harry Hay first conceived of a homosexual rights organization in connection with his work for the Henry Wallace presidential campaign in 1948, nor that Hay and a number of other founders of the Mattachine Society were Communists or fellow travelers. What is more, the Mattachine Society was overtly political from the very beginning; it propagandized homosexuals as an oppressed minority, it actively aimed at consciousness-raising, its organization was structured for growth into a mass movement, and it ventured early on into legal and political activism. By their lights conservatives were quite right to be alarmed.

The Mattachine Society was, however, more than simply the product of the radicalism of the late 1940s as it touched on the homosexual subculture of Los Angeles, thus adding fuel to the fires of political and social reaction. It was from the outset a response to an already ongoing reaction. The politics of anti-Communism dated back to the beginnings of the Cold War in 1947–48 and were first broadened to include homosexuals in early 1950, when an under-secretary of state testified to a Senate committee that most of the government employees dismissed for moral turpitude were in fact homosexual. Sensing that they had uncovered a potentially disastrous weakness in the Truman administration, Republicans took up the issue with enthusiasm, and Democrats, suddenly placed on the defensive, felt compelled to follow suit. The Senate appointed a committee to investigate the employment of homosexuals in the federal government. Though cautious in estimating the number of "sex perverts" in government service, the committee report, issued in December 1950, nonetheless painted an alarming picture of their character, their influence, and their potential threat to the nation's security.

"It is generally believed," the report noted, "that those who engage in overt acts of perversion lack the emotional stability of normal persons. In addition there is an abundance of evidence to sustain the conclusion that indulgence in acts of sexual perversion weakens the moral fiber of an individual to a degree that he is not suitable for a position of responsibility." What is more, the committee "investigation has shown that the presence of a sex pervert in a Government agency tends to have a corrosive influence upon his fellow employees. These perverts will frequently attempt to entice normal individuals to engage in perverted practices. This is particularly true in the case of young and impressionable people who might come under the influence of a pervert. . . . One homosexual can pollute a Government office." The committee report then made the crucial link to the question of national security and the anti-Communist crusade:

> The lack of emotional stability which is found in most sex perverts and the weakness of their moral fiber, makes them susceptible to the blandishments of the foreign espionage agent. . . . The pervert is easy prey to the blackmailer. It follows that if blackmailers can extort money from a homosexual under the threat of disclosure, espionage agents can use the same type of pressure to extort confidential information. . . . It is an accepted fact among intelligence agencies that espionage organizations the world over consider sex perverts . . . to be prime targets where pressure can be exerted.

As proof the report cited the case of Alfred Redl, the chief of Austrian counterintelligence before World War I, whose homosexuality was used by the Russians to recruit him as a double agent. When his treachery was revealed shortly after the outbreak of war, Redl committed suicide. With the United States now at war with Communist North Korea, backed by Soviet Russia, this was especially devastating evidence that the threat might be real and immediate.

Accused in the report of laxity, even permissiveness, in the employment of homosexuals in some government departments, the Truman administration tightened security in hiring, firing, and promotion. The purge quickly spread from sensitive agencies such as the State Department, which dismissed 425 employees with "homosexual proclivities" from 1947 to early 1953, to all federal employees, and then further, from the government itself to government contractors, and from the federal to state and local governments. The Federal Bureau of Investigation (FBI) and local police departments cooperated in compiling lists of known or suspected homosexuals, their meeting places and arrest records, even their friends and associates. The postal service kept track of the recipients of questionable material. Shortly after becoming president Eisenhower signed an executive order officially designating sexual perversion a bar to federal employment.

The lumping together, even equating, of homosexuals and political subversives was now all but complete. After all, both were seen as secretive, wily, and manipulative, as loyal only to their own kind, not to the values of home, family, community, and nation. As Senator Wherry, a Nebraska Republican, who led the charge for a full investigation of homosexuals in government, put it, "I don't say every homosexual is a subversive and I don't say every subversive is a homosexual. But a man of low morality is a menace in the government, whatever he is, and they are all tied together." Subversion, after all, could take many forms; it did not need to be only or directly political. In the long twilight struggle against Communism America had need of strong, virile, resolute leadership, so the argument ran. The stereotypical homosexual, effete and effeminate—a stereotype relentlessly reinforced in popular culture during the 1950s—might, however unintentionally, open the way to political subversion by weakening the moral fiber of the nation.

Colleges and universities were especially vulnerable to this line of thought. As actual or supposed hotbeds of bohemianism and left-wing politics they were open to the charge of corrupting the young. Many institutions of higher learning, like many private employers, hoping to preempt outside pressure or as a condition of keeping contracts or funding, imposed loyalty oaths, and what has received far less notice, academic departments in many of the nation's leading universities (including that at which the author of this book taught) quietly conducted purges of known or suspected homosexuals on their faculties. Such purges could get out of hand, as happened at the University of Florida in 1958–59. There a sometimes indiscreet subculture that spilled out into the surrounding community of Gainesville attracted the attention of a zealous investigator for a state senate committee. Homosexuality was an inviting target for the committee. Although Communists, the Klu Klux

Klan, and the National Association for the Advancement of Colored People (NAACP) also came within its purview, homosexuals, unorganized and unpopular, were particularly easy prey, and revelations about the nature and activities of the subculture made good copy and all but guaranteed continued funding for the committee, as well as political prominence for its members. Convinced that "the greatest danger of a homosexual is his or her recruitment of other people into such practices" and that "a large percentage of young people are susceptible to recruitment," the committee inevitably zeroed in on the public education system, from grade school to university. Over the years the committee investigated, or caused to be investigated, and dismissed dozens of teachers. At the University of Florida sixteen faculty and staff members were purged, and despite strenuous efforts by the university administration to hush the matter up, a practice the publicity-conscious committee deplored, news of the scandal inevitably leaked out.

Entire communities could be overtaken by scandal. The wave of hysteria that swept Boise, Idaho, late in 1955 is by far the best-known instance largely because of John Gerassi's *The Boys of Boise,* a rare example of an objective, in-depth study of a gay issue published in the pre-Stonewall years. Following revelations of homosexual activity in public places, and particularly of the supposed exploitation of, as it turned out, all-too-willing teenage boys by adults, public alarm, although initially whipped up by some local interests in order to discredit others, quickly took on a life of its own. By the time the crisis subsided dozens of men had been arrested or questioned, had lost their jobs or reputations, had fled the state or been imprisoned, or had implicated others in desperate attempts to avert or cushion their own downfall.

Unsupported by professional associations, trade unions, or, until many years later, civil libertarians, and with the homosexual rights movement still only in its infancy, individuals could do little to defend themselves. An extreme though hardly unique example of the lengths to which the authorities were prepared to go in hounding an otherwise law-abiding citizen was provided to the American Civil Liberties Union (ACLU) in 1964 by a man identified only by his initials, BDH. Expelled from the University of Illinois during World War II for making a pass at another student, he worked for some years for the government in Washington. When he returned to the Midwest an FBI agent gained access to his student file. A friend employed in the State Department was subsequently charged with sex perversion; employers and coworkers, informed of his homosexuality, harassed him; following an injury his application for state-aided vocational rehabilitation was denied; and on a number of occasions FBI agents interviewed him at his home, hoping to learn the names of his associates.

Public and private employers, like the police and the FBI, could act almost with impunity since those fired or arrested often feared exposure as much or more than they feared unemployment or police harassment. Thus vice squad activity increased exponentially, all but unchecked by legal niceties. Police entrapment and raids on gay bars (especially in election years) became routine in major cities. Many bars, bathhouses, and other meeting places closed down. Others survived by making payoffs to the police or by accepting protection from the Mafia. While the heyday of the post–World War I gay subculture had lasted for more than a decade before being pushed back underground, the reemergence of the subculture during and after World War II provoked a savage reaction after less than half as many years. That difference is perhaps the best measure of how great a threat to traditional values the larger and more firmly established gay subcultures of the late 1940s had come to represent.

Another measure of the difference was the nature of the initial response to repression from some of the more radical elements within the gay community. While most gay men, as in similar circumstances in the past, hunkered down in their neighborhoods, retreating into near invisibility, others, primarily in cities where the Mattachine Society had established a foothold, refused to go so quietly. After all, the founding of the society had been as much a response to the first signs of repression as a product of postwar radicalism and a more vigorous gay subculture. Not merely despite, but in part because of, a mounting conservative reaction, the Mattachine Society continued to expand its organization and activities through 1952, adding both members and new chapters. The turning point came early in 1953, after the society sent questionnaires to candidates for the Los Angeles city council. This prompted a local reporter to dig into the history of the society, the nature of its organization, and the political affiliations of its leaders. While most of the resulting newspaper coverage was sympathetic, in the context of 1953, with McCarthy at his height and the House Un-American Activities Committee investigating Communist influence in Hollywood, even favorable publicity troubled some members, and the suggestion that this semisecret organization had some far-left-leaning officers produced near panic in the rank and file.

The founders of the Mattachine Society sought to quiet discontent by calling a convention of representatives from every guild to rewrite the society's constitution, transforming it from a hierarchical, cellular organization into an open, democratic, single-membership society. However, they were adamant that the society should remain the core of a movement representing an oppressed minority and that it should resist all pressures toward political conformity. Other, newer members differed, both in theory and pragmatically. Led by Kenneth Burns of Los Angeles and Hal Call from San Francisco, they argued that at a time of growing political and social conservatism it was important for a group of outsiders to demonstrate that it was not in any way subversive and, moreover, to stress the common humanity its members shared with others, not what set them apart. In short, they recommended an integrationist strategy rather than radical or even moderate reformism, let alone an emphasis on a distinct or separate identity.

In the mood of the mid-1950s there was no question which view would ultimately prevail. The founders were able to beat back their most conservative critics at the convention. The delegates rejected anti-Communist declarations and a loyalty oath. Even so, for the sake of unity and to free the society from the imputation of Communist ties, the founders as a body decided to bow out of the leadership. Gradually they drifted away as the moderates took over. Activism, the questioning of majoritarian values, and the raising of gay consciousness gave way to a policy of accommodation in which homosexuals were urged to adopt "a pattern of behavior that is acceptable to society in general and compatible with recognized institutions . . . of home, church and state" and to pursue a program of working with experts in the medical and scientific community to educate and change public perceptions and gain credibility.

By the end of 1953, with the new leadership firmly in control, this approach was enshrined in a revised constitution from which all traces of the society's early militancy had been removed. A majority of the delegates still refused to adopt a loyalty oath, let alone authorize an internal witch-hunt to root out Communist influence, but in all else they opted for accommodation and respectability. As the Southern California chapter had put it some months earlier, "Homosexuals are not seeking to overthrow or destroy any of society's existing institutions, laws or mores, but to be assimilated as constructive, valuable and responsible citizens." The danger, of course, was that they were thus, in effect, acquiescing in second-class citizenship, a stance that was likely to end in internalizing rather than challenging much of the medical, psychoanalytic, and sociological critique of homosexuals as in some measure flawed or deficient. And that, by and large, is precisely what happened.

Nonetheless, the Mattachine Society did survive and, after a sharp decline in membership and morale and a gradual, ultimately official shift of its headquarters to Hal Call's San Francisco, even experienced something of a revival, spawning new chapters in Chicago and New York. The magazine *One,* along with its stable mate, the *One Institute Quarterly of Homophile Studies,* first published in 1958, remained separate from the Mattachine Society and, under the leadership of the likes of Dorr Legg and the scholarly Jim Kepner, maintained its commitment to consciousness-raising within the gay community, which they continued to portray as having a distinct identity as a beleaguered cultural minority. Even more remarkable, in 1955, at the very moment when the Mattachine Society hit bottom a parallel lesbian organization, the Daughters of Bilitis, was founded in San Francisco. The DOB, its title a deliberately obscure reference to a poem by Pierre Louys, was founded and sustained primarily by two women, lovers, Del Martin and Phyllis Lyon. Born in 1921 in San Francisco and raised there, Martin enjoyed dressing in men's clothes as a child and had a number of unexpressed and unfulfilled crushes on other girls but nonetheless felt constrained to lead the life expected of a young middle-class-woman of her generation, even to the point of marrying at the age of nineteen and quitting college when she became pregnant. Unable to quell her feelings for other women, she divorced and struck out on her own, but it was not until she read *The Well of Loneliness* that "for the first time she was able to put a name to what she had been feeling . . . and experienced a release she had never known before." However, neither the San Francisco bar scene nor any of the few published works on the subject provided much sustenance for her new self-identification as a lesbian. At one point she even contemplated suicide. Only after she took a job in Seattle in 1949 and came out to a few coworkers, including Lyon, did she begin to put the pieces of her life together.

Although less plagued by self-doubts than Martin, the slightly younger Lyon took many years to come to terms with, even to comprehend, her sexuality. As a young woman she lived a heterosexual life, though she carefully avoided long-term relationships in college. "It never occurred to me there was any option," she recalled. "If you were a woman, you had to have a man! There was no other way." It was largely through her cautiously developing relationship with Martin that she finally came to accept lesbianism as not only a possible but also a fulfilling way of life. In 1953, now fully committed to each other, they returned to San Francisco, but they soon found the lesbian subculture even in this most open of cities wanting. They disliked the cliquish and confining world of the bars, and, above all, they were uncomfortable with the rigid and pervasive butch/femme stereotypes to which they felt pressed to conform. "We played the roles in public," they recalled, "and then we went home and fought about them." Along with three other couples they founded the DOB primarily to provide themselves with a more congenial social environment.

For Martin and Lyon that was only a beginning. Inspired by the work of the Mattachine Society, of which they had not even heard until after founding the DOB, but frustrated that Mattachine all but ignored women, they wanted their new organization to speak to the needs and aspirations of lesbians, a departure from its predominantly social beginnings that split the nascent movement. Most of the original working-class members, who generally "wanted a supersecret, exclusively Lesbian social club," quit, and the direction of the DOB fell decisively into the hands of its primarily middle-class members, who "had broadened their vision of the scope of the organization." Through cooperation with Mattachine and the editors of *One* early in 1956, and by striking out on their own later that year, sponsoring an open meeting and starting a magazine, the *Ladder,* they hoped to establish the DOB as an equal partner in the homophile movement. Yet, given the temper of the times and because the DOB was both younger and smaller than the Mattachine Society, it was cautious in its activities and always a junior partner in the movement. Its four-point program, reprinted in each issue of the *Ladder,* was clearly influenced by the Mattachine Society's. It did not even mention the word *lesbian:*

1. Education of the variant . . . to enable her to understand herself and make her adjustment to society . . . this to be accomplished by establishing . . . a library . . . on the sex deviant theme; by sponsoring public discussions . . . to be conducted by leading members of the legal, psychiatric, religious and other professions; by advocating a mode of behavior and dress acceptable to society.

2. Education of the public . . . leading to an eventual breakdown of erroneous taboos and prejudices.

3. Participation in research projects by duly authorized and responsible psychologists, sociologists, and other such experts directed towards further knowledge of the homosexual.

4. Investigation of the penal code as it pertains to the homosexual, proposal of changes . . . and promotion of these changes through the due process of law in the state legislatures.

Despite the moderation of its stated goals and methods, the DOB experienced a number of early disappointments. Attempts to sell the *Ladder* at newsstands failed miserably; very few women dared buy it publicly. Dialogue with representatives from a wide range of churches proved fruitless and frustrating until well into the 1960s. And participation in psychiatric research projects produced results that at best were mixed and at worst reaffirmed traditional negative stereotypes. Cautious as the DOB was, or gradually became, it nonetheless had difficulty recruiting professional women fearful for their hard-won advancement. Yet, as an organization primarily of middle-class women, "formed as an alternative to the gay bars," it was unable to attract many working-class members.

Inevitably, therefore, it remained small and was often ignored by its older, bigger brother, Mattachine, much to the annoyance of Martin and Lyon. "At every one of these conventions I attend," Martin complained at a Mattachine convention in 1959,

> year after year, I find I must defend the Daughters of Bilitis as a separate and distinct women's organization. . . . In all your programs and your [Mattachine] Review you speak of the male homosexual and follow this with—oh, yes, and incidentally there are some female homosexuals, too, and because they are homosexuals all this should apply to them as well. *One* has done little better. . . . Quite obviously neither organization has recognized the fact that lesbians are women and that this twentieth century is the era of emancipation of women. Lesbians are not satisfied to be auxiliary members or second-class homosexuals.

Despite such friction the alliance held. The DOB had little choice, really, if it was to survive. And survive it did, even branching out to other cities beginning in 1958 and holding its first national convention two years later, which was no small achievement for an organization of, by, and for lesbians, founded, with no precedents, at the worst possible time in the postwar years.

The experience of the American homophile movement in the 1950s, of tentative advances followed by tactical retreats in the face of public and official hostility, was replicated in most other Western nations. In Germany, once the home of the most open and articulate homosexual subculture, what was left of that subculture after the Holocaust had to rebuild from nothing and did not get very far. Attempts to refound the Scientific Humanitarian Committee in the late 1940s and early 1950s ended in failure, as did a similar later effort by Kurt Hiller, who returned to Germany after exile in England during the Nazi era. The German Society for Sex Research, founded in 1950, which did survive, carefully kept its distance from the efforts to revive the Scientific Humanitarian Committee. At its second congress in 1952, in keeping with the temper of the times, it declared: "In view of the justified scruples that arose and had to arise in conservative and especially church circles against the sex researchers of the earlier period, the notice seemed necessary, that the new German Society for Sex Research is something entirely different from the earlier. There is not the least trace of the spirit of Magnus Hirschfeld to be perceived in this congress." A few, small homophile organizations and low-circulation magazines were established, especially in relatively liberal Hamburg, but even the most prominent of these, such as the Society for Human Rights, founded in 1953, and the magazine *Freund* did not last long and, like the bars, baths, and other meeting places, were subject to regular surveillance and periodic harassment, prosecution, and closure by the authorities.

For a generation after the war the governments in both West and East Germany were totally unsympathetic. In West Germany a coalition dominated by the Christian Democrats, the direct descendant of the pre-Nazi Catholic Center Party, held power until the end of the 1960s, and though a panel of German jurists recommended decriminalization as early as 1951, Paragraph 175, including some of the Nazi embellishments, remained in force. Franz Joseph Strauss, the leader of the right-wing partners in the West German coalition, even attempted to link homosexuality to Communist subversion in emulation of American Cold War political tactics. In Communist East Germany too Paragraph 175 was retained, and additions made during the Third Reich were kept or deleted depending on whether they were seen as serving Nazi ideology or progressive ideas such as the protection of youth. While opponents of decriminalization, like their counterparts in the Soviet Union, viewed homosexuality as a symptom of degeneracy in the capitalist ruling class, supporters of reform countered with the argument that structural (as opposed to real or congenital) homosexuality would disappear in a socialist society. However, proposals that Paragraph 175 be repealed as part of a general law reform fell victim to the instability of the East German regime during the 1950s.

Thus, in both Germanys arrests of homosexuals continued, sometimes at an accelerated pace even by Nazi standards. Moreover, men who had been incarcerated in concentration camps for homosexual offenses were generally regarded by governments and by associations of concentration camp survivors in both Germanys, not as victims of Nazi persecution, but as criminals. Indeed, it was commonly argued that many homosexual prisoners were themselves Nazis, not opponents of the regime. Only those individuals who could demonstrate their political credentials were accepted as victims. Homosexuals as a class were not compensated, and some former inmates were re-arrested for similar offenses after the war.

Both for safety's sake and for a measure of continuity West German homosexuals could at least look abroad and often had to. (East Germans lacked even this support.) The Society for Human Rights was affiliated with the Amsterdam-based International Committee for Sexual Equality, which published a German newsletter during the 1950s, and the longest-lasting German-language homophile magazine, *Der Kreis* (The circle) was published in Zurich and provided extensive coverage of events in Germany as well as an outlet for German authors. Because it was based in neutral Switzerland, *Der Kreis* had also been able to serve as one of the rare sources of continuity between the pre- and postwar homosexual subcultures in Europe. Founded under the name *Menschenrecht* (Human rights) in 1932, the magazine was edited throughout most of the 1930s, when homosexuality was still illegal in a number of Swiss cantons, by Anna Vock, who paid for her outspokenness with the loss of a couple of jobs and a few encounters with the law. Its later, long-time editor was Karl Meier, a Swiss actor. In the late 1920s, as a young man traveling with a touring theatrical company in Germany, he discovered the Berlin subculture and wrote a few articles for Adolph Brand's *Der Eigene*. Shortly after returning to Switzerland in the early 1930s he became a regular contributor to *Menschenrecht*, and in 1942, the same year that homosexual relations between consenting adults in private were decriminalized throughout Switzerland, he took over the magazine, changing its name to *Der Kreis* a year later. Under his pseudonym, Rolf, Meier set the high-minded, idealistic tone that characterized the magazine throughout his twenty-five-year proprietorship. Appropriate, indeed perhaps inevitable, during the forties and fifties, Meier's fastidiousness became increasingly out of touch with the gay subculture as it developed during the 1960s. As one frequent contributor, Samuel Steward (better known as a writer of pornography, though never for *Der Kreis,* by his pen name, Phil Andros) put it, the magazine's "leaders could not keep up with the very changes they had helped to bring about." *Der Kreis* ceased publication at the end of 1967.

That *Der Kreis* had, indeed, helped to bring about the changes that contributed to its demise is undeniable. For many years, especially during the war, and for many of its subscribers it provided a unique source of information, connectedness, and hope. By the early 1950s *Der Kreis* had become a truly international magazine, having added a French-language section during the war and an English-language section in 1951. It also served as the model for *Arcadie,* the leading and longest-lasting French homophile magazine, which began publication in 1954. Its founder, André Baudry, had written for *Der Kreis* under the pseudonym André Romane, and it was out of meetings of French subscribers to the magazine that the idea of publishing *Arcadie* emerged. Like the Club Littéraire et Scientifique des Pays Latins (CLESPALA), established by Baudry three years later, *Arcadie* was avowedly apolitical and, in keeping with the strong homosexual presence among the French literary elite, primarily cultural in aims and content. Never radical, as the Mattachine Society had been at the start, the *Arcadie* circle was similar to what Mattachine became in the mid-1950s: cautious, assimilationist, and intent on demonstrating the essential respectability of the subculture and the common humanity of heterosexuals and homosexuals. Thus, when CLESPALA opened its clubhouse in 1957, it was intended to serve as a socially acceptable alternative to the bar and street scene, sponsoring lectures, conferences, and dances. The rules were carefully written to ensure proper decorum among its members.

That was a necessary strategy in postwar France. Baudry made a point of being on good terms with the clergy (he was a former seminarian) and with the police, and for good reason. The prominent place occupied in France by writers more or less well known to be homosexual—Gide, Cocteau, Peyrefitte, Montherlant, Genet, Geurin—is misleading. So too were the emergence of the St. Germain district as not only the center of intellectual life but the unofficial headquarters of the gay subculture in postwar Paris, and the continued absence of criminal penalties for homosexual relations between consenting adults in private. Most of the postwar generation of gay writers remained, like their predecessors, publicly ambiguous and often privately conflicted about their sexuality. A rare exception was Roger Peyrefitte. Like Gide between the wars, he was increasingly open in his writings, both fictional and autobiographical, and in his actions, as one of the original backers (along with Cocteau) of Baudry in founding *Arcadie* and as a vocal advocate of gay rights. But he paid for his indiscretions both before and after the war with a number of encounters with the police at home and abroad, by being sent home from his diplomatic posting in Greece, and ultimately by being forced out of his position in the Ministry of Foreign Affairs, after which he devoted himself full time to authorship.

The visibility of the subculture and of major literary figures in it was a source of public concern—and of good copy for the tabloid press—into the 1960s. "Paris must not become Berlin of 1925," warned one exposé. Still, the intellectual elite was more or less immune from police harassment and arrest on morals charges (and if the worst happened, a call from Baudry to one of his police contacts could, apparently, get a friend released). Ordinary French-man, even in Paris, and still more in the provinces, were not so lucky. And while the decriminalization of homosexuality a century and a half earlier was not about to be reversed, it was being whittled away at the edges. During World War II the German occupation authorities tolerated the homosexual subculture so long as it did not infect the occupiers. In unoccupied France, however, the puppet Vichy regime adopted a conservative social agenda that included raising the age of consent for homosexual (including lesbian) rela-tions from thirteen to twenty-one. After the war this provision, the first since the decriminalization of sodomy in 1791 to distinguish between heterosexu-ality and homosexuality and treat the latter more severely, was retained in the legal code of France as a whole.

A number of influences, most of them mid-twentieth-century variations on familiar French themes, played into the perpetuation of the rightward trend in social policy: the humiliating defeat of 1940, which seemed to demand greater social discipline as part of a national revival; the influence of the Cath-olic Church, which was itself tending in a conservative direction; the victory of Charles de Gaulle and Gaullism in the face of a Communist challenge in the immediate postwar years; the fear of population stagnation and decline, leading to a greater emphasis on the family and family policy. Thus, the laws on public solicitation were tightened in 1949, as was the regulation of same-sex social events such as dances. *Futur, Arcadie*'s only substantial postwar predecessor as a magazine aimed at a homosexual audience, had an erratic publication history largely because of repeated harassment by the authorities, who claimed that it was offensive to public morals, and *Arcadie,* though more discreet, was fined for the same offense in 1956. Both magazines were pro-hibited from advertising and public display and from distribution to minors. Throughout the postwar period there was recurrent pressure from conserva-tive newspapers and politicians to limit the employment of homosexuals in the civil service and the military.

De Gaulle's return to power in 1959 opened the way to yet another round of restrictions and public denunciation of homosexuality by the government, the church, and the medical profession. Early in the new year, at a confer-ence sponsored by the church and the medical profession, Dr. Marcel Eck summed up the prevailing view of the "homosexual peril." It was, he asserted, "a deviation, a sickness, an anomaly," to which those who lived in "the pseudo civilization of great cities" were most likely to succumb. The adolescent boy was thought to be especially vulnerable; parents and teachers had to be constantly on guard since the wrong experience, an unhappy heterosexual encounter or a satisfying homosexual one, could send him down the wrong path. In July the French National Assembly added homosexuality to a list of "social plagues" including alcoholism and prostitution, to combat which it granted special powers to the government. Four months later the government issued a decree substantially raising the fines for homosexual indecency, making them higher than for similar heterosexual offenses. Police raids on known homosexual meeting places increased markedly.

Yet, for all this, public attitudes toward homosexuality remained mixed. The long history of decriminalization, the anticlericalism of much of the French population, the fragmentation of political parties together with popular suspicion of government authority, particularly when it impinged on individual liberty, combined to limit the virulence of public hostility, at least as compared with Britain or the United States. In a survey of public opinion conducted in 1962, at the height of the official crackdown on the subculture, near majorities viewed homosexuality as a vice or an illness and would not employ a homosexual in a responsible position. But an equal number said that they would not fire someone revealed to be a homosexual, and a slim majority believed homosexuals could lead normal lives. Perhaps most significant, only 22 percent believed that homosexuals should be fined or imprisoned. "Public opinion," the report concluded, "seems clearly in agreement with the civil code which tends to consider homosexuality as a private matter, even while morally disapproving of it."

A rare, if cautious and tentative, exception to the generally conservative trend of official policies toward homosexuality in postwar Western Europe was the Netherlands. During the interwar years the subculture in major Dutch cities had experienced much the same heightened sense of activity, but also many of the same difficulties, as its counterparts elsewhere in northwestern Europe. Although technically homosexuality was not illegal, public sexual activity and semipublic meeting places such as bars were subject, as in France, to periodic crackdowns by police. But perhaps because during the wartime occupation the Nazis had imposed German antihomosexual laws on their Aryan brothers in the Netherlands, the Dutch were, if anything, more committed to a policy of decriminalization after the war than they had been before the war, and this despite constant pressure from the Catholic Church and conservative Protestants for tighter restrictions. This is not to suggest that the other major power blocs in Dutch public life, the liberals and the social-ists, were particularly supportive of homosexual rights. They simply wished to avoid the issue and were, in any case, wary of government interference in private matters and morals. As the leaders of the homosexual subculture in the Netherlands were well aware, therefore, their freedom was more negative than positive. Nonetheless, that freedom provided an opportunity, however limited, to organize openly and seek to advance their interests as perhaps nowhere else in Europe.

In 1946 the surviving editors of the prewar magazine *Levensrecht* and the leaders of what had been the Dutch branch of the Scientific Humanitarian Committee founded the Cultural and Recreational Center (COC). Primarily concerned with providing advice, support, and congenial meeting places for homosexuals, the COC, under the leadership of Nico Engelschman (who at first thought it prudent to work under the pseudonym Bob Angelo), also pur-sued a deliberately low-key policy of working to gain greater acceptance or at least of preventing a conservative reaction, through informal contacts with the leaders of other interest groups, churchmen, politicians, and the police. Although as late as 1950 some Catholic organizations continued to support the criminalization of all homosexual relations, the COC was sufficiently cer-tain of the future that in 1951 it founded the International Committee for Sexual Equality, which served as a refuge and source of contacts and infor-mation for other, weaker homosexual rights groups in Europe and the United States and sponsored a series of international congresses. Baudry, for ex-ample, was its French correspondent and later a member of its executive com-mittee. The COC also provided the model for Baudry's CLESPALA.

In 1952 the COC opened its first dance hall, and from the mid-1950s on, the subculture in Amsterdam could count on an official policy of toleration of gay bars, dance halls, and, in later years, hotels, while police surveillance of sexual activity in public was tightened. It was during these years that Amster-dam developed a lively gay entertainment district centered on and near the Leidsestraat, southwest of the city center, and gained its well-deserved repu-tation as perhaps the most tolerant city in Europe. Indeed, in 1960, at the same time that the French government was embarking on repressive policies toward homosexuality, a number of prominent Dutch theologians, Protestant and Catholic, psychiatrists, and social workers began to call for a rethinking of traditional views of homosexuality and the homosexual in favor of greater un-derstanding, sympathy, and support. The Dutch homophile movement re-sponded to the changing climate by becoming more open. In 1962 Engelschman, long accustomed to working behind the scenes, was succeeded as chairman of the COC by Benno Premsela, who had never used a pseudonym and was an advocate of public dialogue and complete integration. Two years later the COC changed its name to the Dutch Society of Homophiles. In this as in so much else the movement in the Netherlands was well ahead of its contemporaries elsewhere in Western Europe.

If even in France, with its long tradition of distinguishing between public and private moral behavior, the government advocated increasingly repressive attitudes and policies toward homosexuality following World War II, it almost hardly need be added that Britain, with its equally long tradition of blurring distinctions between the public and the private, went much further down the same road. Britain's postwar socialist Labor government, in power until 1951, might have been expected to be more sympathetic toward sexual minorities, but it was overwhelmed from the first by economic crises and its welfare-state policies were uniformly family oriented. Moreover, Britain too was subject to powerful Cold War pressures toward cultural conformity, mostly from its ally (and paymaster) the United States. In this context the defection of Guy Burgess and Donald Maclean to the Soviet Union in 1951 was a disaster. It happened only six months after the United States Senate issued its inflammatory report suggesting that homosexuals were especially likely security risks; unfortunately for the British government and for British homosexuals, Burgess and Maclean fit the stereotypical picture of the homosexual as spy almost perfectly.

Both men came from privileged social backgrounds: Burgess's father was a naval commander, Maclean's a lawyer and member of Parliament. Both were born shortly before World War I and educated between the two world wars at elite private schools and then at Cambridge, where they met. At Cambridge they, like so many in their generation, were drawn to Communism as the only answer to the Great Depression and the threat of fascism, and it was there that they were first recruited as potential Soviet agents. Both were brilliant and able to rise quickly in government service, including the highly selective Foreign Office, despite their reputations as heavy drinkers who were often socially irresponsible when drunk. Both were actively homosexual, Maclean in his youth (he married in his late twenties), Burgess throughout his life.

To what extent their sexual and their political deviance were related or, indeed, fed on each other can only be guessed at. That they were and did is the thesis of the play, later a film, *Another Country,* based on Burgess's brilliant but ultimately thwarted career at Eton. (Interestingly, for their slightly older contemporaries, the Auden-Isherwood group, while their status as sexual outsiders also contributed to their identification with the left, their loyalties in the end remained personal, not political. In this respect they were closer to Forster than they were to Burgess and Maclean. Once again it is worth emphasizing how short a college generation is. The world Isherwood and company plunged into with such enthusiasm after coming down from Oxford and Cambridge was already falling apart by the time Burgess, Maclean, and the other Cambridge spies—Philby and Blunt—entered university.) In any case, whatever the relationship between their sexuality and their politics may have been, Burgess and Maclean amply fulfilled the worst popular prejudices about homosexuals, that they were degenerate, debauched, unreliable, and not only possibly but in this instance undeniably subversive.

Inevitably, as news of their flight and of their checkered personal histories was revealed in the press, pressure on the British government to crack down on potential subversives and on homosexuals increased, especially from Washington, where both Maclean and Burgess had served in the British embassy. Not that the police or successive British governments needed much prodding. Disturbed by the apparent breakdown in sexual morals during World War II, a new director of public prosecutions, appointed in 1944, had embarked on an escalating antihomosexual campaign that climaxed in the early 1950s, following the election of a Conservative government in October 1951, only four months after the Burgess-Maclean story broke. Working closely with the director of public prosecutions and an equally homophobic new Metropolitan (London) Police commissioner, the Home Secretary in the Conservative cabinet made the government's intentions unmistakably clear. "Homosexuals in general," he stated in Parliament, "are exhibitionists and proselytizers, and a danger to others, especially the young. So long as I hold the office of Home Secretary, I shall give no countenance to the view that they should not be prevented from being such a danger."

The results were dramatic. By the mid-1950s the number of arrests and prosecutions for various homosexual offenses—sodomy, indecent assault, gross indecency—was from five to seven times greater than just before the war. To obtain these results the police resorted to entrapment in public places; to grants of immunity to small fry in the hope of snaring more prominent offenders; to so-called chain prosecutions, in which an arrest or threat of arrest could lead to a network of associates; and to charges of conspiracy, in order to cast the net as widely as possible. There were a number of sensational cases in 1953–54, two of which illustrate especially graphically the lengths to which police and prosecutors were willing to go to gain convictions and then to cover their tracks.

The author and critic Rupert Croft-Cooke was arrested (in the middle of the night); his house was searched (without a warrant); he was tried, convicted, and imprisoned solely on the basis of uncorroborated, recanted, and then reaffirmed testimony from two questionable witnesses, sailors arrested on an unrelated charge who had accused Croft-Cooke of committing a gross indecency with them. In return for their testimony the sailors were not charged. After his release, when it became known that he had decided to write a book about his experience, Croft-Cooke was visited by a plainclothes policemen. "I hear you are going to write a book about all this," the policemen said. "Are you going to give details of how your conviction was brought about?" "Of course," Croft-Cooke replied. "I shouldn't do that if I were you," the policeman warned. "It wouldn't do you any good, and might do you irreparable harm. If mistakes were made by anyone—anyone went too far, I mean—it's best forgotten now." To Croft-Cooke this was unthinkable not only for himself but for others. After all, as he pointed out, "This filthy witch hunt is still going on." "That's what I mean," the policeman replied, smiling. "It is. And you know a second conviction is very much more easily obtained. . . . It needs only the word of one person, a policemen perhaps or someone who has been given an interest in the matter. . . . You think it over." Croft-Cooke did indeed think it over but came to a different conclusion; he wrote the book but then went to live abroad in the large and largely homosexual Anglo-American community in Tangier.

Mostly because it was that thing so beloved of the British tabloid press, a sex scandal involving a member of the aristocracy, the Montague-Wildeblood prosecution was the most notorious case, and ultimately the most important, in the antihomosexual campaign of the early 1950s. It had many of the characteristics of the postwar wave of persecutions, including the use of grants of immunity and charges of conspiracy; and it was reminiscent of the Wilde trials six decades earlier in the prosecution's insistence on a retrial following a hung jury and in its emphasis on the age and class differences between the sexual partners as a means of reinforcing popular prejudice against the accused. Charged with committing an unnatural offense and of indecent assault on local boy scouts at his country estate, Lord Montague of Beaulieu's first trial ended in acquittal on the more serious charge and a hung jury on the lesser one. After deciding to pursue the case against him, the prosecution changed and widened its scope, charging not only Lord Montague but a relative, Michael Pitt-Rivers, and a friend, the journalist Peter Wildeblood, with various homosexual acts and with conspiracy to commit them. The chief witnesses for the prosecution were two notoriously promiscuous Royal Air Force airmen, who were themselves never charged. As with Croft-Cooke before him, Wildeblood's residence was searched without a warrant, and again like Croft-Cooke, Wildeblood wrote a scathing account of the whole affair, which ended in convictions and jail sentences of from twelve to eighteen months for all three defendants.

Against this legal onslaught the homosexual subculture had no defense. There was no organization in Britain comparable to the Mattachine Society in the United States, Arcadie in France, or even the Society for Human Rights in Germany, let alone the Dutch COC. The last, tenuous link back to the British Society for the Study of Sex Psychology, which itself had been inspired by Hirschfeld's pioneering efforts in Germany, was severed when its postwar successor, the Sex Education Society, died following the death of its director, Norman Haire, in 1952. Although the small society was not exclusively concerned with homosexuality and was dedicated to providing information, not support, it had provided a front, a forum, and contacts through its publications. Haire had studied at Hirschfeld's institute and was one of the founders of the World League for Sexual Reform and of its British section in 1928. More than anyone else it was he who had kept the issue of sexual reform alive, though only barely, through the lean years of the 1930s and the postwar years in Britain. But following his death there was no organization with even the limited agenda and membership of the Sex Education Society until near the end of the decade. Luck, a degree of discretion, or good connections were the only protections available to the individual homosexual. In a few self-contained professions, such as fashion or the theater, homosexuality was no disadvantage; indeed, as had been the case before the war, not to be homosexual often seemed a disadvantage (though this provided no protection in the outside world, as John Gielgud's arrest in 1953 demonstrated). Networks established in school or university might persist into adult life, and for those with the right contacts private clubs provided not only some protection but also a way around Britain's absurdly restrictive liquor licensing laws.

There were escapes, to Amsterdam for a weekend or, as had long been the case, to Mediterranean Europe or North Africa for a holiday. Wealth or professional responsibilities allowed a few to live abroad, which was especially useful for those with unusual sexual proclivities, say, for underage boys. A rare and surprisingly appealing glimpse into that discomfiting aspect of the sub-culture was provided by Michael Davidson, a foreign correspondent for one of Britain's leading newspapers, whose autobiography, *The World, the Flesh and Myself,* with its opening sentence, "This is the life history of a lover of boys," caused a sensation when it was published in 1962. Arrested twice, imprisoned once, and accosted on another occasion by policemen who reminded him that "we know all about you . . . we got your record," Davidson realized that he had to change his ways, risk going to prison once again, or leave England. Luckily for him his employment as a foreign correspondent beginning shortly after World War II allowed him to avoid the first two alternatives in favor of the third.

For a few it was possible to avoid having to change their ways and to remain at home in relative safety through the cultivation of influence and connections. Perhaps the supreme English example was Tom Driberg, who served for many years as a member of Parliament, on the National Executive of the Labor Party, and finally in the House of Lords, despite his early membership in the Communist Party and a promiscuous homosexual lifestyle dating back to his schooldays. His arrest and trial for indecent assault in 1935 would almost certainly have put an end to any hopes he might have had for a political career, despite his acquittal, had it been reported. But it was not. Driberg was the leading gossip columnist in England, and his employer, the influential Lord Beaverbrook, prevailed on every national newspaper to suppress the story. What is more, the officer who arrested him later indicated that had he known who Driberg was, there would have been no arrest. The Lord Chief Justice of England told Beaverbrook much the same thing. Driberg drew an important practical lesson from his brush with the law, though not the one the authorities must have hoped for. Far from becoming less active and more careful sexually, he was, if anything, more promiscuous (it was not for nothing that he entitled his posthumously published memoirs *Ruling Passions*). He realized that he could use his position as a journalist and later as an MP to overawe potential arresting officers, which he did on two subsequent occasions.

Not many homosexual men had the options available to a Michael Davidson or a Tom Driberg. More representative of the experience of ordinary gay men was Allan Horsfall, later to emerge as one of the leaders of the gay rights movement in England, who spent all of his childhood and much of his adult life in the small industrial and mining towns of northern England. For him and others like him the outlets were few—the bar in a local hotel, a nearby seaside resort—and the risks correspondingly high. "Many people," he later recalled, "took the fatalistic attitude which had been common during the wartime blitz . . . and simply got on with life as best they could." But best was not very good. "There could hardly have been a less satisfactory basis for a social or sexual existence," he concluded. "Had it been possible to produce a gay man's survival guide at that time, it would have urged him never to reveal his name or address, never to discuss how he earned his living or where he worked, never to take anybody to his home or give anybody his telephone number and never to write letters, whether affectionate or not, to anybody with whom he was sexually involved or even to anybody he knew to be gay."

Even the most circumspect, let alone those who frequented such traditional London cruising grounds as St. James's Park, the Thames Embankment, the streets off Shaftesbury Avenue, the Turkish baths in the Imperial Hotel, and any number of West End cottages (as public toilets were called) or the far fewer comparable meeting places in provincial towns and cities, ran a substantial risk of arrest and conviction or of blackmail to avoid exposure. The criminal statistics can only begin to suggest the humiliation of having one's name published in the newspapers, the terrible psychological strain of having always to lead a double life, and the very real prospect of losing family, friends, employment, everything, if the pretense were exposed. If any one man's story demands to be singled out for retelling, it is perhaps that of Alan Turing, in part because his personal sexual and legal history was akin to so many others in the 1950s, and not only in England, but most of all because it ended in the meaningless waste of a good and great man.

One of the great mathematical minds of the twentieth century, Turing was a central figure not only in breaking the German military codes during World War II but in laying the foundations for the computer age. Yet, like many mathematical geniuses, he was something of an innocent when it came to dealing with the harsher aspects of the real world. Born in 1912, he was a few years younger than the Auden-Isherwood group but a contemporary of the Cambridge spies. As the son of a colonial administrator Turing received the training normally accorded young men of his class: boarding school followed by a university education at Cambridge. He had the usual crushes on other boys at school, including a passionate friendship with a boy who died young. Although Turing had his first sexual experience while at university, he was too shy and lived too much in a world of his own to take part in the active homosexual subculture there. His hush-hush wartime work interrupted an otherwise quiet, though immensely productive, academic career, and his personal life was equally uneventful. He was briefly engaged to a coworker with whom he was quite open about the nature of his sexuality, as, indeed, he was with many others. Relatively inexperienced in the ways of the subculture, he nonetheless had a reasonably rewarding sex life, in part because of his openness. Sadly, it was precisely this quality, so rare in the climate of the 1950s, that was to be his undoing.

In December 1951 Turing picked up a nineteen-year-old working-class youth, Arnold Murray, outside a cinema in Manchester. Despite the differences between them in age, intellect, and social status, yet attracted to each other in part because of these differences, they entered into an uneasy relationship. The source—or symbol—of their frequent misunderstandings was money. Murray needed it but did not want to be paid in direct exchange for sex, like a hustler. He preferred gifts or loans for specific purposes and looked to the older, higher-status Turing as a patron, certainly a common enough pattern in the gay world. Turing was willing to give Murray money but was suspicious of the boy's motives and of the truth of much of what he said, a mistrust that was to lead to disaster.

Early in 1952 Turing's house was burgled, and Turing, suspecting Murray, reported the theft to the police and wrote to Murray breaking off all contact. Murray responded by turning up at Turing's house to explain that the burglary had probably been committed by a friend to whom he had boasted of his relationship with Turing. Reconciled with Murray once again, Turing reported the information implicating Murray's friend to the police, but they were far less interested in a minor burglary than in how it was that a man like Turing knew a boy like Murray. In response to clever police questioning and because of his own naiveté—Turing thought there was a government commission looking into homosexual law reform—he finally admitted the nature of his relationship with Murray. In fact, no such commission was appointed until 1954, and no action was taken on its recommendations until 1967, fifteen years after Turing's police interrogation. Turing was not simply naive or misinformed, however; he was just ahead of his time, or perhaps more accurately, outside of it. He saw nothing wrong with his homosexuality and often made a point of mentioning it to friends and colleagues, though not to his immediate family until after his arrest. Neither especially brave nor foolhardy in his dealings with the police, he thought he was acting rationally.

Unfortunately for Turing, the law was not rational and the police were not ahead of their time. Not that the authorities were vindictive; by their standards they were quite enlightened. The police liked him and were impressed by his candor. He was not imprisoned but was placed on probation for a year and ordered to seek a cure. Had Turing lived in the United States, that would probably have meant psychotherapy, but the British psychiatric profession had come to doubt its efficacy in treating homosexuality. Aversion therapy, the use of chemical or electric shock to turn homosexuals (and other sex offenders) away from their usual object choice, was still only in the experimental stage. In the early 1950s the most promising technique appeared to be organotherapy, the use of hormones to alter or suppress sexual drives. Male hormones had been experimented with in the hope of making homosexuals more masculine, but with disappointing results. The sex drive often increased, and sexual orientation was not altered. Hence the idea of utilizing female hormones in men as a means of suppressing the sex drive—chemical castration, in other words—which seemed at the time to produce the desired result. It was that to which Turing was subjected. He found the experience humiliating. Much to his embarrassment his breasts grew. But he came through the treatment with his sex drive unimpaired, though he was careful to go abroad to satisfy it. And then, suddenly and without warning or explanation, he killed himself in June 1954.

Why Alan Turing committed suicide we shall never know for certain, but his biographer has put forward a case that is convincing at its core, if not always at its edges. Turing's offense was committed in 1951, the year of Burgess and Maclean's defection to Moscow; he committed suicide shortly after the Montague scandal and trials early in 1954. And though Britain was well behind the United States in constructing the apparatus of the security state and in automatically categorizing homosexuals as security risks, it was catching up fast. In April 1954, during a debate on the British Atomic Energy Bill, a government spokesman acknowledged, in answer to an opposition question, that homosexuals would now be treated as security risks. Later in the debate the government retreated from such an unequivocal statement, but that was in fact government policy. The nature of Anglo-American cooperation in the field of atomic energy required it, as did coordination between the British and American intelligence services.

For a man like Turing the prospects were ominous. He was essentially apolitical and had no access to atomic secrets. But his head was full of information scarcely less sensitive, and he was eccentric, a loner, an intellectual, and therefore almost automatically a source of nervousness to the security apparatus—and he was homosexual. It was a combination that seemed likely to result in a gradual circumscribing of his personal and intellectual freedom and of his ability to pursue his work. Accepted on the basis of his qualifications and on trust back in the 1930s and 1940s, he would perhaps not have been granted security clearance in the new, postwar climate. It may be more than coincidence that a few days before Turing killed himself it was reported that in the United States Robert Oppenheimer, one of the fathers of the atomic bomb, had been designated a security risk.

To call Alan Turing a homosexual martyr is too simplistic. Rather, he was a martyr to an age increasingly insistent on enforcing norms of belief and behavior. There were any number of ways that one could violate those norms, and a man like Turing was suspect on many counts; but not for the first time in history, nor for the last, homosexuality was seen as an especially flagrant and dangerous deviation that threatened social norms at their very core.

# Chapter 20   Outsiders Abroad and at Home

Accommodation to the politics and prejudices of the 1950s was not the only survival strategy adopted by gay men and lesbians following World War II, but it was certainly the most common. A few courageous or cantankerous individuals refused to accept the tactical necessity of lying low, let alone the dominant view of homosexuality as a negative deviation from social and sexual norms. Like the Mattachine Society, the Daughters of Bilitis, and the Arcadie circle, they tended to turn inward—they had little choice—but in different ways and to different ends. Many in the rising generation of gay American writers dispersed in search of safer, more sympathetic climates. For most of them, as for their English counterparts, this meant spending at least some time abroad as a temporary escape or, especially in the conservative 1950s, as a means of better understanding and criticizing American society and their own less than comfortable place in it.

For young Americans, whatever their sexual persuasion, the grand tour still meant primarily France and Italy, and in 1948, the first postwar year in which extensive European travel was possible, "a pack of queens," as Gore Vidal put it, "was on the move that summer in Europe. . . . The peripatetic group that centered on Tennessee, Capote, the Bowleses" migrated from city to city, primarily Rome and Paris, mingling occasionally with the local literati but for the most part with one another. Vidal sailed for Italy in February, immediately after the publication of *The City and the Pillar,* and quickly discovered that John Horne Burns had been correct in suggesting to him that Italian boys were both attractive and readily available. Tennessee Williams, enjoying the fruits of his first great theatrical successes, also happened to be in Rome, and this unlikely duo hit it off immediately. Before leaving Italy Vidal visited the aged George Santayana and, at a party given by Williams, met Harold Acton, who had ventured down from Florence to inspect, disapprovingly as it turned out, this first wave of the postwar American invasion.

After Rome, Paris, where Williams and Vidal shared a whole floor in a small hotel as well as the boys they picked up on the streets or in bars. "All the writers are here and the atmosphere is heavy with competition," Vidal advised a friend back home. Certainly all the gay writers seemed to be in Paris, including Vidal's present rival and future enemy, Truman Capote. Paul Bowles came up from Tangier to see Williams, and Cocteau, who wanted the French rights to *A Streetcar Named Desire,* invited Williams and Vidal to lunch. Quite by chance Vidal encountered Isherwood, who was back in Europe for the first time since his departure for America before the war. Isherwood introduced him to Lehmann, whose publishing firm had contracted to bring out an English edition of *The City and the Pillar* (though Lehmann, like Isherwood and Williams, disliked the novel's violent and tragic ending). Lehmann in turn introduced Vidal to Gide and invited him and Williams to London to meet the British literary establishment, past and present, including Forster, Spender, Graham Greene, Harold Nicholson, and the Sitwells. Forster invited Vidal and Williams to visit him in Cambridge and showed the young author of *The City and the Pillar* a copy of his still unpublished *Maurice.*

Although most of the postwar generation of American writers were to revisit Europe often in later years, they never again experienced quite the same sense of excitement as in that first summer after a decade of being cut off. Nor, unlike their interwar predecessors, were they as a group inclined to become expatriates. Vidal eventually settled in Italy, but not until many years later. Only one of the young gay writers who arrived in Paris in 1948, James Baldwin, stayed on, and he did so for the sake of racial as much as sexual acceptance. His most openly homosexual novel, *Giovanni's Room,* published in 1956, was written in France. By then the trickle of American visitors to Europe in the late 1940s had become a flood; nonetheless, the doyens of the beat counterculture who descended on Paris in the late 1950s were able to attract quite as much attention as their more mainstream predecessors. The gay contingent among the Beats—Allen Ginsberg, William Burroughs, Harold Norse—generally set the tone. Their unofficial headquarters in Paris was a cheap and seedy residential hotel in the Latin Quarter dubbed the Beat Hotel by one of the lesser lights of the movement. Ginsberg discovered the place in the autumn of 1957 and lived there for almost a year. Burroughs joined him early in 1958, and Norse, who immortalized the Beat Hotel in a novel of the same name, arrived two years later.

Burroughs had come from Tangier, and it marked a significant change in the pattern of American, especially gay American, travels abroad that when Ginsberg embarked on his first trip overseas, he went initially, not to France or Italy, but to Morocco, specifically Tangier, which had become emblematic of the counterculture during the Eisenhower era. As Ginsberg put it, Tangier was a "release from American restraints, and I don't mean sexual, I mean the constraints of anxiety and business, commerce, the civic constraints of the laws on drugs, the constraints of the police state." North Africa was hardly a new destination for northern Europeans in search of the culturally and sexually exotic. Algeria and Egypt had played a pivotal role in their personal self-discovery as homosexuals for some of the most important novelists of the turn of the century: Gide, Forster, Kuzmin. But Morocco, which did not come under direct European control until shortly before World War I, was a relatively late addition to the list of countries commonly visited by Westerners, and Americans were relative latecomers, arriving in significant numbers only from the late 1920s on. As an international zone run by a commission of representatives from the interested European powers, Tangier attracted an extraordinary assortment of colorful and suspect characters: foreign agents and con men, money changers and businessmen, legitimate and otherwise, and expatriates intent on avoiding the laws, sexual mores, high taxes, or simply the colder climates of their homelands. Truman Capote caught the peculiar character of the place and its foreign inhabitants especially well: "Virtually every foreign Tangerine is ensconced there for at least one, if not all, of four reasons: the easy availability of drugs, lustful adolescent prostitutes, tax loopholes, or because he is so undesirable, no place north of Port Said would let him out of the airport or off a ship."

The American presence in Morocco centered to an extraordinary degree on one individual, Paul Bowles. More than any other foreigner, he identified himself with Morocco and defined Morocco in the foreign mind. A near contemporary of George Platt Lynes and a decade younger than Glenway Wescott and Monroe Wheeler, Bowles was one of the last of his generation of American artists, writers, and musicians to embark on the obligatory pilgrimage to Europe before the onset of the Great Depression sent most of them limping back across the Atlantic. The young, blond, and handsome aspiring writer and composer arrived in Paris in 1931 and made the inevitable call on Gertrude Stein. She, in turn, introduced him to a dazzling array of expatriate and French artists, including Virgil Thompson and Gide. Bowles's mentor and teacher, Aaron Copland, arrived in Paris shortly thereafter and almost immediately whisked his reluctant protégé off to Berlin. There he met Isherwood and Spender. They did not hit it off. Bowles found the Englishmen condescending; Isherwood thought Bowles aloof, but he did commandeer his attractive American visitor's last name for the central female character of his Berlin stories. Returning to France, Bowles and Copland visited Stein at her country house, and she advised them to spend the rest of the summer, not on the French Riviera, especially Villefranche—"Everybody's there"—but in Tangier, where she and Alice B. Toklas had spent three pleasant vacations.

Bowles was captivated by the place. He stayed on for some months and visited Morocco three more times in the 1930s. During one long stay in 1933 he hosted Charles Henri Ford and Djuna Barnes on their visit to Tangier. Financial constraints, professional ambition, and World War II kept Bowles in the United States for over a decade, but in 1947 he was drawn irresistibly and permanently back to Tangier. In the interim he had met and married Jane Auer, soon to emerge as an important author in her own right. It was a curious marriage. They may or may not ever have had sexual relations, and if so, it was only in the first years of their marriage. She was openly lesbian and had a number of affairs with other women, including an obsessive relationship with a Moroccan peasant girl, Cherifa. As for Paul Bowles, though intrigued by homosexuality and clearly homoerotically inclined, he was sexually fastidious, even repressed, and his longest lasting relationship in Morocco, with a painter twenty years his junior, Ahmed Yacoubi, was more avuncular than sexual, if indeed it was sexual at all.

Through his writings and personal connections Bowles ensured that Tangier would become a common addition to the itinerary of American writers and intellectuals, as well as the merely curious, traveling in Europe. It was strange and exotic yet close, and it had a reassuringly familiar European quarter next to its mysterious old Arab city. For those in search of cheap and ready access to drugs or to young men and boys, a trip to Tangier became almost obligatory. In 1948 Bowles traveled to New York at Tennessee Williams's request to write incidental music for the production of one of Williams's plays. Bowles returned, accompanied by Williams, who did not like Tangier at first but formed a close friendship with Jane. In 1949 Bowles traveled to Paris, where he met Gore Vidal and Truman Capote and invited them to visit him in Tangier. Vidal made a point of getting there before Capote, found he did not like the place, and "stayed around Tangier only long enough to make Truman believe he was going to spend the whole summer."

Capote stayed longer and partied extravagantly but ultimately tired of the city and its directionless expatriate society. "Among the planet's most pathetic tribes," he later wrote, "are those Americans who elect to make a career of expatriation. If you're young enough, it's okay for a couple of years—but those who pursue it after age twenty-five, thirty at the limit, learn that what seemed paradise is mere scenery, a curtain that, lifting, reveals pitchforks and fire." That was certainly not the case for Paul Bowles, who did his most creative work in Morocco, but it was true of many others, including his wife, who frittered away their creative energies and sank into self-destructive indolence. And it was certainly true of the first of a new wave of American literary visitors to Morocco, William Burroughs. Tangier retained at least a semblance of its old character into the mid-1950s, and it was that that attracted Burroughs in late 1953. "I'm going to steep myself in vice," he declared. And so he did, living for a time in a male brothel and experimenting with a veritable pharmacopoeia of drugs, though he also managed to establish an affectionate relationship with an eighteen-year-old Spanish boy, Kiki, and poured out reams of manuscript for his major novel, *Naked Lunch*. All this Burroughs reported in frequent letters to Ginsberg, and it was primarily in order to visit Burroughs that Ginsberg, preceded by his friend Jack Kerouac, traveled to Morocco early in 1957.

The three had first met in New York in 1944, when Ginsberg, still in his teens, was a student at Columbia. Kerouac, four years older than Ginsberg, and Burroughs, eight years older still, were at least as instrumental as Columbia in educating Ginsberg out of his provincial Paterson, New Jersey, background. They discussed his homosexuality with him and encouraged his coming out; they introduced him to drugs, to an extraordinary range of literature, to the gay bars and bathhouses of New York, and to the criminal subculture of the city, a special interest of Burroughs's. One of Burroughs's discoveries, Herbert Huncke, a petty thief, was taken up by the group as a whole and achieved a certain importance as a source of information on the sexual underworld for Alfred Kinsey (Burroughs, Kerouac, and Ginsberg were also interviewed by Kinsey). Unfortunately for Ginsberg, he inadvertently allowed himself to become implicated in Huncke's criminal activities. Arrested along with Huncke, he avoided prosecution by pleading guilty and committing himself to a psychiatric hospital, where a central aspect of his therapy was an attempt to cure him of his homosexuality.

More than half persuaded that a "normal" sexual orientation was indispensable to a happy and productive life, Ginsberg entered into a number of affairs with women and turned his back on his homosexual past, concluding that "all my queerness was camp, unnecessary, morbid, so lacking in completion and sharing of love as to be almost as bad as impotence and celibacy." Burroughs was skeptical and angry at both Ginsberg and his psychiatrist. "I simply do not recognize such an entity as a 'neurotic heter with strong queer leanings,'" he wrote. "For the Cris sake do you actually think that laying a woman makes someone heter?" In the short run Burroughs was wrong; Ginsberg genuinely enjoyed his heterosexual phase, which was by no means simply a desperate or self-deceiving attempt to cover up a predominant homosexuality. But it was a phase. Gradually he reverted to his homosexual way of life, though in later years he sometimes had sexual relations with women he liked. Burroughs was hardly a disinterested observer of Ginsberg's experiment with heterosexuality, in any case. He fell in love with Ginsberg, who had sex with him, though more out of friendship than out of desire. For his part Ginsberg was attracted to Kerouac, one of a succession of young, blond, athletic, northern or eastern European types, all of them essentially heterosexual, with whom Ginsberg had or wished he might have occasional sex. One of these young men, Peter Orlovsky, accompanied him to Morocco and then to Paris and was to be his most enduring companion.

Mention of Ginsberg and Orlovsky leads back across the Atlantic, indeed across America, to the city where they met, San Francisco, one of the few places in the United States where the counterculture, including the gay subculture, could thrive. As the chief port of embarkation on the West Coast during World War II San Francisco developed an especially active and visible gay social scene, which, despite the concerted efforts of the military, the civilian police, and the state liquor authorities, both during and after the war, survived essentially intact. When Ginsberg arrived in the city in 1953 the North Beach area had already become an identifiably gay neighborhood. It was also home to the city's postwar cultural flowering, the so-called San Francisco renaissance.

No less than in New York in the late 1940s, members of the gay contingent among San Francisco's young postwar writers were optimistically open about their sexuality, and none more so than the poet Robert Duncan. A native Californian, he dropped out of Berkeley in 1938 to accompany his lover to the East Coast. Active in radical literary circles in New York in the early 1940s, in 1944 he wrote for the anarchist journal *Politics* an essay entitled "The Homosexual in Society," which, in arguing that homosexuals must not retreat into a ghetto mentality but should see themselves—and be seen by wider society—as an oppressed minority like Jews or Negroes, anticipated by seven years many of the concerns and prescriptions of both Donald Webster Cory's *The Homosexual in America* and Harry Hay in founding the Mattachine Society. Duncan paid for his frankness, losing a number of outlets for his poetry. He returned to California in 1946 and quickly established himself as one of the central figures of the San Francisco renaissance. Even so, while Duncan and his circle provided a congenial environment for radicals, dropouts, writers, and the homosexual subculture, it was Ginsberg, more than any other individual, who made the San Francisco counterculture a highly publicized national phenomenon.

In October 1955 Ginsberg gave a public reading of his just completed poem *Howl*, a long, rambling, raunchy, sexually explicit, celebratory work very much in the tradition of Walt Whitman. For Ginsberg *Howl* was "the crucial moment of breakthrough" in openly expressing his sexuality. For others in the gay subculture and in the wider Beat counterculture it was a scarcely less decisive moment, and San Francisco soon gained a reputation as a refuge for the disaffected in the Eisenhower era. This was hardly welcome news to the city's elite, but escalating attacks by the authorities only reinforced the movement and brought it to mainstream national attention. In June 1957, shortly after Ginsberg left for Morocco and Europe, the police seized copies of *Howl* from the city's leading avant-garde bookstore, the City Lights Bookstore, and charged its owner with selling obscenity. The defense quickly became a cause célèbre, a test case of fundamental civil liberties that attracted the support of the ACLU and a host of writers. The judge dismissed the case, and *Howl* became that rarity in poetry, a bestseller. National magazines—*Time, Harper's, Look, The Nation*—descended on San Francisco, exposing North Beach and the Beat counterculture to the glare of publicity, almost always critical in tone, often using the prominent gay element among the Beats and in the San Francisco renaissance as a means of discrediting both.

Many longtime North Beach residents resented this lumping together in the press and the public mind of the San Francisco renaissance, the Beats, and the gay subculture, but for the subculture itself, and not only in San Francisco, it was an almost unalloyed blessing. Suddenly it was no longer necessary to look abroad for, let alone go overseas in search of, personal freedom or cultural role models. Right here, in America, there was a movement, many of whose most prominent spokesmen were gay, that sanctioned, even celebrated, intellectual and social dissent. "Through the beats' example, gays could perceive themselves as nonconformists rather than deviates, as rebels against stultifying norms rather than immature, unstable personalities."

So far as the authorities in San Francisco were concerned the situation was clearly getting out of hand, and they responded by stepping up police surveillance in Beat neighborhoods and regulating bars through the Alcoholic

Beverages Control Department (ABC). Political and legal complications soon followed. In the 1959 mayoral race the challenger accused the incumbent, George Christopher, of allowing the city to become "the national headquarters of the organized homosexuals in the United States." Reelected in spite of this, Christopher immediately escalated the ongoing campaign against gay bars. Luckily for the bar owners and their patrons this coincided with a decision by the state supreme court, one of many decisions dating back to the early 1950s, most of them the result of dogged resistance by the owner of the city's most colorful gay bar, the Black Cat, restricting the power of the ABC to withhold or revoke liquor licenses solely on the grounds that bars had a gay clientele. Freed from the threat of losing their licenses, a number of bar owners revealed that ABC employees and police routinely extorted money from them. Using a blatantly homophobic line of defense, the accused officers' lawyers won an acquittal, thus opening the way to an even more virulent campaign against the city's gay subculture. Since the courts now required that some sort of illegal activity be proved if a bar was to be closed down, the police and the ABC cooperated in providing and training decoys to lure, provoke, or entrap the unwary in bars and known cruising areas. The number of arrests, the scale and frequency of raids on bars, both gay and lesbian, and the revocation of liquor licenses skyrocketed during 1960 and 1961, even though the legal basis for these actions was often shaky.

The Mattachine Society and the Daughters of Bilitis, both headquartered in the city, might have been expected to rise to the occasion, but they did not. Weakened by internal divisions (the national structure of Mattachine was dissolved early in 1961), disinclined to activism, and concerned with respectability, they kept their distance from the bar scene. Instead the counterattack was launched by the owners of the bars themselves, led by Bill Plath of the D'Oak Room Bar. In 1962 they formed the Tavern Guild, which contributed to a legal defense fund for arrested members and their customers, financed a handbook on the legal rights of homosexuals, and ran voter-registration drives in the bars at election time. This was not the gay movement's first foray into electoral politics, though it was its first organized effort. A year earlier, the most popular gay entertainer in San Francisco, the Black Cat's own Jose Sarria, had run for city supervisor, establishing in his losing effort an important precedent for the gay community.

The logical next step was taken in 1964, when Plath and others schooled in the activism of the Tavern Guild founded the Society for Individual Rights (SIR), which set out to be what the Mattachine Society had long since ceased to be—militant, political, even confrontational—as well as some things Mattachine had rarely or never been—not elitist but grass roots, anchored in the bars, democratic in structure, and as much a social service as a political organization, sponsoring parties, a recreational club, health clinics, and the like. SIR worked closely with the Council on Religion and the Homosexual (CRH), also founded in 1964, which, as an organization of Protestant ministers, had the enormous advantage over any homosexual organization of being able to take the moral high ground in its dealings with city officials and to enlist the support of other minority groups in exposing and gradually reducing the harassment, entrapment, and physical abuse of homosexuals by the police. The turning point came almost immediately after the founding of the CRH, when the fledging organization decided to sponsor a New Year's Eve dance for the gay community. After failing to pressure the CRH into canceling the event, the police resorted to blatant intimidation, filling the street near the entrance with police and police cars, photographing the guests as they arrived, attempting to enter the hall, and arresting those, including three lawyers, who barred their way. The CRH, and through it the city, was given a graphic illustration that could not be ignored or denied of what the gay subculture had faced for years. The ACLU agreed to defend those arrested, and when the case came to court, the judge instructed the jury to return a verdict of not guilty.

Yet, for all the successes of the San Francisco homophile movement of the mid-1960s, its reach ultimately exceeded its grasp, especially in the political arena, where, despite SIR's initiatives in meeting with and pressuring candidates, it was unable to organize an effective gay voting bloc. The movement's most significant achievement was in reaching out to a wide audience, gay and straight. SIR published a glossy monthly magazine, *Vector*, which was distributed not only by subscription but on newsstands. The scarcity of publications by and about the gay and lesbian community gave *Vector* and the few other such magazines, notably Philadelphia's far more daringly open *Drum*, an importance out of all proportion to their circulation. There was, as yet, relatively little else, although times were changing. Between the late 1950s and the mid-1960s the apparatus of censorship, including the authority of the post office to restrict what was sent through the mails, was gradually dismantled through a series of Supreme Court cases, including a few specifically protecting publications aimed at a gay audience, from the serious journal *One* to the increasingly explicit beefcake magazines (although the authorities did manage to drive the publisher of *Drum*, Clark Polak, who also ran bookstores and ventured into mail-order erotica, out of business in 1969). The "groaning shelf" of gay novels that had appeared in the late 1940s was followed by a steady trickle of fiction on homosexual themes. However, aside from pulp novels, which the attentive reader might happen upon in the racks of paperbacks in bus stations or drug stores, many of the more ambitious novels aimed at a gay audience were published by small presses and were neither widely reviewed nor advertised, let alone readily available in bookstores or public libraries. For lesbians there were the sensational lesbian pulp novels, but often these were written by men for a male audience titillated by descriptions of sex between women. Most gay men had little to fall back on other than the beefcake magazines, pioneered by Bob Mizer's *Physique Pictorial*, which first appeared in 1951, whose hunky models striking exaggerated poses were the direct opposite of the stereotypical effeminate homosexual. Slim pickings indeed, from which SIR's *Vector*, with its blend of news and advocacy, gossip and entertainment, aimed at "creating a sense of community," or *Drum*, with its joyful celebration of sexuality, were rare exceptions.

SIR was unusual in another respect: it welcomed publicity for its wide-ranging social and political activities—and got it. One of the ironies of these years is that the highly publicized police and political crackdowns of the early to mid-1960s, following on the sensational publicity given to the counter-culture, had the unintended consequence of ending the taboo on the public discussion of homosexuality. The publicity may have been bad for the most part, the tone censorious, the attitude one of disgust, though that became less the case in San Francisco as time passed, largely because of the work of SIR and the CRH, but the subject was out there and in the mainstream press, and not only in San Francisco. In the mid-sixties newspapers in other cities began to cover the gay and lesbian subcultures in their own backyards, and national magazines broadened their coverage. Although most of the growing publicity remained negative, treating the subculture as alien and its denizens as lonely and pathetic, coverage nonetheless gradually became more comprehensive, the subject of investigative reporting rather than merely sensational exposés. And whatever its limitations, it had two, once again unintended consequences: it provided information to isolated individuals about the subculture, indeed let them know that there was a subculture, and it opened the way to the dissemination of dissenting opinions.

And dissenting opinions there were, even within the psychiatric profession. A number of psychiatrists and analysts, influenced by the methodologies and findings of other disciplines, primarily in the social sciences, began to question the orthodox view of homosexuality as a pathological condition, at least as traditionally understood. Perhaps, some therapists speculated, rather than being the result of unresolved sexual conflicts or traumas in childhood, homosexuality might be an adaptive response to societal pressures in an age of anxiety, a way of dealing with the stresses of work, rapid technological change, or the fear of nuclear annihilation following on the Depression and World War II. Such a "flight from masculinity," as one practitioner, Abram Kardiner, termed it, might not be a healthy response, and thus therapy might still be required, but now the responsibility was seen as being as much society's as the individual's.

From this it was no great step to the suggestion that many of the supposedly pathological symptoms common in homosexuals were due not so much to any sickness on their part as to the prejudice, discrimination, and persecution they suffered or feared at society's hands. This, ultimately, was the view of Evelyn Hooker, who perhaps did more than anyone else to upset the prevailing psychiatric view of homosexuality. Hooker became involved in research on the subject in the mid-1950s as a result of her acquaintance with a homosexual former student and his friends. Impressed by the variety and apparent emotional health of most of these young men, she did what no researcher had done before: she compared a group of gay men who were not in therapy (the names were supplied by the Mattachine Society) with a group of randomly selected heterosexual men. Her findings, that the psychological profiles of the two groups were virtually indistinguishable, won her near heroic status in the gay community, with which she worked closely in the 1960s, immersing herself nonjudgmentally in the study of its ways and byways.

The validity of her approach was reinforced during the fifties and sixties by a fundamental shift in sociological research into deviant groups, away from the perspective of society at large toward the worldview of the deviant groups themselves. The practical consequences of such social relativism were potentially enormous. To the extent that deviance was in the eye of the beholder, a function of the labels the majority imposed on unpopular minorities, social norms had to be studied and understood as matters of convention, as did majoritarian notions of what was sick or criminal. The actions of individuals and of the subgroups to which they might belong had to be judged not by absolute standards but by the consequences of their actions on society at large, on the subgroups, and on the individuals themselves. For revisionist analysts working with homosexual clients this meant little change in their view of the origins of homosexuality, which they tended still to ascribe primarily to impaired gender identity and childhood trauma, but since they saw sexual orientation as in some measure culturally determined, increasingly they were disinclined to make clear-cut distinctions between the normal and the abnormal and were compelled to rethink the relationship between homosexuals and society and, therefore, how best to treat and counsel them.

As Dr. Judd Marmor put it in his introduction to *Sexual Inversion,* published in 1965, a collection of essays on homosexuality by contributors ranging from Irving Bieber to Evelyn Hooker, "Homosexual behavior and heterosexual behavior are merely different areas on a broad spectrum of human sexual behavior, the sources of which must be determined and understood, and neither can be assumed to be intrinsically more or less 'natural' than the other." That said, however, Marmor was not yet willing to abandon orthodox psychiatric approaches to the treatment of homosexual patients: "The twentieth century psychiatric clinician in the western world inevitably reflects the mores of his time and culture when he regards homosexuality as an undesirable modification of or deviation from optimum personality development and adaptation in our society. . . . In his efforts to help the homosexual achieve a heterosexual adaptation whenever possible, the clinical psychiatrist . . . is endeavoring to help his patient achieve an optimum homeostatic relationship with the environment in which he finds himself." Marmor's suggestion that homosexuality should be treated as a socially dysfunctional condition was hardly likely to endear him to the critics of psychiatry within the gay community, but it was a long way from the orthodox psychiatric view of homosexuality as a pathological condition, and Marmor eventually became one of the leading proponents of the movement within the American Psychiatric Association to remove homosexuality from the list of mental disorders.

Also published in 1965 was Edwin Schur's *Crimes without Victims: Deviant Behavior and Public Policy.* As the title suggests, Schur believed that homosexual men who engaged in consensual sex (like drug users and women seeking abortions) were criminal only because they were labeled as such and that this served no useful purpose other than the self-aggrandizement of the labelers. Elements within the legal profession were coming to a similarly practical conclusion, at least so far as homosexuality was concerned. As early as 1955 the American Law Institute, over strenuous objections from a minority of its members, drafted a model penal code that decriminalized sodomy between consenting adults in private. Illinois adopted the model penal code in 1961, thus becoming the first state to, in effect, repeal its antisodomy laws.

To leave it at that would be misleading, however. The antisodomy laws of Illinois were not actually repealed but rather disappeared, which somewhat diminishes the importance and impact of the change. The antisodomy laws were eliminated almost by stealth as part of a general law reform; the elimination received almost no press commentary until after the reform and most likely would not have passed had it been proposed or widely publicized on its own. Thus it is hardly surprising that Illinois was not only the first state to repeal its antisodomy laws in the 1960s but also the last, and while the model penal code recommended decriminalizing consensual homosexual relations between adults in private, it retained provisions against public solicitation, a matter of greater practical concern to many members of the gay subculture. To the proponents of more sweeping reforms such half-measures were especially galling; although they appeared enlightened, they left intact the apparatus of prejudice and repression. No one outside the gay community took up the cause of even more far-reaching reform or effectively marshaled evidence in support of it from recent developments in psychiatry, sociology, and law to the extent that Dr. Martin Hoffman did. A social psychiatrist, Hoffman undertook in the mid-1960s a comprehensive—and unprecedented—study of the gay subculture in one American city, San Francisco. With the encouragement of other investigators, Evelyn Hooker in particular, he conducted extensive interviews and visited the bars and other institutions of Bay Area gay neighborhoods. The resulting book, *The Gay World*, was almost wholly sympathetic.

Hoffman deliberately personalized his picture of the subculture by recounting the life stories of many of his interviewees, and while he did not skirt controversial topics such as cruising and the central role of the baths and bars as sexual marketplaces, he savagely attacked those who, like Irving Bieber, categorized homosexuality in and of itself as psychopathagenic and laid most of the blame for the ills of the gay world on heterosexual society, as the subtitle of his book suggests: *Male Homosexuality and the Social Creation of Evil*. Hence his prescription for "the best solution to the problem of homosexuality . . . which is modeled on the solution to the problem of religious difference, namely, a radical tolerance for homosexual object choice." In practice that would require not only decriminalizing homosexual relations between consenting adults in private but also ending "police activity against homosexuals in all its forms," ceasing to fire government employees "because they are thought to be homosexual," and encouraging "private industry to cease similar treatment of homosexual employees." That Hoffman spoke for a minority even within his own profession almost need not be said. Nonetheless, the timing of his work was propitious. It coincided with and furthered growing skepticism of generally accepted norms in society at large and within the gay community. *The Gay World* was published by a major press and was widely reviewed when it appeared in 1968, the year after England decriminalized homosexual relations between consenting adults in private; the first paperback edition was published the following June, the month of the Stonewall rebellion.

# Chapter 21    From Wolfenden to Stonewall

As in the United States, so too in western Europe, and with particular significance in England, the conventional wisdom about homosexuality, like the taboo on the public discussion of it, began to erode in the 1950s. That England, with its long—and recent—history of persecuting homosexuality and the near total absence of organized opposition to that persecution, should have emerged as the leader among European nations in advancing the rights of homosexuals is, to say the least, surprising. Ironically, it was the virulence of the official campaign of suppression that began to turn the tide. Like the press fascination with the Beats and the gay subculture in San Francisco, public interest in the British spy scandals of the early 1950s opened the door to press coverage of homosexuality. The publicity was, of course, negative, often sensational. The tabloids led the way with lurid exposés such as the *Sunday Pictorial's* series "Evil Men" in 1952. Purportedly objective book-length studies such as *They Stand Apart,* published in 1955, were scarcely less alarmist, and even scholarly treatments of the subject—*Society and the Homosexual* (1952) by Gordon Westwood (pseudonym of Michael Schofield) and D. J. West's *Homosexuality* (1955)—reiterated the prevailing view of homosexuality as a mental illness, although less dogmatically than their American counterparts.

Nonetheless, even this kind of coverage was better than no coverage at all, if only because it prepared the ground for serious consideration of the legal persecution of homosexuals. The turning point was the Croft-Cooke and Montague-Wildeblood cases in late 1953 and early 1954. So outrageous were the actions of the police and the prosecution in the gathering of evidence, the hounding of defendants, and the use of selective prosecutions that opinion within the social and political establishment began to shift, not yet toward greater sympathy or understanding for homosexuality itself, but against some aspects of the laws that punished it. Immediately after the convictions of Lord Montague, Michael Pitt-Rivers, and Peter Wildeblood in late March, one of the leading weekly newspapers, the *Sunday Times,* lashed out editorially at the government's handling of the case and at its wider implications in undermining the rule of law and in eroding public confidence in the administration of justice. Other newspapers and magazines across the political spectrum followed suit, questioning the methods employed in enforcing the laws against homosexuality and, beyond that, the laws themselves, which seemed to encourage, indeed perhaps inevitably entailed, such methods. "The case for a reform of the law as to acts committed in private between adults is very strong," the *Sunday Times* concluded. "The case for authoritative inquiry into it is overwhelming."

Other voices within the establishment were raised even before these sensational trials. In 1952 the Church of England Moral Welfare Council sponsored a study of homosexuality. Its report, released at a critical moment early in 1954, carefully distinguished between immoral conduct and criminal conduct and recommended reform of the law. Calls for similar changes, or at least for an official inquiry, were echoed by Britain's leading penal reform society and by a number of members of Parliament. Increasingly on the defensive, the government, which had initially resisted demands even for a reexamination of the law, finally gave way and in mid-April created a departmental committee to inquire into the laws relating to homosexuality (and to prostitution, which, as so often before, was regarded as a parallel problem, at least in the official mind).

The Home Secretary appointed Sir John Wolfenden, the vice-chancellor of a provincial university, to chair the committee. It was an odd choice since, as Wolfenden acknowledged, he knew little of either subject and also because his son Jeremy, then twenty years of age and a student at Oxford, was actively and, by the standards of the mid-1950s, openly homosexual. According to Jeremy, following the news of the appointment of the committee, his father wrote to him: "You will probably have seen from the newspapers that I am to chair a committee on Homosexual Offenses and Prostitution. I have only two requests to make of you at the moment. 1) That we stay out of each other's way for the time being. 2) That you wear rather less make-up." Sir John was equally forthright in assessing the prospects for his committee, which seemed likely, whatever it recommended, to be attacked by reformers and conservatives alike. "In short, we can't win," he told a fellow committee member at their first meeting.

In the short run at least he was right. After meeting more than sixty times and interviewing some two hundred witnesses, the committee issued its report in September 1957. Its central recommendation was "that homosexual behavior between consenting adults in private should no longer be a criminal offense." However, this apparently straightforward proposal was hedged around with a number of limitations, particularly regarding the definition of *adult*, and while the report deliberately set out to explode or question some popular myths about the origins, extent, and dangers of homosexuality and drew a clear distinction between the immoral and the criminal, it was at pains to emphasize that decriminalization did not mean indifference to private immorality or that this proposed change in the law should be seen as an opening wedge: "We do not think that it would be expedient at the present time to reduce in any way the penalties attaching to homosexual importuning. It is important that the limited modification of the law which we propose should not be interpreted as an indication that the law can be indifferent to other forms of homosexual behavior, or as a general license to adult homosexuals to behave as they please."

Among the useful functions of a committee or commission of inquiry in a democracy is the shelving of a controversial topic while the inquiry is ongoing and, beyond that, the provision of expert cover for subsequent legislation. The Wolfenden committee admirably served the former purpose but not the latter. Homosexual law reform remained too hot a topic to handle (as opposed to the committee's recommendations concerning prostitution, also based on making a clear distinction between private sexual activity and public importuning, which were implemented in 1959). During a brief debate on the Wolfenden report in the House of Lords in December 1957 a spokesman for the government asserted, no doubt truthfully, that neither Parliament nor the country was ready for even a limited decriminalization of homosexuality. Clearly, if anything was to be done, public opinion would first have to be educated and brought to bear on lawmakers, a process that was begun early in the following year.

On 7 March 1958 the London *Times* published a letter calling on the government to enact the Wolfenden report's recommendations, signed by thirty-three writers, philosophers, churchmen, and others in the nation's intellectual and cultural elite. The man behind the letter was Arthur Dyson, a lecturer in English literature at a Welsh university, who also, along with a handful of friends and supporters, founded the Homosexual Law Reform Society (HLRS) two months later. A classic example of the long British tradition of single-issue reform agitations stretching back almost two centuries, the

HLRS operated at a number of different levels. At the top was an honorary committee, whose roster of famous names was designed to impress and lend respectability, not to do the work of the society. An executive committee, most of whose members were not homosexual, met periodically to plan strategy. The day-to-day operations of the HLRS were carried out by a small group of volunteers, most of whom were homosexual, working out of the home of a gay couple who courageously allowed their address to be published as the head-quarters of the society until an office in central London could be found and afforded.

The founders of the society also created a parallel organization, the Albany Trust, to pursue longer-range goals in research, public education, and social work. The society and the trust were two sides of a coin, sharing a chairman, the prominent psychiatrist and sexologist Kenneth Walker, and after his death, C. H. Rolph, a former chief inspector of police, as well as a succession of secretaries, first Andrew Hallidie Smith, a clergyman and old friend of Dyson's, and finally Antony Grey, whose careers in public relations and jour-nalism proved invaluable. Grey had been a member of the working group of the society from the beginning, and unlike Hallidie Smith, he was himself homosexual, a matter of some concern to the executive committee in view of his prominent public role in the agitation.

Although the founders of the HLRS realized theirs would be a long agita-tion, they initially underestimated the animosity of the opposition. When the House of Commons finally held its first debate on the Wolfenden recom-mendations more than a year after the committee submitted its report, the society sought to prepare the ground by circulating a pamphlet entitled *Ho-mosexuality and the Law,* drafted by Peter Wildeblood, to all members of Parliament. Unfortunately, many MPs were also sent two books, one of them Wildeblood's account of his persecution, by other supporters of reform, but without consulting the HLRS. This only served to further alienate opponents of reform who resented what they saw as undue outside pressure. The HLRS was forced to retreat into a more carefully modulated campaign of gradually widening the circle of support through letters to the press, providing speak-ers, distributing leaflets, and informing potentially sympathetic MPs of espe-cially egregious examples of extortion and blackmail, of police harassment or entrapment, and of prosecutions resulting in personal tragedies such as the loss of jobs or families or, in a few cases, suicides.

By the time of its second anniversary in May 1960, and in preparation for a second major parliamentary debate on homosexual law reform in June, the society had become sufficiently well established to risk holding its first public meeting. The meeting was surprisingly successful, attended by an overflow crowd at one of London's larger meeting halls. The parliamentary response was less encouraging. The proponents of reform were defeated 213 to 99, even though, "knowing that the opposition stemmed largely from deeply irrational feelings of revulsion, they tacitly agreed to concentrate on the anomalies, injustices and unenforceability of the existing law, and were at pains to distance themselves from any charges of acting as champions or agents of the homosexual minority." The Labor backbencher Roy Jenkins, who would be Home Secretary in the government that eased the passage of reform six years later, felt compelled to deny that he represented "a pressure lobby of homosexuals. In considering this question, I am not concerned only with what homosexuals want or even primarily with what they want. I am concerned with what I think is a reasonable law for a civilized country."

Inevitably, the HLRS accommodated itself to these tactics and was criticized by more radical reformers then and later for doing so. But the society had little choice. Its aim was to get a bill through Parliament. Despite the reformers' defeat of more than two to one in 1960, Hallidie Smith correctly assessed that the reformers were on the right track: "After the debate, the question was no longer *whether* the law would be reformed, but *when.* In three years the word 'homosexuality' had ceased to be a dirty joke and had become a topic for serious discussion." That the when was still a long way off remained painfully apparent, however, and to its established methods of cultivating support in the press, among the makers and shapers of opinion, and within Parliament the HLRS added the publication of a newsletter, the sponsoring of public opinion surveys, and close cooperation with the Home Office in the gathering of reliable statistics on homosexual offenses. The Albany Trust launched a more academically oriented periodical, *Man and Society,* as part of a three-pronged strategy of educating the public through research, providing counseling for homosexuals, troubled or in trouble, and ultimately establishing a network of social-service clubs and organizations along the lines of the COC in Amsterdam (which Grey first visited in 1961).

Neither the HLRS nor the Albany Trust was or aimed to be a mass movement (and they received correspondingly little support from the proprietors and patrons of gay pubs and clubs). The trust and especially the HLRS were narrowly focused on a specific objective, and partly for tactical reasons but also out of deference to prevailing views about homosexuality, they tended to portray homosexuals as victims of prejudice and persecution rather than as a cultural minority deserving of rights. The society and the trust remained as small as they were cautious, the work mostly of volunteers, since the campaign was perennially short of funds. They rarely had more than a thousand subscribing supporters and only a few large donors (one of them E. M. Forster, whom Grey visited in Cambridge). However, it was precisely the limited objectives of the society and the respectability of its methods that won it the support of the National Council on Civil Liberties, the Howard League for Penal Reform, and even most of the Conservative quality newspapers and periodicals, as well as generally favorable treatment in television documentaries. When the Labor Party formed a government following the general election of 1964, and still more after it won a larger majority two years later, homosexual law reform seemed a near certainty.

In the event, however, the passage of the Sexual Offenses Act was a tortuous process, occupying more than two years from the time of its introduction in the House of Lords, in May 1965, until it received the royal assent, in July 1967. Although parliamentary time was afforded to the proponents of reform, the government did not sponsor the measure. Backbench members of Parliament moved the bill, and MPs were granted the right—and the responsibility—of voting their consciences. What is more, the bill did not originate in the elected, and therefore vulnerable, House of Commons but in the unelected House of Lords. The government's caution was understandable. Even though opinion polls taken late in 1965 showed that public opposition to decriminalization had substantially decreased, the bill's opponents undoubtedly felt more strongly than all but the most committed reformers, and even many MPs who voted for it did so with misgivings. Richard Crossman, the leader of the House of Commons, was far from unusual in confiding to his diary that "frankly it's an extremely unpleasant bill and I myself didn't like it. It may well be twenty years ahead of public opinion; certainly working class people in the North jeer at their Members at the weekend and ask them why they're looking after the buggers at Westminster instead of looking after the unemployed at home."

To decriminalization's implacable opponents the bill was more than merely unpleasant; its passage, they believed, would lead to a dramatic increase in homosexuality, to the seduction of impressionable young men, to the proliferation of "buggers' clubs," and to Britain's rapid descent into late Roman decadence. Far from seeking to distinguish between immorality and criminality, they argued that one of the primary functions of the law was to uphold and enforce moral standards. As Field Marshal Viscount Montgomery of Alamein put it, they should "build a bulwark which will defy evil influences which are seeking to undermine the foundations of our national character—defy them, do not help them. I have heard . . . that such practices are allowed in France and other NATO countries. We are not French and we are not other nationals. We are BRITISH, thank God!" By the time he delivered this diatribe in May 1965, he and his allies in both houses seemed almost quaintly anachronistic. Lady Gaitskell, the widow of the former Labor Party leader, bested Montgomery in the debate when, after praising him for his "brilliant command of millions of men," expressed her amazement "that he did it with, in a way, so little knowledge of the sex habits of the men under his command." In their fulminations against homosexuality many of the bill's opponents appeared more than a little pathetic. At one point the archbishop of Canterbury, who supported reform, quietly remarked to the leading proponent of the bill in the House of Lords, the earl of Arran, "Oh dear, oh dear! What a terrible time the poor things must have had at their public schools." Clearly the temper of the times was changing.

Belatedly, perhaps, but dramatically the sexual revolution and the revolution in popular culture had reached Britain and, reinforcing each other, worked a dizzyingly rapid shift in the cultural climate. The pivotal year was 1963, the year in which a heterosexual political scandal crippled the Conservative government; in which the Beatles had their first chart-topping hits and the second James Bond movie was released; in which two books on sexuality, *Sex and Society,* by Alex Comfort, and *Towards a Quaker View of Sex,* edited by Alastair Heron, heralded a new openness. So far as gay men were concerned, there were even earlier indications of a shift in public sentiment, not yet toward acceptance of homosexuality, but against the laws that punished it. In 1960, as the House of Commons was decisively rejecting homosexual law reform, two major films on the life and trials of Oscar Wilde were released to favorable reviews. In the following year the evil consequences of current laws were graphically illustrated in the landmark film *Victim.* The film was extraordinarily daring for its time. "It was the first film in which a man said 'I love you' to another man," its star, Dirk Bogarde, recalled. "I wrote that scene in. I said, 'There's no point in half measures. We either make a film about queers or we don't.' . . . I believe that picture made a lot of difference to a lot of people's lives."

It certainly made a difference in the subsequent portrayal of gay characters. By the middle of the decade, with swinging London in full swing, sympathetic (though generally stereotypical) gay characters were commonplace in British plays and films, and the androgynous look in clothing, in hairstyles, and on the pop music scene had become an integral part of British youth culture. Homosexual law reform, far from seeming like a revolutionary departure from generally accepted norms, could be portrayed as a recognition of changes already under way. Certainly it was only one item on a substantial agenda of liberal social reforms—divorce reform, abortion reform, the extension of family-planning services, the abolition of capital punishment, the abolition of theater censorship—enacted during the mid- to late 1960s. What had been regarded as—and was—a radical proposal ten years earlier, at the time the Wolfenden report was published, seemed rather modest in 1967.

And modest it in fact was. Not only did the final bill include all the limitations recommended in the Wolfenden report but Parliament added a few of its own. In addition to setting the age of adulthood high, at twenty-one, exempting the military from the provisions of the act, and actually raising the penalties for an adult convicted of gross indecency with a youth over sixteen, the bill as amended placed the merchant marine, along with the military, off-limits and defined the phrase *in private* as narrowly as possible. Delighted though he was that the central recommendation of the Wolfenden report had become law, Antony Grey was convinced "that a better piece of legislation could have been achieved . . . because the vehemence and volume of opposition to any reform at all remained constant, regardless of the details of what was being proposed." As it was, the proponents of reform in Parliament spent far too much time and energy "placating the implacable." The result, wrote Grey, was "that some provisions of the new Act were severely disappointing to most of our supporters, and I feared that the new law, if restrictively applied, would prolong social difficulties and cause some individual tragedies. I also foresaw that many homosexual people, then and later, would lay much of the blame for this at the HLRS's door."

Grey would be proved right on both counts. There was little, however, that the HLRS could have done differently. Once the issue was before Parliament, reformers had to accommodate themselves to the tactics of their parliamentary allies. They were well aware that this was likely to produce a limited reform, one that would do little to improve the day-to-day lives of ordinary gay men. And so it was to be. Indeed, arrests and prosecutions for some homosexual offenses actually increased after 1967. Hence the tendency of radical critics of the Sexual Offenses Act, such as Jeffrey Weeks, to condemn the Wolfenden report itself and the accommodationist strategy of the HLRS as a "bankrupt policy," since it did little to serve "the longer run need to challenge and transform attitudes."

That is true so far as it goes, but it is hardly fair. The HLRS was a single-issue society whose supporters were united "only in their conviction that . . . the existing law was bad and needed to be changed. There was no 'party line' as to the nature of homosexuality, or the 'correct' attitude towards it, nor could there have been." Any attempt to go beyond their immediate goal would have fragmented their support. Even Weeks admitted that "in the short run, in terms of achieving a limited change in the law, the result was sound." It was, in fact, a great deal more than that. Decriminalization in Illinois in 1961 and in revolutionary France almost two centuries earlier had been achieved by quietly, almost stealthily omitting one among a larger category of crimes without victims from the statute books, but the Sexual Offenses Act in England was a positive reform undertaken in the glare of publicity and pressed by a skillfully managed public agitation.

In addition, while it is easy to ridicule as naive those liberal, utilitarian reforms aimed at nothing more than getting rid of bad laws, it is legitimate to do so only if that goal is pursued as an end in itself. But in this case it was not, at least not by many founders of the HLRS, who created the Albany Trust at the same time to look beyond the issue of law reform. To Antony Grey and many other members of the society, law reform was only a first step. In this they were more than a little duplicitous, assuring potential supporters that law reform would not bring about further substantial changes, while hoping that it would. Not as Weeks suggested, "Almost in spite of itself," but quite often deliberately, "the work of the society . . . did act as a stimulus to homosexual self organization." As Michael Schofield replied when asked if law reform had changed much in people's lives, "No. It has changed things only a little. But I think it was vital and it opens the door to serious change in the future."

And so it—and even the prospect of it—did. Lesbians were the first to organize. Unaffected either by existing laws or by law reform, they were nonetheless inspired by the law reform movement. In 1963 Esme Langley and her companion, Diana Chapman (who lived on the same street as Antony Grey and his partner), founded the innocuously titled Minorities Research Group (MRG), "the earliest gay women's group, and also the earliest overtly homophile group of any kind" in England. It was not all that overt. Although it published a magazine, *Arena Three,* from early 1964 on, offered counseling to troubled lesbians, and provided volunteers for research projects, the MRG remained small and circumspect. *Arena Three* was sold by subscription only and kept to safe topics, such as the sources of lesbianism and the place of lesbians in society, avoiding the explicit discussion of lesbian sexuality. Many of the middle-class members of MRG were critical of those members, often of the working class, who looked and acted butch. Langley herself was very much the mannish lesbian and deliberately cultivated press coverage, but that and her dictatorial style of leadership were sources of friction, and in 1965 a dissident group left to form KENRIC. Named for the fashionable districts of London where most of its members lived—Kensington and Richmond—KENRIC was a social organization that eschewed militancy. Although the two groups were never able to reconcile their differences, both survived, and the MRG was able to spawn a number of provincial societies by the end of the decade.

More directly inspired by the work of the HLRS was the North Western Homosexual Law Reform Committee (NWHLRC), founded in October 1964. The secretary of the committee and its most visible member, Allan Horsfall, had been active in the law reform campaign from the beginning, though in Lancashire, not London. Throughout the agitation he was unusually open in his support of reform and militant in his views on tactics, which led some of his friends to distance themselves from him and ultimately caused a breach between him and the more cautious leaders of the national campaign. In 1958, when he first became involved, Horsfall wrote letters to local newspapers and attempted unsuccessfully to get his local Labor Party leadership to endorse the Wolfenden report; when the NWHLRC could not find a headquarters, he courageously gave his home address. Far more than the national society, the NWHLRC was run by and for homosexuals, and it never affiliated officially with the HLRS. Only a good working relationship between Grey and Horsfall kept the two groups cooperating effectively.

Not surprisingly, that cooperation ended with the passage of the Sexual Offenses Act. The northern group, reconstituted as the Committee (later Campaign) for Homosexual Equality (CHE), proposed setting up a chain of gay social clubs and invited the leaders of the national reform campaign to become patrons. Grey thought the CHE was acting prematurely. "It's still inconceivable that such a group as the Mattachine Society could exist here," he argued with what soon proved to be unwarranted pessimism. "I'd say it won't happen for at least five years." However, he felt that the Albany Trust should not reject the proposal outright; rather, it should offer to cooperate in the creation of something along the lines of the COC in the Netherlands. Michael Schofield and a few others on the trust's board agreed, but the majority were horrified, and none more so than Leo Abse, the Labor MP who had led the fight for law reform in the House of Commons. Not only did the prospect of the proliferation of gay clubs seem to confirm the worst fears of the opponents of the Sexual Offenses Act but many, perhaps most, supporters of law reform, and certainly its parliamentary backers, had not envisaged decriminalization as opening the way to the emergence of a distinct, self-conscious, and militant gay community. Yet that is precisely what did happen, and within months of the enactment of reform, although the catalyst that finally transformed the campaign into a movement was not British or European but developments in the United States.

Nonetheless, as the leaders of the gay liberation movement of the 1970s were compelled to admit, however grudgingly, they could not have responded to events across the Atlantic had it not been for the decade-long struggle to enact the Wolfenden recommendations. But the passage of the Sexual Offenses Act had done a good deal more than that, and it would be unfair to allow the impatient young of the post-Stonewall era to have the last word on the significance of the reform campaign. Gay men of the postwar generation were often indifferent to the issue of law reform and disdainful of what they saw as the pussyfooting of the HLRS. They were determined to get on with their lives and loves regardless of the state of the law, and in the permissive atmosphere of the 1960s they were often able to do so. Thus, many of them failed to appreciate the symbolic significance of a reform that severed the link between law and morality and removed the legal foundation for prejudice. What is more, they were privileged to look back on the old regime from a safer vantage point.

Not so their elders, who had grown up in a more repressive environment in which the Criminal Law Amendment Act appeared fixed and immutable and had experienced persecution or the fear of it either directly or through their friends or relatives. Cecil Beaton, one of the bright young people of the 1920s, a stage designer and photographer of the rich and famous (and later of war), hailed the passage of the Sexual Offenses Act as "one of the most important milestones in English law. . . . this should be a time of great celebration. . . . For myself I am grateful. Selfishly, I wish that this marvelous step forward could have been taken at an earlier age. . . . to feel that one was not a felon and an outcast could have helped enormously."

The moderate reformist tactics of the HLRS had taken nearly a decade to bear fruit. The emergence of a militant gay rights movement out of San Francisco's mix of counterculture and bar culture had taken roughly half as long.

East Coast militancy in the United States, which began later than the movements in either England or the Bay Area and was clearly inspired by both, was aggressive from its beginnings largely owing to the single-mindedness of one man, Frank Kameny.

Armed with a Ph.D. in astronomy, the thirty-two-year-old Kameny was hired by the U.S. Army Map Service in the summer of 1957, only to be fired before the end of the year when investigation of his background revealed a 1956 arrest for lewd conduct. For nearly three years he fought his dismissal. After exhausting every administrative remedy within the government and every legal remedy against it, finally, destitute and desperate, he turned to activism. Working from a list of names in the Washington, D.C., area provided by the New York Mattachine Society, and with the help of Jack Nichols, the openly gay, twenty-two-year-old son of an FBI agent, Kameny spearheaded the formation of the Mattachine Society of Washington in November 1961. Under his leadership the Washington society was different in tone and temper from its older peers in other cities. Social services and public education were all very well, he argued, but the former treated symptoms, not underlying problems, and the latter could not reach the prejudiced mind. Impatient with the results—or the lack of them—of a strategy of accommodation and the debilitating effects of endlessly debating the origins and consequences of sexual orientation, Kameny believed the homophile movement had to become both self-accepting and self-asserting, a civil rights movement, in short:

> We cannot ask for our rights from a position of inferiority. . . . I do not see the NAACP and CORE worrying about which chromosome and gene produce a black skin, or about the possibility of bleaching the Negro. I do not see any great interest on the part of the B'nai B'rith Anti-Defamation League in the possibility of solving problems of anti-semitism by converting Jews to Christians. . . . We are interested in obtaining rights for our respective minorities AS Negroes, AS Jews, and AS HOMOSEXUALS. Why we are Negroes, Jews, or Homosexuals is totally irrelevant.

Given Kameny's personal history and the new society's location in Washington, its primary concern and target, almost inevitably, was federal employment policy. A campaign of letter writing to elected representatives and government bureaucrats and of meetings with government officials produced little apart from compelling the military and the Civil Service Commission to state and clarify their policies of excluding homosexuals. But even that was progress of a sort since it forced the issue into the open and led in 1965 to a ruling by the United States Court of Appeals that the government's reasons for refusing civilian employment to homosexuals were unconstitutionally vague. The local ACLU chapter, also formed in late 1961, with Kameny as a founding member, backed the Mattachine Society in the case, and that too represented a victory since the ACLU elsewhere had refused to treat discrimination against homosexuals as a civil-liberties issue. Tentative steps toward closer cooperation had begun in Washington even earlier, in 1963, when the ACLU supported the Mattachine Society in hearings before Congress and in confronting the local police after a brutal raid on a gay bar. Pressed by its Washington chapter, and with backing from New York and California, in 1964 the national ACLU began to reconsider the hands-off policy it had adopted in the late 1950s, and in 1967 it finally reversed its policy.

Meanwhile, in New York the old guard of the city's Mattachine Society was being shaken out of its lethargy, also largely through the efforts of a lone individual, Randy Wicker, who was, if anything, even more confrontational than Kameny. Schooled in the activism of the civil rights movement, Wicker broke with the cautious conservatism of the local gay establishment by courting publicity wherever he could get it. Beginning in 1962 with a program on a local radio station, he used negative commentary from one source to gain an airing for his views on another, skillfully working the print and broadcast media in order to get access to both and exploiting that press coverage to get himself recognized as a spokesman by left-wing political and cultural groups. Since New York publicity inevitably meant national publicity, Wicker sought and formed contacts with individuals throughout the country and with other radical elements in the homophile movement, and early in 1963 representatives from four groups met in Philadelphia to form ECHO, the East Coast Homophile Organizations.

ECHO convened in Philadelphia because it was convenient, not because the homophile movement there was anywhere near the forefront of the new activism. The local chapter of the Mattachine Society (which changed its name to the Janus Society after the national structure of Mattachine collapsed early in 1961) dated back only to late 1960 and was cautious from the start, in part surely because a preliminary organizational meeting, held on a private suburban estate, was broken up by the police at the instigation of a postal inspector who had intercepted fliers advertising the meeting.

At first ECHO represented the Janus Society, the moderate New York Mattachine Society and Daughters of Bilitis, as well as Kameny's Washington Mattachine Society and individual activists such as Wicker, but by 1965 relations between the coalition partners had reached the breaking point over issues of tactics and, more fundamentally, the proper role of homosexuals and homophile groups in society. In Philadelphia the limits of respectability were tested—and breached—with the appearance of the magazine *Drum* late in 1964. The brainchild of Clark Polak, who had been elected president of the Janus Society the previous year, *Drum* was advertised as offering "news for 'queers,' and fiction for 'perverts,' photo essays for 'fairies,' and laughs for 'faggots'" aimed at a predominantly male audience. That, together with Polak's insistence on managing everything himself, was too much, particularly for many of the former, largely lesbian leadership of the Janus Society, as well as for some of the New York and Washington militants, who feared that *Drum*'s combination of information with entertainment and sexual titillation would distract the movement from its main purpose and confirm the prejudices of the broader public. That *Drum* quickly achieved a readership far greater than the combined circulation of all the serious homophile magazines and newsletters may also have contributed to the resentment and nervousness of his critics. Early in 1965 the Janus Society was drummed out of ECHO and replaced by a new Philadelphia Mattachine Society, headed by Polak's lesbian critics. The new society achieved little else.

Polak, meanwhile, went his own way, applying his organizational and entrepreneurial skills not only to running the Janus Society and the continued publication of *Drum* but also to sponsoring lectures and public demonstrations, successfully winning coverage in the local media, providing legal assistance to gay bars and bar patrons, lobbying in consultation with the ACLU for the adoption of the model penal code in Pennsylvania, founding a Homosexual Law Reform Society to press the issue legislatively and in the courts, and, by no means incidentally, managing local bookstores and a successful mail-order pornography business. While ostensibly committed to cooperation between gay men and lesbians, he never glossed over what he saw as fundamental differences between male and female sexuality and between males' and females' attitudes toward pornography, promiscuity, and sexual relationships, thus at least implicitly raising the question that his own activities raised in the minds of many lesbians, namely, whether the alliance between gay men and lesbians was natural or an artificial one imposed on them by straight society. Apart from SIR in San Francisco, Polak had little use for the mainstream homophile movement, which, in its efforts to win broader acceptance, seemed all too often to internalize homophobia, while ignoring the lives and needs of ordinary homosexuals.

In this Polak was being less than fair, since the mainstream movement was advancing, if less rapidly and less dramatically, toward greater militancy. In April 1965 a few activists, led in Washington by Jack Nichols and in New York by Craig Rodwell, best known as the founder of the Oscar Wilde Memorial Bookstore, decided to picket the White House and U.N. headquarters to protest the U.S. government's and Cuba's repressive policies toward homosexuals. In May ECHO endorsed their actions and scheduled a series of demonstrations in Washington, in New York, and, on the Fourth of July, at Independence Hall in Philadelphia. The numbers involved were tiny, and the protests received correspondingly little publicity. They were conducted, in any case, with the utmost decorum: the women were instructed to wear dresses, the men suits and ties. The conservative leadership of long-established homophile organizations were appalled nonetheless, fearing both that small demonstrations would show weakness and that they might nonetheless alienate public opinion.

Two months earlier the Washington Mattachine Society had made an even more decisive philosophical break with the accommodationist strategy of the 1950s when it resolved "that in the absence of valid evidence to the contrary, homosexuality is not a sickness, disturbance, or other pathology in any sense, but merely a preference, orientation, or propensity, on par with, and not different in kind from, heterosexuality." Infuriated by the unwavering commitment of the psychiatric establishment to the labeling of homosexuality as a mental illness capable of cure, and emboldened by the work of dissidents such as Evelyn Hooker, Nichols and Kameny had publicly rejected the sickness theory as far back as the autumn of 1963. In the summer of 1964 Kameny took the issue to New York in a fiery speech to the local chapter of the Mattachine Society, deliberately encouraging the unwillingness of younger members of homophile groups even to give outside so-called experts a hearing. By the time the Washington society officially repudiated psychiatric orthodoxy a breach within the homophile movement was inevitable.

The breach finally came in May 1965, during a fiercely fought election campaign for control of the board of the New York Mattachine Society. The radicals won overwhelmingly, and most of the old guard dropped out. A watershed event, the election was at least as important in defining the future direction of the movement as was the displacement of the founders of the original Mattachine Society by moderate leaders in the very different political climate of the early 1950s. One of those left behind in the mid-1960s, and surely the most poignant example of the irreversible nature of the split in the movement, was Donald Webster Cory, whose book *The Homosexual in America* had been a beacon and guide to individual homosexuals through the lonely 1950s. But Cory had learned how to survive in lean times too well to make the transition to militancy. For him the primary function of the Mattachine Society was to help homosexuals adjust to society, not to challenge it. Indeed, he accepted much of the medical model, comparing homosexuals to alcoholics, who should be understood, not persecuted, but nonetheless needed counseling.

A turn toward militancy was all but inevitable in the mid-1960s. The civil rights movement had reached its peak, and second-wave feminism was gathering momentum. Which makes the outcome of a similar split within the DOB so surprising, for it was the old guard that won. In the mid-1960s, as Del Martin and Phyllis Lyon shifted their attention to other groups in the homophile movement, in particular the newly formed Council on Religion and the Homosexual, Barbara Gittings emerged as the leading radical voice in the DOB. A diplomat's daughter raised in a sheltered environment, she seemed at first sight an unlikely successor to Martin and Lyon. Following a difficult period of self-discovery in college, searching out medical texts and lesbian novels, and in the bar scene, where she tried not very successfully to fit in with the butch/femme stereotype, Gittings happened on Cory's *The Homosexual in America* and through his publisher contacted the author, who steered her toward the Mattachine Society. Traveling to San Francisco in 1956, she met Hal Call, who introduced her to Martin and Lyon, and it was under their tutelage that two years later, after returning to the East, she took a central role in founding the New York chapter of the DOB.

By the time Gittings took over the editorship of the *Ladder* in late 1962, however, she had already begun to move away from the cautious conservatism of the mainstream West Coast homophile establishment in favor of the new model movement being pioneered in the East by Kameny and Wicker. After first meeting at an ECHO conference in early 1963, she and Kameny became close friends and collaborators. She opened the *Ladder* to Kameny and other radical voices on issues ranging from picketing to opposition to the sickness theory of homosexuality and ultimately paid for her partisanship in 1966, when the DOB board fired her from her post as editor. The national leadership in San Francisco proved equally obdurate in its opposition to direct action. When ECHO endorsed picketing, the moderate leaders of the DOB's New York chapter consulted the national office, which reiterated its policy against political action. After ECHO refused to back off, the DOB withdrew from the coalition. That sparked a revolt by the rank and file in New York, who deposed their moderate leaders. But backed by the national headquarters in San Francisco, the ousted moderates fought a rearguard action that ultimately led their more radical successors to resign in disgust in the summer of 1966, at about the same time that Gittings was released from the editorship of the *Ladder.*

The conservatives had won, but at great cost. Gittings and most of her allies left the DOB, which quickly became a stagnant backwater. The last years of the 1960s were, therefore, an unusually difficult time for lesbians. The perennial problem of being overshadowed or ignored by gay male organizations only worsened, as the cautious DOB declined in comparison with the activism of some branches of the Mattachine Society. Yet radical lesbians had little choice other than to leave the DOB for predominantly male gay organizations, where they inevitably played a secondary role. Some advocated joining the feminist movement, but there too they often felt subordinated, even invisible, welcome as individual women but not so welcome as lesbians. The result was a frustrating and inconclusive debate among lesbians as to which movement and which aspect of their identity as lesbian women should be given priority.

The problems for gay men were less complex but not much easier to solve. All but the most conservative homophile organizations were now committed to building a visible, activist movement. Early in 1966 delegates primarily from the Northeast and California met in Kansas City to create a loose federation, the North American Conference of Homophile Organizations, or NACHO, which inspired and assisted in the formation of affiliates in cities where no such groups had existed before or where earlier attempts to create them had foundered. By early 1969 there were at least fifty such organizations where, at the time NACHO was established, there had been no more than fifteen. Increasingly open and increasingly militant, homophile groups, old and new, deliberately broke with traditional tactics of accommodating themselves to established authorities, be they political, police, legal, religious, or medical.

Harassment and entrapment by the police, probably the most common and certainly the most visible means of regulating and repressing the gay subculture, encountered mounting resistance of a kind previously almost unheard of outside of San Francisco. Often with the assistance of the ACLU, homophile organizations responded with political meetings, petitions, and face-to-face negotiations with city officials, and with a willingness to fight cases in court, sometimes with considerable success, notably in New York in the spring of 1966. Organizations in a number of cities launched protests against local and federal employment practices, with NACHO coordinating their activities in order to maximize pressure and press coverage. Together with actual or threatened lawsuits, once again often backed by the ACLU, these protests began the long, slow process of reducing job discrimination.

Another grievance of long standing was the raiding and closing of gay bars by the police in cooperation with the local licensing authorities. In the spring of 1966 Dick Leitsch, the newly elected president of the New York Mattachine Society, and Craig Rodwell staged a series of well-publicized sip-ins at a string of bars in Greenwich Village to force a change in licensing policy or, failing that, to provoke a test case in the courts. Other cities followed suit, and through either administrative changes or court decisions bars in a number of eastern states won the same protections that similar challenges in California had secured a decade earlier. A New Jersey case fought and won by Polak's HLRS in 1967 was especially sweeping. The movement expanded into entirely new areas of organization and outreach. Students at Columbia University founded the first campus homophile group in the spring of 1967 and inspired similar efforts at New York University, Cornell, and Stanford. Later that year Rodwell opened the Oscar Wilde Memorial Bookstore in Greenwich Village, the first gay bookstore. The *Advocate,* the first of a new generation of radical gay newspapers, appeared in Los Angeles in the fall of 1967, and a year later Troy Perry founded the Metropolitan Community Church.

The new militancy permanently altered relations between the homophile movement and those professions whose opinions and policies impinged most directly on the gay community. No longer willing to enter into a dialogue with their critics, the new breed of homophile leaders sought out allies among liberal lawyers, churchmen, and doctors, while directly confronting or simply bypassing traditionalists in all three professions. Although changes in the official positions of professional societies regarding homosexuality would not take place until the 1970s, there were unmistakable signs of things to come in the late sixties. Illinois remained the only state to adopt the model penal code decriminalizing homosexual relations between consenting adults in private (Connecticut followed in 1971), but the decision of the ACLU to treat discrimination against homosexuals as a civil liberties issue, the growing number of gay rights cases fought—and won—in the federal courts, and, strongly influenced by the recommendations of the Wolfenden report, broadening support for the repeal of antisodomy laws among legal scholars all indicated a historic shift in the weight of legal opinion.

Although virtually all Christian denominations continued to label homosexuality a sin, a number of liberal churchmen and theologians, like their legal counterparts influenced by contemporary events in England, advocated decoupling law from morality, and in 1966 the National Council of Churches sponsored a series of interdenominational conferences on homosexuality, inviting representatives of the homophile movement to speak. Even the psychiatric profession exhibited some movement, though not much. The sickness theory still held sway, and the likes of Irving Bieber were still generally accepted as the authorities on the subject. Inevitably, the homophile movement responded with a policy of confrontation, not cooperation. Nonetheless, in September 1967, three months after the passage of the Sexual Offenses Act in England, the National Institute of Mental Health appointed a committee, chaired by Evelyn Hooker and composed of representatives of a number of professions, to review the state of expert opinion on homosexuality.

For all the signs of change and the homophile movement's important role in bringing them about, the movement remained a collection of fringe groups, the work of a handful of activists, even in New York and San Francisco. In an age of mass popular movements those who led the fight for gay rights were nearly invisible, and their reformist tactics seemed in many ways as oddly old fashioned in the era of black power and the antiwar movement, of the Student Nonviolent Coordinating Committee (SNCC) and Students for a Democratic Society (SDS), as the earlier accommodationist homophile groups had seemed to the young radicals in the movement only a few years earlier. In 1966 Dick Leitsch asserted: "We have to accumulate power and use it sensibly. Power lies not in the number of members. . . . It lies in how effective your organization is in achieving the goals of the homophile movement. This is not a plea for 'Gay power' or 'lavender power.' It is a plea for those charged with leadership positions in homophile organizations to accumulate enough power to implement social change, to make the voice of the homosexual heard in the community." Such a statement would have seemed quite radical five years earlier; in the context of the late 1960s, when numbers did indeed count, it seemed out of date and, more importantly, out of touch with the rank and file. For that to change there would have to be either a new coup from within, as had happened in New York in 1964–65, or a grass-roots challenge from outside, as in San Francisco earlier in the 1960s.

In the event it was a totally unexpected and wholly spontaneous eruption of popular anger and frustration, the Stonewall riot of 27 June 1969, that set off the chain reaction that transformed the gay rights movement. Stonewall has been compared to any number of acts of radical protest and defiance in American history from the Boston Tea Party on. But the best and certainly a more nearly contemporary analogy is with Rosa Parks's refusal to move to the back of the bus in Montgomery, Alabama, in December 1955, which sparked the modern civil rights movement. Within months after Stonewall radical gay liberation groups and newsletters sprang up in cities and on college campuses across America and then across all of northern Europe as well. In an interview right after the riots Allen Ginsberg captured perfectly the new mood, the stunningly rapid change in the character of the movement. "You know," he said, "the guys there were so beautiful. They've lost that wounded look that fags all had ten years ago."

When the vibrant and exciting post-Stonewall gay rights movement is compared with the old, small, diligent homophile groups and the pre-Stonewall cautious and closeted homosexual subculture, an especially revealing coincidence of events that is often noted, sometimes merely ironically, sometimes with more than a touch of malice, is that on the very day the riots began, Judy Garland, that icon of the old gay subculture, was buried. Yet, while it is undeniably the case that a watershed was crossed that day, ushering in a gay rights movement unimaginable except in the climate of the late 1960s, it is equally true but easily forgotten that the emergence of gay liberation would not have been possible but for the long, lonely organizing efforts of the Mattachine Society and the Daughters of Bilitis and, indeed, of the pioneers to whom they looked for inspiration. All gay men and lesbians, whether they know it or not, and by and large they do not, stand on the shoulders of Urnings.

## Chapter 22

**Conclusion to Part 3**

The passage of the Sexual Offenses Act in England in the summer of 1967 and the Stonewall riots in New York in the summer of 1969 were the two most important events, symbolically as well as in fact, leading up to the late-twentieth-century gay rights movement. The one a reform from the top down, the other a rebellion from the bottom up, they met and mingled in an extraordinary outburst of organizing, protesting, demonstrating pressuring—and having a damn good time—all in full view of a startled public.

It is not quite true that if not London in 1967 and New York in 1969, then perhaps Paris or Amsterdam or San Francisco a year or two years later might have sparked a like transformation of the homophile movement. London in the mid-1960s and New York throughout the latter half of the twentieth century occupied unique places in the public mind, and events in these two cities had a resonance elsewhere that events in other cities did not. All the same, in the twenty-three months that separated the royal assent to the Sexual Offenses Act and the first night of the Stonewall riots the ACLU called for the decriminalization of homosexual relations between consenting adults in private in August 1967; the *Advocate* began publication in Los Angeles in September 1967; the Oscar Wilde Memorial Bookstore opened in New York in November 1967; the play *The Boys in the Band* began its long off-Broadway run on Easter weekend 1968; the first radical gay rights group in France emerged during the student uprising of May 1968; the North American Conference of Homophile Organizations adopted the slogan "Gay Is Good" at its annual conference in August 1968; Allan Horsfall announced the formation of Esquire Clubs Ltd. to open and manage a series of gay clubs in northern England in September 1968; the Metropolitan Community Church was founded in Los Angeles in October 1968; a government- and church-sponsored consultation bureau for homosexuals, the Schorer Foundation, began operations in the Netherlands in November 1968; and both Canada and West Germany decriminalized homosexual relations between consenting adults in private in May 1969.

Following on that sequence of events something like the Stonewall riots, erupting probably at much the same time, was all but inevitable. And in the wider context of the 1960s, of the civil rights, feminist, and antiwar movements, a broad-based gay rights movement spanning the whole of the Western world was scarcely less certain, requiring only a catalytic event such as Stonewall. That, however, was only the proximate cause of the transformation during the 1970s of the gay and lesbian subcultures, which, naive, fractious, self-indulgent, and even self destructive though they sometimes were, nonetheless established themselves as permanent players in the public life of the developed world. The roots of that change go much deeper, back through the entire twentieth century, well into the nineteenth century. From a longer perspective, what is perhaps most striking about the history of homosexual subcultures in the twentieth century, what made them fundamentally different from their antecedents, was their tenacity even in the face of savage repression, their ability to resurface if given even the smallest opening.

That had not always been the case. The sodomitical subcultures that emerged in northwestern Europe late in the seventeenth century and again a century later were met with legal persecution and public hostility that ultimately forced them back underground, largely out of sight and out of touch with society at large. Not so the homosexual subcultures of the late nineteenth century, which, though they encountered scarcely less hostility, inspired imitators, in some instances even direct descendants, in every generation since. In the 1920s, again in the 1940s, and finally, and as it turned out permanently, in the 1960s gay and lesbian subcultures surfaced with ever greater boldness. The difference lay in part in external circumstances: the dislocating effects of two world wars and the influence of feminism and, in the United States, of the civil rights movement. In addition, the late-nineteenth-century labeling of homosexuals, in particular by the medical profession, as a category of persons apart had the effect of crystallizing attitudes not only toward these subcultures but within them more firmly than ever before. But that was not a new development; it was the culmination of a process dating back to the emergence and recognition of the sodomite as in some measure a distinct personality type early in the previous century, as well as to the first medical studies of sodomy nearly a hundred years before Krafft-Ebing. What was new in the mid- to late nineteenth century was the long-drawn-out search for self-definition, operating in tandem with medicalization, both influencing and influenced by it, occupying some six or seven decades, from Whitman and Ulrichs through Hirschfeld, Friedländer, and Carpenter to Gide and Hall. Whatever its limitations and however halting its progress, it was a process that endowed these subcultures with a self-awareness, self-confidence, and resilience, what John Addington Symonds had called self-effectuation, even in the face of repression, that they are unlikely ever to lose.

# Notes

## Preface

x "Immoral and unacceptable": U.S. Supreme Court, "Bowers v. Hardwick," in Rubenstein, 135.

x "Hidden from history": Duberman, Vicinus, and Chauncey.

xi "Effects a number of exclusions": Howard, 12.

xi "'Phenomenon' . . . 'concept'": ibid., 15.

xii "The unknown, the unfamous": Porter and Weeks, 2.

## Chapter 1. Origins

Edward Stein has gathered together the major contributors, from Foucault on, to the debate between the essentialists and the social constructionists. The most important sources of information on these early subcultures are the collections of essays edited by Gerard and Hekma, Dynes and Donaldson, Maccubin, Higgs, Fout, and Herdt. Coward on France and, on a more popular level, Norton (*Mother Clap's Molly House*) on England, Rey on Paris, and Trumbach on London are especially noteworthy.

3 On Kertbeny: Feray and Herzer.

4 "The sodomite had been": Foucault, 1:43.

5 "It interests me": Mass, 2:209.

6 "The late nineteenth century": Weeks, 2.

6 "A basic but creative response": ibid., 1.

6 "Signs of the emergence": ibid., 4.

9 "His whore on one arm": Trumbach, "Sodomitical Assaults," 408.

10 "Sodomy was intimately connected": Rocke, 191.

10 "Truly autonomous and distinctive": ibid.

10 Fairies: Chauncey, *Gay New York*, ch. 2.

12 "There is no crime": Norton, *Mother Clap's Molly House*, 116.

14 "Taste . . . was not for women": Oresko, 113–14.

14 "Is more than ever taken": ibid., 117.

14 "Vices were of two sorts": Rubini, 363.

15 Affective Individualism: Stone, 7–8 and ch. 6.

## Chapter 2. Patterns of Repression

In addition to the works cited in Chapter 1, see Rocke and Perry on Renaissance southern Europe. The essays on the Netherlands in Gerard and Hekma are invaluable.

17 "Against nature": Rom. 1:27.
17 "Shall surely be": Lev. 20:13.
18 "The detestable and abominable vice": Norton, *Mother Clap's Molly House,* 15.
18 "Who commits lewdness": Huussen, 252–53.
21 "School and bordello of sodomy": Coward, 237.
21 "That an example must be made": Rey, 136.
26 "Exterminate this vice": van der Meer, 141.
32 "Throughout the century": Coward, 249.

## Chapter 3. Sodomy and the Enlightenment

The context for the writings of the philosophes is provided by Stockinger and Ragan. On eighteenth-century Prussia see Steakley's "Sodomy in Enlightenment Prussia."

34 "In his states": Steakley, "Sodomy in Enlightenment Prussia," 166.
35 "A vice which would destroy": Voltaire, 76.
35 "Infamy," "a crime": Montesquieu, 189.
35 "Once a philosophe": Stockinger, 162.
35 "Nothing that exists": Ragan, 24.
36 "How did it come about": Voltaire, 76.
36 "Let there be no customs": Montesquieu, 189.
36 "It is very odd": ibid.
36 "A victim was needed": Voltaire, 79.
37 "Sodomy, so long as": Ragan, 22.
37 "My stomach turned over": Rousseau, bk. 2, 71.
37 "There was nothing": ibid., 72.
37 "The whole matter": ibid.
38 "To other subjects": Bentham, pt. 1, 384–85.
38 "I am ashamed": ibid., 385.
38 "At any rate": ibid.
38 "Giving one sex the weaknesses": Montesquieu, 189.
39 "It might well be said": Bentham, pt. 1, 402.
39 "If pleasure is not a good": ibid., pt. 2, 96.
39 "The persecution they meet": ibid., pt. 1, 403.
40 "Offense of a still deeper malignity": Blackstone, vol. 4, ch. 15, sec. 4.
40 "The awkward and ugly instrument": Crompton, 32.
41 "Imaginary crimes": Courouve, 9.
42 "It makes absolutely no difference": Sade, 326.
42 "New governments will require new manners": ibid., 307.
42 "We wonder that savagery": ibid., 325.
43 "There are very few criminal actions": ibid., 307.

43 "We are fully convinced": ibid., 316.
45 "Physicians are all agreed": Bentham, pt. 2, 102.
46 "We are responsible": Mosse, *Nationalism and Sexuality,* 27.

## Chapter 4. Europe Divided

For unusually interesting discussions on developments in Germany and England, see, on Germany, Aldrich (on Winckelmann) and the contributions to Kuzniar; on England, Crompton; and on both countries, Mosse, *Nationalism and Sexuality.* See also Norton, *Mother Clap's Molly House;* and Harvey on scandals and punishments in England.

49 "The quiet and repose": Mosse, *Nationalism and Sexuality,* 14.
50 "Completely separated his intellectual ideal": Aldrich, 44.
51 "The age of Winckelmann": Richter, 45.
51 "As long as a person": Hull, *Sexuality, State, and Civil Society in Germany,* 349–50.
54 "I know that by regulating": Furneaux, 54.
54 "Proclamation for the Encouragement": Bristow, 38.
57 "That which you get for five pounds": Crompton, 161.
59 "It is by the power of names": ibid., 262–64.
59 "Irregular," "the improlific appetite," "the Attic mode": ibid., 263–24.
60 "Never did work appear": ibid., 255.

## Chapter 5. Conclusion to Part 1

On the Netherlands, see Salden.

61 "Any person who shall have committed": Sibalis, "Regulation of Male Homosexuality in Revolutionary and Napoleonic France," 83.
62 "Would do great violence": Crompton, 359.
62 "A nameless offense of great enormity": ibid., 358.
63 "Punishment, however severe": ibid., 252.
65 "If such crimes were effectively checked": ibid., 231.

## Chapter 6. Pioneers: The United States

Of the huge literature on Whitman, Justin Kaplan's is perhaps the best traditional biography, Shively's the most relevant to this subject. See also the autobiography of Hartland and the biography of Alger by Scharnhorst and Bales, as well as the articles by Duberman and Martin in Duberman, Vicinus, and Chauncey.

70 "Sexual inversion": Symonds, "Problem in Modern Ethics," 101.
70 "I have traced": Symonds, *Letters,* 2:201–2.
70 "There is no one": Shively, 10.
71 "Line of transmission": Leyland, *Gay Sunshine Interviews,* 1:106.
71 "Buggery is twofold": Katz, *Gay American History,* 24.
72 "A friendship I deemed": Martin, 178.

72 "Met one day a young man": Higginson, *Cheerful Yesterdays,* 107.

73 "I never loved but one male friend": Higginson, *Thomas Wentworth Higginson,* 126.

73 "Their letters were more like those": ibid., 125.

73 "Moral deterioration": Higginson, *Cheerful Yesterdays,* 108.

73 "Romantic attachment": Higginson, *Thomas Wentworth Higginson,* 72.

73 "Concede to any person": Wells, 80–81.

73 "I strongly suspect": Higginson, *Cheerful Yesterdays,* 110.

73 "It is possible": Martin, 180.

73 "Whether you yet have": Duberman, "'Writhing Bedfellows' in Antebellum South Carolina," 155.

74 "Frequent and swift flash of eyes": Shively, 206.

74 "O I saw one passing alone": ibid., 217.

74 "I too . . . was called": Whitman, *Complete Poetry and Prose,* 1:170.

75 "I share the midnight orgies of young men": ibid., 129–30.

75 "There is never a day": Shively, 50.

75 "To celebrate the need of love": ibid., 190.

76 "Dreamed . . . of a city": ibid., 206.

76 "Love of athletic comrades": ibid., 190.

76 "The brotherhood of lovers": ibid., 212.

78 "Affection . . . is sometimes": ibid., 65.

78 "Every now and then": Whitman, "Spiritual Characters among the Soldiers," in *Specimen Days,* 43–44.

78 "As the most extraordinary piece of wit": Kaplan, *Walt Whitman,* 17.

78 "It is believed you are not ashamed": ibid., 276.

79 "In your conception of comradeship": Symonds, *Letters,* 3:482.

79 "Gratuitous and quite at the time": Katz, *Gay American History,* 349.

79 "I feel sure he could not have written it": Symonds, *Letters,* 3:808.

79 "Depress the adhesive nature": Kaplan, *Walt Whitman,* 316.

80 "I often say to myself": Katz, *Gay American History,* 345.

81 "Self abuse": Hartland, 41.

81 "Scores of such nights": ibid., 40.

81 "If my parents could have seen": ibid., 7–8.

81 "My love for my own sex": ibid., 91.

81 "Unnatural . . . perverted nature": ibid., 5–7.

81 "A prisoner for life": ibid., 89.

82 "The guardians of public purity . . .": Thomas Wentworth Higginson, editorial, *Women's Journal,* 4 February 1882.

83 "A I lay with my head": Whitman, *Complete Poetry and Prose,* 1:294.

83 "It is to the development": Whitman, *Democratic Vistas,* n. 10, 262.

84 "You do not know": Symonds, *Letters,* 3:667.

## Chapter 7. Pioneers: Germany

The most important writings of the central figures—Ulrichs, Hirschfeld, and (in Oosterhuis and Kennedy) Friedländer—are available in excellent translations. Ulrichs is well served biographically by Kennedy, not so Hirschfeld by Wolff. Steakley, *Homosexual Emancipation Movement,* is indispensable.

87 "My poor and . . . innocently persecuted comrades": Kennedy, *Ulrichs,* 52.
87 "I am an insurgent": ibid., 70.
89 "For the repeal of the legal punishment": ibid., 148.
89 "The people's consciousness of right": ibid., 147–48.
90 "One of the men I prized": Symonds, *Letters,* 3:815.
90 "Thanks pours out to you": Kennedy, *Ulrichs,* 174.
91 "Virtually proven": Le Vay, 23.
91 "Subject to feelings": ibid.
91 "Condemns very many upright": ibid.
92 "It is no coincidence": Steakley, *Homosexual Emancipation Movement,* 24–26.
93 "Quest for truth, justice and humanity": Le Vay, 24.
93 "The government's hands": Steakley, *Homosexual Emancipation Movement,* 31.
94 "Through Knowledge to Justice": ibid., 30.
95 "In the interests of the welfare": Fout, "Sexual Politics in Wilhelmine Germany," 285.
95 "Chivalric love," "love of friends": Oosterhuis and Kennedy, 30.
95 "Journal of male culture": ibid., 3.
97 "The more spiritualized": Friedlander, "Male and Female Culture," 215.
97 "Same sex intercourse": ibid.
97 "Esteem for the beauty of youths": ibid.
97 "With sicknesses one can have pity": Friedlander, "Memoir for the Friends and Contributors of the Scientific Humanitarian Committee," 75.
97 "From the standpoint of natural rights": ibid., 71.
97 "The whole modern sexual freedom movement": ibid., 83.
98 "Since we renounce in principle": ibid., 84.
98 "One thing has been achieved": Lauritsen and Thorstad, 22.
98 "Path over corpses": Steakley, *Homosexual Emancipation Movement,* 33.

## Chapter 8. Pioneers: England

In addition to their own writings, the major figures—Symonds, Carpenter, and Ellis—are the subjects of good to excellent biographies by Grosskurth and Tsuzuki. Weeks is as central to the subject in modern England as Steakley, *Homosexual Emancipation Movement,* is for Germany.

101 "Self effectuation": Grosskurth, *John Addington Symonds,* 112.
103 "A few special friends": Tsuzuki, 42.
103 "Within the limits of good sense": Symonds, *Memoirs,* 202.
103 "To have the imaginative and sensuous side": ibid., 207.
104 "Brawny young soldier": ibid., 253.
104 "That the physical appetite": ibid., 254–55.
104 "Very dull lectures": ibid., 255.
105 "If I were to publish it now": Symonds, *Letters,* 3:419.

106 "I know of all you speak of": Grosskurth, *John Addington Symonds*, 280–81.

107 "The opportunity of talking over this question": ibid., 286.

107 "Ought to be scientifically": ibid.

108 "Sexual inversion is in a vast number of cases": Carpenter, "Intermediate Sex," 207–8.

109 "That they exist": ibid., 199.

109 "Great genius for attachment": ibid., 187.

## Chapter 9. Wilde

See especially Ellman on Wilde and Bristow on the general climate in England. The writings of H. Montgomery Hyde are particularly relevant for this period.

112 "Any male person who in public": Smith, "Labouchere's Amendment," 165.

114 "Smart looking lads": Smith, *Love in Earnest,* 193.

117 "I would [let Wilde off]": Hyde, *Oscar Wilde,* 271.

117 "It was like feasting with panthers": Wilde, *Selected Letters,* 220.

117 "Unwholesome . . . morbid and perfumed manner. I resent": Symonds, *Letters,* 3:477–79.

118 "Posing as a sodomite": Hyde, *Oscar Wilde,* 196.

118 "It was worse": ibid., 211.

118 "A man who was not an artist": ibid., 213.

118 "Everything I write": ibid., 214.

118 "It is the first I have heard": ibid., 216.

118 "Oh dear no": ibid., 219.

119 "That I do not know": ibid., 259.

119 "Truth may be found": ibid., 260.

119 "The love that dare not speak its name": ibid., 257–58.

119 "I decided that it was nobler": Ellman, 471.

120 "The crime of which you have been convicted": Hyde, *Oscar Wilde,* 293.

120 "Every train to Dover": Hyde, *The Love That Dared Not Speak Its Name,* 152.

121 "A nice little gang of Secularists": Brome, 102.

125 "His unhappy fate": Hyde, *The Love That Dared Not Speak Its Name,* 3.

125 "I didn't know what homosexuality was": Porter and Weeks, 23.

125 "I didn't realize the significance of it": ibid., 6.

125 "The Oscar Wilde trial": Ellis, 352.

126 "Reviewing the results of the trial": ibid., 352–53.

## Chapter 10. Degeneracy and Atavism

On the medicalization of homosexuality, see Greenberg, ch. 9; and Symonds, "Problem in Modern Ethics." On French attitudes during the this period, see Copley, chs. 4 and 6; and Merrick and Ragan, *Homosexuality in Modern France,* chs. 5–7.

127 "To a class of people": Hyde, *Oscar Wilde,* 266.

128 "The heinousness of the crime": Hyde, *The Love That Dared Not Speak Its Name,* 149–50.

128 "Another contrast": ibid., 150.

128  "If such be 'Artists'": Schmidgall, 209.
128  "Unwholesome tendencies": Cohen, 206.
128  "Righteous sentence": Hyde, *The Love That Dared Not Speak Its Name,* 149.
129  "Open the windows!": Ellman, 479.
129  "Throwing the search-light of justice": Schmidgall, 273.
129  "There is not a man or woman": ibid.
129  "True pederasts": Thompson, 114.
130  "Traces of the habits of pederasty": Copley, 106.
131  "I do not claim to explain": ibid.
131  "In the majority of persons": Symonds, "Problem in Modern Ethics," 115.
131  "Contrary sexual feeling": Greenberg, 380.
132  "In almost all cases": ibid., 414.
134  "Man with all his noble qualities": Darwin, 276.
134  "Sexual perverts in general": Greenberg, 419.

## Chapter 11. Purity and Impurity

On the Netherlands, see the essays by Hekma and Salden in Naerssen and by Hekma in Higgs. On the United States, see ch. 7 of D'Emilio and Freedman on the purity movement, Gustav-Wrathall on the YMCA, and above all Chauncey on New York. On Germany, see Fout's essay on Wilhelmine Germany, Steakley on the Eulenburg scandal in Duberman, Vicinus, and Chauncey, and, most comprehensively, Hull, *Entourage of Kaiser Wilhelm II.*

139  "Now we have come so far": Salden, 167.
141  "That there is a community": Katz, *Gay/Lesbian Almanac,* 294.
141  "Queers": Chauncey, *Gay New York,* 101.
142  "Fairies": ibid., 35.
145  "The very institutions established": Gustav-Wrathall, 6.
145  "Indecent and degenerate": ibid., 161.
147  "Highly idealized effusive male friendships": Hull, *Entourage of Kaiser Wilhelm II,* 51.
149  "In 1908 I first learned": ibid., 136.
149  "Abnormal sexual instincts": ibid., 137.
151  "One of the finest German virtues": Oosterhuis, 17.

## Chapter 12. The Cult of Youth

Of the extensive literature on the English public schools, Honey, in the latter half of ch. 3, is perhaps the most reliable on issues of sexuality, as is Jeal, ch. 3, on Baden-Powell. Reade and Smith, *Love in Earnest,* open windows on the strange world of the Uranian poets. On the German youth movement, in addition to Steakley, *Homosexual Emancipation Movement,* see Bluher and, in Oosterhuis and Kennedy, the introduction to pt. 4 and the essays by Brand, Reiffegg, Lucifer, and Waldecke.

155  "A strange mixture": Hyde, *The Love That Dared Not Speak Its Name,* 120.
156  "Such boys are to be seen": Marcus, *The Other Victorians,* 19.

158 "Sensuous, dreamy, Greece-haunted": Reade, 54.

159 "Stripped for the sea your tender form": ibid., 348.

160 "Exaltation of the youthful female ideal": ibid., 315.

161 "The authorities in their desire": Honey, 183.

162 "Character factory": Rosenthal, 6.

162 "Girlitis": Jeal, 88.

162 "Sentimentalism": ibid., 94–95.

163 "That deeper form of subordination": ibid., 101.

164 "The typus inversus": Bluher, 47.

166 "I have in my mind's eye": Honey, 179.

166 "Every old public school boy": ibid., 181.

## Chapter 13. Forster and Gide

In addition to the writings of Gide and Forster, they are well served biographically, Gide by Sheriden (among many others more directly concerned with his sexuality—Pollard, Lucey, and Hanna), and Forster by Furbank. See also Parker and Ackerley himself on Ackerley. Gadd untangles the complex love lives of the Bloomsbury group and, in Ch. 6 of *Scandal in the Ink,* Robinson treats the pederastic tradition in France.

169 "The great pleasure of the debauchee": Gide, *If It Die,* 286.

170 "Awakening . . . authorization": Copley, 170.

170 "Attempt at objectivity": Rivers, 267.

171 "This leads to a much greater sense": Robinson, *Scandal in the Ink,* 145.

172 "Normal pederasty": Gide, *Corydon,* 120.

173 "I can think of no opinion": ibid., 115–16.

173 "To make a posthumous masquerade": Pollard, 231.

174 "However dangerous that truth may be": Hanna, 206.

174 "They all denied": Gide, *Corydon,* 8.

174 "I would probably lose courage": ibid.

174 "I am merely a little boy": Copley, 166.

174 "To transmit through his writings": Forster, "Gide's Death," 232–33.

176 "The Ideal Friend": Ackerley, 131.

176 "I am not romantic": Furbank, 2:162–63.

177 "I was writing the latter half": ibid., 40.

177 "In my loneliness": Forster, *Maurice,* 245.

177 "The general plan": ibid., 246.

178 "Not to express myself": Furbank 1:200.

178 "If it ended unhappily": Forster, *Maurice,* 246.

178 "Clive, on the bench": ibid., 251.

178 "May get off": ibid.

179 "But Gide hasn't got a mother": Parker, 138.

179 "Only connect": Furbank, 1:188.

179 "Defense at any last judgment": ibid., 2:14.

179 "The central preoccupation of his life": ibid., 295.

180 "So long as no one": Skidelsky, 2:129.

181 "I really think the whole conception": Furbank, 2:16.
182 "If I had to choose": Forster, "What I Believe," 68.

## Chapter 14. Conclusion to Part 2

On homosexuality in World War I, contrast ch. 7 of Hirschfeld's *Sexual History of the Great War* with ch. 8 of Fussell. On Gloeden and List, see ch. 5 of Aldrich. Perhaps the best of the many collections of historical photographs are Ellenzweig and Weiermair. On Warren, the official life by Burdett and Goddard is all but unobtainable, but Green, *Mount Vernon Street Warrens* and Sox cover much the same ground. Shand-Tucci provides the Boston background.

183 "No matter how catastrophic": Hirschfeld, *Sexual History of the World War,* 11.
184 "While it is perfectly true": ibid., 119–20.
184 "Feminine constitution": ibid., 121.
185 "I came out in order to help": Fussell, 296.
186 "If you could hear, at every jolt": ibid., 294.
187 "Bed and boy": Holroyd, 281.
188 "Was effeminate by the standards": Shand-Tucci, 221.
190 "There is in the modern world": Burdett and Goddard, 376.
191 "Finds no place in modern life": Thwaite, 182.
191 "The weight of law and custom": Symonds, *Letters,* 3:347.
191 "I wrote it neither for my friends": Forster, *Selected Letters,* 1:222.
191 "Does it date?": Isherwood, 126.
191 "The transformed England": Forster, *Maurice,* 250.

## Chapter 15. Between the Wars

The real or fictionalized memoirs of Isherwood, Spender, Lehmann, and Worsley provide an evocative portrait of the lives of a select group of gay men between the two world wars. Humphrey Carpenter, Hynes, Annan, and Martin Green (in *Children of the Sun*) provide context, while Porter and Weeks open a window onto that era as seen through the eyes of ordinary men. On Germany, besides Steakley, *Homosexual Emancipation Movement,* there is a wealth of sources on homosexuality under the Nazis: Grau, Plant, Heger, Lautmann. On Russia, see Karlinsky's essay in Duberman, Vicinus, and Chauncey; and Engelstein.

195 "It would be fair to say": Hyde, *The Love That Dared Not Speak Its Name,* 201.
196 "Bright Young Things": Carpenter, *Brideshead Generation,* 167.
196 "When Auden went up to Oxford": Annan, 119.
196 "What was inexcusable": Isherwood, 216.
197 "Essentially masculine . . . utterly feminine": Weinberg, 147.
198 "Berlin meant boys": Isherwood, 2.
198 "For them drink, for us sex": Spender, *Temple,* x.
199 "The guilty feeling of being a misfit": Lehmann, 7–8.
199 "His tribe": Isherwood, 17.

200 "The silly solemn old professor": ibid.

200 "He loved Hirschfeld": ibid.

200 "A slim boy of about seventeen": ibid., 91.

200 "Everything became politics": Spender, *Temple*, xi.

201 "As soon as I saw": Isherwood, 162.

201 "The England of Nearly Everybody": ibid., 164.

201 "Suppose, Christopher now said to himself": ibid., 335–36.

202 "[He] had done his best": ibid., 334–35.

203 "Homosexuality never served": Engelstein, 58.

203 "The criminality of [which] is deeply rooted": ibid., 63.

206 "Whether the political relations": Steakley, *Homosexual Emancipation Movement*, 92–95.

209 "Except for a few minor cliques": ibid., 82.

210 "I thought of Röhm": MacDonald, 220–21.

210 "It is not necessary that you and I live": Steakley, *Homosexual Emancipation Movement*, 84.

211 "The police be purged": Plant, 48.

211 "Immoral purposes": Grau, 29.

211 "In the interests of the moral renewal": ibid.

212 "Not an institution for the moral education": Plant, 61.

212 "Pure and cleanly": ibid., 67.

212 "Any sex offense against males": Grau, 66.

213 We have a full account: Dijk.

213 "A symptom of racial degeneracy": Plant, 111.

214 "Acted out of a predisposition": Grau, 176.

215 "Because their subculture": Lautmann, 78–80.

215 "If one lost his 'friend'": Steakley, *Homosexual Emancipation Movement*, 116.

215 "That homosexuals were able": Lautmann, 86–87.

217 "Remnants of the exploiting classes": Karlinsky, 362.

217 "Lived my life, not I his": Spender, *World within World*, 177.

218 "Someone I loved had gone into the war": ibid., 214.

218 "An effective number of those": ibid., 252.

219 "Divide himself in two": Worsley, 222.

## Chapter 16. The Making of a Lesbian Subculture

On love between women in the eighteenth century, see Donaghue, Mavor, and pt. 1 of Faderman, *Surpassing the Love of Men*. The greater portion of that pioneering work is devoted to the modern era, as is the slim volume on German lesbianism Faderman co-authored with Eriksson. There are important articles by Vicinus, Smith-Rosenberg, Newton, and Benstock in Duberman, Vicinus, and Chauncey. See also chs. 7 and 8 of Robinson's *Scandal in the Ink*, Benstock's study of the Paris lesbian subculture, and the biographies of a number of its leading lights by Herring (Djuna Barnes), Wineapple (Janet Flanner), and Wickes (Natalie Barney). On British lesbianism, see pt. 3 of Weeks, and Cline's biography of Radclyffe Hall.

220 Auden Generation: Hynes.

221 "Implying subordination": Donaghue, 221.

225 "So utterly abandoned": Faderman, *Surpassing the Love of Men,* 149.

226 "A union—there is no truer word": ibid., 190.

226 "Friendship occupied": Sherman, 69.

227 "But the growth of true friendship": ibid., 72.

229 "The masculine soul": Smith-Rosenberg, 270.

229 "While influences of the modern": Ellis, 262.

229 "A woman's life": Faderman, *Surpassing the Love of Men,* 251.

230 "Our lives were on a much higher plane": Faderman, *Odd Girls and Twilight Lovers,* 54.

230 "I considered myself without shame": ibid., 58.

230 "The homosexual woman": Rueling, 91.

231 "Considering the contribution": ibid.

234 "Paris has always seemed": Wickes, 44.

234 "Is undoubtedly the most important": Robinson, *Scandal in the Ink,* 211.

234 "Was either ignored": Marks, 362.

235 "Spectrum of human sexuality": Robinson, *Scandal in the Ink,* 215.

235 "Will speak sadly of pleasure": ibid.

237 "Placid and self assured": Wickes, 177.

237 "The homosexual woman possesses": Rueling, 84–85.

238 "I wrote the book": Weeks, 107.

239 "Neutral and natural sexual variation": Hamer, 97.

239 "Further morbidified the most natural": Faderman, *Surpassing the Love of Men,* 323.

239 "For bourgeois women": Newton, 291.

## Chapter 17. Homosexuality and Psychiatry

Lewes and Bayer are the most important studies of the psychiatric profession and homosexuality.

243 "General love of mankind": Bayer, 22

243 "External motives": Lewes, 34.

244 "Homosexuality is surely no advantage": Bayer, 27.

245 "Suffering, unhappiness, limitations": Lewes, 116.

246 "I have no bias against homosexuality": ibid., 15.

246 "The great percentage of homosexuals": ibid., 114.

246 "The common judgment that homosexuality": ibid., 149.

246 "The passive homosexual": ibid., 115.

246 "The new freedom that women": Faderman, *Odd Girls and Twilight Lovers,* 134.

247 "All psychoanalytic theories": Bieber, 18.

247 "That heterosexuality is the biologic norm": ibid., 319.

247 "A homosexual adaptation is a result": ibid., 303.

247 "The homosexual adaptation is an outcome": ibid., 173.

247 "Non psychotic mental disorders": Bayer, 40.

248 "That the historical trauma": Lewes, 232.

## Chapter 18. False Starts and New Beginnings

The interwar years are excellently covered in the latter part of Chauncey and the early chapters of Loughery. The glamorous world of Lynes and his circle is conveyed in words and pictures by Leddick and by Poherilenko and Crump. Berube has written definitively on World War II, and Kaiser, Loughery, and above all D'Emilio are equally authoritative on the postwar era. Hay is well served biographically by Timmons.

249 "There were many of us": Green, *Love in America,* 156.

249 "The shame of antiquity": ibid., 50.

250 "Was no longer alone": ibid., 206.

250 "Immoral conditions": Chauncey, "Christian Brotherhood or Sexual Perversion?" 294.

251 "Husbands": ibid., 299.

252 "If your men don't knock it off": ibid., 305.

254 "Short haired women": Chauncey, *Gay New York,* 242.

254 "Pansies": ibid., 15, 314.

256 "Men for the purpose of committing": ibid., 172.

256 "Depicting or dealing with the subject": ibid., 313.

256 "If the cops have their way": ibid., 340.

257 "Sex perversion or any reference": Loughery, 63.

259 "I didn't like him": Leddick, *Intimate Companions,* 23.

260 "Where odd, frightening things": Miller, *On Being Different,* 24–25.

261 "The army is an utterly simplified": Berube, 98.

261 "Then suddenly, into the feast": Crisp, 151–52.

263 "Sexual psychopaths": Berube, 14.

263 "Yessir. If the general pleases": Faderman, *Odd Girls and Twilight Lovers,* 118.

265 "An arrest of psychosexual development": Menninger, 225.

265 "General [American] attitude": ibid., 222.

265 "In a technical, psychiatric sense": ibid., 223.

265 "For every homosexual who was referred": ibid., 227.

266 "That is more than one male": Kinsey, Pomeroy, and Martin, 623.

266 "It is difficult to maintain": ibid., 659.

266 "Might very well reexamine": ibid., 660.

266 "The police force and court officials": ibid., 665.

267 "Whether such a program": ibid.

267 "If all persons with any trace": ibid., 666.

268 "A groaning shelf": Katz, *Gay/Lesbian Almanac,* 630.

268 "I set out to shatter the stereotype": Vidal, *City and the Pillar,* 246.

269 "Spiritual autobiography": Cory, xiv.

269 "Straight," "gay": ibid.

269 "The homosexual desires freedom of expression": ibid., 233.

269 "Until the world is able to accept us": ibid., 14.

270 "Child molestation": Timmons, 36.

270 "I'm sorry but you're too obvious": ibid., 71.

271 "Maybe instead of a girlish boy": ibid., 97–98.

271 "Casting couch for society": ibid., 96.

271 "Somehow or other my [life]": D'Emilio, 60.

273 "We took the name Mattachine": Katz, *Gay American History,* 413.

273 "Your father knew Cecil Rhodes": Timmons, 8.

273 "TO UNIFY, TO EDUCATE, TO LEAD": ibid., 154.

275 "The postwar reaction, the shutting down": ibid., 135.

## Chapter 19. Reaction

Loughery and Kaiser complement D'Emilio on the postwar United States, much as David complements Weeks on England. See also Martin and Lyon (on the origins of the postwar lesbian subculture). On continental Europe during these years see Kennedy on the homophile magazine *Der Kreis,* ch. 9 of Copley on France, and Tielman's essay in Naerssen and Hekma's in Higgs on the Netherlands. Weeks and David again make a good pairing on England, and Hodges's biography of Turing is both comprehensive and moving.

277 "It is generally believed": United States Senate, 244–45.

278 "Homosexual proclivities": *New York Times,* 13 April 1953.

278 "I don't say every homosexual": Katz, *Gay American History,* 95.

279 "The greatest danger": Sullivan, 65.

281 "A pattern of behavior": D'Emilio, 81.

281 "Homosexuals are not seeking": ibid., 84.

282 "For the first time she was able": Martin and Lyon, 29.

282 "It never occurred to me": Tobin and Wicker, 48.

283 "We played the roles in public": Martin and Lyon, 12.

283 "Wanted a supersecret, exclusively lesbian": ibid., 222.

283 "Education of the variant": Daughters of Bilitis.

284 "Formed as an alternative": Martin and Lyon, 234.

284 "At every one of these conventions": Katz, *Gay American History,* 431.

285 "In view of the justified scruples": Kennedy, *Ideal Man,* 85.

286 "Leaders could not keep up": ibid., 3.

287 "Paris must not become Berlin": Sibalis, "Paris," 30.

288 "Homosexual peril": Copley, 217.

289 "Social plagues": Adam, 67.

289 "Public opinion seems clearly": Copley, 220.

292 "Homosexuals in general": Hyde, *The Love That Dared Not Speak Its Name,* 215.

293 "I hear you are going to write": Croft-Cooke, *Verdict of You All,* 251–52.

295 "This is the life history": Davidson, 1.

295 "We know all about you": ibid., 221.

295 "Many people took the fatalistic attitude": Horsfall, 18.

298 His biographer has put forward a case: Hodges, 487–527.

## Chapter 20. Outsiders Abroad and at Home

On Americans abroad after World War II, in addition to Finlayson on Tangier, see the memoirs of Vidal and Norse, and the biographies of Vidal by Kaplan, Bowles by Green, and Ginsberg by Miles. D'Emilio is particularly good on San Francisco.

300 "A pack of queens": Vidal, *Palimpsest*, 176.
301 "All the writers are here": Kaplan, *Gore Vidal*, 276.
302 "Release from American restraints": Finlayson, 215.
302 "Virtually every foreign Tangerine": ibid., 244.
303 "Everybody's there": ibid., 91.
303 "Stayed around Tangier": ibid., 126.
303 "Among the planet's most": Green, *Dream at the End of the World*, 69–70.
304 "I'm going to steep myself": Finlayson, 185.
304 "All my queerness was camp": Miles, 129.
304 "I simply do not recognize": ibid., 130.
306 "The crucial moment": Leyland, *Gay Sunshine Interviews*, 1:103.
306 "Through the beats' example": D'Emilio, 181.
307 "The national headquarters": ibid., 121.
309 "Creating a sense of community": Loughery, 280.
310 "Flight from masculinity": Lewes, 168 and 275.
311 "Homosexual behavior": Marmor, 17.
311 "The twentieth century psychiatric clinician": ibid., 17–18.
312 "The best solution to the problem": Hoffman, 198.

## Chapter 21. From Wolfenden to Stonewall

On the law reform movement in England, Grey is the central source, to which Weeks provides a useful corrective. To the familiar trio of Loughery, Kaiser, and D'Emilio on the pre-Stonewall years should be added Marc Stein's detailed study of Philadelphia.

315 "The case for reform": *Sunday Times*, 28 March 1954.
315 "You will probably have seen": Faulks, 242.
315 "In short, we can't win": Wolfenden, 135.
316 "That homosexual behavior between consenting adults": "Wolfenden Report," 262.
316 "We do not think that it would be expedient": ibid., 272.
318 "Knowing that the opposition": Grey, 44.
318 "A pressure lobby of homosexuals": ibid.
318 "After the debate": ibid., 44–45.
319 "Frankly it's an extremely unpleasant bill": Crossman, 2:407.
319 "Buggers' clubs": Hyde, *The Love That Dared Not Speak Its Name*, 262.
319 "Build a bulwark which will defy": Grey, 94.
320 "Brilliant command of millions of men": ibid.
320 "Oh dear, oh dear": ibid., 90.
320 "It was the first film": Jivani, 144.
321 "That a better piece of legislation": Grey, 128.

321 "Bankrupt policy": Weeks, 173.

322 "Only in their conviction": Grey, 128.

322 "In the short run": Weeks, 173.

322 "Almost in spite of itself": ibid., 177.

322 "No. It has changed things only a little": ibid., 178.

322 "The earliest gay women's group": Grey, 136.

323 "It's still inconceivable": ibid., 182.

324 "One of the most important milestones": Jivani, 149.

325 "We cannot ask": D'Emilio, 153.

327 "News for 'queers'": Stein, *City of Sisterly and Brotherly Love*, 232.

328 "That in the absence": D'Emilio, 164.

332 "We have to accumulate power": ibid., 210.

333 "You know, the guys there were so beautiful": *Village Voice*, 3 July 1969.

# Selected Bibliography

Ackerley, J. R. *My Father and Myself.* New York, 1969.

Adam, Barry. *The Rise of the Gay and Lesbian Movement.* Boston, 1987.

Aldrich, Robert. *The Seduction of the Mediterranean: Writing, Art, and Homosexual Fantasy.* London, 1993.

Aldrich, Robert, and Garry Witherspoon, eds. *Who's Who in Gay and Lesbian History: From Antiquity to World War II.* London, 2001.

———. *Who's Who in Contemporary Gay and Lesbian History: From World War II to the Present Day.* London, 2001.

Alexander, Jeb. *Jeb and Dash: A Diary of Gay Life, 1918–1945.* Edited by Ina Russell. Boston, 1993.

Annan, Noel. *Our Age: English Intellectuals between the World Wars—A Group Portrait.* New York, 1990.

Bayer, Ronald. *Homosexuality and American Psychiatry: The Politics of Diagnosis.* Princeton, N.J., 1987.

Beemyn, Brett, ed. *Creating a Place for Ourselves: Lesbian, Gay, and Bisexual Histories.* London, 1997.

Benstock, Shari. *Women of the Left Bank: Paris, 1900–1940.* Austin, Tex., 1986.

Bentham, Jeremy. "Paederasty." Edited and with an introduction by Louis Crompton. Parts 1 and 2. *Journal of Homosexuality* 3, no. 4, and 4, no. 1 (1978).

Bergman, David. *Gaiety Transfigured: Gay Self-Representation in American Literature.* Madison, Wis., 1991.

Berube, Allan. *Coming Out under Fire.* New York, 1990.

Bieber, Irving. *Homosexuality: A Psychiatric Study.* New York, 1962.

Birkin, Andrew. *J. M. Barrie and the Lost Boys: The Love Story That Gave Birth to Peter Pan.* New York, 1979.

Blackstone, William. *Commentaries on the Laws of England.* 4 vols. London, 1765–69.

Bland, Lucy, and Laura Doan, eds. *Sexology in Culture: Labelling Bodies and Desires.* Chicago, 1998.

Blasius, Mark, and Shane Phelan, eds. *We Are Everywhere: A Historical Source Book of Gay and Lesbian Politics.* New York, 1997.

Blüher, Hans. *Family and Male Fraternity.* Paris, 1994.

Bristow, Edward. *Vice and Vigilance: Purity Movements in Britain since 1700.* London, 1977.

Brome, Vincent. *Havelock Ellis, Philosopher of Sex: A Biography.* London, 1979.

Burdett, Osbert, and R. H. Goddard. *Edward Perry Warren: The Biography of a Connoisseur.* London, 1941.

Cant, Bob, and Susan Hemmings, eds. *Radical Records: Thirty Years of Lesbian and Gay History.* London, 1988.

Carpenter, Edward. "The Intermediate Sex." In *Selected Writings. Vol. 1: Sex,* 185–244. London, 1984.

Carpenter, Humphrey. *The Brideshead Generation: Evelyn Waugh and His Friends.* Boston, 1990.

Chauncey, George. "Christian Brotherhood or Sexual Perversion? Homosexual Identities and the Construction of Sexual Boundaries in the World War I Era." In Duberman, Vicinus, and Chauncey, 294–317.

———. *Gay New York: Gender, Urban Culture, and the Making of the Gay Male World, 1870–1940.* New York, 1994.

Cline, Sally. *Radclyffe Hall: A Woman Called John.* New York, 1998.

Cohen, Ed. *Talk on the Wilde Side: Toward a Genealogy of a Discourse on Male Sexualities.* New York, 1993.

Colette [Sidonie-Gabrielle Colette]. *The Pure and the Impure.* Translated by Herma Briffault. New York, 2000.

Cooper, Emmanuel. *The Sexual Perspective: Homosexuality and Art in the Last One Hundred Years in the West.* London, 1986.

Copley, Antony. *Sexual Moralities in France, 1780–1980: New Ideas on the Family, Divorce, and Homosexuality.* London, 1989.

Cory, Donald Webster. *The Homosexual in America: A Subjective Approach.* New York, 1951.

Courouve, Claude. "1791 Law Reform in France." *Cabirion* 12 (spring/summer 1985).

Coward, D. A. "Attitudes to Homosexuality in Eighteenth-Century France." *Journal of European Studies* 10, no. 4 (1980): 231–55.

Crisp, Quentin. *The Naked Civil Servant.* New York, 1977.

Croft-Cooke, Rupert. *Feasting with Panthers: A New Consideration of Some Late Victorian Writers.* New York, 1967.

———. *The Verdict of You All.* London, 1955.

Crompton, Louis. *Byron and Greek Love: Homophobia in Nineteenth-Century England.* Berkeley, 1985.

Crossman, Richard. *The Diaries of a Cabinet Minister.* 3 vols. New York, 1975–77.

Darwin, Charles. *Darwin: A Norton Critical Edition.* Edited by Philip Appleman. New York, 1970.

Daughters of Bilitis. "Statement of Purpose." In Blasius and Phelan, 328.

Davenport-Hines, Richard. *Sex, Death, and Punishment: Attitudes to Sex and Sexuality in Britain since the Renaissance.* London, 1991.

David, Hugh. *On Queer Street: A Social History of British Homosexuality, 1895–1995.* London, 1997.

Davidson, Michael. *The World, the Flesh, and Myself.* London, 1985.

D'Emilio, John. *Sexual Politics, Sexual Communities: The Making of a Homosexual Minority in the United States, 1940–1970.* Chicago, 1983.

D'Emilio, John, and Estella Freedman. *Intimate Matters: A History of Sexuality in America.* New York, 1988.

Dijk, Lutz van. *Damned Strong Love: The True Story of Willi G. and Stephan K.* New York, 1995.

Donaghue, Emma. *Passions between Women: British Lesbian Culture, 1668–1801.* New York, 1996.

Driberg, Tom. *Ruling Passions.* London, 1978.

Duberman, Martin. *About Time: Exploring the Gay Past.* London, 1991.

———. "'Writhing Bedfellows' in Antebellum South Carolina: Historical Interpretation and the Politics of Evidence." In Duberman, Vicinus, and Chauncey, 153–68.

Duberman, Martin, Martha Vicinus, and George Chauncey. *Hidden from History: Reclaiming the Gay and Lesbian Past.* New York, 1990.

Dynes, Wayne, ed. *Encyclopedia of Homosexuality.* 2 vols. New York, 1990.

Dynes, Wayne, and Stephan Donaldson, eds. *History of Homosexuality in Europe and America.* New York, 1992.

Ellenzweig, Allen. *The Homoerotic Photograph: Male Images from Durieu/Delacroix to Mapplethorpe.* New York, 1992.

Ellis, Havelock. "Sexual Inversion." In *Studies in the Psychology of Sex,* vol. 1, pt. 4. New York, 1942.

Ellman, Richard. *Oscar Wilde.* New York, 1988.

Engelstein, Laura. *The Keys to Happiness: Sex and the Search for Modernity in Fin-de-Siècle Russia.* Ithaca, N.Y., 1992.

Faderman, Lillian. *Odd Girls and Twilight Lovers: A History of Lesbian Life in Twentieth-Century America.* New York, 1991.

———. *Surpassing the Love of Men: Romantic Friendship and Love between Women from the Renaissance to the Present.* New York, 1981.

Faderman, Lillian, and Brigitte Eriksson. *Lesbians in Germany, 1890s–1920s.* Tallahassee, Fla., 1980.

Faulks, Sebastian. *The Fatal Englishman: Three Short Lives.* London, 1997.

Feray, Jean-Claude, and Manfred Herzer. "Homosexual Studies and Politics in the Nineteenth Century: Karl Maria Kertbeny." *Journal of Homosexuality* 19, no. 1 (1990): 23–47.

Finlayson, Ian. *Tangier: City of the Dream.* London, 1993.

Fone, Byrne. *A Road to Stonewall: Male Homosexuality and Homophobia in English and American Literature, 1750–1969.* New York, 1995.

Forster, E. M. "Gide's Death." In Forster, *Two Cheers for Democracy,* 232–33.

———. *Maurice.* New York, 1973.

———. *Selected Letters of E. M. Forster.* Edited by Mary Furbank and P. N. Furbank. 2 vols. Cambridge, Mass., 1983.

———. *Two Cheers for Democracy.* New York, 1951.

———. "What I Believe." In Forster, *Two Cheers for Democracy,* 67–76.

Foucault, Michel. *History of Sexuality.* Translated by Robert Hurley. 2 vols. New York, 1978–85.

Fout, John. "Sexual Politics in Wilhelmine Germany: The Male Gender Crisis, Moral Purity, and Homophobia." In Fout, *Forbidden History,* 259–92.

————, ed. *Forbidden History: The State, Society, and the Regulation of Sexuality in Modern Europe.* Chicago, 1992.

Friedländer, Benedict. "Male and Female Culture: A Causal Historical View." In Oosterhuis and Kennedy, 207–17.

————. "Memoir for the Friends and Contributors of the Scientific Humanitarian Committee in the Name of the Secession of the Scientific Humanitarian Committee." In Oosterhuis and Kennedy, 71–84.

Furbank, P. N. *E. M. Forster: A Life.* 2 vols. New York, 1978.

Furneaux, Robin. *William Wilberforce.* London, 1974.

Fussell, Paul. *The Great War and Modern Memory.* Oxford, 1975.

Gadd, David. *The Loving Friends: A Portrait of Bloomsbury.* New York, 1974.

Gardiner, James. *Who's a Pretty Boy Then? One Hundred and Fifty Years of Gay Life in Pictures.* London, 1997.

Gerard, Kent, and Gert Hekma, eds. *The Pursuit of Sodomy: Male Homosexuality in Renaissance and Enlightenment Europe.* New York, 1989. Published simultaneously in *Journal of Homosexuality* 16, nos. 1/2 (1988).

Gerassi, John. *The Boys of Boise: Furor, Vice, and Folly in an American City.* New York, 1966.

Gide, André. *Corydon.* London, 1985.

————. *If It Die.* New York, 1935.

Gilbert, Arthur. "Sexual Deviance and Disaster during the Napoleonic Wars." *Albion* 9, no. 1 (1977): 98–113.

Grau, Gunter. *Hidden Holocaust: Gay and Lesbian Persecution in Germany, 1933–45.* London, 1995.

Green, Julian. *Love in America: Autobiography Vol. III (1919–1922).* New York, 1994.

Green, Martin. *Children of the Sun: A Narrative of "Decadence" in England after 1918.* New York, 1976.

————. *The Mount Vernon Street Warrens: A Boston Story, 1860–1910.* New York, 1989.

Green, Michelle. *The Dream at the End of the World: Paul Bowles and the Literary Renegades in Tangier.* New York, 1991.

Greenberg, David. *The Construction of Homosexuality.* Chicago, 1988.

Grey, Antony. *Quest for Justice: Towards Homosexual Emancipation.* London, 1992.

Gross, Larry, and James Woods. *The Columbia Reader on Lesbians and Gay Men in Media, Society, and Politics.* New York, 1999.

Grosskurth, Phyllis. *Havelock Ellis: A Biography.* London, 1980.

————. *John Addington Symonds: A Biography.* London, 1964.

Gustav-Wrathall, John Donald. *Take the Young Stranger by the Hand: Same Sex Relations and the YMCA.* Chicago, 1998.

Hamer, Emily. *Britannia's Glory: A History of Twentieth-Century Lesbians.* London, 1996.

Hanna, Martha. "Natalism, Homosexuality, and the Controversy over *Corydon*." In Merrick and Ragan, *Homosexuality in Modern France,* 202–24.

Hartland, Claude. *The Story of a Life: For the Consideration of the Medical Community.* 1901. Reprint, with a foreword by C. A. Tripp. San Francisco, 1985.

Harvey, A. D. "Prosecutions for Sodomy in England at the Beginning of the Nineteenth Century." *Historical Journal* 21 (1978): 939–48.

Hay, Harry. *Radically Gay: Gay Liberation in the Words of Its Founder.* Boston, 1996.

Heger, Heinz. *The Men with the Pink Triangle.* London, 1986.

Hekma, Gert, Harry Oosterhuis, and James Steakley, eds. *Gay Men and the Sexual History of the Political Left.* Binghamton, N.Y., 1995. Published simultaneously in *Journal of Homosexuality* 29, nos. 2/3 and 4 (1995).

Helms, Alan. *Young Man from the Provinces: A Gay Life before Stonewall.* New York, 1997.

Herdt, Gilbert, ed. *Third Sex, Third Gender: Beyond Sexual Dimorphism in Culture and History.* New York, 1994.

Herring, Phillip. *Djuna: The Life and Work of Djuna Barnes.* New York, 1996.

Higgins, Patrick. *Heterosexual Dictatorship: Male Homosexuality in Postwar Britain.* London, 1996.

Higginson, Mary Thacher. *Thomas Wentworth Higginson: The Story of His Life.* Boston, 1914.

Higginson, Thomas Wentworth. *Cheerful Yesterdays.* Boston, 1898.

Higgs, David, ed. *Queer Sites: Gay Urban Histories since 1600.* London, 1999.

Hirschfeld, Magnus. *The Homosexuality of Men and Women.* Amherst, N.Y., 2000.

———. *The Sexual History of the Great War.* New York, 1946.

History Project (Boston). *Improper Bostonians: Lesbian and Gay History from the Puritans to Playland.* Boston, 1998.

Hoare, Philip. *Oscar Wilde's Last Stand: Decadence, Conspiracy, and the Most Outrageous Trial of the Century.* New York, 1998.

Hodges, Andrew. *Alan Turing: The Enigma.* New York, 1983.

Hoffman, Martin. *The Gay World: Male Homosexuality and the Social Creation of Evil.* New York, 1968.

Hogan, Steve, and Lee Hudson, eds. *Completely Queer: The Gay and Lesbian Encyclopedia.* New York, 1998.

Holroyd, Michael. *Lytton Strachey: The New Biography.* New York, 1994.

Honey, John Raymond. *Tom Brown's Universe: The Development of the English Public School in the Nineteenth Century.* London, 1977.

Hooven, F. Valentine. *Beefcake: The Muscle Magazines of America, 1950–1970.* Cologne, 1995.

Horsfall, Allan. "Battling for Wolfenden." In Cant and Hemmings, 15–33.

Howard, John. *Men Like That: Southern Queer History.* Chicago, 1999.

Hull, Isabel. *The Entourage of Kaiser Wilhelm II, 1888–1918.* Cambridge, 1982.

———. *Sexuality, State, and Civil Society in Germany, 1700–1815.* Ithaca, N.Y., 1996.

Huussen, Arend. "Prosecution of Sodomy in Eighteenth-Century Frisia, Netherlands." In Gerard and Hekma, 249–62.

Hyam, Ronald. *Empire and Sexuality: The British Experience.* Manchester, 1991.

Hyde, H. Montgomery. *The Cleveland Street Scandal.* New York, 1976.

———. *The Love That Dared Not Speak Its Name.* Boston, 1970. Published in England as *The Other Love* (London, 1972).

———. *Oscar Wilde.* New York, 1975.

Hyde, Louis, ed. *Rat and Devil: Journal Letters of F. O. Matthiessen and Russell Cheney*. Boston, 1988.

Hynes, Samuel. *The Auden Generation: Literature and Politics in England in the 1930s*. New York, 1972.

Isherwood, Christopher. *Christopher and His Kind, 1929–1939*. New York, 1976.

Jeal, Tim. *The Boy-Man: The Life of Lord Baden-Powell*. New York, 1990.

Jivani, Alkarim. *Its Not Unusual: A History of Lesbian and Gay Britain in the Twentieth Century*. Bloomington, Ind., 1997.

Kaiser, Charles. *The Gay Metropolis, 1940–1996*. Boston, 1997.

Kaplan, Fred. *Gore Vidal: A Biography*. New York, 1999.

Kaplan, Justin. *Walt Whitman: A Life*. New York, 1980.

Karlinsky, Simon. "Russia's Gay Literature and Culture: The Impact of the October Revolution." In Duberman, Vicinus, and Chauncey, 347–64.

Katz, Jonathan. *Gay American History: Lesbians and Gay Men in the U.S.A.: A Documentary*. New York, 1976.

———. *Gay/Lesbian Almanac: A New Documentary*. New York, 1983.

Kennedy, Hubert. *The Ideal Man: The Story of "Der Kreis."* Binghamton, N.Y., 1999. Published simultaneously in *Journal of Homosexuality* 38, nos. 1/2 (1999).

———. *Ulrichs: The Life and Works of Karl Heinrich Ulrichs, Pioneer of the Modern Gay Movement*. Boston, 1988.

Kinsey, Alfred, Wardell Pomeroy, and Clyde Martin. *Sexual Behavior in the Human Male*. Philadelphia, 1948.

Kuzniar, Alice, ed. *Outing Goethe and His Age*. Stanford, Calif., 1996.

Lauritsen, John, and David Thorstad. *The Early Homosexual Rights Movement*. New York, 1974.

Lautmann, Rudiger. "Categorization in Concentration Camps as a Collective Fate: A Comparison of Homosexuals, Jehovah's Witnesses, and Political Prisoners." *Journal of Homosexuality* 19, no. 1 (1990): 67–87.

Leddick, David. *Intimate Companions: A Trilogy of George Platt Lynes, Paul Cadmus, Lincoln Kersten, and Their Circle*. New York, 2000.

———. *Naked Men: Pioneering Male Nudes, 1935–1955*. New York, 1997.

Lehmann, John. *In the Purely Pagan Sense*. London, 1985.

Le Vay, Simon. *Queer Science: The Use and Abuse of Research into Homosexuality*. Cambridge, 1996.

Lewes, Kenneth. *The Psychiatric Theory of Male Homosexuality*. New York, 1988.

Leyland, Winston, ed. *Gay Roots: Twenty Years of "Gay Sunshine": An Anthology of Gay History, Sex, Politics, and Culture*. San Francisco, 1991.

———. *Gay Sunshine Interviews*. 2 vols. San Francisco, 1978–1982.

Licata, Salvatore, and Robert Peterson, eds. *Historical Perspectives on Homosexuality*. New York, 1981. Published simultaneously in *Journal of Homosexuality* 6, nos. 1/2 (1980–81).

Loughery, John. *The Other Side of Silence: Men's Lives and Gay Identity: A Twentieth-Century History*. New York, 1998.

Lucey, Michael. *Gide's Bent: Sexuality, Politics, Writing*. Oxford, 1995.

Lynch, Michael. "'Here Is Adhesiveness': From Friendship to Homosexuality." *Victorian Studies* 29, no. 1 (1985): 67–96.

Maccubin, Robert, ed. *'Tis Nature's Fault: Unauthorized Sexuality during the Enlightenment*. Cambridge, 1988.

MacDonald, Ross. *Dark Tunnel*. New York, 1972. Originally published in 1944 under the name Kenneth Millar.

Mangan, J. A., and James Walvin, eds. *Manliness and Morality: Middle-Class Masculinity in Britain and America, 1800–1940*. New York, 1987.

Marcus, Eric. *Making History: The Struggle for Gay and Lesbian Equal Rights, 1945–1990: An Oral History*. New York, 1993.

Marcus, Steven. *The Other Victorians: A Study of Sexuality and Pornography in Mid-Nineteenth-Century England*. New York, 1977.

Marks, Elaine. "Lesbian Intertextuality." In Stambolian and Marks, 353–77.

Marmor, Judd, ed. *Sexual Inversion: The Multiple Roots of Homosexuality*. New York, 1965.

Martin, Del, and Phyllis Lyon. *Lesbian/Woman*. San Francisco, 1972.

Martin, Robert K. "Knights-errant and Gothic Seducers: The Representation of Male Friendship in Mid-Nineteenth-Century America." In Duberman, Vicinus, and Chauncey, 169–82.

Mass, Lawrence D. *Homosexuality and Sexuality: Dialogues of the Sexual Revolution*. 2 vols. Binghamton, N.Y., 1990.

Mavor, Elizabeth. *The Ladies of Llangollen*. London, 1971.

McCormick, Ian, ed. *Secret Sexualities: A Sourcebook of Seventeenth- and Eighteenth-Century Writing*. London, 1997.

McGilligan, Patrick. *George Cukor: A Double Life*. New York, 1991.

Menninger, William. *Psychiatry in a Troubled World: Yesterday's War and Today's Challenge*. New York, 1948.

Merrick, Jeffrey, and Bryant Ragan, eds. *Homosexuality in Early Modern France: A Documentary Collection*. Oxford, 2001.

———. *Homosexuality in Modern France*. Oxford, 1996.

Miles, Barry. *Ginsberg: A Biography*. New York, 1989.

Miller, Merle. *On Being Different*. New York, 1971.

Miller, Neil. *Out of the Past: Gay and Lesbian History from 1869 to the Present*. New York, 1995.

Montesquieu, Charles de Secondat, baron de. "Of Crimes against Nature." In *Spirit of the Laws*, 189–90. Translated by Thomas Nugent. New York, 1966.

Mosse, George. *The Image of Man: The Creation of Modern Masculinity*. Oxford, 1996.

———. *Nationalism and Sexuality: Respectability and Abnormal Sexuality in Modern Europe*. New York, 1985.

Murphy, Lawrence. "Defining the Crime against Nature: Sodomy in the United States Appeals Courts, 1810–1940." *Journal of Homosexuality* 19, no. 1 (1990): 49–66.

Naerssen, A. X. van, ed. *Gay Life in Dutch Society*. New York, 1987.

Nardi, Peter, David Sanders, and Judd Marmor, eds. *Growing Up before Stonewall: Life Stories of Some Gay Men*. London, 1994.

Newton, Esther. "The Mythic Mannish Lesbian: Radclyffe Hall and the New Woman." In Duberman, Vicinus, and Chauncey, 281–93.

Nicolson, Nigel. *Portrait of a Marriage*. New York, 1973.

Norse, Harold. *Memoirs of a Bastard Angel*. New York, 1989.

Norton, Rictor. *Mother Clap's Molly House: The Gay Subculture in England, 1700–1830.* London, 1992.

———. *The Myth of the Modern Homosexual: Queer History and the Search for Cultural Identity.* London, 1997.

Nye, Robert. *Masculinity and Male Codes of Honor in Modern France.* Oxford, 1993.

Oosterhuis, Harry. "Homosexual Emancipation in Germany before 1933: Two Traditions." In Oosterhuis and Kennedy, 1–27.

Oosterhuis, Harry, and Hubert Kennedy. *Homosexuality and Male Bonding in Pre-Nazi Germany.* Binghamton, N.Y., 1991. Published simultaneously in *Journal of Homosexuality* 22, nos. 1/2 (1991).

Oresko, Robert. "Homosexuality and the Court Elites of Early Modern France: Some Problems, Some Suggestions, and an Example." In Gerard and Hekma, 105–28.

Parker, Peter. *Ackerley.* New York, 1989.

Perry, Mary. *Gender and Disorder in Early Modern Seville.* Princeton, 1990.

Plant, Richard. *The Pink Triangle: The Nazi War against Homosexuals.* New York, 1986.

Plummer, Kenneth. *The Making of the Modern Homosexual.* Totowa, N.J., 1981.

Poherilenko, Anatole, and James Crump. *When We Were Three.* Santa Fe, N.M., 1998.

Pollard, Patrick. *André Gide: Homosexual Moralist.* New Haven, Conn., 1991.

Porter, Kevin, and Jeffrey Weeks, eds. *Between the Acts: Lives of Homosexual Men.* London, 1991.

Prater, Donald. *Thomas Mann: A Life.* Oxford, 1995.

Ragan, Bryant. "The Enlightenment Confronts Homosexuality." In Merrick and Ragan, *Homosexuality in Modern France,* 8–29.

Reade, Brian. *Sexual Heretics.* New York, 1970.

Rey, Michel. "Police and Sodomy in Eighteenth-Century Paris: From Sin to Disorder." In Gerard and Hekma, 129–46.

Richter, Simon. "Wieland and the Homoerotics of Reading." In Kuzniar, 47–60.

Rivers, J. E. "The Myth and Science of Homosexuality in *A la Recherche du Temps Perdu.*" In Stambolian and Marks, 262–78.

Robinson, Christopher. *Scandal in the Ink: Male and Female Homosexuality in Twentieth-Century French Literature.* London, 1995.

Robinson, Paul. *Gay Lives: Homosexual Autobiography from John Addington Symonds to Paul Monette.* Chicago, 1999.

Rocke, Michael. *Forbidden Friendships: Homosexuality and Male Culture in Renaissance Florence.* Oxford, 1996.

Roll, Wolfgang. "Homosexual Inmates in the Buchenwald Concentration Camp." *Journal of Homosexuality* 31, no. 4 (1996).

Rosenthal, Michael. *The Character Factory: Baden-Powell and the Origins of the Boy Scout Movement.* New York, 1986.

Rousseau, Jean-Jacques. *The Confessions.* Translated by J. M. Cohen. Baltimore, 1971.

Rubenstein, William, ed. *Lesbians, Gay Men, and the Law.* New York, 1993.

Rubini, Dennis. "Sexuality and Augustan England: Sodomy, Politics, Elite Circles, and Society." In Gerard and Hekma, 349–81.

Rueling, Anna. "What Interest Does the Women's Movement Have in the Homosexual Question?" In Faderman and Ericksson, 83–94.

Russo, Vito. *The Celluloid Closet: Homosexuality in the Movies.* New York, 1981.

Sade, Donatien-Alphonse-François, comte de. "Yet Another Effort, Frenchmen, If You Would Become Republicans." In *Justine, Philosophy in the Bedroom, and Other Writings,* 296–339. Translated by Richard Seaver and Austryn Wainhouse. New York, 1965.

Sadownick, Douglas. *Sex between Men: An Intimate History of the Sex Lives of Gay Men Postwar to Present.* San Francisco, 1996.

Salden, Maarten. "The Dutch Penal Law and Homosexual Conduct." In Naerson, 155–79.

Saslow, James. *Pictures and Passions: A History of Homosexuality in the Visual Arts.* New York, 1999.

Sawyer-Laucanno, Christopher. *An Invisible Spectator: A Biography of Paul Bowles.* New York, 1989.

Scharnhorst, Gary, and Jack Bales. *The Lost Life of Horatio Alger, Jr.* Bloomington, Ind., 1985.

Schmidgall, Gary. *The Stranger Wilde: Integrating Oscar.* New York, 1994.

Shand-Tucci, Douglass. *Boston Bohemia, 1881–1900: Ralph Adams Cram, Life and Architecture.* Amherst, Mass., 1995.

Sheriden, Alan. *André Gide: A Life in Present.* Cambridge, 1999.

Sherman, Sarah. *Sarah Orne Jewett: An American Persephone.* Hanover, N.H., 1989.

Shively, Charles. *Calamus Lovers: Walt Whitman's Working-Class Camerados.* San Francisco, 1987.

Sibalis, Michael David. "Paris." In Higgs, 10–37.

———. "The Regulation of Male Homosexuality in Revolutionary and Napoleonic France, 1789–1815." In Merrick and Ragan, *Homosexuality in Modern France,* 80–101.

Skidelsky, Robert. *John Maynard Keynes.* 2 vols. New York, 1986–1994.

Smith, F. B. "Labouchere's Amendment to the Criminal Law Amendment Act." *Historical Studies* (Melbourne, Australia) 17 (1976–77): 165–75.

Smith, Timothy d'Arch. *Love in Earnest: Some Notes on the Lives and Writings of the English Uranian Poets from 1889–1930.* London, 1970.

Smith-Rosenberg, Carroll. "Discourses of Sexuality and Subjectivity: The New Woman, 1870–1936." In Duberman, Vicinus, and Chauncey, 264–80.

Sox, David. *Bachelors of Art: Edward Perry Warren and the Lewes House Brotherhood.* London, 1991.

Spender, Stephen. *The Temple.* New York, 1988.

———. *World within World.* New York, 1994.

Stambolian, George, and Elaine Marks, eds. *Homosexualities and French Literature.* Ithaca, N.Y., 1979.

Steakley, James. *The Homosexual Emancipation Movement in Germany.* 1975. Reprint, Salem, N.H., 1993.

———. "Sodomy in Enlightenment Prussia." In Gerard and Hekma, 163–75.

Steegmuller, Francis. *Cocteau: A Biography.* Boston, 1992.

Stein, Edward, ed. *Forms of Desire: Sexual Orientation and the Social Constructionist Theory.* New York, 1992.

Stein, Marc. *City of Sisterly and Brotherly Love: Lesbian and Gay Philadelphia, 1945–1972*. Chicago, 2000.

Stockinger, Jacob. "Homosexuality and the French Enlightenment." In Stambolian and Marks, 161–85.

Stone, Lawrence. *The Family, Sex, and Marriage in England, 1500–1800*. London, 1977.

Stryker, Susan, and Jim van Buskirk. *Gay by the Bay: A History of Queer Culture in the San Francisco Bay Area*. San Francisco, 1996.

Sullivan, Gerard. "Political Opportunism and the Harassment of Homosexuals in Florida, 1952–1965." *Journal of Homosexuality* 37, no. 4 (1999): 57–79.

Summers, Claude, ed. *The Gay and Lesbian Literary Heritage:*
*A Reader's Companion to the Writers and Their Works, from Antiquity to the Present*. New York, 1995.

Symonds, John Addington. *The Letters of John Addington Symonds*. Edited by Herbert M. Schueller and Robert L. Peters. 3 vols. Detroit, 1967–69.

———. *The Memoirs of John Addington Symonds*. Edited by Phyllis Grosskurth. New York, 1984.

———. "A Problem in Modern Ethics." In *Sexual Inversion*, 101–91. New York, 1984.

Thompson, Victoria. "Creating Boundaries: Homosexuality and the Changing Social Order in France, 1830–1870." In Merrick and Ragan, *Homosexuality in Modern France*, 102–27.

Thwaite, Ann. *Edmund Gosse: A Literary Landscape, 1849–1928*. London, 1984.

Timmons, Stuart. *The Trouble with Harry Hay: Founder of the Modern Gay Movement*. Boston, 1990.

Tobin, Kay, and Randy Wicker. *The Gay Crusaders*. New York, 1972.

Trumbach, Randolph. "London's Sodomites: Homosexual Behavior and Western Culture in the Eighteenth Century." *Journal of Social History* 11 (1977): 1–33..

———. *Sex and the Gender Revolution*. Vol. 1, *Heterosexuality and the Third Gender in Enlightenment London*. Chicago, 1998.

———. "Sodomitical Assaults, Gender Role, and Sexual Development in Eighteenth Century London." In Gerard and Hekma, 407–29.

———. "Sodomy Transformed: Aristocratic Libertinage, Public Reputation, and the Gender Revolution of the Eighteenth Century." *Journal of Homosexuality* 19, no. 2 (1990): 105–24.

Tsuzuki, Chushichi. *Edward Carpenter, 1844–1929: Prophet of Human Fellowship*. Cambridge, 1980.

U.K. Parliamentary Committee on Homosexuality and Prostitution. "The Wolfenden Report: Part Two, Homosexual Offenses." In Blasius and Phelan, 252–73.

Ulrichs, Karl. *The Riddle of Man-Manly Love: The Pioneering Work on Male Homosexuality*. 2 vols. Buffalo, N.Y., 1994.

United States Senate. "Employment of Homosexuals and Other Sex Perverts in the U.S. Government." In Blasius and Phelan, 241–51.

Van der Meer, Theo. "Sodomy and the Pursuit of a Third Sex in the Early Modern Period." In Herdt, 137–212.

Vidal, Gore. *The City and the Pillar*. New York, 1965.

———. *Palimpsest: A Memoir.* New York, 1995.

———. *Sexually Speaking: Collected Sex Writings.* San Francisco, 1999.

Voltaire. "So-called Socratic Love." In *Philosophical Dictionary,* translated by Peter Gay, 76–79. New York, 1962.

Wainwright, David, and Katherine Dinn. *Henry Scott Tuke, 1858–1929: Under Canvas.* Carshalton, Surrey, 1989.

Waugh, Thomas. *Gay Male Eroticism in Photography and Film from Their Beginnings to Stonewall.* New York, 1996.

Weeks, Jeffrey. *Coming Out: Homosexual Politics in Britain from the Nineteenth Century to the Present Day.* London, 1979.

Weiermair, Peter. *The Hidden Image: Photographs of the Male Nude in the Nineteenth and Twentieth Centuries.* Cambridge, 1988.

Weinberg, Jonathan. *Speaking for Vice: Homosexuality in the Art of Charles Demuth, Marsden Hartley, and the First American Avant-Garde.* New Haven, 1993.

Wells, Anna Mary. *Dear Preceptor: The Life and Times of Thomas Wentworth Higginson.* Boston, 1963.

Whitman, Walt. *The Complete Poetry and Prose of Walt Whitman.* 2 vols. New York, 1948.

———. *Democratic Vistas.* In Whitman, *Complete Poetry and Prose,* 2:208–63.

———. *Specimen Days.* In Whitman, *Complete Poetry and Prose,* 2:2–206.

Wickes, George. *The Amazon of Letters: The Life and Loves of Natalie Barney.* New York, 1976.

Wilde, Oscar. *Selected Letters of Oscar Wilde.* Edited by Rupert Hart-Davis. Oxford, 1979.

Wineapple, Brenda. *Genet: A Biography of Janet Flanner.* New York, 1989.

Wolfenden, Sir John. *Turning Point.* London, 1976.

Wolff, Charlotte. *Magnus Hirschfeld: A Portrait of a Pioneer in Sexology.* London, 1986.

Worsley, T. C. *Fellow Travelers.* London, 1984.

# Index

Greenwich Village, 235, 253–55, 256, 331
Grey, Antony, 317, 319, 321, 322, 323
Groningen, 27
Guerin, Daniel, 287
gymnast movement, 50–51, 86

Haan, Jacob Israel de, 139
Hague, the, 7, 15
Haire, Norman, 294
Hall, Radclyffe, 236–37, 237–40, 336
Hallidie Smith, Andrew, 317, 318
Hamburg, 217, 285
Hammond, Charles, 114, 115, 116
Hannover, 85, 86, 88, 210
Harden, Maximilian, 148–51
Harlem, 253–55
*Harper's*, 306
Harris, Frank, 120, 121
Harrow, 57, 103, 154, 160
Hartland, Claude, 80–81
Hartley, Marsden, 197–98, 236, 255
Harvard University, 72, 78, 188
Hay, Harry, 269–75, 276, 305
Healey, Tim, 113
Hemingway, Ernest, 198
Henry VIII, king of England, 18
Higginson, Mary, 72, 73
Higginson, Thomas Wentworth, 72–73, 82
Hiller, Kurt, 207–8, 209, 211, 284
Himmler, Heinrich, 212–13
Hirschfeld, Magnus: background and early career, 90–95, 96, 98–99, 135, 146, 149, 154, 164–65, 265; and England, 121, 122, 294; and Eulenburg scandal, 151; André Gide on, 172; later career, 199–200, 205–7, 209, 211; and the Netherlands, 139; and Russia, 203, 216; and the United States, 141; and the women's movement, 230–31; and World War I, 183–84
Hitler, Adolph, 200, 201, 209, 211, 212, 219
Hoening, Margaret, 259
Hoffman, Martin, 312–13
Holland, 36, 37. *See also* Netherlands, the
Holroyd, Michael, 181
homoerotic attraction: between ethnic groups, 50, 57, 72, 104, 167–68, 175–76,

186–87, 197–98, 199, 204, 300–301, 302, 303, 304; between friends, 10, 31, 50–51, 57–58, 72–73, 80, 96–97, 147, 151, 152, 157, 160–61, 164, 171, 173, 184–85, 226–28, 229; between generations, 8–9, 10, 14, 21, 50, 74, 76, 96–97, 114, 118, 145, 152, 154–55, 157–60, 162, 164, 165, 167–68, 171–73, 186–87, 189, 215, 234, 270, 279, 293, 294–95, 297, 300–301, 302; between social classes, 8–9, 21, 74, 75, 103, 104, 114, 118, 119, 127, 130, 142, 147, 155, 175–76, 177, 199, 293, 297, 304
*Homogenic Love* (Carpenter), 108, 109, 121, 122
homosexual/homosexuality, definitions and uses of terminology: adhesiveness, 77; Bentham's coinages, 59; buggery, 18, 71; contrary sexual feeling, 131; gay, 77, 197, 269, 270; homophile, 273; homosexual, 3–4, 90, 95, 105, 108, 190, 264, 270; lesbian, 221; pederasty, 30, 171, 172; sexual inversion, 70, 105; Sapphic, 221; slang terms, 141, 142, 221, 251, 254, 259; sodomy, 3–4, 30, 71, 264; Urning/Uranian, 86–87, 90, 93, 95, 105, 108, 190
*Homosexual in America, The* (Cory), 269, 305, 328–29
Homosexual Law Reform Society, 316–19, 321–22, 323–24
homosexual subcultures: Renaissance, 10, 19; early modern, 7–16, 33; early nineteenth-century, 56–57, 66, 74; late nineteenth- and early twentieth-century, 92, 104, 114, 115, 118, 130, 138, 141–43; interwar, 196, 198, 208, 232–33, 235, 250–55, 257, 259, 270; World War II and after, 264, 268, 278–79, 280, 285, 290, 294, 295–96, 304, 305, 306, 307–8, 309, 312
homosexuality
—classical antiquity as an inspiration for: decline in use of, 186, 187–92; in England, 58, 105, 123, 155, 158–60, 185; in France, 170–71, 173, 233; in Germany, 49–50, 86–87, 96, 164, 186–87, 236; in the United States, 189, 233, 236